Language of Inequality

Contributions to the Sociology of Language

36

Editor
Joshua A. Fishman

MOUTON PUBLISHERS · BERLIN · NEW YORK · AMSTERDAM

Language of Inequality

Edited by
Nessa Wolfson
and Joan Manes

MOUTON PUBLISHERS · BERLIN · NEW YORK · AMSTERDAM

CIP-Kurztitelaufnahme der Deutschen Bibliothek

Language of inequality / ed. by Nessa Wolfson and Joan Manes. –
Berlin ; New York ; Amsterdam : Mouton, 1985.
(Contributions to the sociology of languages ; 36)
ISBN 3-11-009946-2 geb.
ISBN 3-11-009947-0 Pb.
NE: Wolfson, Nessa [Hrsg.]; GT

Library of Congress Cataloging in Publication Data

Main entry under title:
Language of inequality.
(Contributions to the sociology of language ; 36)
   1. Linguistic minorities–Addresses, essays, lectures. 2. Languages in contact–Addresses, essays, lectures. 3. Language planning-Addresses, essays, lectures. 4. Multilingualism–Addresses, essays, lectures.
I. Wolfson, Nessa. II. Manes, Joan. III. Series.
P119.315.L36   1985   401'.9   85-2899
ISBN 0-89-925052-1
ISBN 0-89-925053-X (pbk.)

Printed on acid free paper

Typesetting: COPO Typesetting, Bangkok, Thailand. – Printing: Druckerei Hildebrand, Berlin. – Binding: Dieter Mikolai, Berlin. Printed in Germany.

PREFACE

The sociologist Morris Janowitz once said that the goal of theory is to make the obvious inescapable. By that criterion, this book contributes to theory. To be sure, its articles are about specific places and regions. Each tells about a particular situation. There is little or nothing of causal hypothesis and correlation, of typology and dimensions for comparative framework, or model building of other kinds. And such things should be a goal, whether we call the sphere of our activity 'sociology of language', 'sociolinguistics', 'ethnography of communication', or something else. But it is difficult to reach that stage of theory, when so many find the obvious quite escapable indeed.

This book contributes to theory, then, by helping to make palpable the pervasive linguistic inequality of our world. It is not that there are writers who deny that multilingualism exists, that standard languages exist, that language minorities exist, that languages sometimes are dominated, sometimes die. It is just that the part of the mind or the faculty which knows these things is isolated from the part that knows what is called 'theoretical linguistics'. Nor is this a new thing. It stems from the beginnings of modern linguistics in the United States. The functional equality of all languages has been a tenet of the faith from the founders of structural linguistics to most practitioners of linguistics today. It is unacceptable in most respectable linguistic circles to suggest that one language is less capable in some respect than another, or that some users of a language are different in one or more abilities from other users. These facts of everyday experience, these realities of language use in so much of the world and every educational system, 'fade into air, into thin air', when linguists speak in their professional capacities as linguists.

The tenet, indeed, has been a progressive force. In terms of it Boas, Sapir, Bloomfield and others were able to criticize the received beliefs of our civilization as to the superiority of European languages to languages of other types, as to the presumed lack of structure and stability in languages not written, etc. A space was cleared for appreciation of the marvelous variety of forms taken by human linguistic creativity. From the standpoint of reconstructing the past or understanding the working of language in general, the speech of a community of a few hundred, such as Hopi in Arizona, Eyak in Alaska, or Toda in southern India, might count for as much as the speech of an empire. But there was a latent professional interest in this progressive critique. To define all languages as equal in the eyes of science was to expand the scope of linguistic science itself, and at the same time to excuse linguists from attending to certain kinds of fact. The first effect was necessary and proper, the second understandable, but in the long run debilitating. If one does not attend to the loss of narrative abilities in American Indian communities whose traditions of myth have been extinguished; if one does not attend to the difference in life chances between the child in Nigeria who acquires a command of English and the child who does not; if one has no principled way of accounting for the fact that economic security in a society may require some kinds of linguistic ability to which only some have ensured access; then one has no purchase on the world to which grammars bearing language names, such as 'English', presumably refer. A once progressive critique has come to function as the defense of an academic elite against intellectual change. Radicals champion a liberal idea to conservative effect.

To think of linguistics as having a responsibility to describe, analyze and theorize about such situations is to challenge accepted assumptions of the discipline today. Simplification of data and theoretical argument seem to go hand in hand. Models that connect universal mind with universal kinds of situation seem to be preferred, as against consideration of historically derived patterns of cultural practice and belief. Yet the recognition of linguistic inequality requires methods of description and analysis that integrate linguistics with aspects of the social sciences and humanities. This is not the place to sketch such things (cf. Hymes 1980, 1983), and it would be quite misleading to imply that there are not a certain number of scholars who do address these matters. But they are few in proportion to those who do not; their work is slower to accumulate critical mass.

Perhaps there is something in language itself that works against the comprehensive understanding of language in human life. A page may contain many recurrences of a phoneme; a text may contain many recurrences of essential morphemes and types of word order. Understanding of language choice and ability requires the observation of a range of settings and activities; it calls for a combination of linguistic and ethnographic skills. It is inherently more complex and time-consuming. Or so it seems at least if one compares the rapidity with which one might challenge observations of one's own language or think of counterarguments in a formal system, to the pace at which one may come to understand a community way of life.

In any case, the testing of such general hypotheses and dimensions of typology as we have proceeds very slowly, and will continue to do so, I fear, so long as the empirical work required is so little valued by so many. It often seems in the academy that work which has the most to do with actual life is the least valued. The issues raised by the reality of inequality in language are inseparable from issues of education, for example. The theory that emerges from knowledge such as provided in this book will be necessarily in part a theory of education as well as of language. Yet that pervasive force in shaping communities, countries and the world is often looked down upon.

There are encouraging signs, to be sure, in the growth of attention to discourse on the part of linguists today. An important part of the work in discourse addresses social settings, such as courtrooms, hospitals, class rooms, work places. Perhaps the increased attention to verbal interaction in such settings will reinforce the efforts of those who address whole communities and regions. Perhaps before too long most of us will find analyses of language whose only relation to an actual place and group of people is a language name simply too unsatisfying to read. Matters most of us will want to know about will not be addressed. Who uses this language or this style or this feature? when? to what purpose? instead of what? with what meaning to those around them? Of whom are these things true? of whom perhaps not true? what part does this play within the verbal repertoire or resources of the group as a whole?

For a half-century or so the dominant thrust in linguistics has been precision in terms of form and structure. Work which could not satisfy standards as to the facts of language, as to relevant features and the relations among them, was set aside. The challenge now is to make the dominant thrust in linguistics the connection between form and structure, feature and relation, on the one hand, and abilities and events, on the other. The structures of languages and the structures of societies are mediated by ways of speaking, ways in which verbal means are selected and grouped together in activities by definite people in definite settings, in short, by situated competence.

Were there no political domination or social stratification in the world, there would still be linguistic inequality, of course, the kind of linguistic inequality inevitably given by individual variation in ability and by the ways in which one or another ability, one or another use of language, is encouraged or discouraged in a habitat, a home, a community, a culture. In the world we live in that natural diversity, which one could respect and value, is pervaded by diversity of access and opportunity stemming from regional, national and world systems. Varieties of language themselves become reintegrated into complex dependencies, their possibilities of development shaped by functional niche. It is impossible to think of the world's languages now as spread about in space, one to a place and way of life. Allocation and hierarchy are intrinsic. Nor should the investments of many, perhaps even including ourselves, in some existing arrangements be underestimated. Effective change in the direction of greater equality will only partly be change in attitude, or removal of external domination; it will be inseparable in many cases from change of social system.

Whatever the future brings, planned or unplanned, we can hope that linguistics will have become theoretically adequate to it. A book such as this is an essential step.

Dell Hymes

References

Hymes, Dell. 1980. *Language in education: Ethnolinguistic essays.* (Language and Ethnography Series 1) Washington, D.C.: Centre for Applied Linguistics.
−   , 1983. Report from an underdeveloped country: Toward linguistic competence in the United States. In Bruce Bain, (ed.), *The Sociogenesis of language and human conduct*, 189-224. New York: Plenum

FOREWORD

Linguistic inequality, like other forms of social inequality, is a problem of major dimensions in the modern world. Indeed, linguistic inequality may be particularly pernicious. Often, discrimination on the basis of language ability is not seen as truly prejudicial—anyone can learn to speak the 'correct' language, whatever that may be, and if they don't do so, it is clearly their own fault! However, one's native language is so much a part of one's identity that to denigrate it is to effectively deny one's human ability to communicate.

This collection of articles attempts to give the reader an overview of sociolinguistic problems arising from situations of language contact. We have not aimed at covering the field entirely. What we have done rather, is to bring together articles which focus on the specific problems of a community, nation or area in which different languages are differently valued. In such situations we find that language use reflects and indeed influences social, economic or political inequality. Some papers present in-depth studies of particular communities while others focus more broadly, using the community or area of study as an example of a general sociolinguistic situation. We feel that both approaches are extremely valuable and that a collection which combines them is the more likely to give readers a clear picture of the causes and effects of linguistic inequality. For the same reason, we have not limited ourselves to any one region or aspect of the problem.

The articles in the first section of this book focus on problems of language choice: how linguistic diversity has arisen; how speakers select a language for a particular interaction or type of interaction; what the significance of these choices are; what attitudes speakers have towards specific languages and linguistic choices; what factors result in a language being lost or being maintained for at least some functions within the community. Although specific situations differ, a number of recurrent themes appear. Language imposition and shift as a result of military conquest and economic power, and interethnic conflict at both the societal level and the level of face-to-face interaction are treated from differing perspectives.

We begin with an article by John Fought in which a history of linguistic imposition and diversity in a particular area is traced. Here we are offered a taxonomy of bilingual situations which reflects the interaction of language choice and sociopolitical dominance. The articles by Zentella, Darnell, Heller, Woolard and Rubin provide concrete examples of such patterns of language choice. The first four, and most particularly those by Zentella and Darnell, call attention to the problems of interaction between members of communities which are linguistically distinct and at the same time unequal with respect to power and influence. Heller, Woolard and Rubin focus on those factors which affect an individual's selection of one language over another in specific social situations, an issue which Zentella also addresses. In addition, Rubin's and Woolard's papers, like those by Wald and Rickford which follow, emphasize the importance of language attitudes within the context of multilingual communities. The last four articles deal with language choice on the societal rather than the individual level, and turn our attention to the factors involved in language shift vs. language maintenance, language death vs. language survival. Both Day and Hardman are concerned with the imposition of non-native languages upon speech communities: Hardman uses place names and borrowings to trace an ancient and long-standing regional pattern of conquest and language imposition; Day gives us a close-up view of a modern instance of such imposition, describing the pressures which result in the ultimate acceptance and use of a colonial language and the ensuing death of the traditional native language. Clyne and Fishman both discuss the effects of population movement: Clyne from the point of view of immigration, examining different patterns of language use and linguistic and cultural assimilation among different groups of immigrants; Fishman from the point of view of emigration or dispersion, considering the effects of such dispersion and the ability of one language, Yiddish, to adapt and survive in changing circumstances. In this final article of the section, Fishman emphasizes that 'language death', the loss of its native speakers, is not the only possible fate for an oppressed language.

The second section of the book is concerned with the problems faced by post-colonial peoples in the areas of language policy, language development, and education. Southworth's article deals specifically with the question of language standardization. Taking India as an example, he shows that despite a declared policy of equality of opportunity, language standardization choices reflect and perpetuate a well-established pattern of social stratification. Zuengler contrasts two closely related post-colonial nations, Kenya and Tanzania, where divergent sets of national goals have resulted in very different solutions to the problems of language in education. The next four articles, by Sato, Craig, Dada and Briggs, give additional concrete examples of the problems and effects of language policies as these relate to education. Brigg's article also joins those by Philips and Edwards in focusing directly on the interaction between classroom teachers and non-standard speaking children. From there we move to larger aspects of language planning development and change in multilingual societies. An excellent example of the effects of economic pressures on both individual language choice and language policy decisions at the national level is given in Kuo's description of the present situation in Singapore. In discussing a very different multilingual situation, that of India, Dua points up the problems inherent in the attempt to develop minority languages for expanded functions. In contrast, Wurm demonstrates how a stigmatized variety, New Guinea Pidgin, has developed into a national language and describes the relevance of changing attitudes towards the language. We end with two articles which present widely differing views on the nature and value of multilingualism in post-colonial societies. Spencer argues that multilingualism beyond a certain point becomes counterproductive to the evolution of a modern, economically sound, technologically developed society. Pattanayak, on the other hand, argues that the European monolingual model is neither applicable to nor in the best interests of multilingual societies such as his own.

The differing viewpoints and different theoretical and methodological approches, not to meantion the very wide range of spedicifc situations described in this collection, reflect both the complexity and the generality of the problems of social and linguistic inequality. No issue discussed here is relevant solely to the speech community or communities used to exemplify it, nor is any issue unrelated to others discussed in other sections of the book. Speakers' linguistic choices cannot be separated, for example, from their own and others' attitudes towards those choices. Language planning, to be in any way successful, must reflect and grow out of speakers' actual linguistic patterns and must take into account their beliefs and feelings about the value, beauty and significance of different varieties of speech. At the same time, both the attitudes of speakers towards a language and the status (official or unnofficial) of that language are in fact a reflection of the status of its speakers, and language 'choices' are often determined by economic, political and social pressures. Thus as various themes recur, the problem of social inequality and its effects on linguistic behavior, language attitudes and language policy remains central to every article in the volume and unites them into a coherent whole.

Nessa Wolfson and Joan Manes

Contents

XIV

CLASSROOM INTERACTION AND EDUCATIONAL POLICY

LANGUAGE DEVELOPMENT AND THE FUNCTIONS OF MULTILINGUALISM

INTRODUCTION

Einar Haugen

The Language of Imperialism:
Unity or Pluralism?*

Some may wonder why I have chosen to call this paper 'linguistic pluralism'
rather than 'bilingualism' or 'multilingualism', since that is in fact what I
mean. One reason is that the term 'bilingualism' has become so loaded with
emotional value judgments that one can hardly mention it without raising
someone's hackles. Especially is this true in a country like Canada, where it is
a perennial topic of discussion and conflict. In the United States we have
suddenly reversed ourselves, after two centuries of linguistic homogenization
resulting from the theory of the infamous 'melting pot'. We have gingerly and
somewhat tentatively embarked on a subsidized program of what we call
'bilingual education'. A good many of my colleagues in linguistics, in language
teaching, and in education are involved in this program. Volumes are
appearing and learned articles are breeding like guinea pigs, so that old hands
in the game like myself (if I may mix my metaphors) are unable to keep our
heads above water in this new deluge of print and near-print. (See Gray's
review of Abrahams and Troike 1975; for a critical survey see Paulston 1975.)
    What none of us can know at the moment is how long the present
enthusiasm will be sustained. In education as in linguistics the fads come and
go, especially when ideas are closely tied to current ideological and economic
climates. One never knows when today's enthusiasm will become tomorrow's
yawn. For this reason I do not wish to tie my discussion today either to the
current situation in the United States, which is abnormal, nor to that of
Canada, which is normal in the sense that it appears to be endemic to your
national life. So I have chosen a term that is in some ways more neutral
because it is less well-known and less well-worn. That is the term 'pluralism',
usually preceded by the word 'cultural'; but instead of encompassing all of
'cultural pluralism', I shall try to limit myself to that facet of it which relates
to language.
    'Language pluralism', as we may also call it, is not precisely the same as
'language diversity'. The latter is an objective fact of life which can be
measured by census takers and sociologists (e.g. Lieberson et al. 1974, 1975a,

1975b). It is a fact, for example, that in a country like Nigeria, the former British protectorate, more than two hundred different native languages and dialects are spoken. That is language diversity with a vengeance, and it is hardly a desirable goal, nor a 'consummation devoutly to be wished' for any country that is to have a viable government or a successful school system. When we speak of 'pluralism', we imply not a state of affairs, but a goal that may make it possible for diverse language groups to live together. It is a more subjective term, implying a policy of deliberate planning and official action, which may or may not be desirable. The very suffix of the word, '-ism', implies that it is a doctrine, a theory, in short a goal which some desire and others deplore (Berry 1974).

Most people take for granted the language into which they are born, the one spoken in their home and by their playmates. They learn it as a matter of course, and it appears to be of no more consequence to them than the air they breathe. Yet without either one they could not grow up to be human beings: lack of air would kill their bodies, but lack of language would kill their minds. Each of us speaks the one or more languages we do speak as the result of a long history involving not only ourselves and our ancestors, but our ethnic group and our nation. One part of this history is a set of linguistic policies and decisions made far away and long ago without our knowledge and certainly without our consent. On the other hand, those of us who are alive today may by our decisions and our policies be able to influence the lives of those who come after us. To do so as well as possible requires that we know both the past and the present situations that have influenced the use and the disuse of languages and dialects.

The issue as it is presented to us today is one of centralism and assimilation versus coexistence and pluralism. On every hand we see how the steamroller of uniformation is wiping out ethnic groups and their languages through the spread of national and international languages by radio and TV. On the other hand we see new nations coming into being, nations that struggle to create or preserve their own national languages. In so doing they are following the example of the old nations that threw off the yoke of Latin, which was western Europe's 'world language' until the sixteenth century and later.

We see within nation after nation a struggle on the part of minority groups to assert their own linguistic rights: the Catalonians in Spain, the Basques in Spain and France, the Welsh in England, the Lapps in Scandinavia, the Chinese in Malaysia, and even the Guarani Indians in Paraguay: The Guarani have only minority status although they are a majority of the population (Rubin 1968). This struggle between dominated and dominant groups for the right to survive includes what I have called 'the ecology of language' (Haugen 1972). By this I mean that the preservation of language is a part of human ecology, which in turn is a branch of the larger disciplines of sociology and political science.

As the center of the struggle stands language, which is the special province of linguistic science. But for the individuals involved language also becomes a psychological, social, and political problem, requiring the cooperation of all the social sciences. Special interdisciplinary fields of study have sprung up across the borders of traditional disciplines. Just as we have biophysics and social anthropology, so we now have psycholinguistics and sociolinguistics. Most recently I discovered 'geolinguistics', the title of a journal appearing since 1974, published by a newly founded American Society of Geolinguistics. The last term is reminiscent of the German term *Geopolitik* or geopolitics, which is probably closely related to the concerns of these new geolinguistics. In the journal I found an article on 'linguistic imperialism' by Allen Walker Read, which has helped to inspire some of my reflections here (Read 1974).

These are some of the problems I shall be discussing:

How did language diversity within nations come about and why is it a problem? What policies have major powers adopted to meet this problem? And finally: can a policy of linguistic pluralism be implemented as a satisfactory solution of the problem?

First the origin of language diversity. We must face the fact that most nations have been established by military conquest and without regard for the language of their masses. When President Wilson tried after World War I to implement a policy of linguistic self-determination in Europe, it may have been the first time in history that statesmen paid any attention to the wishes of their subjects in such matters. But it was implemented largely to break up the Austro-Hungarian empire and to tear the Baltic countries away from Russia. In World War II most of his plan came unstuck. The Baltic countries, except for Finland, reverted to Russia, while the successor countries to the Austro-Hungarian and Turkish empires, like Hungary. Romania, Yugoslavia, and Czecho-Slovakia still turned out to be multilingual.

Today it would actually be hard to point out a single European nation that does not have a minority problem, in the sense of having within its borders a population speaking some language that cannot be regarded as just a dialect of the national tongue. Those nations that have been strong enough to extend their power beyond their European borders into overseas lands have not hesitated to incorporate into their empires populations of different languages and ethnicities. The results are rampant today in the form of internal conflicts at home and colonial collapse abroad. The policy of ethnic incorporation is of course not limited to modern Europe. It appears to be immemorial: China, Mongolia, Japan followed it in the Far East, India in South Asia, the Egyptians, the Chaldeans, the Assyrians, anyone you can mention in the Middle and Near East, the Incas and the Aztecs in the Americas and in some far-distant time, our most remote linguistic ancestors, the Indo-Europeans, Within historical time the Greeks, Romans, French, Germans, Russians, Spaniards, Portuguese, and English have carried on the grand tradition of encircling and suppressing racial and linguistic minorities wherever they had the power to do so. Even the small and now pacific nations of the Scandinavian North, cradle of my ancestors, have a history that does not in the least free them from an accusation of linguistic and cultural suppression.

Recent years have seen a growing interest on the part of social scientists in the study of minority groups, particularly those that are held together by ethnic identity in which language is often a strong component. Earlier sociologists were either disinterested or hostile, reflecting the prevalent views of national and chauvinist ideologies. They regarded minority groups as an obstacle to national unity, a roadblock on the path to modernization of society, or in Marxist terms, 'a survival of barbarism'. In a generally objective study of 'ethnic stratification' written as recently as 1965 by Shibutani and Kwan, the authors could say that "most Americans who profess humanitarian ideals favor assimilation". They even found it ironic that the same presumably 'liberal' Americans who condemned 'separate but equal' facilities for Blacks and Whites often favored pluralism for European nations (Shibutani and Kwan 1965: 533). Yet Nathan Glazer and Daniel Moynihan of Harvard had just two years earlier published their classic book, *Beyond the Melting Pot* (1963), in which they put forth the thesis that "the ethnic group in American society" had become "not a survival from the age of mass immigration but a new social form" (Glazer and Moynihan 1963: 16). And in a recent article, which has become the first chapter of a book entitled *Ethnicity*, they could ask the question, "Why Ethnicity?", and answer it by declaring that ethnicity is "no mere survival but intimately and organically bound up with major trends of modern societies." (Glazer and Moynihan 1974: 39; 1975).

Other scholars have also put forth theories to account for the behavior and continued existence of minority groups within a modern society. Schermerhorn has suggested a two-dimensional model, which involves "cultural distinctiveness on the one hand and some form of subjection on the other" (Schermerhorn 1964: 238). This is one way of saying that a 'minority group' need not be a minority at all: it is simply a cultural group that lacks political autonomy and power. So 'minority group' becomes a mere euphemism for a *dominated* group, in contrast to the *dominant* minority, for which he reserves the word 'elite'. In another study Hubert Blalock speaks of 'dominant-group' and 'minority-group', and he makes the point that each of these has its resources of power, and even has the potential of mobilizing these resources, if it wishes to achieve certain goals (Blalock 1967: 111—113). We conclude that the élite is itself a minority group. It has the option of imposing its way of life, including its language, on other groups under its sway, or it may stay aloof from them, while keeping them unmobilized as long as possible. The dominated group may, as one alternative, choose to accept whatever crumbs fall from the rich man's table, growing ever more acculturated to his way of life. If some or all of the members of the dominated group are accepted into membership by the élite, they may become wholly assimilated. If not, the 'minority' may mobilize its resources in opposition and revolt, refusing to recognize the legitimacy of the élite, thereby seeking either total autonomy or some kind of federation with equal rights, in other words a share of the power. (On 'mobilization' see Deutsch 1953).

One of the resources which is available either to the élite or the minority is language, both as a symbol and as an instrument. Wherever language problems have appeared, there has been some form of what we have chosen to call 'language planning', a form of social planning. In the Europe of yesterday as in the Africa and India of today procedures have been developed to determine language *choice* and language *codification*, which are two essential ingredients in a program of language planning. There are two further ingredients, if the program is to be successful; these I have chosen to call *elaboration* and *implementation*. By elaboration I am thinking primarily of the development of terminology to meet the needs of a modern written language. By implementation I mean the effective introduction of language teaching into the schools and from them into the public and private life of the nation (Haugen 1966; Rubin and Jernudd, eds. 1971; Fishman, ed. 1974; Rubin, ed., *Language Planning Newsletter*, 1975ff.).

In this wide sense of the word, language planning may be either *overt* or *covert*, and it may be either *official* or *private*. By 'overt' I mean consciously formulated in handbooks or grammars and dictionaries, with rules of correctness and policies of exclusion and inclusion that define a norm. This codification makes them available for teaching in schools or for self-improvement by reading. By 'covert' language planning I mean the absence of such expressed formulation, often in the form of shared understandings within a group of what is appropriate on given occasions. The overt rules may be prepared and propagated by an official institution, such as a government, a church, a school (which may be under the control of either). Or they may be formulated by private groups or even individual citizens, who choose to establish special codes that mark the groups and hold them together. Such groups can of course have covert rules as well, ways of speaking and acting that are learned only by association and training, as in an upper class or in an occupational group. In reading about the development of languages like English one often gets the impression that like Topsy, they 'just grew'. But this is an illusion. It is merely that the guidance may have been private and covert, and that today it can be disinterred only by the diligent student who looks for it. Covert rules are indeed often more rigid than overt ones, since they are enforced by the pressure of one's peers, who punish by exclusion and reward by admission. Overt rules are more like written laws, which can be broken or ignored, often with impunity, or at least with only mild correction.

Let us now turn from these rather general and perhaps rather dry theoretical models to the real practice of some of the major powers of the world. How can we characterize the policies they have adopted toward ethnic minorities within their sway?

We begin with Spain, which was not only one of the first great colonizing powers, but also one that had a clear and firm policy about language. The first grammar of a modern European language was written for Spanish in the year 1492 and presented to Queen Isabella as an 'instrument of empire'. This work by her biographer Nebrija was a codification of Castilian, the language of Isabella's court, which established it as the élite language. It did so at the expense of other Spanish dialects like those of León and Navarra, as well as such potentially distinct languages as Galician and Catalonian. Isabella and her successors unhesitatingly imposed Castilian on all their subjects, including the conquered Moors, and in 1536 Emperor Charles V even ventured to address the Pope in Castilian instead of Latin. It was a turning point, a clear recognition on the one hand that the day of Latin was passing and on the other that like the Romans the Spaniards were about to make their language the language of their empire (Heath 1972; 1974: 16).

The *conquistadores* who followed Columbus into the New World accordingly had their instructions: the Laws of Burgos (1512) required them to train the Indians in the Catholic faith and the Castilian tongue, first via the training of teachers who would then spread these to other Indians. Eventually this task proved too burdensome for these men of affairs, and they turned it over to the friars. But the empires which Spain destroyed, those of the Aztecs in Mexico and the Incas in Peru, had already established and spread their own languages, Nahuatl and Quechua respectively, so that in many cases the friars found it simpler to learn these languages and teach Christianity to the natives in their own tongues. The Spanish government vacillated over the enforcement of its policies, but from time to time the offers to teach the Indians Spanish were renewed. By the time of independence in the early nineteenth century, the Latin-American nations had established the supremacy of Spanish in all of their territories, but they were still far from having taught the language to all their Indians. From Argentina and Chile in the south to Mexico and Cuba in the north (excepting of course Portuguese Brazil), Spanish was the language of the élite, while the masses continued to use their native tongues in all intimate contacts. Not until the late 1930s did Mexico begin to institute bilingual education programs in its Indian languages as a measure against illiteracy and of assimilating the Indians into the life of the nation.

We now turn to England and look for her language policy, both within and then without her tight little island. I shall introduce the topic by a sentence from Shirley Brice Heath's excellent comparison of the policies of Spain and England as colonial powers: "The English viewed language as the mark of an individual's reward of a proper birth or successful educational and social achievements mixed with a careful consciousness about language" (Heath 1974: 9). She adds that in England "the matter of individual choice in language was an habitually instilled ideal" (Heath 1974: 10). I would put it a little less respectfully: to an Englishman his language was his badge of status. The way he spoke it marked his personal status, while the *fact* that he spoke it demonstrated his superiority to 'the lesser breeds without the law.' The great turning point for the English language came with the defeat of the Spanish Armada in 1588. By opening up North America and giving England undisputed mastery of the seas, it established English as one of the languages of empire. But contrary to the Spanish, the English did not have an overt language policy. They took the purely practical view that others ought to see the advantage to themselves of learning English. Anyone who did not was either a fool or a barbarian. Language was a personal issue: you were either born to it or you achieved it, and it was not the government's business to prescribe it.

Curiously enough, this *laissez-faire* policy worked reasonably well within Great Britain, wiping out most of the remains of Celtic both in Ireland and Scotland during the nineteenth century. In Wales it met a strong minority resistance because language was allied with religion: the nonconformists used Welsh as a weapon against the Church of England. The English terms for their élite dialect are tinged with moral overtones: 'proper' English is associated with proper morals, 'correct' language with correct behavior, and words like 'good' or 'bad' are equally applicable to a person's language and his moral character. While one might not exactly be thrown in jail for his language, one could be and often was frozen out of good society, which could mean loss of jobs or restricted opportunities. Shaw's *Pygmalion* was not just a comedy, but an Irishman's biting satire on the English attitude to language.

It is significant that in the eighteenth century a number of English men of letters and grammarians, as distinguished as Defoe and Swift, wanted to found an English academy after the model of the French. But this plan was denounced as a tyranny unworthy of free Englishmen by no less an authority than Samuel Johnson and others, and nothing came of it. But what happened? In 1755 the same Samuel Johnson, by his own private enterprise (supported by the booksellers of London), produced a dictionary of English, which for a century fixed the norms of English just as effectively as any

Academy could have done. Similarly in the United States, when the colonies had won their independence and wished to defy the dictates of London in matters of language as well, a new lexicographer rose from the ranks and became the lawgiver of private enterprise. This was of course Noah Webster, whose name has become synonymous with linguistic propriety, although he was in fact a radical reformer. We owe to him those few differences in spelling that still set us off from the English in words like 'humor' and 'labor', 'center' and 'theater'.

The consequence of this English background was that in the colonies of North America, as in India and elsewhere, the English administrators arrived with no stated policy concerning language. (On English in India see Khubchandani 1972.) In North America they also met an entirely different kind of social organization among the natives than did the Spanish. The Castilians simply incorporated the well-organized Indians into their own hierarchy, while the English pushed the largely hunting and gathering Indians aside and set up their own social hierarchiy to the exclusion of the Indians. Contrary to the Castilians, the English government had no policy for converting the Indians to Christianity. This, too, became a matter for private enterprise, left to missionary organizations set up by the churches themselves.

The North America Indians proved unwilling to perform hard manual labor for the colonizers, so that when labor was needed, it was obtained either by trading for slaves from Africa or by enticing European immigrants to fill the vast open spaces of the temperate and subarctic zones of the continent. So long as these immigrants did their work, they were left severely alone to speak as they wished. The Blacks were segregated by color even after liberation, and by that time their tribal languages had been virtually lost and their English was shaking off its creolized forms. The white immigrants were admissible to society once they had seen the light and had given up their native tongues. The major instrument in this process was the universal public school, where the much-maligned schoolmarm provided models of 'correct' speaking. She not only taught a heterogeneous population the three R's, but also served as a cultural and linguistic missionary among the 'barbarian' hordes from Norway, Germany, Poland, Italy, or Russia, who became the backbone of the American labor force in the nineteenth and early twentieth centuries. (On language policy in the U.S. see Leibowitz 1974).

We turn now to France and her relationship to the ethnic and linguistic diversity which the French met at home and abroad. Like the other languages, French was created by an élite clustering around a center of political and military power, in this case of course Paris and the surrounding Île-de-France. Its centralization dates back to the fifteenth century when Charles VII with the aid of Joan of Arc succeeded in expelling the English and making Paris his capital (Dauzat 1930). In 1539 King Francis I in one blow eliminated its classical rival Latin and its provincial competitors in France by making French the language of the law courts. In the seventeenth century poets and grammarians like Malherbe (1555–1628) and Vaugelas (1595–1650) codified it according to the usage of the élite. In 1635 Cardinal Richelieu shrewdly established the Académie Française to regulate the language and make it an instrument of political and cultural centralization. In the words of one French writer, "It was in reality a question of raising the French language out from among other languages and giving it that universality, that preeminence, and accordingly that perfection which Greek and Latin had had in the ancient world" (*La Grande Encyclopédie*, 1.185). Once this codification had been accomplished, French writers and scholars elaborated it into one of the world's great instruments of culture. French armies and French diplomats carried it around the world, with a single-minded devotion far greater than that of either the Spaniards or the English for their languages.

The difference stands out in full clarity in the contrasting behavior of the two great powers while colonizing Africa. The English generally made it a policy to introduce vernacular education at the lower levels and gradually introduce English as the student progressed. The French have almost everywhere disregarded local vernaculars entirely and given all education in French. This carries on the home country policy of disregarding and actively discouraging enclaves of Bretons or Basques, Germans in Alsace or Italians in Corsica not to speak of the Occitanian language of the South of France. France is one of the few nations that has never included a question on language in its census, so we have nothing but educated guesses concerning the number of native speakers of non-French languages or dialects. A study by John Spencer (1971) of French and English policies in Africa confirms this view. Spencer finds that in Africa the French policy was determined by the concept of 'identity': "In the long run the metropolitan community and the African peoples subject to their rule must share a common political destiny." The English, on the other hand, "maintained a social and cultural gap between European and African" (Spencer 1971: 542; also in Fishman, ed. 1974: 169; the distinction goes back to Lord Hailey's, *An African Survey*, London: Oxford, 1957.) Or to put it more bluntly: the English were tolerant of native tongues but unwilling to accept their speakers as social equals. The French were willing to receive natives of all colors into the French community provided they gave up their identity and learned French!

We shall now conclude our survey of imperial policies with a perspective of language planning in the Soviet Union. Here, again, I can refer to a recent and exhaustively analytical work, written by Glyn Lewis, a Welshman who for years has been director of the program of bilingual education in the United Kingdom (Lewis 1972).

Of the four languages surveyed, Russian is the latest to be standardized. One can hardly speak of modern stndard Russian before the eighteenth century and the time of Peter the Great. Czar Peter and his successors were able to extend the use of this language all the way from the Baltic to the Pacific across northern Europe and Asia (and even into Alaska) and to establish dominion over an amazingly multilingual area. The dominated languages included representatives of many major language families, from the Indo-European Baltic languages of Latvia and Lithuania to Eskimo and Aleut on the Bering Strait, in all some 180 different languages. The language policy of the Czars was simple enough: to forbid the teaching and writing of any other language than Russian. After the revolution of 1917 this policy was replaced by one that deliberately tried to accommodate linguistic pluralism within a Russian-dominated totalitarian regime. The enormous complexity of the Soviet domain makes it difficult to delineate the policy briefly or simply, especially since we are all inclined to look with suspicion on any policy initiated by a government predicated on a totalitarian philosophy.

As Lewis outlines it, the early Communists were faced with the need of securing the allegiance of the peoples under their regime. Lenin, following Marx, was committed to the "theory of self-determination of all nations which enter into the composition of the state" (Lewis 1972: 67). The first decade of Soviet existence was therefore one in which enormous forward strides were made toward giving national and ethnic groups the opportunity to read and write their own languages, many of them for the first time in history. The prevailing theory was that socialist ideology, the *content* of Communism, could be expressed in any language, or as their slogan ran: 'national in form, socialist in content'.

But the 1930s, under Stalin, saw a growing Russian chauvinism, with the emphasis shifted to the dangers of 'local nationalism' and 'national languages' (Stalin 1961, in Lewis 1972: 71). So policy swung away from pluralism to a greater stress on centralism. In 1938 the teaching of Russian as a second language was decreed for all monorities; scripts that had been Arabic or Latin were replaced with Cyrillic; and Russian loanwords were required for new intellectual and technical concepts. Then, on Stalin's death in 1953, there was a political 'thaw', and with it a swing back toward emphasis on pluralism. Khrushchev maintained in 1956 that "love for one's country" did not contradict "the international solidarity of the workers"; "only a great attentiveness to the interests of the various nations removes the grounds for conflicts and removes mutual distrust" (*Pravda*, Feb. 15, 1956, in Lewis 1972: 74). But Khrushchev fell, and since then there has been a new reversion in favor of centralism. At the 24th Congress of the Communist Party Brezhnev established his own line, emphasizing the "diligence and selflessness of the Russians which had enabled them to offer such outstanding leadership to other nationalities". He declared his implacable opposition to all manifestations of nationalism (Lewis 1972: 80).

Our conclusion concerning Russian policy is that in promoting literacy the Communists have encouraged the local languages as instruments of spreading their social gospel. It is interesting to consider that Christian missionaries have similarly been the most eager among westerners in the use of the local languages. In both cases it was realized that only through the languages of infancy and home is it possible to reach into the very hearts and roots of personality. The ruling Communist Party has behaved much like the élites of birth or wealth or education in other countries in its singleminded devotion to expanding its power over the hearts and minds of its subjects. In this process the local languages have been used as an instrument, not as a goal. One can hardly overlook the fact that the goal is assimilation, uniformation, the creation of what Lewis calls a 'civic' culture. As in the United States, this culture uproots old allegiances and small groups, only to replace them with an abstract allegiance to some kind of wider vision, which may be cold comfort for those who are deprived of their old ways of life.

Let us now try to sum up and characterize the policies of the great powers I have chosen to describe, ever so superficially, in terms of the model suggested earlier. Spain, like Czarist Russia, had a policy that was both public and overt, aimed at spreading the élite language and the orthodox doctrine as instruments of imperial dominance. In America the Castilian policy, like the Russian, has vacillated, and its American agents sabotaged it by not implementing it through a universal school system. The result is that Latin America has a great heritage of developed pluralism, which only in Mexico enjoys official encouragement. England had no overt or public policy, but a covert one, which it was left to local officials and private organizations to implement. Assimilation was left to individual initiative, which was eventually encouraged by the establishment of the public grade school. Until recently this school did nothing for the native American Indians, the Mexican Chicanos, or the Blacks. Today it is being used tentatively for experiments in pluralistic language teaching, more with an eye to eventual assimilation than to the preservation of the respective ethnicities. The French had a public and overt policy of imposing their language, and they succeeded in creating an extraordinary allegiance to the language, in part because their lesser color prejudice enabled them to live their lives in closer contact with the native populations of the old and the new world. Implementation was enforced both privately and through the school system, thus engendering a deep sense of pride in being part of the francophone world. The Russians are the most obviously public in their planning and give overt support to pluralism, but with strong covert insistence on centralization and the ultimate goal of turning all subject peoples into good Russian Communists.

It is clear that those who advocate centralism and assimilation are in a position to do so because of their superior power. One cannot therefore condemm them offhand as mere power seekers. It is clear that there are great practical advantages in having any one code in governing a country. But from this purely practical point of view we might as well have only one language in the whole world, a solution which has had plenty of advocates. To my mind this is a purely bureaucratic solution, worthy of an efficiency expert, but not of a human being. It fails to take into account the fact that in a lifetime most people have no need to communicate with the whole world. Most of us live circumscribed, comfortable lives, in which the things that matter take place within our homes, among our friends, at our jobs. Here the imposition of a new language merely because it has some national or international advantage, is disruptive of the life pattern. It leaves people uprooted, lonely, aggressive, unsocial.

The solution would rather seem to be a thoughtfully planned bilingualism which leaves each of us with a native, homely, familiar everyday language in which we can live and love. Then we can learn a language of wider communication that will enable us to travel to the ends of the world if occasion arises (Haugen 1973 b). Bilingualism has been with us since time began, and it has been an indispensable link between people (Lewis 1974). When it is rightly introduced and taught, and is not made to seem desirable by the larger society in which we also live, it is not only not harmful, but mind-expanding and infinitely rewarding.

In making these flat and unsupported statements I can only plead that in one lecture there is not time to explore the problem of bilingualism more deeply. I have already done so in numerous publications, to which I can only refer you, and note that others have now carried the topic far beyond my ability to deal with it (Haugen 1972, 1973a).

If bilingual education raises problems in the school, these must not be sought primarily in the schoolroom. If it fails to produce the desired effects, we must look back at the ultimate policies, overt or covert, public or private, of the society in which the education is taking place. If the language of the home is also dominant in the life of the nation and is supported by the prestige of an élite then the introduction into the school of another language can become a valuable supplement to one's native competence. It can become the means of access to another, friendly group. It is therefore no problem to immerse English-speaking Canadians in French; they will learn English anyhow. But if the language of the home is looked down upon and is not supported by the prestige of an élite, then the acquisition of a second language which does have prestige may be disastrous to the pride and cohesion of the pupil's ethnic group. This is why there are problems when we set up bilingual programs for Mexican and Indian speakers in the United

States. In each case we must keep an eye on the larger issues involved. If parents do not wish their children to learn a second language, or if they are indifferent about their own native language because of its low prestige, bilingualism is bound to fail. If the parents are favorable, the program will succeed, whatever teaching methods may be used (Paulston 1975). In the first case we have what Lambert has recently called 'additive' bilingualism, in addition to one's repertoire of a new language; in the second one we have 'subtractive' bilingualism, which may promote transition to the new language and loss of one's mother tongue (Lambert 1976).

Is there then any nation in which bilingualism is wholly acceptable as an educational program and where linguistic pluralism is a fact? I point to Switzerland, not as necessarily an ideal commonwealth, but as one country where no one is trying force their language or culture upon anyone else. The historical basis of this is of course that as a nation it is almost unique in not having been created by conquest, but by voluntary federation. The central government has no ambition to homogenize or uniform the languages of its population. Each canton has its own language, and the national government operates with as many languages as the cantons wish. So the country is able to survive while maintaining three official and four national languages, and its German population speaks its own Swiss German which is virtually a national idiom. But it is only because no one part dominates the others; and each one leaves the rest alone. It is a truly pluralistic country, because each group is left to live its own life, which then fits into a larger and unmistakably Swiss national pattern.

Perhaps the moral to all this is that real pluralism requires some degree of segregation, of separate but equal facilities; but the cement that holds it all together is the body of bilinguals, who can transcend their own group without denying it.

Notes

* First appeared in *Language and Society*(1969: 65-82) under the title, "Linguistic Pluralism as a Goal of National Policy".

·References

Berry, J. W., 1974. Psychological aspects of cultural pluralism: Unity and identity reconsidered. *Topics in Culture Learning* (Honolulu, Hawaii: East-West Center), 2.17-22.
Blalock, Hubert M., Jr., 1967. *Toward a theory of minority-group relations*. New York: Wiley.

Dauzat, Albert, 1930. *Histoire de la langue française*. Paris: Payot.
Deutsch, Karl W., 1953. *Nationalism and social communication*. Cambridge, Mass.: MIT Press.
Fishman, Joshua A., ed., 1974. *Advances in language planning*. The Hague / Paris: Mouton.
Glazer, Nathan and Daniel Patrick Moynihan, 1963. *Beyond the melting pot*. Cambridge, Mass.: M. I. T. Press and Harvard University Press.
– 1974. Why ethnicity? *Commentary*, 58.33-39.
– 1975. *Ethnicity*. Cambridge, Mass.: Harvard University Press.
Gray, Norman, 1975. Review of Roger D. Abrahams and Rudolph C. Troike, *Language and cultural diversity in American education*. (Englewood Cliffs, N. J.: Prentice-Hall, 1972); *Language*, 51.720-730.
Haugen, Einar, 1966. Linguistics and language planning, *Sociolinguistics*, ed. Wm. Bright (The Hague: Mouton), 50-71.
– 1972. *The ecology of language*. Essays, selected and introduced by Anwar S. Dil, Stanford, Cal.: Stanford University Press.
– 1973a. Bilingualism, language contact, and immigrant languages in the United States: A research report 1956-1970, *Current Trends in Linguistics*, ed. T. Sebeok (The Hague / Paris: Mouton), 10.505-591.
– 1973b. The curse of Babel, *Language as a human problem*, ed. M. Bloomfield and E. Haugen (New York: Norton), 33-43.
Heath, Shirley Brice, 1972. *Telling tongues: Language policy in Mexico, colony to nation*. New York: Teachers College Press.
– 1974. Colonial language status achievement: Mexico, Peru, and the United States. Paper presented at VIII World Congress of Sociology, Toronto, Canada, August 1974.
Khubhandani, Lachman M. C., 1972. English in India: A sociolinguistic appraisal, *International Journal of Dravidian Linguistics*, 2.199-211.
La Grande Encyclopédie, C. 1900. Paris.
Lambert, Wallace, 1976. Effects of bilingualism . . . , *Bilingualism* (Conference, Plattsburg, New York, March 12, 1976).
Leibowitz, Arnold H., 1974. Language as a means of social control: The United States experience, Paper given at VIII World Congress of Sociology, Toronto, Canada, August 1974.
Lewis, E. Glyn, 1972. *Multilingualism in the Soviet Union*. The Hague / Paris: Mouton.
– 1974. Bilingual education in the classical world, Appendix 1.1 in Joshua A. Fishman, *A sociology of bilingual education* (Final report, stenciled), 173-232.
Lieberson, Stanley, and Lynn K. Hansen, 1974. National development, mother tongue diversity, and the comparative study of nations, *American Sociological Review*, 39. 523-541.
Lieberson, Stanley, and James F. O'Connor, 1975a. Language diversity in a nation and its regions, *Multilingual political systems: problems and solutions*, ed. by Jean-Guy Savard and Richard Vigneault (Québec: Les presses de l'Université Laval), 161-181.
Lieberson, Stanley, Guy Dalto, Mary Ellen Johnson, 1975b. The course of mother-tongue diversity in nations, *American Journal of Sociology*, 81.34-61.
Paulston, Christina Bratt, 1975. Ethnic relations and bilingual education: Accounting for contradictory data, *Working paper in bilingualism* (Ontario Institute for Studies in Education), 6.1-44.
Read, Allen Walker, 1974. What is 'linguistic imperialism'? *Geolinguistics*, 1.5-10.
Rubin, Joan, 1968. Language education in Paraguay, *Language problems of developing nations* (ed. Fishman, Ferguson, and Das Gupta, New York: John Wiley), 477-488.
– ed., 1975ff. *Language planning newsletter*, vol. 1ff. Honolulu, Hawaii: East-West Center.
– and Björn H. Jernudd, eds., 1971. *Can language be planned? Sociolinguistic theory and practice for developing nations*. Honolulu: East-West Center, University Press of Hawaii.

Shermerhorn, R. A., 1964. Toward a general theory of minority groups, *Phylon*, 25. 238-246. (Expanded into his *Comparative ethnic relations: A framework for theory and research*. New York: Random House, 1970.)

Shibutani, Tamotsu, and Kian M. Kwan, 1965. *Ethnic stratification*. N.Y.: Macmillan.

Spencer, John, 1971. Colonial language policies and their legacies in Sub-Saharan Africa, *Current Trends in Linguistics*, ed. T. Sebeok (The Hague / Paris: Mouton), 537-547. (Reprinted in Fishman, ed. 1974, 163-175).

SECTION ONE: ORIGINS AND PATTERNS OF DIVERSITY

LANGUAGE CONTACT AND THE EFFECTS OF SOCIAL INEQUALITY

John Fought

Patterns of Sociolinguistic Inequality in Mesoamerica*

In ancient times, Mesoamerica, like Peru, was the homeland of a succession of
high cultures. What is known or inferred about these cultures adds a dimension
to the picture of language use and social organization lacking in other regions of
native America. This paper will first sketch some traits of Mesoamerican
sociolinguistics; it will then look more closely, as well as more personally, at
three Mayan towns I visited between 1965 and 1972; next it will look
backward, speculating on antecedent and parallel patterns of inequality in
Mesoamerica before the coming of the Spanish; finally, it will offer sugges-
tions for a general classification of complex speech communities. It must
be remembered that a brief sketch of such a complex topic is like a very large
scale map in leaving out a great deal of information that someone actually
walking over the ground would want to know. It is meant only to give a
general idea of the shape of things in a territory which has received, as Diebold (1962) remarked, relatively little attention from sociolinguistics.

The territory archeologists call Mesoamerica is made up of two parts
joined by the Isthmus of Tehuantepec in southern Mexico. The focus of the
western part is the great valley containing the present-day capital, Mexico
City, and opening into several eastward routes; the eastern part is made up of
Yucatan and the rest of Mexico beyond the Isthmus, all of Belize and
Guatemala, and the adjoining portions of Honduras and El Salvador.

Considered from a national or urban perspective, Mesoamerica is a part of
the Spanish-speaking world, with a hierarchical social system whose élite has
cosmopolitan connections, with significant economic development (especially
in Mexico) and the attendant working class and middle class specialists, and
with a substantial class of agriculturalists, including large numbers both of
laborers working land belonging to others and of peasant farmers working land
owned by themselves or administered for them by the government through a
system of common lands.

Considering these agriculturalists in their own rural setting, however,
brings into focus the importance of their ethnic identities. Some are monolingual speakers of Spanish, and may be regarded as primarily a component of
the national culture. Others have as a first language one of the many Native

American languages spoken in Mesoamerica, whose territories divide the area up into a mosaic of communities with mutually unintelligible, often unrelated, forms of speech, and distinct cultura norms and traditions. Collectively, these Native American langauges are a social fact of enormous importance in the life of the region. More than half of the population of Guatemala has as a first language one of the two dozen or so modern Mayan languages. In the Yucatan and Belize, hundreds of thousands of Indiana speak one of these, Yucatec Maya, some of them as monolinguals. In some highland towns, a majority, sometimes a large majority, is functionally monolingual in an indigenous language. But individually, each of these languages, even one with a large number of speakers, is of negligible importance in the national life.

In general, the indigenous languages of Mesoamerica retain their importance as cultural vehicles only in proportion to their isolation from Spanish and the dominant national culture. The more closely a town is integrated into the national communication network of transportation and the media, the more powerful is the influence of the national language and culture over the local norms. As the network of all-weather roads and railroads, schools, and broadcasting grows, the sphere left to indigenous culture and speech diminishes.

In the northern lowland zone of Chiapas, for example, timber companies have built a road network and a system of work camps opening up to wheeled traffic an area accessible previously only by canoe. Small bands of Lacandon Mayas living in this territory are among the least assimilated groups of Native Americans in Mexico. Soon after the opening of the roads in 1970 at least one of these bands had begun hitching or paying for rides to the nearby cities of Tabasco, particularly the capital, Villahermosa, bringing sets of bows and arrows hastily made in imitation of those they used not long ago for hunting. With this change in their mode of subsistence, admittedly incomplete, from hunting and gathering to door-to-door selling, has come a need for at least rudimentary proficiency in Spanish. As their territory is developed, that is, integrated further into the national system, this need will grow greater as well. Presumably the impact on their lives of the ethnographic film crew that had been visiting them for some weeks will be more transitory.

The Lacandon are perhaps the most recent subjects of this process, which began centuries ago, and is far advanced in their immediate vicinity.

The Chontal of San Carlos, Tabasco — *largely Hispanicized*

Near the cities visited by the Lacandon, in the low, swampy plain of Tabasco, are the towns of San Carlos and San Fernando. The town centers look very similar: a plaza with cement benches and a bandstand is bordered by a wide street. Part of one side is taken up by a large shed housing the town market. There are a few municipal offices and several bars. Near the plaza, most buildings are of masonry, and face on interior courts in the Colonial style; farther out, many are like the farm houses, of vertical canes laced together, with thatched roofs. The first language of the Indians here is the Yocot'an dialect of Mayan Chontal.

Despite the swampy ground and the numerous rivers meandering through the countryside, interspersed with bayous and ponds, it is relatively easy to build roads. For some time, the earlier system of peasant farming has been losing ground to large landholdings devoted to cattle. Pemex, the national petroleum monopoly, has developed major oil fields in the nearby countryside and a large refinery complex is in operation on the coast not far away. In keeping with the advanced economic and social integration of this part of Mexico into the national system, Spanish is relatively more important in this town, even for Indians who also speak Chontal. There are no monolingual Chontal speakers, except perhaps for very young children. It is not unusual for families to deny that they know or use Chontal; often one branch of an extended family will take this step while another remains overtly Indian in ethnic identity. Chontal is heavily influenced by Spanish. There are many borrowings, not only of nouns designating objects from the national culture and its technology, but also of verbs and constructions which have, or once had, Chontal equivalents but which have been lost. Most conjunctions and prepositions are Spanish in origin, and clause structure appears to follow Spanish models more closely than Mayan. The domain of Chontal use is largely restricted to family settings. In public, Spanish is likely to be used even for conversation among bilinguals. Many households follow a pattern whereby one or more adults have little or no capability in Chontal; in such instances, bilinguals rarely have occasion to use Chontal even in the family.

Crafts and lore follow the same pattern. Hardly anyone now makes houses or pottery in the old style. Folklore is largely Spanish in theme and content, with emphasis on the Revolution as a remote period. In outlying fields, one can still see traditional agricultural methods in use, but the farmer planting with a dibble stick is likely to wear manufactured rubber boots, and he will be fluent in Spanish. Indian culture, like the Chontal language, is not prized, even by those who participate in it, and it is clearly perceived as disappearing. Indeed, there is now little to distinguish San Carlos and San Fernando from the towns around them where the process of Hispanization has gone to completion, as it doubtless will in these two remaining towns as well.

Within the same small portion of Mayan Mesoamerica, then, we can see the process of sociolinguistic change in operation, and see its effects at varying stages of completion, ranging from the beginning of functional bilingualism and cultural contact, propelled by economic forces, and moving quite literally along the roadways of the national system, through several phases of progressively greater influence of Spanish, ending with the disappearance of the indigenous language and culture. The size of the indigenous speech community is one obvious variable affecting the rate and completeness of the process: the small bands of Lacandons are subject to much more rapid and complete influence than is the larger social unit made up of the Yocot'an Chontal of the two neighboring and well-populated towns.

The two other communities to be discussed are larger in area and in number of speakers than the Chontal, and differ significantly from it and from each other in accessibility to outside influence.

The Chortí of Jocotan   *oppression - substrate*

One of three neighboring towns in Chiquimula state, eastern Guatemala, serving as economic and ceremonial centers for the Chortí-speaking Mayans living around them, Jocotan is at the center of a large, oval valley, on both banks of the Jocotan river. Not far to the East is the major Mayan archeological site of Copan, in Honduras. The town center of Jocotan is a plaza bordered by a stone church on one side, and by dwellings, an office or two, and permanent stores on the other sides, and along the wide streets entering the plaza at the corners. Of the two thousand or so permanent inhabitants of the town itself, the great majority are monolingual Spanish speakers, the *ladinos*.

A web of trails leads outward and upward from Jocotan. The hills around the town are low and rounded at first, but form progressively higher ridges, cut by gulleys of all sizes, with a few cliffs of bare rock around the rim of the valley, perhaps a thousand feet above the river. The Chortí live in the hills, in hamlets made up of widely dispersed dwellings, with one family of three or four generations living in each cluster of buildings—one or two houses, a kitchen lean-to, and a few outbuildings. From Jocotan, nothing resembling a village can be seen up in the hills, though there are a few close to the town, also inhabited by *ladino* farmers. From each house in a Chortí hamlet, one or two other clusters of buildings may be visible, but none is likely to be nearer than a quarter of a mile, and many are more widely separated still. Except for children, all the Chortí are bilingual, with Spanish as a second language.

Although the Chortí are eight or ten times more numerous than the *ladinos* of Jocotan, it is they and not the *ladinos* who become bilingual. That is the key effect of the social system on language use, and the fundamental reason for it, of course, is that political and economic power are securely controlled by the *ladinos*. Upward mobility in this society is movement into the *ladino* world, and this requires the use of Spanish. But even without regard to social mobility, to an actual transition from one group to another, everyday contact with the national culture in stores, government offices, and schools takes place through the medium of Spanish.

Conversely, the surest token of Indian identity in Jocotan is the use of Chortí in the family. In those relatively infrequent cases where an Indian decides to give up his ethnic identity and join the *ladino* community without leaving Jocotan, the use of Chortí is given up too. One such person, an aunt of my principal informant, was pointed out to me. With sadness and understanding, I was told that she had left her native hamlet, moved into town, married a *ladino*, and now not only refused to speak or admit to understanding Chortí, but also denied knowing any of her former kinsmen when encountering them in the streets of the town.

Sociolinguistic inequality, the positive valuation of one code and the stigmatization of others, is manifested in more prosaic ways in Jocotan also. Twice each week, on Thursday and Sunday mornings, a market is held in Jocotan. The stores in the buildings around the plaza are open, selling tools, supplies, fabrics, staple foods, and liquor, Indian and *ladino* vendors display goods of many kinds in the streets and plaza. From dawn until early afternoon the market is crowded with people, most of them Indians down from the hamlets for the day. The social activity is as intense as the economic: market days are practically the only occasion for social contact between Indians and *ladinos* (except for contact between employee and employer) and between Indians from different hamlets (apart from occasional group activities such as house-raisings). Everyone is dressed up; marriageable girls are very much on display.

Service and conversational encounters of every kind accompany the buying and selling. In the store buildings owned by the more prosperous *ladino* families and patronized by all, including the poorest Indians, one can see the greatest differences of status and of ways of speaking illustrated over and over again. A typical encounter in such a store begins when an Indian, or more often an Indian couple, steps in through the wide doorway and begins to examine the stock of items on display. The Chortí are silent much of the time, exchanging a few words in their language in low, somewhat urgent tones. The *ladino* storekeeper watches, and after a time starts the commercial transaction with a question in Spanish about what is wanted. The Chortí man, or more rarely, a woman, may ask a price, or it may be volunteered by the storekeeper, who may at this point show off a word or two of Chortí, naming an item or its price in Chortí numbers. The customers may hesitate, decide, or leave the store. If there is hesitation, it rarely leads to a lowering of the asking price by the storekeeper, as it often would if the customer were another *ladino* with whom one might bargain. If a purchase is made, the transaction may end with a few loudly spoken words of good will directed to the departing, still silent customers. The encounter displays throughout the most striking contrasts between the verbal styles of the Chortí, who speak softly and very little, and the *ladinos*, who speak loudly and quite a lot. The encounter is begun and controlled by the server, rather than by the customer. The attitude of social superiority displayed by the storekeeper is plainly evident throughout, and unchallenged by the Chortí, whose uncertainty and discomfort are equally patent. The same contrast of styles and attitudes is seen in transactions between the local government, whose officials are *ladinos*, and the Chortí citizens. It was painful to observe the careful, patient display of ritualized subservience required of my principal informant by a local official (who from my vantage point seemed far inferior to him in human terms) before the documents needed for a visa application could be gathered.

If the customer, like the server, is a *ladino* resident of the town, the transaction is likely to be framed by a social encounter, a brief greeting and conversation about matters and people of common concern. Names will be used, and there will be at least a display of cordiality. There will be a conventional leavetaking at the end. The elaboration and warmth of all this is of course dependent on the closeness of the social and personal relationship between server and customer, but it is in general quite distinct from the pattern of *ladino*-Indian encounters.

Although the two ethnic groups share the valley, and have many encounters in the town, however superficial these may be, it is striking how limited the knowledge of Chortí is of even the most receptive *ladino* merchants. Their vocabulary scarcely exceeds the names of the commonest items of trade, and the numerals from one to four, coupled with the general classifier. The pronunciation of *ladinos* invariably omits certain phonological features of high frequency and significance in Chortí, such as the distinction between plain and glottalized stop consonants ([t] and [t'], for instance) or between long and short vowels.

The Chortí, on the other hand, learn Spanish well enough to conduct necessary business in it, and often become highly proficient speakers. Pronunciation is accurate and interference from Chortí is usually confined to some grammatical patterns, such as gender agreement or the sequence of tenses, where the Mayan system is most different from the Spanish. Schooling is a neglible factor in the acquisition of Spanish, since most of the time the sessions are abbreviated, or skipped entirely, and the quality of instruction is as low as the motivation of the pupils. Although I never was able to observe a school in session while I was in the hamlets around Jocotan, I did see many of the buildings, and I heard a number of stories about how the schools were used. A token effort was made to teach the alphabet, generally with the help of the crudest equipment, such as a chalkboard consisting of a short length of smooth gray planking. Much of the time of the pupils was devoted to fetching and carrying for the schoolmaster, I was told, and the pupils rarely devoted more than a few months of their lives to what was commonly regarded as a useless undertaking. The medium of this instruction, of course, is Spanish, which many of the young children had not yet mastered, but literacy, rather than language teaching, appears to have been the sole objective of the curriculum.

The actual learning of Spanish begins during family trips to Jocotan for the markets, and to a lesser degree in other work-related contacts with *ladinos*. Chortí is stigmatized, being considered a mere *lenguaje* rather than a true *idioma*, or roughly a 'dialect' in the traditionally disparaging sense, rather than a real 'language'. Skilled use of Chortí is respected within the Indian community, but more tangible rewards go to those with fluent Spanish, and a few individuals with high levels of skill in both languages are able to support themselves as intermediaries between the *ladinos* or the foreign priests or missionaries and the Indians. One such job is the consecutive translation of sermons in both Roman Catholic and other churches. The use of Chortí for religious instruction by both denominations is based on a familiar ideology of affective linkage between a language and the social group identified with it: to truly reach the Chortí, even though they are bilingual, one should use Chortí, thus avoiding unfavorable associations with the dominant, Spanish-speaking class. Thus, both the Belgian Roman Catholic priests and the American Quaker missionaries of the 1960s in Jocotan devoted some effort to language learning, and used translators. In folk religious material, however, there is considerable syncretism of Mayan and Catholic elements, and a good deal of lexical borrowing from Spanish. Some Chortí shamans, who are among other things specialists in the formal and artistic use of Chortí, incorporate a high proportion of Spanish vocabulary into their ritual utterances, perhaps in order to acquire the personal prestige accorded those with evident command of Spanish, and perhaps also in accordance with an older ideology associating the power of a social group with the power of its language.

Both outsiders and insiders, then, appear to understand the attitudes surrounding the relatively stable pattern of language use in Jocotan, and both are willing to try to exploit these attitudes for social effect or personal gain. Overall, there is a long-range trend toward dilution of Chortí forms and content by Spanish borrowings. This is apparent in the distribution of loans, including a number of frequent conjunctions and prepositions as well as nouns and verbs, in the content of prayers and traditional narratives, and in the fading of Chortí social and religious institutions and practices over the years remembered by my informants.[1]

The Chol of Tila, Chiapas

A few miles south of the crest of the ridge line overlooking the plains of Tabasco, the mountain town of Tila stands on a spur connected to one of a series of long ridges separated by deep valleys. The terrain here is more rugged than in the Chortí territory in Guatemala, and the road to Tila in the early 1970s was not open to wheeled traffic in the rainy season. The cash crop here is coffee; a surprising amount of it is flown out in single-engined planes from the small, sloping local airfield.

A majority, perhaps as many as two-thirds, of the Chol speakers around Tila are functionally monolingual. Many service encounters in the town stores are practically silent, or involve the exchange of only a few words relating to price and payment. Some of the help in the busiest stores is hired from the ranks of the more assimilated bilingual Indians.

Chol hamlets are not dispersed like those of their close linguistic relatives, the Chortí. They are much more European in organization, perhaps because the Chol were brought up into this country by the early Colonial administrators, and forcibly settled in towns for easier administration and control, in the aptly named process of 'reduction'. After arriving in one of these villages, however, the sense of familiarity produced by the sight of 'houses' grouped into 'streets' is soon dissipated by the characteristically reserved interactional style of the Chol inhabitants. The shyness and the hushed conversations found among the Chortí are the norm here also; inside the houses, the traditional Mayan arrangement of functions and furniture, and the three-stone hearth used since ancient times, reinforce the impression of a carefully guarded traditional culture.

The Chol have indeed maintained more of their language and lore than the Chortí, and far more than the easily accessible Chontal in the lowlands. The ruggedness of their territory is doubtless a major factor in this, together with its lack of any tempting natural resources and its location off main corridors of transportation. Among the Chontal I was able to find only scraps of traditional Mayan religious lore (though I may have missed some of what remains); some of the Chortí have retained much more than this, and memories if not current practices keep many of the old ceremonies alive. The Mayan Rain God, for example, is easily recognizable in the Working Angel, who chops up clouds with his sword to make rain. Among the Chol, this deity is still known as *Chahc* (the noise of lightning), and his angelic characteristics are lacking. Maintenance of the language is on a par with the conservatism of this cultural material. Spanish lexical and structural elements are far less frequent in Chol, and more closely confined to cultural borrowings associated with the national system. Interestingly, the numeral system of these three Mayan peoples has been almost completely replaced by Spanish, with only the numbers from one to three, four, or five in common use in their Mayan forms.

Effective command of Spanish is found mostly among the younger Chol men. Quite a few of them have made an effort to learn Spanish in preparation for leaving the Chol territory either temporarily, to do wage labor in the lowlands, or permanently, to settle there or elsewhere in Mexico, perhaps someday in the capital. Those I knew seemed well aware of the gamble involved, balancing the emotionally secure but hard and narrow peasant life against the risks and opportunities presumed to exist in the national culture.

Certainly there was a clear understanding among these outward-looking Chol men that to leave the community meant to leave the language and the life of their culture behind, for most of them knew of others who had already left, and the high social pressures of urban life were known at least in principle. The lure of the cities, and of Mexico City especially, is so strong that the urban migration from rural Mexico is virtually an avalanche, however, and the net gain of urban residents each year has greatly over-stressed the municipal institutions and facilities, with consequences familiar not just in Mexico but in many parts of Latin America and the rest of the world.

Looking Backward[2]

The picture drawn here is familiar indeed: an urban center homogenizes the native cultures by its two-fold action, sending the national culture outward along the communication network and drawing the more venturesome natives inward along the same routes. The product is a levelled-out but only partly assimilated version of the formerly colonial national culture, growing always at the expense of the indigenous cultures, whatever their intrinsic merits. As a sketch of the third world over recent decades many would recognize it immediately.

In Mesoamerica, however, this process is not new. It can be traced back through the succession of indigenous high cultures that occupied the same territory.

Just before the Spanish conquest, the Aztec empire was at its peak. Thanks to the efforts of its chroniclers, we know a good deal about the daily life of its people five centuries ago. It was the Aztec capital of Tenochtitlán that the Spanish occupied, destroyed, and rebuilt into Mexico City: where the principal temple-pyramid of the Aztecs once stood is now the Cathedral; its great plaza is now the central square; the imperial residences have been replaced by the offices of the current political and economic institutions. The symbolism could not be more perfect.

Aztec culture was highly stratified. There was a small, very wealthy elite from which the Emperor was chosen, and all of whose members enjoyed many hereditary privileges. There was a wealthy caste of merchant travelers, many orders of priests to serve the numerous temples, a large and influential military establishment, schools of various kinds including some for artists, musicians, scribes, and poets, and a large class of peasants. There were a number of layers of serfs and bondsmen, with slaves at the bottom of the system; the numerous peoples subjugated by the Aztecs were heavily represented in these lower strata.

Aztec hegemony in the western part of Mesoamerica, rapidly consolidated in the few centuries just before the Spanish came, rested on military force and commercial power. Taxes, tribute, and profits flowed into the capital, which grew very rapidly. Though cosmopolitan in many respects, the imperial center displayed some strikingly familiar symptoms of condescension toward those less fortunate. Fluency in the favored Texcoco dialect of Nahuatl spoken by the elite of the capital was highly prized as a mark of cultivation:

> The Mexican language is considered the mother-tongue, and that of Texcoco is thought the noblest and the purest. All the languages other than this were held to be coarse and vulgar. . . . The Mexican language spreads over the whole of New Spain . . . and the others are thought barbarous and strange. . . . It is the richest and fullest language that is to be found. It is not only dignified but also soft and pleasing, lordly and of a high nobility, succinct, easy, and flexible.[3]

Those lacking the necessary skill in Nahuatl to be considered fully civilized were 'barbarians', literally 'babblers', people who could not speak properly. The Nahuatl word was strikingly parallel to the Greek one in both sound and sense, and that is how a number of unrelated languages of the area came to be called *Popoluca* or *Popoloca*. Even speakers of the very closely related Nahuatl dialect of Aztecan were called *Pipil* for the same reason. And the *Chontal*, both the Mayan Chontal of Tabasco and the unrelated Hokan Chontal of Oaxaca, are the *chontalli*, the 'forest people', or hillbillies.

Looking back still farther, beyond the Toltec culture that influenced both the Aztecs and the Mayas of Postclassic Yucatan, to a period seven or eight centuries before the arrival of the Spanish, one can dimly see a Mesoamerican pattern of civilization with some interesting parallels to both the Aztec culture and the modern Mexican one, though obviously much more must be inferred about the earlier periods for lack of documentary evidence. Astride one of outlets of the Valley of Mexico was the great city of Teotihuacan, the capital of a powerful and highly developed civilization which had then dominated the western part of Mesoamerica for centuries, and apparently was a major influence throughout the eastern part as well. Its distinctive art and architectural styles have been found in site after site throughout the region of its economic and political influence, suggesting the maintenance of a system of colonies, diplomatic missions, or trade outposts. During roughly this same period, the eastern part of Mesoamerica was the seat of the Mayan civilization. One of its major archeological sites, and one of the longest inhabited, is Kaminaljuyú, now mostly surrounded or covered by modern Guatemala City. Within the archeological zone an important Teotihuacan enclave has been found. These and other materials and their distribution have made it clear that there was trade and cultural contact of major importance linking the two parts of Mesoamerica during ancient times, with trade routes criss-crossing the Mayan culture area as well as the Mexican.

It is no exaggeration to call these ancient Mesoamerican cultures civilizations. The ceremonial centers and their surrounding residential zones were of impressive size. The pyramids of Teotihuacan are among the largest structures of the ancient world: the largest is 210 meters square at the base and 64 meters high; smaller variations on the temple-pyramid theme are one of the unifying traits of the Mesoamerican cultural area. At its greatest extent, the residential zone of Teotihuacan covered about seven square miles. Excavation has only sampled this area outside the main ceremonial center, but there is evidence of the clustering of some occupational specialists in districts (e.g. obsidian workers). Writing was used, though little survives. Another trait of the Mesoamerican zone doubtless present at Teotihuacan was the calendar, based on a cycle of 18,980 days (365 x 52 or 260 x 73). This appears to have originated with the Olmecs on the Gulf coast of Vera Cruz in the Middle Preclassic period (between 1000 and 300 BC) and was taken up by most of the later cultures, becoming especially elaborated in the Mayan civilization. There it was supported by a well-developed system of naked-eye astronomy that included knowledge of eclipse cycles, the movements of the visible planets and the Moon, and of the relation between the movement of the Sun and the cycle of rainy and dry seasons of the tropical year. Astronomical and calendrical calculations were made using a system of arithmetic employing a place notation and a symbol for zero. Perhaps most impressive of all, in the case of the Mayan civilization, was the development, before 300 AD, of a full-fledged writing system, of mixed logographic and phonetic type, attested in many inscriptions, in ceramic and mural painting, and in a few surviving books. This writing system, now partially deciphered, was used for historical and religious purposes at least, presumably by a caste of specialist scribes.[4]

Recent archeological discoveries have led to a sharp revision of estimates of the economic base of Mayan civilization. Water-borne trade in salt and other goods over the entire region was an important factor in deciding the location of the political-ceremonial centers themselves. Systems of raised fields covering very large tracts of swampy lowlands have been found; the canals separating them, formed by excavating the soil and plant material used for the raised fields themselves, were perhaps an extension of the transportation system used for moving the surplus from this very productive type of agriculture whose carrying capacity would have supported a population far larger than previous estimates had allowed for.

All of this—the complex architectural and artistic developments, the mathematics, science, and writing, the vast engineering effort required for the raised fields, and the evidence of dynastic interrelationships contained in the inscriptions, makes it clear that the Mayan culture was intricately structured and complex.

Surviving examples of Mayan graphic arts—ceramics, carvings on wood and stone, a few frescos, and three books—are sophisticated in technique and obviously complex in their symbolism. Some specimens depict musicians and costumed performers dancing, and perhaps enacting dramas or pageants. The degree of specialization implied by the availability of highly skilled artists, performers, scribes, and carvers, not to mention priests, would surely not be found without a parallel development of verbal art. Indeed, one finds few societies of any kind without verbal art, and the modern Mayans have kept theirs alive here and there. And a tradition of verbal art necessarily embodies notions of style and taste, a system of valuation imposed on the range of usage and dialect diversity of the community it serves. Mayan hieroglyphic writing itself, as it is now known from the partial decipherment so far achieved, incorporates an elaborate symbolism of sounds and cultural content, drawing upon religious, astronomical, astrological, and numerological lore. It is most unlikely that the Mayans, who even today are ready to volunteer judgements about dialects, giving the relative merits of their own (superior), their neighbors' (inferior), and more remote ones (best of all), would have developed the intricate artistic superstructure of their classic period without a fully developed canon of linguistic purity and excellence in verbal art.

Having stated these assumptions, however, which make the very existence of the writing system and the other arts evidence of a kind in favor of inequalities in the sociolinguistic fabric of the culture, it is hard to find more than scraps of evidence to support them. Decipherments of certain hieroglyphic signs, however, interpreted in the context of this paper, may give some insight into the values and attitudes of the late postclassic Yucatecan scribal tradition. It is a characteristic of primarily logographic writing systems such as the Mayan, the Chinese, and the Near Eastern Cuneiform systems that a word-sign may be read with the same meaning by readers with different dialects or languages each pronouncing the sign in his own quite distinct way. This capability has often been cited as an advantage of writing systems of this type for multilingual societies, as in the case of China. But the phonetic neutrality of the logograms, arbitrary word symbols whose 'pronunciation' must be memorized, also allows a quite different kind of flexibility that has been exploited in the case of late Mayan writing. The diversity within the Mayan language family is such that cognate words from different languages within the family have quite different, though regularly patterned, consonant and vowel values. Some of these differences are traceable in the hieroglyphic writing system in contexts where particular signs are used for their phonetic value alone, rather than their meaning, in what amounts to a kind of rebus writing. Thus, the sign for the day named 'deer' in many versions of the Mesoamerican calendar is written in Mayan texts with the same sign that appears as one constituent in the glyph group for the direction 'West', which is *chikin* in Yucatec Maya. But the Yucatec word for 'deer' is *ceh* with a plain 'hard' *c* and an [e] vowel like English *bed*. In Cholan, however, a Central Mayan linguistic subfamily, the word for 'deer' is *chih*, with the right consonant and vowel values. And it was in Cholan territory that the great development of Classic Mayan culture seems to have taken place. Another calendrical sign, the vague year or 'period of 360 days', also meaning 'stone', displays a similarly Cholan value, being read *tun* instead of the Yucatecan *ton*.[5] If the interpretation suggested here is correct, the writing system was used in this way to evoke an earlier, more pure era of the culture, in somewhat the same way a 'cultivated' speaker of American English might affect a 'British' pronunciation of certain words, or a preacher might strive for a 'King James' style of usage in his sermons. The interpretation of the month signs in the hieroglyphic writing system harks back even farther in the history of Mayan, fitting best with the names of the months in the languages of the northwestern shoulder of Guatemala, a region that was largely left out of the classical developments but had been important in the formation of the Mayan culture and the early diversification of the language family. The appropriate analogy here with the history of English might be the 'Anglo-Saxon' element of modern English vocabulary, used sometimes deliberately for its connotations of downrightness and vigor. Unfortunately, these interpretations are necessarily speculative, and must remain so.

The broad outlines of the system, however, are very securely known from the documentary and archeological record. Mesoamerica has been literally 'civilized' for about two thousand years, and in that time, the development of social and political stratification linking peasant farmers to their local and regional political-ceremonial centers, and linking these in turn into a hierarchy of dynastic power, has been a nearly constant process through much of the region. The mosaic of relatively small ethnic and linguistic groups living on the land has participated, sometimes as victors, and sometimes as victims, in the formation, destruction, and reformation of multilingual, multicultural states and empires. The languages now stigmatized as emblems of inferiority were in some cases in the past symbols of cultural superiority, and may be so again, for all that can be known now. Other languages now the object of scorn by Spanish speakers were once scorned by Nahuatl speakers, or Mayan speakers, or Totonac speakers, or Zapotecs, and indeed are so scorned today, given the continuing and seemingly universal effect of ethnocentrism. The current hierarchy of culture and language has Spanish at the top, but that is only the latest episode in a long story.

Complex Speech Communities

Although sociolinguistic systems like those described here in general outline are very commonly encountered in the 'third world', there is nevertheless no really satisfactory classification to fit them into. Diebold (1961, 1962) focused on the early stages of the process of hispanization in his accounts of the Huave community of San Mateo del Mar, chosen for study because of its high proportion of monolinguals. His description introduced the term *incipient bilingualism*. Despite some differences apparently due to cultural attitudes, there are many parallels between San Mateo del Mar and Tila. Despite the somewhat lower proportion of monolinguals in Tila, the factors governing the use and spread of Spanish seem to be nearly the same for both groups of Indians.

Linguistics has taken notice of bilingual or multilingual societies for a long time, of course. Bloomfield devoted a chapter of his textbook to what he called *intimate borrowing*; for its time (1933) it was very good. He considered the various outcomes of language contact resulting from conquest bringing about different durations and intensities of contact between groups. He distinguished an upper language (spoken by the dominant or privileged group) and a lower language, and weighed the factors sometimes leading to the extinction of the one or the other, and sometimes to the formation of a pidginized interlanguage. He mentioned as examples of different outcomes the conquest of the British Isles by West Germanic peoples in the fifth century, leaving Celtic speakers on the periphery, and later conquest by the Normans that established French as a dominant language for several centuries, although for much of that time the Anglo-Normans were bilingual, and English remained the only language spoken by most of the inhabitants. Bloomfield might have added the Roman conquest of Britain as an example of brief contact followed by extinction of the upper language. The factors he regarded as important in the process of change were the relative size of the groups in contact, their territorial relationships, the cultural and linguistic attitudes of each, and the degree of isolation. He attended only indirectly to the idea of a linguistic repertoire or code switching. His focus was macroscopic, and like Diebold and many others, Bloomfield implicitly treated bilingualism as a transitional state rather than as a potentially stable organization of a speech community.

With increased interest in code switching and the complexity of verbal repertoires in all kinds of communities has come a focus on multilingual and multidialectal communities as they are, without regard to change, or with change as a distinctly secondary matter. Perhaps the best known accounts of code switching on a comparable large scale are Ferguson's classic paper on *diglossia* (1959) and Joan Rubin's discussions of national bilingualism in Paraguay (1962, 1963). Diglossic societies as described by Ferguson employ two varieties of a language, which he called *high* and *low*, each used in a subset of speech situations mutually exclusive with the domain of the other. Everyone begins by learning *low* as a family language, and it remains associated with intimate or informal situations; some (not necessarily all) go on to learn *high*, typically at school, and it remains associated with formal situations. The term and the notion of diglossia have sometimes been abused since their introduction into linguistics. Many patterns of code switching have been called diglossia by now, including some of quite different structure from the original systems mentioned by Ferguson. His model focused on switching between just two codes, presented for the sake of simplicity as if the same for all, and not explicitly connected with social stratification. A closer approximation would point out the variability of both *high* and *low* codes, and correlate this with significant differences in speech situation and in social relationships among interactants. Joan Rubin's work moved in this direction, showing parallels between the use of Spanish (*high*) and Guaraní (*low*) in Paraguay and the model of pronoun usage constructed by Roger Brown. Rubin added a consideration of speech situation (and speaker attitudes), social class, and community structure to the diglossia model. Garvin and Mathiot (1956) discuss what might be called the incipient standardization of Guaraní. This paper and Rubin's work, in their treatment of a bilingual society in equilibrium, represent a significant departure from most earlier work, with its concern for change or remediation.

What is still lacking is a single system of classification integrating the dimensions of social stratification situation, and code diversity.

The accompanying diagrams can only suggest some of the relationships such a classification would take into account. Each square is a schematic representation of a speech community, with social class or prestige increasing along the vertical dimension and formality of speech situation increasing along the horizontal dimension. Each of two codes is represented by a distinct pattern of hatching; the use of both codes in alternation in a given situation is shown by cross hatching. A horizontal line between apexes divides the community into two distinct ethnic groups; a line without apexes at the margins is a linguistic boundary separating two distinct codes or code alternation patterns.

Diagram 1 shows a situation typically arising through conquest, with an upper sociolinguistic group (a superstrate) using one language, and a lower sociolinguistic group (a substrate) using another. Each group uses its own code across the entire spectrum of speech situations. There are in principle no bilingual individuals. Diagram 2, on the other hand, shows a society made up entirely of bilingual individuals, where everyone has both codes available in all situations. There are no monolingual individuals. Both are idealizations. The original model of diglossia is shown in Diagram 3: everyone in the society has two codes available, but one is used in all informal speech situations, and the other in all formal ones. The code boundary in Diagram 3 is therefore vertical, cutting across social class distinctions, and dividing possible speech situations into two groups, whereas the ethnic-linguistic boundary in diagram 1 is horizontal, dividing the community into two distinct social groups each having a single code for all situations.

The community schematized in Diagram 4 has an upper language used by one ethnic group and a lower language used by another ethnic group; in addition, some members of the substrate group are bilinguals. The Huave-Spanish relationship described by Diebold (1962) is like this; so is the Chol community of Tila. A different outcome of contact is shown in Diagram 5, where the superstrate instead of the substrate has become bilingual. Within a few generations of the conquest, the Anglo-Norman superstrate in English-speaking Britain had become bilingual in this way. The use of French and Russian by Czarist aristocrats was similar.

Economically and educationally advanced societies with diglossia, Switzerland being perhaps the best example, are somewhat more accurately represented as in Diagram 6 than in Diagram 3. The sloping code boundary reflects the fact that the higher social strata use the H code in more situations (and in closer conformity to standard usage) than the lower strata, who rely more on the L code. The last three figures are meant to add a further refinement to the notion of diglossia. They introduce a variety I will call *split diglossia*, because it affects only a part of the community. Some eastern European communities match rather well with Diagram 7: lower social groups use little or no H, whereas the higher strata alternate in the way one expects to find in diglossic communities. Urban Austria (i.e., Vienna) is close to Diagram 6, but other districts, such as the Tyrol or Vorarlberg, are like Diagram 7. In Diagram 8, on the other hand, most of the upper social group uses the H code in all situations, but the lower group is diglossic. This arrangement prevails in communities in the United States where one part of the community is diglossic in Black English Vernacular (as the L code) and in Standard English (as the H code), while another part of the same community uses only Standard English. It should be taken for granted, of course, that nobody in any of these communities follows a homogeneous and

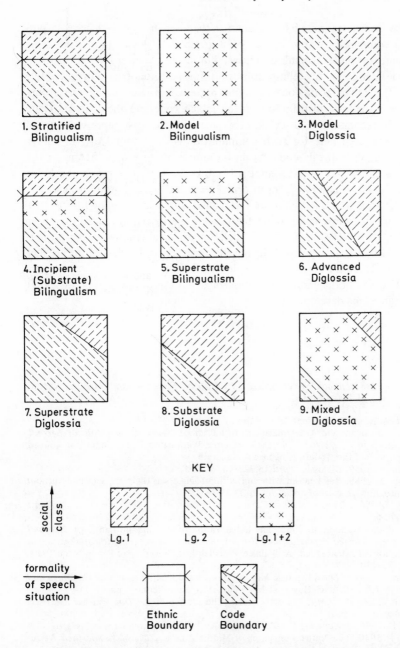

1. Stratified Bilingualism

2. Model Bilingualism

3. Model Diglossia

4. Incipient (Substrate) Bilingualism

5. Superstrate Bilingualism

6. Advanced Diglossia

7. Superstrate Diglossia

8. Substrate Diglossia

9. Mixed Diglossia

KEY

social class

Lg. 1   Lg. 2   Lg. 1+2

formality of speech situation

Ethnic Boundary   Code Boundary

uniform pattern of usage, whatever the code. A pattern like that in Diagram 8 for Mesoamerica is the Chorti community of Jocotan, where the Indians use Chorti as L and Spanish as H, while the monolinguals use Spanish alone.

More issues are raised by diagram 9 than can be resolved here. It por-
trays a community whose upper social group is 'diglossic' in a sense, using
one code in more formal situations, but using a pattern of alternation,
of code switching or bilingualism in informal situations. For a middle
group, this bilingual or code-switching pattern is usual. For a lower group,
there is a diglossic distribution of the mixed code and the L code. There
are such communities, I think. This may be the best representation of
those considered here for such communities as the Chontal of San Carlos,
where Spanish is the H code, Spanish-Chontal mixture or switching is the
intermediate pattern, and Chontal is the L code. Thus, one group uses H for
formal situations and H + L for informal ones, and another group reverses the
picture, using H + L for its more formal utterances, and L alone for informal
situations. The proportion of H features in the speech produced in a given
situation then serves as a possible social index, or alternatively, the proportion of H in a situation reveals its relative formality if the class of the speaker
is known. There is a great deal to be done before such a system is more than a
suggestive way of diagramming relationships, but there is enough promise in it
to warrant some development.

References

Baugh, J. (1983). *Black Street Speech: Its History, Structure, and Survival.* Austin:
    University of Texas Press.
Bloomfield, L. 1933. *Language.* New York: Holt.
Diebold, A. R. 1961. Incipient Bilingualism. *Language* 37.97-112.
–   1962. Mexican and Guatemalan Bilingualism. *A Study of the Role of Second
    Languages in Asia, Africa, and Latin America.* Washington, D. C.: Center for Applied
    Linguistics of the Modern Language Association.
Ferguson, C. 1959. Diglossia. *Word* 15.325-40.
Fishman, J. 1969. Bilingualism with and without Diglossia; Diglossia with and without
    Bilingualism. *Journal of Social Issues* 23.29-38.
Fought, J. 1969. Chortí (Mayan) Ceremonial Organization. *American Anthropologist*
    71.472-6.
Garvin, P. and Mathiot, M. 1956. The Urbanization of the Guaraní Language. *Men and
    Cultures: Selected Papers of the Fifth International Congress of Anthropological and
    Ethnological Sciences,* ed. A. Wallace. Philadelphia: University of Pennsylvania Press,
    pp. 783-790.
Johnson, F. 1940. The Linguistic Map of Mexico and Central America. *The Maya and
    their Neighbors,* ed. C. Hay et al. New York: Appleton-Century, pp. 88-114.
Justeson, J. and Matthews, P. Forthcoming. The Seating of the *Tun:* Further Evidence.
    American Antiquity.
Kelley, D. 1976. *Deciphering the Maya Script.* Austin: University of Texas Press.
Mason, J. 1940. The Native Languages of Middle America. *The Maya and their Neigh-
    bors,* ed. C. Hay et al. New York: Appleton-Century, pp. 52-87.
Muñoz Camargo, Diego. 1892. *Crónica de Tlaxcals.* Mexico:
Rubin, J. 1962. Bilingualism in Paraguay. *Anthropological Linguistics* 4.52-8.
–   1963 National Bilingualism in Paraguay. Yale University Dissertation.

Sanders, W. and Price, B. 1968. *Mesoamerica: The Evolution of a Civilization.* New York: Random House.
Sharer, R. Forthcoming. *The Ancient Maya.* (New Edition) Palo Alto: Stanford University Press.
Soustelle, J. 1970. *The Daily Life of the Aztecs.* Stanford CA: Stanford University Press.
Willey, G., ed. 1966. *An Introduction to American Archaeology, vol. 1: North and Middle America.* Englewood Cliffs, N. J.: Prentice Hall.

Notes

* I thank Lee Ann Draud, Joan Manes, and Nessa Wolfson for their help in giving this paper its present form. In particular, I am grateful to Nessa Wolfson for helping me to see the significance of the treatment of diglossia sketched here. Responsibility for the content of the paper rests with me alone, however.

1. In Fought 1969, I traced the influence of customs and institutions from the Guatemalan Highlands and beyond (these being blended with Hispanic influences) on the ceremonial organizations of the Chortí. These influences were passed eastward along the routes to the major pilgrimage site of Esquipulas on the eastern frontier of Guatemala. The note also deals with the decline of these ceremonial organizations in recent years.

2. The literature on Mesoamerica is large and rapidly growing. For a broad and conservative view of the archeology, see Willey (1966); on the Mayans, see Sharer (forthcoming). A perspective on the cultural evolution of the region is given by Sanders and Price (1968). Soustelle (1970) is a popular and accessible treatment of the life of the Aztecs. On the linguistic geography of Mesoamerica, I still prefer the papers by Mason (1940) and Johnson (1940).

3. Munoz Camargo (1892), quoted in Soustelle (1970: 233-4).

4. On Mayan hieroglyphic writing see Kelley 1976.

5. On this point, see Justeson and Matthews (forthcoming).

Ana Celia Zentella

The Fate of Spanish in the United States:
The Puerto Rican Experience.

The 1980s have been widely heralded as the decade of Hispanics in the United States. Residents from Spanish speaking countries, now the fastest growing minority, are expected to become the largest minority group in the country before the 1990 census. This has encouraged many to hope that the government will address the social and economic ills that plague all Hispanic communities, especially the Puerto Rican and Chicano ghettoes. But Hispanics, who have been a significant presence in the United States since its earliest days, are coming of age at a time when national priorities are being redirected in the name of fiscal restraint. As a result, programs tailored to meet Hispanic needs for housing, job training, education, etc., are judged impractical and unaffordable. More and more, national priorities and official pronouncements recall the parochialism and xenophobia of the post World War I period. American families fear immigrant families as threats to their standard of living. Many of the children of the familes who settled in the USA during the late nineteenth and early twentieth centuries have joined the attack on the latest immigrants. At the same time that poor immigrant communities are being made the scapegoats for the country's economic crisis, the US government has reinitiated massive loans to Latin American regimes who flagrantly violate the civil rights of their citizens, causing more of them to flee to the US each year.

In this climate, there is an urgent need to convince the American public that, like the previous waves of immigrants before them, Hispanics are making contributions to the American way of life that far outweigh the problems they seem to present. National priorities must be re-directed so that these contributions can become a permanent thread in the fabric of US life. Present attitudes and policies aid in condemning millions of people to a life of poverty and dependency.

The US has reached a point in its development when it can and must take advantage of the opportunities presented by the presence of 12 million Hispanics in the USA. One of the most invaluable contributions that can be made is to break the linguistic isolationism of the US, often a source of amazement and ridicule in Europe, Africa, and the rest of the world, where monolingualism is the exception, not the rule. The narrow view that Americans should speak only English was decidedly not part of the philosophy of the founding fathers (Heath 1977). The leading citizens of the new United States understood such a position to be impractical and antithetical to the democratic principles they sought to establish. When the US became intolerant of different linguistic and cultural minorities, particularly after World War I, an incalculable price was paid in the loss of linguistic resources; massive efforts were required in order to undo the damage when the country found itself unprepared for the linguistic demands of a second world war (Kloss 1977). A recent federal study that documents the negative impact of monolingualism on the US has led universities and educational agencies across the nation to re-evaluate and invigorate their language programs (Commission on Foreign Language and International Studies 1979). The premise is that an educated North American should learn to appreciate different linguistic and cultural realities.

Within the heart of the nation, in every state, there are some of the 25 to 30 million people whose mother tongue is a language other than English; these speakers of other languages could be the key to a US effort to open its linguistic frontiers. The sad experience of most of these new Americans is that they are pressured into forgetting their native language and replacing it with English. Some steps to reverse this process were undertaken in the 1960s, culminating in the 1968 *Bilingual Education Act* which provided the first federal funds for instruction in the native language as well as English. As the 1980s begin, before these initiatives have had the opportunity to establish themselves, and before the new wave of Hispanics can take advantage of them, they are being decimated by budget cuts. Along with the hopes of the Hispanics and others for a better future that are being washed away, the linguistic resources of the nation are being squandered. This chapter documents how the oldest and largest group of Spanish speakers on the east coast of the United States have fared as subjects of US language policies.

United States Language Policy in Puerto Rico

The Puerto Rican case is significant because, unlike the major waves of late eighteenth and early nineteenth century migrations, it shares many characteristics with the most recent groups of immigrants from Latin America, i.e., they are considered non-white, non-European, and they are arriving when technology and closed union policies are denying jobs to low skilled workers with minimal education. One major factor distinguishes the Puerto Rican experience from that of today's Dominican, Cuban, Colombian, etc. migrations; the US control of the governmental, educational, and linguistic policies affecting Puerto Ricans pre-dated their arrival in the US. Puerto Rico has been a colony of the US since the US invasion of the island on July 25, 1898. During the next fifty years, US policies attempted to undo 400 years of Spanish language and culture. Military governors and colonial educational officials began with a relentless Americanization of the island that forbade the use of Spanish throughout the legal and educational systems (Negron de Montilla 1975). Practically overnight, the classes and the courts were required to function in English only; teachers could not be certified if they did not pass English exams (Figueroa 1972). Early documents reflect the negative opinion the new leaders had of their subjects' language:

> Their language is a patois almost unintelligible to the native of Barcelona and Madrid. It possesses no literature and has little value as an intellectual medium. There is a bare possibility that it will be nearly as easy to educate these people out of their patois into English as it would be to educate them into the elegant tongue of Castile (Osuna 1949: 324).

In fact, the Spanish of Puerto Rico in 1898 and today was/is easily understood by any native of Spain or Latin America; it is as legitimate a variety of Spanish as is the Castilian dialect, just as US English and British English are equally legitimate dialects of English. We elaborate on the importance of recognizing the legitimacy of Puerto Rican Spanish in our discussion of The Puerto Rican Experience on the Mainland: Crisis in Cultural Identity, below.

When widespread island resistance and new US economic interests demanded different tactics, the more subtle penetration of English and replacement of Spanish began (Language Policy Task Force 1978, Zentella 1981 b). Language policies changed at least eight times during the first 50 years of US rule. Some required English in early grades; others changed it to later grades or to particular subjects. Extensive damage was done to the educational future of that and succeeding generations of Puerto Ricans by the alternation of these culturally insensitive and linguistically inappropriate policies (International Institute of Columbia Teachers College 1926). After three decades of control by various Secretaries of Education from the US, 80 percent of the students had failed both Spanish and English and had dropped out of school. Widespread resistance to the replacement of Spanish with English resulted in strikes and demonstrations. No self-respecting Puerto Rican educator would assume the position of Secretary of Education between 1936–37 and 1945–48 because the US Senate required that they formally commit themselves in writing to a policy favoring English. In 1952, Puerto Rican officials were allowed to reinstate Spanish as the language of instruction, in an effort to deflect the independence movement's ability to organize around the language issue. English, however, was, and still is, compulsory in all grades, and English instruction counts on administrative and material support that far exceeds that given to Spanish. Although the imposition of English is bitterly resented in some quarters, harsh realities, e.g., per capita income below $3000 per annum in 1980, make many Puerto Ricans link English with economic survival—either as a ticket to a job serving tourists, or as the price of a ticket to the mainland.

The Puerto Rican Experience on the Mainland: Crisis in Cultural Identity

The dominant themes of the US practices and policies on the island, i.e., that Puerto Rican Spanish is inferior to that of Spain, that English is corrupting Puerto Rican Spanish, and that progress means becoming American by adopting the English language and North American cultural values, are the legacy that is part of the baggage that Puerto Ricans take with them to the mainland.

The economic well being and the linguistic status of Puerto Ricans continue to suffer on the mainland. Sixty years after the first 1000 Puerto Ricans were recorded in the US census of 1916, the most comprehensive government analysis of conditions in the US Puerto Rican community found little improvement and 'an uncertain future' (US Commission on Civil Rights 1976). Throughout the US, and especially in New York City, where 57 percent of all Puerto Ricans in the US live, Puerto Ricans are the poorest of all groups: compared with Anglos, Afro-americans, Chicanos, Dominicans, Cubans and other Latin Americans, they have the highest percent of families with children living in poverty, the lowest percent of people in the work force, and the lowest median income (National Puerto Rican Forum 1981).

The Puerto Rican struggle to earn a living in the US is exacerbated by the obstacles of racism, cultural conflicts, and linguistic ignorance. To cite an example, Puerto Rican respondents to census and other questionnaires were traditionally asked to select among Black-White-Other, or Black-White-Puerto Rican; in this way they learned that US racial categories convert the Puerto Rican culture or nationality into a race. Such classifications ignore the fact that, unlike the US, where geno-typic theories classify persons with one drop of black blood as black and all others as white, people in Latin America with fair features are considered *blancos* 'white', those whose features are African are considered *negros* 'black', and the more prevalent combinations of these groups, and others, are also recognized, e.g., *trigueño* (olive skin), *jabáo* (African and European features, light hair), *grifo* (African and European features, dark hair), *mulato* (light skinned black), *indio* (indian features), etc. Moreover, whereas racial identification supercedes cultural identity in the US, the reverse is true for Latin America (Rodriguez 1980). This inversion of the primary factors of identification contributes to the identity conflict of Puerto Ricans and other Latin Americans, particularly among the second generation. In response to the conflicting pressures they feel between their parent's cultural identity, the US denigration of blackness, and the Afro-American's reaffirmation of black pride, many mainland born/raised youth of all complexions have chosen to identify themselves as 'non-white' (Rodriguez 1980).

The racial aspect of the identity crisis that Puerto Ricans in the U.S. face is shared by many other Latin Americans, but other aspects are unique to Puerto Ricans; they stem from the political status of Puerto Rico. Whereas Dominicans, Mexicans, etc., are citizens of their respective countries until they apply for and are granted US citizenship, Puerto Ricans on the island are citizens of the US at birth; they have been since several weeks before the US began drafting men to fight in World War I. As a result, American citizenship conflicts with Puerto Rican identity even in the native land. Most parents raise their children to believe that those who were born in Puerto Rico are Puerto Ricans, and those who were born in the US are Americans. This cleavage within families, often based on accidents of birth, given the massive back and forth migration, contributes to the confusion of the children, especially when they find that they are rejected by other Americans. The first parent whose cooperation I sought for my research on how Puerto Rican children become bilingual was accompanied by his eight year old daughter. She immediately interjected, "But I'm not Puerto Rican, I was born here". Nevertheless, the next years of taping and observation revealed that she shared patterns of behavior with other children her age who were born and raised in Puerto Rico, and which are not part of the lives of the majority of US-born children. Thus, in addition to the confusion about race and nationality, the Puerto Rican second generation is confused by too simplistic a link between culture and place of birth.

These identity conflicts are perhaps best exemplified by the consistent attacks on how Puerto Ricans speak, attacks mounted most effectively by the schools and the media, and which recall the dominant themes of US policy in Puerto Rico, i.e., the inferiority of Puerto Rico and its Spanish and the superiority of the US and English. One of the most effective lessons learned in US schools is that Spanish and Spanish speakers enjoy low status in the US. This is achieved by various practices. Students' names are often anglicized in spelling and/or pronunciation. Their Spanish is constantly corrected and denounced, e.g., they are told to pronounce syllable final *s* at all times, e.g., mucha*s* gracia*s*, never to omit intervocalic *d*, e.g., esta(d)o, habla(d)o, to say *naranja* and *autobús* instead of *china* 'orange' and *guagua* 'bus'. Words in their vocabulary such as *roofo* 'roof', *hol* 'hall', *beihman* 'basement' are called barbarisms. And, as if to clinch the argument, Puerto Ricans are told they speak a dialect of Spanish that is not 'real' Spanish, harkening back to the anti-linguistic posture of the early colonial administrator cited above. Although there has been no consistent documentation of the psychological and emotional harm caused by these attitudes, case studies of disturbed Puerto Rican children frequently mention language harassment as a significant source of friction and distress (Montalvo 1972).

It is surprising, given the enormity of the pressures to the contrary, that many Puerto Ricans have managed to survive with a positive sense of identity, and with both Spanish and English as integral parts of that identity. Many more could become fluent bilinguals if they and those who design and implement policies that affect them understood the historical linguistic processes that characterize languages in contact. For example, the 'barbarisms' that cause such alarm are so few in number that they pose no threat to the Spanish vocabulary. More important, they constitute additions that reflect a new or different sociocultural reality, e.g. roofs, lunches and blocks are not the same in Puerto Rico as they are in the US and *roofo*, *lonche*, and *bloque* capture the new connotations. The detractors of Puerto Rican Spanish are as unaware of these processes, known as borrowing, loan translation, etc., as they are of basic notions of language variety and its social correlates. Speakers of every language share certain features of pronunciation, grammar, and word formation with others, and these become important symbols of membership in a particular group. This variety is what is meant by the word dialect; dialects distinguish each geographical region, class, ethnic group and race from each other. Just as people of Great Britain say *lift* and [šedyul] for what North Americans call *elevator* and [skedyul], Puerto Ricans say *china* and [grasyah] instead of *naranja* and [grasyas]. Except in the minds of some arch anglophiles, British English is not considered superior to US English. Similarly, it is worth repeating that Puerto Rican Spanish, part of the Caribbean variety, should not be considered inferior to any other dialect.

The noxious self image with which many Hispanic children leave elementary schools is exacerbated in the advanced grades, where their English and Spanish come under attack by language teachers ignorant of these basic linguistic facts. Many junior and senior high school students recall the anguished embarrassment they felt when the teacher of Spanish introduced the course with the injunction that the class was about to learn 'correct' Spanish, not what Puerto Ricans spoke, and that those members of the class who were not Puerto Rican would be at an advantage because they would not have to unlearn what they knew. It is not surprising to learn that many Puerto Rican students dread Spanish classes and often fail them. On the other hand, those who overcome these odds and do well are also punished; they are belittled for taking 'snap courses', although no similar accusation is made of native English speakers who enroll in English courses. This double standard is most unjustly applied at award time. On more that one occasion a Spanish medal has been denied to a Puerto Rican student with the highest average in Spanish in favor of the non Puerto Rican who earned the second highest grades. Nevertheless, the same Puerto Rican student was not awarded the English medal when he/she had the second best English grades; it was awarded to the Anglos with the highest grades. Students who observe or are subjected to such injustices can only become cynical about the 'work hard and you'll make it' theory.

Perhaps the most frequent accusation hurled at Puerto Ricans in the US is that they speak neither English nor Spanish, but Spanglish, a non-defined mixture. This criticism is so prevalent that it is not uncommon to see it referred to in newspapers and magazines (Fernández 1972, *New York Daily News* 1980). The most notorious example of a large scale effort to establish Spanglish as the language of Puerto Ricans in New York occurred in 1970 when a well known university, the New School for Social Research, offered courses in Spanglish to Anglo professionals. Picketing by irate community groups and condemning editorials in the Spanish daily forced the cancellation of the classes (Varo 1971). My own research in the Puerto Rican community in New York, to be discussed below, not only rebuts the myth that Puerto Ricans are degenerating Spanish and English, it also proves that Spanish-English alternation is a dynamic communicative strategy that serves important discourse functions and maintains the grammatical integrity of both languages.

Puerto Ricans in the US are caught in a double bind: their Spanish is unacceptable to the educational institutions and the mass media, and so is their English. Many New Yorkers with characteristic New York accents ridicule the Spanish accented English of island born/reared Puerto Ricans; qualified teacher applicants from this first generation have received poor grades on the New York City Board of Education's oral exam because of their accents. Puerto Ricans are not blind to the fact that while many North Americans consider French and other accents elegant, Spanish accents are often considered laughable and/or repulsive. Inevitably, their children, the second generation, learn to be ashamed of their parents' speech, and parents in turn lose their confidence in their ability to speak English; many depend on young children to negotiate their way through bureaucracies. These experiences tear at the strong family fabric characteristic of Puerto Rican culture, and help destroy traditional notions of 'respeto' (respect) in child-adult relationships.

Of course, the difficulties we have discussed are not unique to the Puerto Rican community; they have been the experience of every immigrant group in the United States. Prevalent sociological theory maintains that these growing pains are overcome when the second and third generation achieve the level of cultural and social assimilation that now marks the earlier migrations (Senior 1965, Fitzpatrick 1971). These theorists fail to distinguish between the eras in which the different migrations occurred, and contrasting political and geographic constraints. They also ignore such crucial factors as voluntary vs. involuntary migration, European vs. non-European status, and white vs. non-white classification. These differences account for the fact that the forces that have led previous immigrant groups to replace their mother tongue with English have not taken effect on Puerto Ricans in the same way. For example, as US citizens free to migrate back and forth from their nearby homeland, Puerto Ricans have maintained Spanish longer than other groups have maintained their mother tongue. According to the 1970 census data, Spanish is the mother tongue of more than 83 percent of the Puerto Ricans in the US, and 72 percent speak Spanish at home.

Another difference between the language history of Puerto Ricans in the US and that of previous immigrant groups is the assimilation of the Puerto Rican second generations' English to surrounding Black dialects. Some young Puerto Ricans learn to speak like the Afro-Americans with whom they share the schools and ghettoes. These youngsters become the object of a new epithet; 'You sound like as Spic' is replaced by 'You sound like a nigger'.

Anglos and other non-Puerto Ricans are not the only harsh critics. Some of the most damaging judgements come from Puerto Ricans, particularly professionals, who use the term 'Nuyorican' with disparaging connotations. In 1968 Fishman found that 80 percent of the Puerto Rican professionals he interviewed in New York believed that it was necessary to speak Spanish to be a Puerto Rican, and that *nuyorquinos* spoke Spanish badly. In contrast, the 'ordinary' Puerto Ricans saw no inextricable link between an ability to speak Spanish and Puerto Rican identity, although they considered *nuyorquinos* good Spanish speakers (Fishman 1971).

El Bloque: A Bilingual Community

Most commentaries on the way Puerto Ricans speak are based on hearsay and/or isolated examples. The linguistic data reported on here were gathered during two years of participant observation on a block in New York City's El Barrio, East Harlem; a wide range of home and street activities were tape recorded (Zentella 1981a). The speakers included the nineteen families of *el bloque* (the block) and their thirty-four children between four and sixteen years of age. The members of the community varied as to number of years in the US and proficiency in English and Spanish, but they shared desperate socio-economic conditions and limited education. Not all of the families of *el bloque* communicate the same way at home, but all of the bilingual speakers, young and old, display an ability to alternate the languages in their repertoire, i.e., to code switch from Spanish to English or vice versa for productive discourse purposes. Our analysis of the valuable communicative role played by intra-turn code switching follows a general description of language behavior in the home.

Four distinct communication patterns exist in the homes on the block; they differ in terms of the language(s) that the parents speak to each other, the language(s) the parents speak to the children and vice versa, and the language(s) the children speak among themselves. These dyads can be diagrammed on Figure 1.

In the majority of the families (twelve of nineteen, containing seventeen of the thirty-four children studied, Figure 1 (I and II)) the children hear their parents speak Spanish at home to each other, and are always spoken to in Spanish by at least one parent. Their parents had migrated to the United States after spending their youth, including early adolescence, in Puerto Rico.

Parents who were born and raised in New York City, or left Puerto Rico before late adolescence, or married an Anglo, speak mainly English to each other and their children. These account for five families which include thirteen children (Fig. 1. (III)). Two young couples frequently switch from English to Spanish with each other and their four young children (Fig. 1. (IV)).

Contrasting language patterns at home notwithstanding, we can say that these differences may make no difference in the proficiency levels of the children of each group of families, i.e., children from each group may end up with very similar language abilities, and children from the same family may differ markedly in their ability to speak, read, and/or write Spanish or English. It is true, as the diagram indicates, that the children of group I spoke more Spanish to each other than those of group III, i.e., it seems that English among the children increases in proportion with the amount of English understood and spoken by their parents. By the end of the study, however, the school age children in group I were speaking to each other almost exclusively in English except for limited code switches, despite the fact that their primary caretakers did not demonstrate visible improvement in their English skills. Nor are these isolated cases; communication in English is the norm for school age sisters and brothers. The principal exceptions are among those siblings who migrated to the United States during or after their teen years. This holds true even for older sisters and brothers who have lived more years in New York than in Puerto Rico, e.g., many of those who arrived at fourteen and sixteen still speak Spanish to each other at forty-two and forty-four, or sixty-two and sixty-four. They may, however, speak only English to their children. In this way the Puerto Rican community is similar to all other linguistic minorities in the United States whose fate it has been to lose their

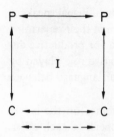

I.

The parents speak only Spanish
to each other and the children,
who respond to them in Spanish
but speak English and Spanish
to each other.

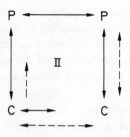

II.

The parents speak Spanish to
each other and the children;
one of them sometimes speaks
English as a second language
to them. The children respond
in both languages, preferring
Spanish for their parents and
English for each other.

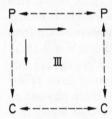

III.

The parents speak English to
each other and to the children;
one speaks some Spanish to them.
The children respond in English
and speak it to each other.

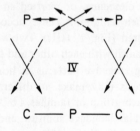

IV.

The parents code switch
frequently among themselves
and to the children, who
are too young to speak yet.

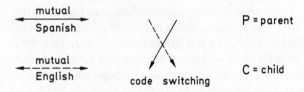

Figure 1. Communication patterns in the home.

mother tongue by the third generation. More significant, however, are the differences that may interfere with or impede the expected replacement of Spanish. Primary factors involve macro social and economic issues, e.g., the rate and residential patterns of the migration flow to and from Puerto Rico, out-marriage rates, female and male employment opportunities, public housing desegregation policies, urban renewal, etc. In the block that is home to our subjects, the prevalent configurations of these factors favored the continued presence of Spanish during the period of the study, i.e., a greater number of residents came from Puerto Rico than left, the overwhelming majority of households included Puerto Ricans only (one Anglo spouse was the only exception), the tenements allowed for frequent und extensive interaction among the families and for housing for relatives, the presence of one dominant family network intensified the residents' complex and dense relationships, and the high percent of unemployed residents contributed to the continuous presence on the block of members of diverse networks. Therefore, the children of all of the families were in contact with various patterns of English-Spanish dyads outside of their homes.

Within each family different members will be subject to Spanish and English influences to varying degrees; this affects each child's personal language history and development. One child may visit Puerto Rico more frequently or for longer stays than another, one may have a Spanish speaking caretaker and the others not, one may be enrolled in a bilingual program and the other may be in a monolingual English class, one may spend more hours out on the block and others may be more confined to the apartment, one may identify more with Afro-Americans than with Puerto Ricans, one may participate in religious programs that require literacy in English or Spanish, etc.

In sum, the pattern of linguistic dyads within the family is only one strand of the multiple threads in the web that is the language diversity of the block. Previous studies that focused on the languages that parents spoke to children and to each other within communities with stable economic, demographic, and social parameters, cannot be adequately compared to the language experiences of the children on the block. It is precisely the complexity of linguistic patterns, of linguistic norms and their interpretation within the community, that characterize the process of growing up bilingual in *el Barrio*. Attempts to judge or interpret this process via the principle of one language – one environment, or classic diglossia, fall short of capturing the diversity and strength of the language abilities of the children of the block. Perhaps the most misunderstood of these abilities is the frequent and rapid alternation of English and Spanish known in the literature as code switching. The question of cultural identification is central in this process, i.e., children love people who speak Spanish and English, they love Puerto Rico and New

York, and they feel like Puerto Ricans and New Yorkers. They learn to admire members of the community who are fluent and verbal and for whom code switching is one of the ways of speaking. They communicate on a daily, often hourly, basis with interlocutors who run the gamut from English monolinguals to Spanish monolinguals.

Everyone who is bilingual alternates the languages in his/her repertoire in accordance with the primary community norm: speak the best language of the addressee. Language choices for initiation and response to discourse on the block are invariably linked primarily to the identity of the interlocutors and their level of proficiency in both languages, whatever the social situation, locale, or topic might be. Although school reading scores are more likely to be discussed in English and making *pasteles* is more likely to be discussed in Spanish, each can, and does, occur in the other language, particularly if the linguistic limitations of the addressee demand it. As the children develop the ability to switch between the phonological and grammatical systems of languages in their repertoire for different addressees, they also learn to extend this ability to switches for stylistic purposes, and to accomplish it within the boundaries of a sentence.

In our focus on code switching, we found it useful to separate what it is that we can observe, what we must interpret as being in the knowledge of the speaker, and what it is that we can with precision analyze in the language itself. The catchword labels that capture this tripartite approach to factors are 'on the spot', 'in the head', and 'out of the mouth'. At any given moment of a situation, several 'on the spot' factors can be observed: the physical setting, as well as the speakers and addressees. The particular location and human participants in a given situation, their particular mix and changing configurations contribute to the choices the children make as they use Spanish and English or switch from one to the other. At an early age, Puerto Rican children of the block become junior ethnographers, capable of assessing each speech situation in terms of what they observe at the moment of interaction. Three on-the-spot observables of participants help determine language choice for the children: physical features, i.e., Spanish for Latinos and English for Anglos; sex, i.e., Spanish for women and English for men; and age, i.e., Spanish for infants and the elderly, and English for others. Given the configuration of these variables on the block, it is older Puerto Rican women and migrants, more than any other groups, who maintain Spanish in the community.

After the child responds to or initiates discourse, she/he may switch languages to achieve particular communicative purposes; major ones are: to change styles from casual to formal or vice versa, to cover gaps in his/her knowledge ('crutching') to realign the roles of speaker-hearer ('footing') to convince and/or control ('appeal and control'). For this s/he must depend on the kind of in-the-head knowledge that co-members in a speech community share. On *el bloque*, children learn to switch into either English or Spanish to accomplish any of these purposes. The language of the switch carries less importance than the switch itself, which serves to highlight the discourse strategy. For example, a mother may chastise her child by switching from Spanish to English (A) or by switching from English to Spanish (B):[1]

A: *Cállate*. Shut up. (Shut up.)
B: See that chair over there, go squash your seat in it.
   Go sit down, go. *SIEN-TA-TE:* (SIT DOWN!)

The switch itself strengthens the admonition, often regardless of the language.

Certain styles produce more switches, e.g., the children switched more frequently in narratives than during interviews, games, telling jokes, or teaching lessons. In general, switches are more likely to occur in the most informal styles of speaking. This is corroborated by bilingual classroom research which found that children code switched more during domino games than during interviews or classroom lessons (Zentella 1978, 1981c).

Within the same style, code switches may be employed to smooth over spots where the speaker is at a temporary loss for words in one language:

1. s/he uses the other language as a crutch to fill the gap,

   e.g., *Necesito un* string *para la* kite. (I need a string for the kite.)

2. for taboo words,

   e.g., They should blow an ash can up his *huevos* (balls)

Other types of what I term 'crutching' are:

3. repairs of ill formed switches,

   e.g., Tu don't go—*tu no vas*. (You aren't going.)

4. repetition of the previous speaker's switch,

   e.g., Pito: My mother got the *pasajes* already. (plane tickets)

   Maria: My *pasajes* are for the twelfth.

5. switches triggered by their similar form in both languages,

   e.g., My name *es Juan*. (is Juan.)

When the parents of *el bloque* were asked why they or their children shifted between Spanish and English, they all attributed it to a lack of linguistic knowledge, i.e., they believed that switches occurred only when the speaker did not know the word/construction in the language they were speaking at the moment, or could not remember it, and so they turned to the other language, as in 'Necesito un string para la kite'. Bilinguals are likely to remember these lapses and generalize that all code switches serve the same purpose. Code switching is indeed employed to this advantage, and in this role it plays a useful function in resolving a potential lapse in communication. But it is far from being the only reason why bilinguals switch. Contrary to widespread belief, switches for the five types of crutching listed above constituted less than 10 percent of the entire corpus (162/1639).

The most productive communicative strategy achieved by code switching is what I call 'footing', in line with Goffman's belief that "a change in footing implies a change in the aligment we take up to ourselves and others present as expressed in the way we manage the production or reception of an utterance" (Goffman 1979: 5). Some examples of code switches for a change in footing are:

1. switching from statement to question or vice versa,

    e.g., I wiggle my fingers. *Qué más?* (What else?)

2. shifting topic,

    e.g., *Vamos a preguntarle.* It's raining! (Let's ask them.)

3. tags that check with the listener,

    e.g., She is, *verdad?* (right?)

4. quotations,

    e.g., *El me dijo,* "Call the police". (He told me)

The third category of discourse strategies that code switching accomplishes for the children and adults of the community involves a special type of footing, they are attempts to convince or control the addressee. Most of these switches attempt to persuade the hearer via:

1. repetitions or translations that intensify/emphasize,

    e.g., *Límpiate la boca,* clean your mouth.

The chastising mother's examples (above) also belong in this category. Others seek to control the interlocutor by means of commands that are tinged with threats:

2. aggravated requests,

    e.g., Give me a kiss *o te pego.* (or I'll hit you)

or commands tinged with appeals:

3. mitigated requests/threats,

    e.g., *Dále un beso a Pucho.* Julie, please. (Give Pucho a kiss)

or commands accompanied by explanations:

4. accounting for requests,

    e.g., *Véte Eddie, véte,* so you could see. (Go Eddie, go)

Several of these discourse strategies, e.g., quotation and mitigation or aggravation of requests, had previously been noted in the switching of Mexican-American bilingual adults (Gumperz and Hernández Chavez 1975, Valdes 1981) or children (McClure 1977). However, not every code switch can be assigned a specific communicative purpose because there is a good deal of switching for switching's sake. In a community where different languages are in close contact, code switching is another style of speaking; on *el bloque* it exists alongside monolingual English and monolingual Spanish, and it has become a badge of community membership. In our data, only 48 percent of the code switches were attributed to one of the 22 crutching, footing and appeal and control strategies we found at work. We can expect to expand and refine these categories as research in discourse analysis progresses, but we must recognize that the key to the dynamic of code switching lies in its reflection of the dual cultural strains in the community. Code switchers are in effect saying to each other. "We belong to two worlds, and can function in either, but we are most at ease when we can shift back and forth from one to the other" (cf. Lavandera 1978).

Previous research has documented that code switching is an in-group behavior, i.e., code switching is more frequent when Puerto Ricans speak to each other than when they speak to other Spanish speakers (Marlos and Zentella 1978, Poplack 1978). Even what comes 'out of the mouth', as we have labelled it, i.e., the type of constituents that are switched, is affected by in or out membership in the speech community, e.g., switches for non-community members include higher percentages of nouns/noun phrases for cultural items that might be unfamiliar to the out-group member, such as *santería* (spiritism) and *bochinche* (gossip).

In addition to knowledge about when and why to code switch, and to whom, bilinguals in a code switching community share complex grammatical knowledge about how to alternate the languages in their repertoire within the confines of a single sentence (intra-sententially). Most switchers display their control of the grammar of two languages by linking one language to the other at just the equivalent points, i.e., the overwhelming majority of switches link constituents that are grammatical in one language with constituents that are grammatical in the other (Poplack 1981). The shift is accomplished in a way that does justice to both grammars simultaneously. One consequence of this is that proficient code switching is also a mark of proficiency in each of the bilingual's languages. In fact, our data showed that the most prolific intra-sentential code switchers were also the best speakers of English and Spanish.

Our investigation of the specific points at which syntactic constituents are alternated led to the discovery that, among the children of *el bloque*, age and language dominance were crucial influences. There was a tendency for the younger Spanish dominant bilinguals to switch into English for tags, e.g., *Esto es una peseta*, right? (This is a quarter.), conjunction, e.g., *El viene* but *ella no lo sabe.* (He's coming but she doesn't know it.), nouns/noun phrases, e.g., *un* string *para la* kite (a string for the kite). The older English dominant children switched into Spanish for the same easily insertable constituents. In this way, both groups display their bilinguality by switching into their weaker language for the constructions most under their control.

Both younger and older children honor the same syntactic constraints regarding what can be switched and where, except that the older girls produce a greater percent of infrequent switches; I attribute this to the fact that they switch more often, and are thereby running afoul of the linguistic constraints more frequently. Also, just as friends who know each other well relax their taboos against *ain't* and double negatives, code switchers sometimes jump from one language to another at points that break up constituents that are usually kept together, e.g., between determiner and subject noun as in 'the *demonio*' (devil).

What then of the charge that young second generation Hispanics are 'ruining' both English and Spanish, and creating a new language, a Spanglish? In response several facts should be kept in mind:

1. Word borrowing and code switching are not unique to poor minority communities in the US, they are time honored linguistic practices wherever languages are in contact (Hoenigswald 1960).
2. Code switchers do not violate the grammatical rules of either language; they speak English and then switch to Spanish or vice versa. They are not speaking a new language.
3. Neither linguistic not cognitive deficiency can be attributed to speakers of non standard ways of speaking (Labov 1972b).

The implications for educational policy are obvious:

> The attribution of deficient linguistic or cognitive ability on the basis of either non-standard dialects or code-switching and the consequent instruction designed to eradicate these different forms of language use is likely to succeed only in alienating bilingual students both from their own communities and from intrinsically-motivated involvement in the educational process (Cummins 1981: 33).

In fact, given the important cultural meaning and discourse strategies linked to code switching, efforts to eradicate it may do harm to a child's linguistic and social development. By the same token, it is equally unfair to assume that children need no exposure to standard English and Spanish and their appropriate use in monolingual settings. While it is true that for most of the activities in their communities Puerto Rican bilinguals in the US can speak non-standard varieties of English and Spanish and code-switch among them, there are other settings in the US and Puerto Rico which require command of standard English or standard Spanish. The youngster who is not prepared with an expanded linguistic repertoire will find certain doors closed to him/her.

To date, public schools have not prepared children to enter any door they wish or need to. Classrooms have focused on standard English only and rejected the mother tongue of the nation's immigrants, effectively locking them out of their grandmother's house. Immigrants and the nation as a whole have paid a heavy price in trauma and underdevelopment as a result of this short sighted policy, a price that advances in many disciplines, notably psychology, sociology, anthropology and linguistics, now tell us need no longer be paid.

References

American Institutes for Research (AIR). 1978. *Evaluation of the Impact of ESEA Title VII Spanish/English Bilingual Education Programs.* Bilingual Education Paper Series, National Dissemination and Assessment Center, Los Angeles.

Blom, Jan-Peter and John Gumperz. 1972. Social Meaning in Linguistic Structures: Code Switching in Norway. In *Directions in Sociolinguistics: The Ethnography of Communication.* John J. Gumperz and Dell Hymes, eds., 407-435. New York: Holt, Rinehart and Winston, Inc.

Commission on Foreign Language and International Studies. 1979. *Strength through Wisdom.*

Cummins, James. 1981. Four Misconceptions about Language Proficiency in Bilingual Education. *NABE Journal.* Vol V, no. 3:31-45.

Epstein, Noel. 1977. *Language, Ethnicity and the Schools: Policy Alternatives for Bilingual-Bicultural Education.* Washington, D.C. Institute for Educational Leadership, George Washington University.

Figueroa, Loida. 1972. La Cuestión del Idioma en Puerto Rico: Una Batalla Inconclusa. In *Tres Puntos Claves.* San Juan: Editorial Edil.

Fernández, Micho. 1972. A Glossary of Spanglish Terms. *New York Magazine,* August 7:46.

Fitzpatrick, Joseph. 1971. *Puerto Rican Americans: The Meaning of Migration to the Mainland.* Englewood Cliffs, New Jersey: Prentice Hall, Inc.

Gal, Susan. 1979. *Language Shift: Social Determinants of Language Change in Bilingual Austria,* London: Academic Press.

Genishi, Celia. 1976. Rules for Code Switching in Young Spanish-English Speakers: An Exploratory Study of Language Socialization. Ph.D. Dissertation, University of California, Berkeley.

Goffman, Erving. 1979. Footing. *Semiotica* 25: 1-29.

Gumperz, John J. and Eduardo Hernández Chávez. 1975. Cognitive Aspects of Bilingual Communication. In *El Lenguaje de los Chicanos.* Eduardo Hernández Chávez, Andrew Cohen and Anthony Beltramo, eds. Arlington: Center for Applied Linguistics.

Heath, Shirley Brice. 1977. Language and Politics in the United States. In *Georgetown University Round Table on Languages and Linguistics 1977.* M. Saville Troike, ed., Washington, D.CL: Georgetown University Press.

– 1979. Questioning at Home and at School: A Comparative Study. In *The Ethnography of Schooling: Educational Anthropology in Action.* George Spindler ed.

– forthcoming. *Ways with Words: Ethnography of Communication, Communities and Classrooms.*

Hoenigswald, Henry M. 1960. *Language Change and Linguistic Reconstruction.* Chicago: University of Chicago Press.

International Institute of Columbia Teachers College. 1926. *A Survey of the Public Educational System in Puerto Rico.* New York: Columbia University.

Kachru, Braj. 1975. *Toward Structuring the Form and Function of Code-mixing: An Indian Perspective.* Studies in the Linguistic Sciences 5 a. Department of Linguistics, University of Illinois at Urbana.

Kloss, Heinz. 1977. *The American Bilingual Tradition.* Rowley MA: Newbury House.

Labov, William. 1972a. *Language in the Inner City: Studies in the Black English Vernacular.* Philadelphia: University of Pennsylvania Press.

– 1972b. *Sociolinguisitc Patterns.* Philadelphia: University of Pennsylvania Press.

Language Policy Task Force. 1978. Language Policy and the Puerto Rican Community. Working Paper No. 1, reprinted in *The Bilingual Review/La Revista Bilingüe.* Vol. V, Nos. 1 and 2. New York: York College.

Lavandera, Beatriz R. 1978. The Variable Component in Bilingual Performance. In *Georgetown University Roundtable on Languages and Linguistics 1978.* James E. Alatis, ed. Washington, D.C: Georgetown University Press.

López, Adalberto. 1980. The Puerto Rican Diaspora: A Survey. In *The Puerto Ricans: Their History, Culture and Society*. Adalberto López, ed., 313-344. Cambridge, Ma: Schenkmann Publishing Co.

Marlos, Litsa, and Ana Celia Zentella. 1978. A Quantified Analysis of Code Switching by Four Philadelphia Puerto Rican Adolescents. *University of Pennsylvania Review of Linguistics* 3: 46-57.

McClure, Erica. 1977. Aspects of Code Switching in the Discourse of Bilingual Mexican-American Children. In *Linguistics and Anthropology*. M. Saville-Troike, ed., 93-117. Washington, D.C: Georgetown University Press.

Montalvo, Braulio. 1974. Home-School Conflict and the Puerto Rican Child. *Social Casework*: Vol. 55, no. 2: 100-110.

National Institute of Education. 1975. Spanish-English Bilingual Education in the United States: current issues, resources, and recommended funding priorities for research. Unpublished MS.

National Puerto Rican Forum. 1981. *The Next Step Toward Equality: A Comprehensive Study of Puerto Ricans in the U.S. Mainland*. New York: National Puerto Rican Forum, Inc.

Negrón de Montilla, Aida. 1975. *Americanization in Puerto Rico and the Public School System 1900-1930*. San Juan. Universidad de Puerto Rico: Editorial Universitaria.

Osuna, Juan José. 1949. *A History of Education in Puerto Rico*. Rio Piedras: Editorial de la Universidad de Puerto Rico.

Philips, Susan U. 1972. Participation Structures and Communicative Competence: Warm Springs Children in Community and Classroom. In *Functions of Language in the Classroom*, Cazden, John, and Hymes, eds. New York: Teachers College Press. .

Poplack, Shana 1981. Quantitative Analysis of a Functional and Formal Constraint on Code Switching. In *Latino Language and Communicative Behavior*. R. Duran, ed. New York: Ablex Publishing Corp.

Rodriguez, Clara. 1980. Puerto Ricans: Between Black and White. In *The Puerto Rican Struggle: Essays on Survival in the United States*. Clara Rodriguez, V. Sanchez Korrol, Jose Oscar Alers, eds., 20-30. New York: Puerto Rican Migration Research Consortium.

Santiago, Isaura. 1578. *A Community's Struggle for Equal Educational Opportunity: Aspira vs Board of Education*. Princeton, New Jersey: Office for Minority Education, Educational Testing Service.

Senior, Clarence. 1965. *The Puerto Ricans: Strangers, then Neighbors*. New York: Quadrangle Books.

Swain, Merrill. 1979. Bilingual Education: Research and its Implications. In *On TESOL 79: The Learner in Focus*. C.A. Yorio, K. Perkins, J. Schachter, eds. Washington, D.C.: TESOL.

Timm, L.A. 1975. Spanish-English Code Switching: el porqué and how not to. *Romance Philology* 28: 473-482.

U.S. Commission on Civil Rights. 1976. *Puerto Ricans in the Continental United States: An Uncertain Future*. Washington, D.C: United States Commission on Civil Rights.

Valdés, Guadalupe. Code Switching as Deliberate Verbal Strategy. In *Latino Language and Communicative Behavior*. R.P. Duran, ed. Norwood, New Jersey: Ablex Publishing Corporation.

Varo, Carlos. 1971. *Consideraciones Antropológicas y Políticas en torno a la Enseñanza de 'Spanglish' en Nueva York*. Rio Piedras: Ediciones Librería Internacional.

Waggoner, Dorothy. 1981. Statistics on Language Use. In *Language in the USA. Charles Ferguson and Shirley Brice Heath*, eds. 486-515. Cambridge: Cambridge University Press.

Wolfram, Walt. 1981. Varieties of American English. In *Language in the USA*. Charles Ferguson and Shirley Brice Heath, eds., 4-68. Cambridge, University Press.

Zentella, Ana Celia. 1978. *Code Switching and Interactions among Puerto Rican Children*. Working Papers in Sociolinguistics, no. 50. Austin, Tex: Southwest Education Devel-

opment Laboratory.
- 1981a. "Hablamos los dos, we speak both": Growing Up Bilingual in el Barrio. Ph. D. Dissertation, University of Pennsylvania, Philadelphia.
- 1981b. Language Variety among Puerto Ricans. *In Language in the USA.* C. Ferguson and S. B. Heath, eds. Cambridge: Cambridge University Press.
- 1981c. . . . 'Tá bien, you could answer me en cualquier idioma. . .' Puerto Rican Code-switching in Bilingual Classrooms. In *Latino Language and Communicative Behavior.* R. Duran, ed, Norwood, New Jersey: Ablex Publishing Corp.

Note

1. Spanish, in italics, is followed by English translation in parentheses.

Regna Darnell

The Language of Power in
Cree Interethnic Communication*

Introduction: Problems of Cross-Cultural Communication

Contact between cultural systems is necessarily fraught with uncertainty and difficulty. Patterns of interaction and ways of speaking are learned in childhood socialization, in part before the onset of speech itself. Each child learns first a communicative system which is appropriate among intimates of family and community. Even within a single cultural system, new rules must be learned as the child's world expands to include outsiders and strangers. To the extent that strangers do not share underlying assumptions about the nature of communication, the threatening potential of interaction with them is exaggerated—until strangers become enemies (a common lexical equivalence in many native American languages). When the salient fact about cultural contact is asymmetrical access to power, as it is in the case of all native Americans when interacting with whitemen it could be nothing short of miraculous if Indian persons acted without tension and discomfort.

Group stereotyping is inevitable in cultural contact. Much of it is based not on the content of specific interactions but on the ineffective progress of typical interactions. The frustration is on both sides. Native people perceive whitemen as aggressive and insensitive. Whitemen perceive Indians as reticent, withdrawn, sullen and verbally incompetent. Neither party leaves an interaction with a feeling that effective communication has been established and maintained. In subsequent interactions, both parties expect, and actively court, disaster—their expectations are often met.

Unfortunately, contact between groups rarely occurs on a symmetrical basis. When one party holds the power, as a representative of his group, the interactional burden falls on the subordinate party, who is usually least able to bear it and transcend the cultural barrier. The result of the conflicting interactional systems is not only miscommunication but confirmation for both parties of the unequal sociopolitical relationships between their respective groups.

Moreover, the majority of cross-cultural interactions proceed in institutional contexts, guaranteeing that the power differential is paramount in the minds of native participants. Government, legal and educational institutions are imposed upon native people regardless of the personal openness of the whiteman who represents the system. Even in service encounters, there is a stigmatization of native person which operates to restrict their access to the resources of the larger society. Any effort to improve interethnic communication between Indians and whites must start from a recognition of the stacked deck resulting from the allotment of power in that larger society.

The situation is not, however, hopeless. Indians know a lot about whitemen and are certainly able to judge deviations from the ethnocentric and egocentric norm. Because they lack power, they must be careful and self-aware in dealing with the dangerous and ambivalent whiteman. Individual whitemen may certainly learn to appreciate and respond to native interactional patterns, attempting not to give offense without relinquishing their own cultural identity. Whitemen in administrative and service roles can be trained to deal more effectively and sensitively with their native clients.

In order for this process of increased communicative effectiveness to work, some of us at least must take the time and energy to learn how the native system works and to provide effective translation for whitemen who deal with native people. This is the first responsibility of the anthropologist. The second is to change the access to power so that the two groups can meet on a more nearly equal basis. The interactional consequences of differential access to power will not go away. It is impossible for the native person who is always in the subordinate role vis-à-vis whitemen to act with openness and self-confidence. Interethnic miscommunication cannot be alleviated within the realm of interaction alone. On the other hand, sophistication on both sides about interaction is a good start in negotiations toward political and social change.

A few methodological strictures are in order before proceeding to an examination of the details of the interactional system. First, examples from the Cree of northern Alberta will be used throughout the paper. This is solely a product of availability of first-hand data. Many of the patterns described appear to be widespread in native North America, and it is not surprising that this should be so. Native Americans share an areal tradition which has grown up historically over a long period of time. They further share a contact history of dealings with the whiteman under conditions of asymmetrical access to power.

Second, group stereotypes do reflect reality to a great extent. It is impossible to perceive without categorizing and whitemen are recognized in large part by their behavior. Surely there are exceptions to the group stereotypes, but this does not mitigate against their usefulness. Statements about cultural systems of interaction are necessarily normative (or even stereotypic). Not every individual all the time will act in accord with the interactional norms of his society. Personalities differ and individuals are 'typical' of their groups to varying degrees. Assessment of situational variables by individuals will produce further divergence from expected normative behavior. This does not, however, invalidate the process of understanding a cultural system of behavior. It will be normative rather than predictive. By focusing not on the actor but on the interpretation of his action by members of his own and other groups, the normative validity is retained. In no society do people expect all behavior to be normative, but in all societies observers recognize behavior that is not normative and evaluate it appropriately.

Finally, it is important to stress that the native system does not depend on speaking a native language. Cree English retains a basically Cree semantic system and is used in Cree interactional contexts. Language code is, then, a trivial determinant of communicative effectiveness. In fact, the native person whose first or only language is English may be subject to greater communicative difficulty simply because both parties to interethnic communication assume incorrectly that they speak the same laguage. In reality, however, they are applying quite different systems for its use and quite different semantic interpretations of many common concepts. The result is miscommunication without realization that messages and relationships are being understood in different and incompatible ways.

Cree people frequently feel inadequate in interactions with whitemen because they recognize the ineffectiveness of their communications in English. Although this is usually perceived as a purely linguistic difficulty, it is rooted in contrasting communicative economies. Increasing emphasis on the use of native languages functions to increase self-confidence and pride, a process of which many native leaders are fully aware. For example, some years ago, the Alberta Indian Education Center suggested that job upgrading should depend heavily on increasing verbal fluency among native people. Their program focused on native language fluency to increase self-confidence and expressive capacity, only later turning to bilingual fluency in English. The expectation was that the native languages provided better, more precise mechanisms for self- expression and were not subject to outside (white) interference which would allow power differentials to inhibit self-expression on the part of native people. The Province of Alberta has 42 bands speaking seven major languages. However, difficulties of translation and native language multilingualism were perceived as a small price to pay for the privilege of unimpeded expression.

Decision-Making: Consensus vs. Majority

One of the most common arenas of interethnic communication is the political meeting, typically including a small number of English-speaking bureaucrats and a larger number of native people. The direction of the meeting is set by the whiteman who explains the position of the group he represents and expects that his role is to provide information so that a decision can be made efficiently and action can proceed on the basis of the meeting. Any discussion which leads up to a 'decision' is irrelevant once that decision has been arrived at. He expects that there will be differences of opinion but that the decision of the majority will rule, the basic premise of his notion of democratic government.[1]

The native person has a quite divergent notion of what is taking place. A meeting is an occasion for finding out what the issues are and beginning to think about what opinions will have to be part of a consensus-based decision. If the issue is an important one, there will be considerable divergence of opinion, such that a decision cannot be reached hastily just by knowing the facts as seen by the whiteman. The majority is unable to act until there is consensus. A decision which is taken without such consensus will not produce effective action. When a decision seems to him to have been forced, the native person will withdraw from the whole program or policy, usually impeding its implementation by passive resistance. This strategy is the only one open under relations of asymmetrical power, from the native point of view. To the great frustration of the whiteman who wants to implement his program, the individuals who support the program are often most vociferous in their withdrawal from further action. The whiteman interprets this as lack of commitment and indecisiveness.

An illustration with reference to the school system comes from a young man who was always good at mathematics and regretted not having learned much of it in school. He explained that he realized others in the class did not understand and were not sufficiently confident to ask questions. Because he did understand, he was the one with the responsibility to ask questions until everyone understood. He recalls the frustration of his teachers at his questions. It never occurred to him to explain why he was asking questions and it never occurred to the teachers that he was not asking for himself. Learning is supposed to take place for the group as a whole, and it is the responsibility of the leader to make sure that consensus is attained before proceeding to a new point.

A political meeting, because of the need for ultimate consensus, must operate with strategies that avoid confrontation. The style is that anyone may express their concerns, often on points which are only tangentially related to the topic of the meeting. Compartmentalization is not encouraged. Part of the definition of a problem requiring action is to determine how far its ramifications may extend. Rarely are there answers provided to a comment; it is equally rare that direct questions will be asked. The floor does not return to the original speaker to respond. In fact, the proponent of an issue would be foolhardy to respond to particular points before all of the concerns are on the floor. Further speakers may refer back to previous points but normally do so without noting the connection.

Confrontation through differences of opinion is a reality, but its expression is carefully depersonalized. Proper names, and other forms of direct address, are avoided. Comments are made, in a sense, to the floor. Eye contact with any particular adversary is inappropriate. It is normally expected that a decision will not be reached in a meeting, but that the decision-making process will begin after the meeting.

The role of moderator or political leader is not highly valued. It puts people on the spot and makes them feel foolish. Cree make a distinction between *okimaw*, the leader whose judgment is informally followed, usually an elder, and *okimahkan*, the official chief, the individual who puts himself in the unenviable position of speaking for others and negotiating with outsiders. The *-hkan* suffix means fake or secondary (e.g. *awasis*, child vs. *awasihkan*, doll, or *totos*, breast vs. *totosihkan*, brassiere). The connotation is not necessarily negative, but the secondary thing should not be confused with or used in place of the real thing.[2]

A similar role phenomenon is observed at pow-wows, where there is always an M.C. who carries on a running commentary about what is going on, who is present, where to buy food, whose car needs to be moved from the parking lot, etc. It is hard to find someone to do this job and it is always a position held by someone of low status. He is playing the fool and everyone knows it.

The real decision-makers, the *okimawak*, are often not even present when a decision has to be made. They are protected from the potential for conflict. Even if present, rarely will an elder speak during a meeting. If he does so, his words will be cryptic; usually he tells a story whose relevance to the sequence of action is far from obvious. His input to the decision will be made at a later time, when consensus can be attained.[3]

Much of the work of arriving at decisions is done by mediators, or 'consensus brokers', some of whom may be whitemen. In the old days of Indian treaties, the translators served in this role (interestingly enough, many of them were half-breeds who had some understanding of both sides). When an individual expresses his concerns to the mediator, depersonalization is maintained. Discussion is in the third person; the enemy is the person/group favoring the decision. The sympathetic broker encourages expression of disagreement and agrees with the factional position he listens to. Both then try to figure out how to get the other guy to act reasonably. It is expected that compromise will be necessary on both sides. Only when the outlines of this consensus have been predetermined will the parties to the dispute again meet publicly or discuss their disagreement. It is then that a decision can be made.

Of course, it is not always possible to attain consensus. Simultaneously, decisions do have to be made. In the old days, the group splintered, the minority faction setting up a new community. Today, this is not always possible, since people are no longer nomadic. Often, decisions cannot be made, or the decisions which are made are never intended to be implemented.

For example, in a discussion of standardized Cree teaching materials, teachers from various areas of Alberta reached consensus by agreeing that they would take the dialect of 'central Alberta' as their standard. This was duly recorded in the minutes and cited as evidence of a successful meeting. Cree language teachers from Hobbema understood 'central' to mean central of the geographical range of the province, their reserve is at the southern end of the Cree area but central within the province. Teachers from Saddle Lake understood 'central' to mean central to the area of Alberta and the Northwest Territories in which Cree is spoken. The decision everyone felt good about had no effect at all on disputes about how to spell particular words in the curriculum content. However, the people continued to be able to talk to one another, even if they could not all endorse particular materials. Each major area has continued to produce its own curriculum. Dialect standardization is a subject on which consensus is not presently possible. But relations among teachers from different areas do not break down as a result.

Speakers and Listeners

Most Cree people believe that whitemen do not know how to attain consensus. They have a common binary standard of behavioral evaluation, distinguishing between *nehiyaw*, a Cree person, and *moniyaw*, a white person. The most common gloss for *moniyaw* is 'loud-mouthed'. Although the terms have their origin in ethnic distinctions (Frenchmen are called by a different term in this use), normative behaviors are associated with the ethnic identities. An Indian person who is behaving like the negative stereotype of the whiteman and forcing his opinion on others will be called *moniyaw*, with a hope that he will modify his behavior, although this does not always occur.[4] The whiteman who behaves with restraint and respect for the autonomy of others will be called *nehiyaw*, although most often when he is not present.

Loudness of voice is not the issue, although it is correlated with the behavioral syndrome. The question is one of interactional framing and timing. For Cree speakers, pauses between speeches are longer, as well as those whithin speeches. The whiteman assumes that the native person is finished speaking and is perceived as interrupting with his own continued conversation. The Indian person is consistently in the position of opening his mouth to speak at the appropriate time and finding that the whiteman has already begun his speech. The whiteman becomes increasingly nervous because he is receiving no response and talks even faster.

Cree persons perceive a clear relationship between silence and listening. Anything serious enough to be worth responding to requires a pause to register and evaluate the words, before speaking in answer. Respect for the speaker requires the hearer to consider before he begins his own turn at talk. In fact, the role of listener is more highly valued than that of speaker—the listener is learning something from the words of another.

A speaker will not continue if he feels that no one is listening to him. The listener(s) is/are expected to respond at pauses within a speech, to murmur *ehe*, 'yes'. This is an acknowledgement of what is said, not an agreement with it. A stronger response, but one rarely heard until an argument has been fully presented is *tāpwe*, 'truly'. Segmentation of speech is provided by these markers of attentiveness. The respondent is expected not to interrupt the flow of speech by raising his own concerns.

In fact, the listener may not get an opportunity to express his opinion at all. For Cree persons, *who* speaks is usually more important than *what* is said. Sex and relative age are the markers of right to speak and right to perform. It is obvious in most gatherings who has the right, and obligation, to speak. Younger people will not tell a traditional story if there is an old man present, although many will do so if they are the oldest Cree person present. Even children will practice telling the traditional stories (*atayohkewina*, sacred stories, are distinguished from *achimowana*, narratives about witnessed experience, often glossed as 'news') when there is no adult present. Practicing of traditional speaking skills is done in private until the learner has attained the status through age and relationship to other elders to speak publicly.

It is not the individual who has the right to speak. The individual speaks because he has the status or experience to do so. His speaking must not convey that he puts himself above others in importance. If the audience includes strangers, native or white, he will usually begin with a validation of his right to speak, noting his age, status as a hunter, or healer, often with reference to his spirit guides (visions). Even biographical details, however, will be presented in a non-egocentric manner, avoiding use of the first person pronoun, referring to the self as a channel or vehicle through which power manifests itself (suffixes are added to the verb indicating direction of movement of natural forces and objects of the movement; the actor need not be mentioned at all).

The speaking of an elder is the example par excellence of what speaking is. Its ideal form is a monologue, in which the listener may, at certain segments of the speaking, ask questions of information or clarification, but has no other input. The notion of conversational exchange through dyadic inter-action does not apply in such cases. It tends to be the only model for talk available to the whiteman. The typical Cree interaction is asymmetrical on the basis of age and status; interactional control is residual to the person of highest status and this is not negotiable.

All respected elders are called *nimosōm*, 'my grandfather', even if they are not personally known to the speaker. It is a term of respect for age and status. E.g., children unknown to an old man working with them to develop teaching materials fell automatically into this traditional role with a new grandfather. Indeed, the Cree word for the ancestors, the bearers of their cultural tradition, is *nimosōmipanak*, 'my grandfathers who are dead'. The *-ipan* suffix meaning 'no longer living' may be added to any kinship term, but only in the instance of grandfather is the term extended beyond actual biological or adopted relatives.

What the old man says is a product of his experience Therefore it cannot be understood fully by someone who lacks that experience and wisdom. The speaking of an elder is referred to as a 'telling' rather than a 'teaching'. The interaction is open-ended, in the sense that its closure comes only when the meaning of the lesson has been incorporated into the life experience of the student. The message is not, then, intrinsically verbal; its verbal expression is merely a guide to action in the future. The responsibility of the old man is to pass on what he knows so that it will not be lost, and to choose well his listeners. It is unlikely that he will be alive when the effectiveness of his teaching can be assessed. All of the interactional work must be done by the listener, over a long period of time, to understand what he has been taught. This process is supposed to be difficult. It is fully appropriate for the elder to speak in opaque terms. Indeed, because life experiences and essential attributes of person-ness differ, each listener will receive a different 'meaning', which is valid for him.

This method of teaching is characteristic of Cree culture, although only cultural and moral teaching is verbal. Moral lessons are absorbed by the learner and stored until he is prepared by his experience to apply the lesson in action without help from the teacher. In the case of teaching of skills, the teacher simply illustrates the skill and the learner observes until he can himself attempt the act. In both types of teaching, responsibility rests with the learner for his own effective use of what he taught.

The open-endedness of Cree learning and teaching is carried over into other kinds of ongoing social interaction. Formal greetings and farewells are avoided because they give the impression that the relationship is restricted to that occasion. Although specific interactional events have beginnings and endings, ongoing social relationships do not. The whiteman's effort to summarize and effect closure on a given occasion is interpreted as an unwillingness to pick up the same relationship and topic at an unspecified future time. The continuity of social relations is the key to effective action in all areas of native life.

Conflict in the Classroom

These assumptions about the nature of interaction differ quite substantially from those common within the white-dominated educational system. The importance of conflicts in the classroom cannot be overemphasized, given the enforced presence of Indian children in school during the years when they must also learn their own native traditions and ways of learning. Some of the reasons for the consistent lack of success of native children in the school systems are structural — e.g., teachers are usually young women and Indian children are accustomed to learning from old men. Others are interactional and can be corrected by attention to native interactional premises.

For example, native people do not correct a mistake directly. Most white teachers cannot understand how you convey that an answer is 'wrong' without saying so. An old man discussing number words in Cree and English first established with the children that one cannot say 'one *moswa*' or '*peyak* moose'. The students were left to make the general observation that both words have to be in the same language. The old man then showed them the symbol 1 and asked them which language that was in. The unanimous response was 'English'. The old man appeared startled but recovered quickly and began to make his point in a different way. He asked the children if the Ukrainians had a word for one and, after a moment of silence, was told that they did. He then asked about the Chinese and the children agreed that they too had a word for one. The old man sat back with an expression of satisfaction on his face and waited for them to volunteer the generalization. One boy then said, "I guess everybody has a word for one". The old man acknowledged that statement by saying, "Oh, I see", and, after a moment of silence, went on to a new topic. This bit of pedagogical improvisation reflects the respect for persons, even if they are children, which characterizes interaction among Cree persons.

Another example may be found in the classroom notion that all children should be paying attention all of the time. The native teacher will begin speaking quietly to a single listener. Because the children already assume that his words will be important, they will gather around him to share what is happening. There is no effort to force anyone to accept teaching. The role of listener or learner is an active, participatory one and cannot be forced.

Cree persons do not talk much about talk; nor do they verbalize their feelings. The valued style of self-expression is a terse, laconic one by white standards. The Cree do not state the obvious. Classroom tasks which single out a child, even one who is doing good work, and force him into a framework of embarrassing self-relevation are counter-productive. Writing in a journal on a topic of the student's own choice is a far more effective way of encouraging verbal fluency, because it does not put him on the spot in front of his classmates.

A common source of difficulty for teachers is the Cree avoidance of direct eye contact. The white teacher tends to assume that eye contact is a measure of attention. For Cree children, however, listening is a receptive process which takes place within the self. The old man who talks to children will usually be focusing his eyes on some point in middle space, as though concentrating on a mental image which is not part of the immediate interaction. The child who listens does not invade the privacy and personal space of the old man by staring at him. Visual contact is maintained through fluctuating peripheral vision rather than by direct eye focus. Each participant in an interaction remains essentially self-contained. This is part of the respect for autonomy of person.

There is a further conflict with the school system which arises from conceptualizations of what it means to be a child. The Cree child is treated as an autonomous person long before he comes to school. He is responsible for his own actions and belongings, as well as for his own learning process, in which he is understood to be an active participant. He is accustomed to caring for younger children and participating meaningfully in the work of his household. He is not excluded from adult activities as long as he does not disrupt their progress, and expects to be a silent observer of and learner from what goes on around him. The schoolteacher is used to thinking of children as incompetent by adult standards, and frequently insults the autonomy of students by treating them as white children.

Native teacher aides, even when they lack formal teaching credentials and are young women, have been remarkably effective in native classrooms. Their presence in such classrooms has been justified largely on the grounds of linguistic difficulty; they are expected to help the teacher translate when children are not fluent in English. In fact, many have served to translate the concepts of how learning is expected to be accomplished and to present the curriculum content in ways which relate to the experience and learning styles of the students. The teaching techniques of such teacher aides provide an easily-available model for the white teacher, though few seem aware of its potentials.

The trend toward inviting native elders into classrooms to teach native language and culture has also been growing. The difficulty here has been that many are not fluent in English and feel uncomfortable in the institutional setting of the school. When these difficulties are overcome, however, students seem to respond by feeling a less insurmountable distance between school and community. It is interesting that many native elders choose to speak to the children in the native language so as to assure that their words will not be understood by the teacher. This is true even when fluency in English is sufficient to make a real choice possible. When materials are presented in both languages, the old man will usually include many asides to the children in Cree, especially regarding their behavior in the classroom, which are not present in English.

Conclusion: Establishing True Communication

There is currently a trend toward training of native teachers, and placing of native persons in administrative roles in native communities. Although this is, of course, a major route to native political autonomy and self-determination, it does not solve the problems of interethnic communication. At some level or another, all native people have to deal with white people. Their confidence in their native identity is at stake whenever communication fails. What is needed is a compromise between interactional systems which rests on respect for the autonomy of both parties and recognition of the differences in their habitual ways of treating people. It is certainly not necessary that the whiteman who wants to communicate effectively with native people become a native person, at least in interactional style. To try too hard is to lose the spontaneity and mutual acceptance which is the basis of effective communication regardless of the cultures involved.

The language of power—in which the interactional norms of evaluating the progress of social relationships are those of the group with power—provides an incredible stumbling block to the establishment of social relationships across cultures which can lead to effective mutual action. Cree persons are taciturn with strangers because they are unknown. One must observe people's actions in order to know them and understand how to talk to them. Silence is a mechanism of self-defense, protecting autonomy of person. When the Cree person has made up his mind about an individual whiteman, he becomes voluable and talkative. Talk is a marker of established intimacy and trust, of consensus as to the nature of relationships. Differences of power remain, but do not disrupt the relationship, any more than does the existential asymmetry between old man and child he teaches. It is possible, though rare enough in present reality, for Cree and whiteman to work together for a more egalitarian social system to be shared by both of their groups.

Notes

* Although examples are based on my own ongoing fieldwork with the Cree of northern Alberta, this paper profits greatly from talk about Indian interaction and politics with a number of colleagues, most particularly Keith Basso, Susan Philips, Ron and Suzanne Scollon, Anthony L. Vanek, and DiAnn Watson. I have drawn on their insights in ways of which I am too often not fully aware but gratefully acknowledge. This paper is in memory of Roseanna Houle who shared with me her teaching of the Cree language. I also thank our grandmother Frances Thompson who has had a large part in making our family what it is, and my grandfathers, who know who they are and whose tellings I continue to ponder.

1. A fairly common strategy in meetings where only the Cree persons are bilingual is for discussion to proceed in Cree and continue for what the whiteman considers an interminable length of time. At its conclusion, the native spokesman will report in one or two sentences in English. If consensus has not been reached, the summary statement will be non-committal but polite, leaving the witheman under the impression that everyone agrees with him. Such a misconception has disastrous consequences when translated into future action. The whiteman is seen as a fool for not understanding the process of political decision-making and the plans he implements will be ridiculed.
2. In the old days, the distinction was between the warrior and the elder. The warrior was the man of action, as the chief is today. The elder was responsible for directing the actions of the warrior, counseling wisdom and moderation in the affairs of the people. For example, at a conference a few years ago, the late Dan George spoke on the same program with Harold Cardinal, then president of the Indian Association of Alberta. Both received standing ovations from the audience, but for diametrically opposed performances. Chief Dan George presented a poetic oration on the nature of Indian perceptions of the social and natural world. Harold Cardinal took such a recognition of the validity of native wisdom for granted, and solicited political support from the audience for a then-current battle with the Department of Indian Affairs. The complementarity between leader, or wise man, and leader as man of action is necessary and inevitable to Cree persons.
3. The prestige and authority of leaders is fluid. Holders of official positions are elected frequently, usually annually. The elders are respected as long as their judgment proves effective and people are willing to follow their advice. A leader of either variety would find his power gone if he attempted to enforce it.
4. The pronoun 'he' is used throughout for purposes of convenience, and because it is more often men who are involved in the institutional contacts between native and white.

PATTERNS OF LANGUAGE CHOICE

Monica Heller

Ethnic Relations and Language Use in Montréal

Not long ago I was in the hallway of a Montréal company with one of the older employees. We were talking in English (our mother tongue) when a younger man came by. The latter was also a native speaker of English; however, it happened that he and I had only ever heard each other speak French, and so neither of us knew that the other was an anglophone. So French was the language we used when he stopped to talk. After several minutes our older friend interrupted us: "You having a personal conversation here?".

This story is revealing of the sorts of things that are happening in Québec these days, of the ways in which social change affects how people interact in their daily lives, and of how they feel about their interactions. The reason our friend felt offended was that he knew each of us (albeit separately) and knew we were anglophones—and yet, here we were, speaking French. In his world anglophones speak English to each other, especially in the presence of another anglophone. To make matters worse our friend is monolingual, having grown up in a Montréal where the French spoke English but the English did not have to speak French. The two of us who were younger, however, were operating under a different set of assumptions. According to Québec law French is the language of work; people whose mother tongue is not French must prove their competence in French to the employer and to the government. As anglophones, then, we had a certain amount of face to maintain (Goffman 1959; Brown and Levinson 1974) with respect to the rest of the company. Further, we both knew that because of the social context of work in present-day Québec our 'significant others' in the department were the francophones and not the low-status, indeed marginal, few older anglophones. So since we could not be sure the other was really anglophone we each thought that we might have to maintain face with respect to each other; and in any case we were standing in a well-travelled hallway and would therefore not risk damaging our own face or each other's with respect to our colleagues.

How did this come to be, that two anglophones should find it normal to speak French to each other in the presence of a third, who should find the choice of language upsetting, if not downright rude? What sorts of changes had taken place in interethnic relations in Québec such that different generations should have different norms of verbal behaviour? In this paper I will first briefly discuss the historical context of social, political and economic events and processes that have led to the present situation, in which language use is both part of the process of changing interethnic relations and symbolic of those relations. The rest of the paper will be concerned with describing the role that language plays in daily interaction. Here language is being used to create or to mediate the change between the old status quo, in which the francophone majority of Québec was dominated by the anglophone minority, and the future (whether hoped-for or feared), in which francophones are, if not dominant, at least equal, and the use of the French language normal rather than stigmatized.

Social and Historical Background

Québec is a society organized, for historical reasons, along lines of ethnic divisions. Originally a French colony, Québec was conquered by the British in 1759. When the French administrative élite returned to France, they left behind a peasantry, landowners, and the institutions of the Catholic Church which organized French social life. The Protestant British took over the province's administration and commerce, which they controlled from urban areas. The French were largely rural and agricultural. With the Industrial Revolution many of the French moved into towns to form an urban working class. The French upper class, educated by the Church, went into the liberal professions and became doctors, lawyers, notaries and clergymen. After Canada became independent in 1867, provincial politics became for the French another attractive sphere which they came to dominate; the English were more concerned with federal politics.

This state of affairs characterized Québec life until after World War II. French and English lived in separate areas, formed different classes, engaged in different economic activities, had different religions, different languages and different schools and other institutions. Contact between francophones and anglophones was confined to limited interactions in the public arena and to the more prolonged contact between anglophone employer and francophone employee. It was the francophone employees, naturally, who became bilingual; other francophones, and most anglophones, were effectively monolingual. Although immigrants tended to learn English, largely because English was the language of economic advancement, francophones remained the majority group of Québec.

After World War II, economic development caused a series of changes whose immediate impact was felt in French society. Increased wealth encouraged the rise of a new French middle class which was involved with the expansion of the provincial government. As the government grew stronger it began appropriating control over various domains of social life such as education and health. Institutional divisions between ethnic groups began to crumble, and religious divisions began to pale.

Further, increased government control created a necessity for a larger bureaucracy which absorbed educated francophones until, in the 1960s, it became saturated. As a result, the francophone middle class found itself with expectations that were hard to fulfill. The logical place in which to seek advancement became the private sector. However, private enterprise was controlled by anglophones and entry at the management level was difficult to obtain. In any case, the entry of francophones was a process involving individuals, and was therefore a slow one entailing loss of cultural identity, since individuals were isolated from their cultural milieu. A more efficient and satisfactory method had to involve the French as a group, thus avoiding the perceived danger of assimilation.

At the same time as the bureaucracy was reaching the point of saturation a vacuum was being created in Québec by a westward shift of capital and economic decision-making. Many corporate head offices left Québec, taking many anglophones with them and indirectly causing others to leave. This left room for new personnel to take regional control (Clift and Arnopoulos 1979). Further, the francophone middle class found an ally among the francophone intellectuals. The latter had control of the political parties in the province and wished to retain that control, the basis of which was being threatened by shifting demographics. The francophone birth rate had plummeted, while the anglophone group continued to recruit most of the immigrants. The interests of the French intellectuals and of the French middle class were served by the same cause, that of French nationalism, and by the same means, that of political power.

Beginning in the mid 1960s laws were enacted which were designed to allow the French access to all sectors of social and economic activity in Québec. This was accomplished by increasing the power of the one remaining salient factor left differentiating the French from the English: their language. The last of these laws (Bill 101, the Charter of the French Language, 1977) had the effect of making French the language of work. Everyone now seeking a job or a promotion must speak French, and only French is required unless the employer can prove that another language is necessary. In this fashion, monolingual francophones were favoured for employment.

Ethnic divisions of Québec had served to unequally allocate roles and resources. Bill 101 was designed to rectify some of the inequalities, by giving the French as a group favoured access to those roles and resources. But there is an irony involved in Bill 101: it had to favour the French as a group by rewarding knowledge of the French language. This had the advantage of appearing non-discriminatory, since knowledge of a language is something anybody can achieve. Both French and non-French can use the language to gain access to all roles and resources valued in Québec society. But if this were to happen then the breakdown of boundaries between the groups must inevitably result (cf. Barth 1969). Tension is produced as a result of the fact that both groups have an interest in maintaining those boundaries, since they protect French group interests (principally job opportunities) within Québec, and similar English interests outside Québec. Thus language is at the centre of the process of re-definition of boundaries, and the source of a conflict in which the language criterion is both discriminatory and non-discriminatory, and in which it serves both to maintain and to destroy ethnic boundaries.

Language and Ethnicity in Social Interaction

It is in this context that people in Québec must carry out their daily lives. In the past the unequal relationship of French to English was accepted by both groups: everyone knew what to expect, everyone knew how to act. Norms of behaviour, including norms of language use, were based on this shared frame of reference, which was made up of what people knew about social reality (Gumperz 1978). Since social reality consisted of, among other things, English dominance, clearly English was the language to be used in interethnic interaction. However, the changes described above had the effect of making the old norms invalid. The re-definition of social boundaries entails the re-definition of norms of social interaction.

In order for this re-definition to take place a certain amount of social knowledge must be shared. This starts with an awareness that language is symbolic of group relations and that language choice can convey information about an individual's views on those relations, and therefore on his frame of reference—whether old, new, or in a state of change. The exclusive use of French, for example, can indicate the new French nationalist goal of universal use of French. The exclusive use of English may indicate resistance to that nationalism, based on protection of the old status quo. For example, here is a conversation at a government bureau between a bilingual receptionist and an anglophone who has come to take the official French test:

> 1. (face-to-face):
> Man: Could you tell me where
>   the French test is?

Receptionist (in French): Pardon?
Man: Could you tell me where
             the French test is?
Receptionist: En français?   (IN FRENCH?)
Man: I have the right to be
             addressed in English by
             the government of Québec
             according to Bill 101.
Receptionist (to 3rd person):
             Qu'est-ce qu'il dit?   (WHAT'S HE SAYING?)

However, the exclusive use of one or the other language may merely indicate value-free monolingualism. What exactly is the case cannot be determined a priori, but rather must be elicited or discovered in conversation. In order to do so participants in a conversation must have information about each other's position with respect to ethnic group membership and knowledge of languages. This is a process of sorting out language as a tool from language as a symbol, and of sorting out one's own and one's interlocutor's expectations and assumptions based on group membership. Only on that basis can the negotiation of norms proceed.

Speakers start on the assumption that some frame of reference holds, whether or not that is the case. In order to find out what that frame might be they elicit social information, on the supposition that social experience, as constrained by social identity, affects the way individuals see and define the world. Even if no frames of reference exist this social information is still valuable as a basis for the establishment of new norms and of new definitions of role and situation, in the context of a new frame of reference. The rest of this paper is concerned with describing some aspects of the negotiation of norms, where frames of reference are either not shared or are in a state of change, as revealed in interethnic interaction in Montréal.

There are two arenas in which language use is particularly problematic and important, because interethnic contact there is frequent and the outcome of interaction therein has a large impact on people's lives. The first arena is that of public service encounters, encounters in which members of the general public request services from people whose job it is to provide those services. These encounters are manifold, especially in a society like Québec where so many services are provided more or less publicly (rather than, for example, by one's family). The second arena is that of the workplace, especially in private enterprise, where the ethnic composition is in a state of transition and which is the specific focus of much official language policy.

Observed interactions in an out-patient clinic and in a restaurant, both in downtown Montréal, provide some data concerning public service encounters.[1] Downtown is a buffer zone between ethnic areas; it is neutral territory. The hospital in which the clinic is located was originally an English hospital; its staff is largely anglophone, but its patient population is very mixed with a high percentage of francophones. Thus contact between francophones and non-francophones often occurs.

The most basic aspect of this contact concerns choice of the language to be used in the interaction. It used to be English, of course. Such a solution can no longer, however, be taken for granted. Clerks and patients, waiters and patrons, and others in similar configurations, find themselves in an uncertain situation, where language choice is potentially a political statement, but where it is impossible to determine a priori whether a political statement is intended, or what, if one is intended, it might be. One has to know a great deal about the person with whom one is speaking to understand what, if anything, they mean by speaking a particular language. This creates a dilemma in a typical public service encounter: the participants have never seen each other before and have no knowledge of each other's background or expectations.

It should first be made clear that ethnic categorization in Montréal is far from obvious. There are no physical manifestations of it, nor do language spoken, family name and ethnicity always coincide. Someone with a French name, speaking perfect and colloquial French, may categorize him/herself as English; someone with an Irish name may be a monolingual francophone. This can create certain interactional difficulties, as evidenced by these examples from interaction between hospital clerks and patients with identity cards:

2. (face-to-face):
Clerk:	Lombard, Anne-Marie?
Patient:	(Silence. Glare.)
Clerk:	C'est bien ça votre nom? (ISN'T THAT YOUR NAME?)
Patient:	(Silence. Glare.)
Clerk:	Is this your name?
Patient:	yes.

3. (telephone):
Clerk (in French): St-Pierre, Robert?
Patient (angrily, in English): St. Pierre. Robert.

In both these cases the patients resorted to inexplicit strategies to tell the clerk that they wished to be addressed in English. Another way to accomplish the same thing is to simply use the language of choice or to ask directly, but these can lead to conversational difficulties also. Either can be interpreted as political and therefore potentially hostile acts; or alternatively they may be taken as an admission of inability to cope with two languages.

A more interesting situation is that which arises when participants have no particular political axe to grind. Consider the following examples:

4. (telephone):
Clerk:	Central Booking, may I help you?

Patient:	Oui, allô?	
Clerk:	Bureau de rendez-vous, est-ce que je peux vous aider?[2]	(APPOINTMENTS DESK, MAY I HELP YOU?)
Patient:	(French)	(The patient begins
Clerk:	(French)	to try to make an
Patient:	(English)	appointment)
Clerk:	(English)	
Patient:	(French)	
Clerk:	(French)	
Patient:	Ètes-vous française ou anglaise?	(ARE YOU FRENCH OR ENGLISH?)
Clerk:	N'importe j'suis ni l'une ni l'autre.	(IT DOESN'T MATTER, I'M NEITHER ONE NOR THE OTHER.)
Patient:	Mais. . .	(BUT. . .)
Clerk:	Ça ne fait rien.	(IT DOESN'T MATTER.)
Patient:	(French)	

(The conversation continues in French)

5. (face-to-face):

Waiter:	Je reviens dans une minute. (Pause. Second look.) Anglais ou français, English or French?	(I'LL BE BACK IN A MINUTE.)
Patron:	Ben, les deux.	(WELL, BOTH.)
Waiter:	Non, mais, anglais ou français?	(NO, BUT, ENGLISH OR FRENCH?)
Patron:	It doesn't matter, c'est comme vous voulez.	(. . . AS YOU LIKE)
Waiter	(sighing): Okay, okay, I'll be back in a minute.	

In both these cases it appeared that one party to the interaction was not comfortable until a norm of language choice was established for the interaction. Further, that norm was to be based on the preference of the other party. Several ways of eliciting that preference are illustrated in the above examples. These strategies are:

A. Pretend you do not hear what your interlocutor said and make him/her repeat. This assumes the repetition will be in the speaker's preferred language. On the other hand, lack of comprehension is conventionally interpreted to mean a preference for the language other than the one used, thereby automatically engendering a code-switch:

6. (face-to-face):

Clerk:	May I help you?	
Patient:	(Silence.)	
Clerk:	Est-ce que je peux vous aider?	(MAY I HELP YOU?)
Patient:	(Confused look.)	
Clerk:	Anglais ou francais?	(ENGLISH OR FRENCH?)
Patient:	WHAT?	
Clerk:	MAY I HELP YOU?	

Patient: Oh, yes, yes, I'm just a little
                deaf.
                (See also example 2 in this regard.)

B. Code-switch. If you do it often enough you may either wear your
interlocutor out (and it is well known that in situations of fatigue one prefers
one's mother tongue) or catch him/her making a mistake; in either case you
find out what his/her mother tongue really is. The name of the game among
supporters of neutrality is not to make a choice, and therefore to give as little
compromising information as possible (cf. Scotton 1976 for a discussion of
similar phenomena in some African cities). Consider the following example:

7. (face-to-face):
Patient: Bonjour, English or
                French, français ou
                anglais?
Clerk: Czechoslovak.
Patient: Bon, est-ce qu'il y a un   (WELL, IS THERE A
                endroit où je peux acheter   PLACE WHERE I CAN
                un journal?   BUY A NEWSPAPER?)
Clerk: (Puzzled look.)
Patient: Can I buy a newspaper
                somewhere?
Clerk: Un journal?   (A NEWSPAPER?)
Patient: Oui.   (YES.)
Clerk: At the tuck shop, au bout   (. . . AT THE END OF THE
                du couloir.   HALLWAY.)

In this exchange it is worth noting two other things: the balanced pattern of
alternations, and the fact that the clerk responds to a question phrased in
terms of languages with an answer phrased in terms of nationality.

C. Ask explicitly what language the interlocutor wishes to speak (as in
example 7, and probably 5 and 6).

D. Ask the interlocutor explicitly to what ethnic group s/he belongs
(example 4).

The frequency of occurrence and seeming interchangeability of Strategies
C and D indicate two things: first, that language of preference and ethnic
origin are often confused (this elicits violent reactions from those who would
prefer to keep them separate); and second, that a certain amount of social
knowledge about one's interlocutor is a necessary part of negotiations about
language choice. Besides language preference and ethnic origin, questions
frequently asked of total strangers include birthplace, school attended,
birthplace of parents and language spoken at home. This knowledge gives one
clues as to one's interlocutor's expectations, assumptions, and view of social
reality. Eliciting such information is thus a step towards establishing a shared
frame of reference, such that norms of behaviour might be created, i.e. such
that behaviour might be interpreted in a conventional manner (Gumperz

1977; Tannen 1979). Only on this basis is interaction towards a goal possible, as illustrated in example 4. The point of the conversation (getting an appointment) was temporarily abandoned until a frame of reference could be established.

One other aspect of these conversational strategies should be discussed: the interlocutor who begins the negotiation may appear deferent by giving the choice of language to the other interlocutor. However, in situations where interlocutors wish to be equals, or to occupy a neutral position, this may be seen differently. It is not control of choice that is coveted, but rather an exhibition of flexibility and mastery of both languages (and therefore control over and access to a wider range of social roles and situations). If a speaker tries to make his interlocutor choose, this can be interpreted as an attempted put-down (i.e. 'Don't pretend you can compete with me!'); this is especially true if the strategy used is switching from one's mother tongue to one's second language. For these reasons the clerk in example 4 refuses to divulge her identity, the patron in example 5 refuses to choose, the waiter in example 5 sighs, and the clerk in example 7 classifies herself as a (phonetically and ethnically neutral) Czech.

In this type of public encounter, then, people have coped with change by using linguistic strategies to elicit the social information they need to establish new norms of interaction based on shared knowledge and shared expectations, in light of the fact that participants at least share knowledge about the basic purpose of the interaction (obtaining a service) and about the potential political interpretations of their use of language. What they must discover includes which language to use to get the job done without stirring up a conflict, since the provider wants to be seen as having given services efficiently and courteously, and the client wants to be seen as a legitimate recipient of such services. Negotiations of language choice are thus a means of neutralizing potential underlying conflict, by the establishment of a frame of reference in which interlocutors are enlisted on the same side, relative rights or duties are asserted as a function of newly-defined roles, or the issue is avoided altogether; as a result the main purpose of the interaction can be accomplished.

The workplace represents another critical area where language use in daily interaction is affected by and affects social change. Conversations in this domain occupy a space somewhere between the rapidity and impersonality of service encounters and the duration and intimacy of most private inter-actions. Employees may work together over prolonged periods of time, and interact at regular intervals. Their identity, largely defined by their jobs and hierarchical position, is widely known. They participate in a restricted set of situations, using a restricted set of channels of communication. All these factors affect their interaction; equally important, however, are the ways in which social change in the wider community is manifested inside the workplace.

This relationship between verbal interaction, social situation and social change in the workplace was examined during a study of a large Montréal company (Heller et al. in press). The company is a large one and was founded about 200 years ago. Montréal used to be the company's sole location until it expanded its operations in the 1950s and 1960s to include the rest of Canada plus U.S. subsidiaries. Up until recent years the Montréal branch was typical of old-style Québec enterprises: the anglophones formed the management, francophones and immigrants made up the vast majority of workers. In the 1960s the branch implemented a policy of recruiting and training francophones at the management level. As this was done on an individual basis, and since trainees were usually trained in English (often outside Québec), they soon functioned in English. However, in the early 1970s many of the anglophone management were sent to take over operations in the company's new western plants; many of the others, of a generation hired just after World War II, were approaching retirement. Hiring had been very limited on all levels for about 15 years, during a period of mechanization. In the early 1970s enough personnel had retired or been transferred to warrant a new phase of intense hiring. There are thus now two distinct generations in the branch: the senior is of mixed ethnic origin (with ethnic groups hierarchically stratified), and the junior is almost exclusively French. Especially at the management level the company is pursuing a policy of recruitment and rapid promotion of francophones, to replace personnel lost through transfer or retirement, and to simultaneously satisfy in the most efficient way the government's regulations concerning the use of French in the workplace. Anglophones in line for promotions are passed over if their knowledge of French (as measured by government tests) is inadequate. It remains the case that knowledge of English is necessary in the higher positions for dealing with the world outside of Québec; francophones who do not already have this knowledge can acquire it with a few years' training at another branch.

These changes have affected both informal and formal settings at work. Possibly as a result of their decreasing numbers, for example, anglophones now tend to seek each other out, from different hierarchical levels and different departments, for such informal activities as having coffee, a beer, or lunch. Francophones, on the other hand, tend to spend their breaks with the people they work with. So informal encounters tend to be monolingual. Two areas, however, are open to interethnic contact: formal meetings, restricted to top management, which is now ethnically mixed due to the promotion of francophones; and certain departments which are ethnically mixed at lower levels due to the change in recruitment policy and in the pool from which personnel are drawn.

In both cases it used to be that all, or almost all, participants in interaction in these areas were anglophone, and the language used was English. In formal meetings now the proportions have quite suddently been reversed, but the language used tends to remain English if the old anglophone department head has not been replaced. This is less and less frequently the case, however, as the rate of replacement is high. In formal meetings, then, participants have to work out a new set of norms that will enable them to do their work and to simultaneously maintain good working relations. It is clear all the while that the young francophones have a vested interest in French as the language of work, since the language policy is the same one that favours their promotion.

In some departments the use of French in meetings was decreed by fiat, at the risk of alienating the older anglophones. (Some of them do say that they feel 'out of it', 'stupid', or 'like a dumb-dumb', but that they try not to let it bother them; they accept the use of French as the new norm and are not much threatened by it since they will soon retire.) In other departments the change has not been so abrupt. Consider the following examples from a tape-recorded meeting chaired by Albert, a young department head recently promoted to replace an anglophone, and attended by Bob, an older Scot who would under other circumstances have gotten Albert's job, by Claude, an older francophone accustomed to working in English, and by Daniel, a monolingual young francophone recently promoted to a position originally slated for a monolingual anglophone:

8.

| Albert: | Tout le monde connaît Monica? Bob, have you met Monica? | (EVERYONE KNOWS MONICA?...) |

9. (Albert is criticizing Claude for the excessive detail of his reports):

| Albert: | ... il nous reste plus de temps après ça pour discuter les problèmes majeurs t' sais les choses qui vraiment you understand that Bob? I say if we lose less time in going over the routine we have more time to discuss the important uh. ... | (WE'LL HAVE MORE TIME AFTER THAT FOR DISCUSSING MAJOR PROBLEMS YOU KNOW THE THINGS THAT REALLY....) |

In both these cases Albert has solved the problem of which language to speak in the following manner: whenever he wants Bob to participate in the conversation Albert addresses him in English, translating his previous remarks if necessary. In general Albert and Claude also speak English whenever Bob is participating in the conversation. For example:

10.

| Albert: | ... so if we can manage to handle buckets on that floor okay |

Claude:	on the first floor	
Bob:	deuxième étage	(SECOND FLOOR)
Claude:	second floor	

11.

Albert:	. . . meeting de mardi brass- age six brasses de moins que prévu (unintelligible) huit point deux pour cent (unintelligible) budget	(TUESDAY MEETING BREW- ING SIX BREWS LESS THAN FORECAST. . .EIGHT POINT TWO PER CENT . . . BUDGET)
Bob:	eight point two	
Claude:	which means that	
Albert:	ah M.L. opened the subject again. . .	

Notice that Albert and Claude speak English regardless whether Bob speaks French or English. However, when Bob is not involved in the conversation Albert and Claude speak French to each other. In fact, Albert sometimes seems to make a point of it, since Claude still reads his reports in English having long been accustomed to do so. Thus, for example:

12.

Claude:	. . . I have one to hire to replace Monsieur Edmond who's leaving next year	
Albert:	bon avant d'aller plus loin avez-vous des nou- velles uh de l'affichage?	(OKAY BEFORE GOING ANY FURTHER DO YOU HAVE ANY NEWS UH OF THE SIGN- POSTING?)
Claude:	ben, c'est fait	(WELL, IT'S DONE)

Although Claude reads his reports in English his side comments to Albert are in French, e.g.:

13.

| Claude: | oui uh vacation staff R.M.,
L.P., again temp D.B., he's
on the lubrication survey,
L.R. working on the expense
budget but he's going off
for two weeks hein il prend
deux semaines de vacances
ça je l'avais donné ça y a
un bout de temps, ben, des
vacances, des vacances à
see frais, on les paie à 4
per cent | (EH HE'S TAKING TWO
WEEKS VACATION THAT
I GAVE THAT A WHILE
AGO, WELL, VACATION,
VACATION AT HIS OWN
EXPENSE, THEY PAY 4
PERCENT) |

Through various means, predominantly through code-switching, Albert, Bob and Claude are trying to cope with a change in norms and with new roles in the context of a given situation. Albert, for example, has to balance expectations that he use French with courtesy to an older man whose job he has, essentially, usurped; Bob must keep his dignity while showing flexible adaptation to new terms; and Claude must please both his new boss and his old colleague. It is interesting to note that example 9 is part of a long negotiation concerning the purpose of the weekly meeting and how best to achieve it. Only Daniel, the most junior member of the group in both age and rank, as well as the most recently arrived, seems out of the negotiations; he speaks only when spoken to and only in French. He is thus more part of the context than of the process.

In another situation, in the laboratory, the acting head is a young francophone, François, who is now temporarily the superior of a young anglophone from another province, George. François and George are normally of the same rank, although George is younger than François and has not worked for the company as long. He was given his job on the condition that he learn French, to which he agreed since the job represented career advancement; further, by doing so he demonstrated a certain amount of initiative. Consider the following exchange between François and George:

14. (face-to-face):

François:	Je reviens dans dix minutes.	(I'LL BE BACK IN TEN MINUTES.)
	(Pause.)	
	I'll be back in ten minutes.	
George:	I can never figure out if you're speaking French or English. My ear's not attuned to it.	
François:	With me the trouble's not my ear, it's my tongue.	

George's failure to answer François immediately caused François to code-switch to make sure that he was understood. As George's failure to respond to French could be seen as a failure to live up to expectations, George felt obliged to explain himself. In order to avoid offending George by allowing him to continue to feel inadequate, François makes a small joke, designed to put himself down concerning the same subject, inadequate mastery of one's second language, and thereby restores relations to an equilibrium. François has re-defined the assumptions to be shared for the purposes of the inter-action in order to do so: rather than judge people on the basis of their knowledge of French, he is suggesting that they be judged on the basis of their knowledge of a second language.

In another case, also involving lab technicians, an equilibrium is achieved through means that have already been conventionalized. Ian is an anglophone who has been working for this company for many years. Hélène is the second francophone ever to be hired in the labs; she has been working there for above twelve years. Since her arrival the French/English proportions have reversed: there are now four anglophone and thirteen francophone employees. Hélène is the only francophone colleague with whom Ian interacts. Here is an example of the reason that Ian feels comfortable with her:

15. (face-to-face):

Hélène:	Va-t-on manger de la soupe aujourd'hui?	(ARE WE GOING TO HAVE SOUP TO-DAY?)
Ian:	I'm going to, I don't know if anyone wants to join me.	
Hélène:	Je veux bien, qu'est-ce qu'on mange?	(SURE, I DO, WHAT WILL WE HAVE?)
Ian:	Oh, I'll take care of it.	

In both these situations, the formal meetings and the daily working relationships, the over-arching norm of language use is shared: everyone agrees that the language of work should be French. But everyone is also aware that cannot be accomplished overnight, so that in their daily behaviour they are coping with what they know about each other, about the situation in which their interaction is taking place, and with the gap between experienced and idealized social reality. They are, in effect, doing the work of changing social life by changing the norms of behaviour of which it is constituted.

Conclusion

In Québec, then, the relationship between language, social interaction and interethnic group relations must be seen on two levels. On one level language is symbolic of interethnic relations. The use of one, the other, both, or neither language can constitute in itself a statement about the speaker's perceptions of ethnic relations. However, these statements are only inter-pretable in the context of what the speakers know about each other and about various aspects of the world in which they are operating. That is, any given utterance can have many social significances (or none at all) as a function of the way language has been used in that utterance; the intended degree and kind of significance is discoverable only if interlocutors share a frame of reference. This frame is something that is constituted via social interaction. When the world is stable it can be indicated by conventional means. In times of change, however, that frame may not be shared or may no longer exist. Rather, in order to avoid insult or injury, or to permit interaction to occur at all, a frame must be established for the interaction as a whole. The construction of a frame of reference takes place through communication, and it is on this level of daily interaction that language plays its most direct role in ethnic relations. It is used as a tool to convey and elicit that social information which is a pre-condition to the establishment of a shared set of expectations and assumptions based on shared knowledge. In the absence of other clues (as in public service encounters) language is used to elicit information and to negotiate a frame of reference and a norm of interaction. In the workplace language is used to mediate between old and new norms, since the frame is shared and the new norm is imposed. It is also used to mediate between an egalitarian ideology which judges people on the basis of merit and a reality in which people are favoured as a result of belonging to an ethnic group. In both cases what is often involved is the creation through negotiation of norms appropriate to specific interactions (as opposed to classes of interactions).

The norms are designed to create islands of certainty in an uncertain world—to allow life to go on by suspending, for the moment, some of the more difficult questions of inequality that might otherwise permanently disrupt social interaction. In this way negotiation can lead to a conventionalization of norms covering ever-widening circles of social activity, and eventually to a world where assumptions are shared, whatever social conflicts they may hide.

Acknowledgements

I would like to thank John Gumperz, Timothy Kaiser, Andrew Roth and Cristina Roth for their valuable comments on earlier drafts of this paper. Part of the research on which the paper is based was carried out under grants from the Social Sciences and Humanities Research Council of Canada and from the Ministere du Developpement Culturel, Québec.

References

Barth, F. (ed.) 1969. *Ethnic Groups and Boundaries,* Boston: Little, Brown.
Brown, P. and Levinson, S. 1974. Universals of language usage: politeness phenomena. Ms. Department of Anthropology, University of California, Berkeley.
Clift, D. and Arnopoulos, S. 1979. *Le fait anglais au Québec,* Montréal: Editions Libre Expression.
Goffman, E. 1959. *The Presentation of Self in Everyday Life,* New York: Doubleday.
Gumperz, J.J. 1977. Sociocultural knowledge in conversational inference. In: *28th Annual Round Table on Languages and Linguistics.* Washington D.C.: Georgetown University Press.
– 1978. The conversational analysis of interethnic communication. In: Ross, L. (ed.), *Interethnic Communication.* Athens, Georgia: The University of Georgia Press.
Heller, M., Bartholomot, J.-P., Lévy, L. and Ostiguy, L., in press. *Le rôle de la langue dans les processus sociaux: une étude de cas sociolinguistique d'une entreprise montréalaise,* Québec: L'Editeur Officiel.

Scotton, C.M. 1976. Strategies of neutrality: language choice in uncertain situations. *Language* 52(4):919-941.

Tannen, D. 1979. What's in a frame? Surface evidence for underlying expectations. In: Freedle, R. (ed.), *New Directions in Discourse Processing.* Norwood, New Jersey: Ablex.

Notes

1. Another analysis of the same examples appears in: Monica Heller, 'Bonjour, hello?': Negotiations of Language Choice in Montreal'. In *Communication, Language* and *Social-Identity.* Cambridge: Cambridge University Press, 1982, edited by John J. Gumperz.
2. This appears to be a calque on the English formula; I am indebted to John Gumperz for pointing this out.

Kathryn A. Woolard

Catalonia: The Dilemma of Language Rights

In most cases, minority languages in complex societies are associated with educational, economic, and political inequality.[1] The coincidence of difference and isadvantage in all its manifestations is so pervasive that much of our thinking about minority language rights pointedly addresses socioeconomic and political problems as much as linguistic ones. The issue of bilingual education in the United States is an example of this.

Unlike the majority of bilingual situations that have been studied, in Catalonia the inferior status of the regional language in terms of official policy has NOT been accompanied by socioeconomic inferiority for its speakers (Arnau 1980).[2] Because the relation of linguistic, economic and political power is complex and violates many of our expectations, Catalonia provides an opportunity to examine and test some of our assumptions about difference and dominance. However, it also raises difficult new questions about the nature of language rights and linguistic equality. This chapter presents a descriptive overview of the sociolinguistic situation in Catalonia, based on ethnographic and experimental research in the capital city of Barcelona in 1979-80.

The Languages

The two languages that are spoken in Barcelona are Catalan and Castilian, as Spanish is known on the Iberian peninsula and will be referred to here. As a Romance language, Catalan is a sister to Castilian, although its historical development is more closely tied to that of Occitan, the language of southern France which is now experiencing its own revival (Sanchis Guarner 1980). Catalan is spoken in the 'Catalan Countries' (*Els Països Catalans*) of the Mediterranean area; in addition to Catalonia proper (the northeastern area of Spain comprising four provinces), these include Valencia, the Balearic Isles, the Pyrenean principality of Andorra, the Roussillon region of southern France, and the Sardinian city of Alghero.

As sister languages, Castilian and Catalan share many linguistic features but are distinguished by others. The most striking differences are phonetic and phonological; to the unacquainted ear, Catalan sounds more like Italian or Portuguese than Castilian. The phonemic inventory of Catalan incudes several fricatives and affricates not present in Castilian (š, z, ž, dž) and a more complex vowel system, including both open and closed versions of 'e' and 'o' (ɛ, e, ɔ,o). Some phonemes shared by the two languages are distributed differently. For example, word-final palatals (λ and η) are permitted in Catalan while they are not in Castilian, and are especially characteristic in proper names (e.g., *Capmany, Palafrugell*). Phonological rules are also quite distinctive; for example, unstressed 'a' and 'e' reduce to schwa (ə) and unstressed 'o' becomes 'u' in Catalan, but there are no comparable phenomena in Castilian. Catalan does not favor the canonical consonant-vowel syllable structure of Castilian, so that more consonant clusters are permissable and plurals may be formed by adding 's' directly to a final consonant (e.g. *gat, gats*). Liaison between words is obligatory, giving rise, for example, to voicing of word-final 's' and other voiceless consonants before an initial vowel. These features of Catalan are among the most difficult to master for a native Castilian speaker, and thus often serve as markers of a speaker's origin.

Syntactically Catalan is quite like Castilian in many respects (as it is similar to other Romance languages), but there are several distinguishing features such as a complex system of pronominal clitics and obligatory use of the definite article before a possessive adjective (e.g. *la meva mare* 'my mother'). The periphrastic past tense used in oral Catalan is not found in Castilian, and is deceptively similar to the Castilian periphrastic future. Thus, the Catalan past is formed by an auxiliary plus the infinitive of the main verb; all but the first and second person plural forms of the auxiliary are identical to the present tense of the verb 'to go' (*anar*). In Castilian, in contrast, the periphrastic future is formed from the conjugated 'to go' (*ir*) + *a* + infinitive.

Catalan: 'they go' *van*; 'they learned' *van aprendre*.
Castilian: 'they go' *van*; 'they are going to learn' *van a aprender*.

The many lexical similarities between Catalan and Castilian are counter-balanced by important differences, especially at the level of basic vocabulary (see Table 1). Both children and adult learners are able to formulate phonological rules of thumb to transform Castilian vocabulary to Catalan, and vice versa, and by applying these rules one can produce a correct form much of the time. However, almost as often one will produce a 'barbarism' (a prescriptively incorrect but commonly accepted term) or a completely unacceptable form. Because misconceptions abound, it should be stressed that although they are closely related and there is substantial borrowing and interference, Catalan is not a dialect of Castilian but rather a separate Romance language by linguists' standards.[3]

Historical Background

Politics and Language

A city of approximately two million inhabitants surrounded by an industrial belt housing another two million people, Barcelona is one of the largest and most important urban areas in Spain; it has long been an economic leader as well as a cosmopolitan cultural rival to Madrid. However, Barcelona is also the capital of the once independent state of Catalonia, which was joined to Castile through the marriage of Ferdinand, ruler of the Catalano-Aragonese federation, and Isabel of Castile in the fifteenth century. This political union has often proved an uncomfortable one, and there is a long (although not continuous) history of strife between Spain, as represented by Castile, and Catalonia.

The conflict has focused on various themes through the centuries, from feudal privileges to royal succession to tariff policies; in most cases such conflict was an expression of underlying structural differences between an agrarian-based society, Castile, and a mercantile and industrial society, Catalonia (Vilar 1964). In the mid-nineteenth century, the Catalan capitalist elite initiated an attempt to identify Catalonia's industrial and commercial interests as the central interests of Spain as a whole. In its frustration, this movement took on a nationalist cast. – i.e., Catalan nationalism versus the Spanish centralist state–that continues to exert force in current politics.

Nineteenth century Catalan nationalism was typical of Romantic movements in Europe and united cultural, linguistic, economic and political concerns. As a former independent polity which once dominated Mediterranean trade and controlled parts of Italy and Greece, Catalonia had its own 'illustrious tradition' (Fishman 1972) in statescraft, commerce and the arts, as well as its own language with an early history of distinguished literary achievements. All these were resources for the flowering nationalism, but language became the most powerful symbol of the tension between the Spanish center and the Catalan periphery. Firmly rooted as the vernacular language of the populace, Catalan had lost ground to Castilian among urban elites in Barcelona and in literary use during the eighteenth and early nineteenth centuries, partly due to official policy. The literary and cultural revival (*Renaixença*, commonly dated to the 1833 publication of Aribau's nostalgic poem, *Oda a la Pàtria*) led to remarkably successful movements to standardize the language and broaden its functions in the early twentieth century.

The Catalan nationalist movement has experienced ups and downs and important political transformations over the past century, changing from a solidly bourgeois orientation to the predominantly liberal and leftist stance of the Republican, Civil War, and Franco periods. The greatest political and linguistic gains were made during the short-lived Second Spanish Republic (1931–1939), when partial political autonomy was granted to Catalonia and the Catalan language was made co-official with Castilian and used actively in schools, government, and the information media. The greatest losses were sustained after the defeat of the Republican forces in the Spanish Civil War (1936–1939) and during the ensuing forty-year Franco dictatorship.

During the Franco years, many of the forces which enter into play in the current situation took on their modern form. Franco's government targeted the Catalan language as a tool and symbol of Catalan rejection of the Fascist state (Barcelona had been a major leftist and Republican stronghold), and Catalan was indeed used for political protest. Severe repression of the language was instituted, including prohibition of its use in public domains such as schools, government offices and the information media under penalty of law. Through propaganda in school texts and other literature, official policy encouraged dialectalization, the reduction of Catalan to a spoken 'patois' with Castilian perceived as its standard counterpart (Kloss 1967, Azevedo forthcoming). Because of this institutionalized diglossia, today there are virtually no monolingual speakers of Catalan, and a high proportion of Catalan speakers are illiterate in their native language. Nonetheless, for the most part Catalans maintained a tenacious loyalty to their language. Catalan was never displaced from informal communication between native speakers of most social strata, and its use in public was a significant aspect of the leftist and nationalist political protests that arose in the 1960s.

With the death of Franco in 1975, political and particularly regional possibilities began to open up again in Spain, and changes began to be negotiated in the fragile new democracy. Limited regional autonomy was again granted to Catalonia in 1979, the Catalan language was again made co-official, and the new Catalan government (*Generalitat*) has worked to gain administrative control over the region and the educational process in particular, and to implant Catalan in the bureaucracy, school system, and mass media. Teaching of Catalan as a subject matter in the schools, for example, is now required by law. The *Generalitat* has established an Office of Linguistic Policy charged with 'normalizing' the use of Catalan, and a law for the defense and normalization of the language was passed in 1983.

Economic Development and Immigration

Linguistically and politically, the situation of Catalonia is the familiar one of a 'submerged people' struggling for control over its affairs as has happened often in Europe and is happening in many other parts of the world. However, in social and economic terms there are two extremely important differences between the usual center-periphery or dominant-submerged group situation and that of Catalonia.

First, rather than lagging behind the center in industrial and economic development as did, for example, Québec, Flanders and the Celtic fringe of Britain, Catalonia has long been a leading commercial and industrial force in agrarian Spain. Catalan nationalism arose directly from the struggle of Catalan industrialists to identify the Spanish state's interests with their own rather than those of the land-based Castilian oligarchy. Catalonia is in fact one of the richest and most developed regions of the Spanish state and, with the highest per capita income in Spain, its inhabitants enjoy privileged economic status in comparison to most other regions (Medina 1975). This early economic development has created the second major difference between Catalonia and other seats of regional movements: the presence of a primarily non-native working class.

To fill the need for manual labor in construction and other burgeoning industries, since the early twentieth century there has been a heavy influx into Catalonia of monolingual Castilian-speaking workers from the impoverished agricultural regions of southern Spain. With the advent of economic stagnation and crisis, immigration has now tapered off, but its impact is massive. In 1970, 40 percent of the population of Catalonia was non-native born, mostly from Andalucia and Murcia; in Barcelona province the proportion of immigrants reaches 47 percent (Sàez 1980). Of the Catalonia-born, a high percentage are in fact children of Castilian-speaking immigrants, who have a higher fertility rate than autochthonous Catalans (Pinilla de las Heras 1979).

Thus, one of the greatest fears that small European countries might harbor about their 'guest workers'—that they will numerically overwhelm the native population—has virtually come to pass in Catalonia. It is particularly crucial that this has occurred in a region with a strong sense of nationhood but none of the institutional mechanisms for protecting this identity. Moreover, the situation is made critical by the fact that these immigrant workers are speakers of dialects of the official state language, Castilian, and consider themselves Spaniards (*españoles*). In all of Catalonia, only about 52 percent of the adult population speaks Catalan as the home or habitual language; this figure falls to about 40 percent in the city and has been estimated at as low as 25 percent in parts of the heavily immigrant urban periphery (Junyent 1979,

Strubell 1978). These data reflect actual demographic change rather than linguistic shift on the part of Catalans. Given the differences in fertility rates between Catalans and immigrants, due both to age and cultural factors, it is not surprising that in the province of Barcelona only about 37 percent of primary school children are native speakers of Catalan (Arnau 1980) (see Table 2).

The population of Catalonia is not simply divided linguistically and ethnically; the importance of this division lies in the fact that it largely coincides with class divisions. As unskilled labor was brought in to fill the lowest rungs of the occupational ladder, the autochthonous labor force moved up into skilled positions. The socio-economic differences between native Catalans and immigrants, who are almost all of Castilian-speaking origin, are striking. (See Table 3).

In spite of the presence of a Castilian political and administrative elite placed in Catalonia by the Franco government, native Catalans are heavily concentrated in the highest occupations and immigrants in the lower levels of manual labor. Education levels and the distribution of children in public and private schools reported in Table 2 are additional reflections of this social inequality. While these patterns are due primarily to the unskilled character of the immigrating forces rather than to discrimination, they generate potentially long-term consequences.

Pre-Civil War immigration, mostly from Murcia, was absorbed into several of the large Catalan working class neighborhoods in the city proper of Barcelona. It is generally claimed that these immigrants integrated into the fabric of Catalan life and assimilated to the Catalan language. While there are no data on this assimilation, it is certainly the case that there are many older immigrants who speak Catalan, and many Castilian-surnamed descendents who are linguistically and ethnically Catalan.

Post-Civil War immigration, however, has met a different fate. Because of the rapid rate of immigration and the sheer numbers involved, much of the second wave of immigration was forced into crowded, high-rise living in worker suburbs where services are inadequate and integration into the life of Catalonia is minimal. Because of the enclave nature of these suburbs, many Castilian-speaking inhabitants rarely enter into direct contact with the Catalan language. Since until very recently (1975) Catalan was generally prohibited in schools and other public use, there has been little opportunity to learn the language for the vast majority of these immigrants, although many express the desire to do so. Given the existing physical and social separation of the two communities, there is real danger that the coincidence of linguistic and class divisions will become a permanent phenomenon. This tendency is exacerbated by the current limitations on economic expansion induced by the state of the world economy.

It is ironic that the same factor has created the strengths and weaknesses of the Catalan nationalist position. Relatively early economic development gave Catalonia the material resources to maintain a strong sense of identity and the power to adopt a defiantly independent stance toward the central government (Medina 1975). However, it has also led to the undermining of the ethnic homogeneity of the region, the implantation of the Castilian language at the vernacular level, and the accentuation of the divisiveness of class in attempts at political mobilization.

Contemporary Sociolinguistic-Development

Language and Politics

Catalonia is a region in a larger state in which the language has been doubly threatened by two radically different factors: externally, by official repression on the part of the central government, and internally, by a large immigrant population. Because linguistic repression was linked to political repression, Catalan has logically become a prime symbol of the quest for political liberalization and autonomy for native Catalans; indeed, language rights are the major substantive issue for many. More problematic is the symbolic value of this language for the immigrant half of the population, for the most part monolingual speakers of a non-standard dialect of the wider state language. The political subjugation of Catalonia was not linked to economic subordination, and the majority of the working class and the most disadvantaged strata in Catalonia are in fact not speakers of the language which is being defended. These facts make expressive manipulations of the language ambiguous. When a Catalan university professor refuses to offer his class in Castilian because it is the 'language of the Civil Guard', he is also rejecting the native language of part of his audience. Such complexities create a difficult and potentially explosive problem for nationalist politicians and language policy makers.

Nationalist political strategies, be they of the left or the right, mobilize support on the basis of appeals to ethnic or regional identity. Since demographic changes over the last forty years have made the definition of Catalan identity problematic, who and what is to be considered 'Catalan' has become the focus of public debate. During the 1979 campaign for approval of the referendum on regional autonomy (*Estatut d'Autonomia*), appeals from almost the entire spectrum of Catalan political parties were directed at formulating the broadest possible base for nationalist mobilization by including the immigrants. The key slogans of the campaign were '*Més que mai, un sol poble*' ('Now more than ever, one single people') and '*Es català tothom qui viu i treballa a Catalunya'* ('Everyone who lives and works in Catalonia is Catalan'). Highly sensitive to the need for immigrant support, political strategists worked to avoid dividing the populace into two communities on the basis of language or place of birth.

Because the working class shares with the non-Castilian regions a history of oppression under the Franco regime, there has been an implicit if uneasy pact between Catalan nationalists and Castilian-speaking workers in their political efforts. For this reason, the appeals made in the campaign for the *Estatut* were relatively (although not resoundingly) successful; the referendum passed with a 40 percent abstention rate. However, the slogans of the campaign did not reflect the reality of ethnic identity in everyday life, wherein only Catalan speakers are normally considered 'Catalan' while Castilian speakers are 'Castilians', regardless of birthplace (although both euphemistic and pejorative labels, as well as regional referents, have developed for the latter group). Thus the validity of the slogans and more global definitions of identity began to be called into question publicly in the year that followed, especially during the electoral campaign for the Catalan parliament (*Parlament*). As each party attempted to define its constituency, variation in public positions on the meaning of Catalan identity and the role of the Catalan language emerged. A relatively conservative, expressly Catalan nationalist party, which clung to the broad definition of identity but found its voters primarily among natives, gained the presidency of the government. However, a specifically immigrant political party which rejected Catalan identity for its constituency managed to gain two seats in *Parlament*, despite the outcry from leftist groups against their tactics as demagogic and divisive.

At the same time, Catalan intellectuals wrote of a 'crisis in the concept of Catalan identity', levelling their criticism at the all-inclusive slogans (Argente et al. 1979). Underlying this sense of crisis were two main questions:

(1) How is the Catalan nation to be distinguished from Spain if not by its language? No more powerful or legitimate traditional symbol is available; most of the remaining cultural differences are largely a matter of the degree of modern industrialization. What other than language makes Catalonia a nation?

(2) If not the defining criterion of Catalonia, what then is the role of the Catalan language? If those who do not speak Catalan are to be considered Catalan, then the language is not an integral, defining feature of identity. What role beside redundancy remains for a minority language in modern society? These concerns led to an insistent chorusing of the Herderian concept of a people as defined by their language, and a rejection of the claim that one who does not speak Catalan can be Catalan.

Linguistic Etiquette

The insistence that ethnic identity is linked to language is of course not novel to the Catalan movement. However, the urgency of the question in this case results from deep and not unreasonable fears for the fate of Catalan in its struggle against Castilian. If Catalan is not indispensable but merely optional in the new Catalonia, many fear that it will have no power to maintain itself against a world language such as Castilian which has already made so many inroads into the dominion of Catalan. Thus some believe that if as a political expedient and a gesture of acceptance toward the Castilian-speaking population Catalan remains only co-official rather than the primary language of Catalonia, it will die of attrition.

A look at recent and current norms of language use will explain the fears of Catalan speakers. Four basic (although conflicting) norms of correct language choice can be abstracted, varying in the degree to which they are generalized in the community. The first two can be termed the 'traditional norms', by which is meant only the tradition of the past forty years. They are the result of three primary factors discussed above: (1) the earlier process of shift toward Castilian as a prestige language for public and literary use among the elite and upper middle classes (McDonogh 1981); (2) the legally enforced diglossia; and (3) the influx of monolingual Castilian speakers. The combined effects of these influences resulted in the characteristic situation in which a minority language is reserved for in-group domains and functions, and the state language for all other uses.

NORM 1. The first traditional norm dictated situational choice, and selection of language in most formal and public situations was automatically enforced for all community members. In schools, government offices, public speeches, radio and television, and in almost all kinds of writing, Castilian was mandated by the situation, even when the majority of participants were Catalan speakers.

Because this norm was mostly externally imposed, it has broken down rapidly, especially for oral language. Catalan has quickly come to be considered appropriate, at times even obligatory, in public speech. For example, it is a rare and comic moment when the President of Catalonia is heard to speak Castilian, reserved for campaign advertisements directed at immigrants or short formal welcomes to the King of Spain. Almost all legislators in the Catalan *Parlament* use Catalan, and one representative absented himself in protest on the few occasions when a fellow legislator employed Castilian. In other isolated incidents public use of Castilian has provoked furor: a university professor was questioned and severely criticized for using Castilian in a public forum even though he was defending Catalan language rights.

In spite of this sometimes militant shift to the public use of Catalan, the traditional situational norm still had profound effects on many activities in 1980. At the time, throughout the city of Barcelona, almost all advertising was in Castilian, and only one daily newspaper of a half dozen was published in Catalan. The state-run television provides only 57 hours monthly in Catalan, although the situation was remedial in 1983 by the attainment of a Catalan-language channel. On an individual, but even more telling level, over half of all Catalan speakers use Castilian in personal note-taking (Subirats 1980).

NORM 2. A second and even more enduring norm developed out of the Franco period, the traditional interpersonal norm for informal situations. By this standard, language choice is dictated not simply by the situation, but by the linguistic identity of the interlocutor. Traditionally, Catalan is reserved for use with co-members of the Catalan group only. Although the majority of Castilian speakers easily acquire passive competence in Catalan, it is 'polite' to speak Catalan only to those who are identified as native speakers of Catalan, or for whom there are fairly clear signals of this identity, such as physical or accent cues. Catalan is the marked case and Catilian the unmarked case to be used with all unknown quantities as well as known outsiders. Thus a person who uses Castilian in response to Catalan, even when giving every indication of perfect comprehension, traditionally provokes an automatic shift to Castilian on the part of the interlocutor. Any sign that an unfamiliar interlocutor has not fully understood a Catalan statement provokes a similar shift, even though the addressee may simply have been unable to hear.

This norm is double-edged in significance. On the one hand it signals defense and accommodation to the Castilian speaker, but on the other hand it serves to sharply define a Catalan in-group and to exclude outsiders. While Catalan speakers may be offended by what they see as Castilian expectations of accommodation, Castilian speakers can sometimes also be frustrated and offended by what they perceive as rebuffs or patronization when they attempt to join Catalan speakers. That the norm indeed represents politeness can be seen from the apologies speakers offer for lapses into Catalan. But that it is also a selective solidarity mechanism can be seen in the shifts to Castilian that are triggered by the detection of an unfamiliar accent in otherwise fluent Catalan. This chagrins those who are in fact native speakers from different areas, such as Valencia, or who were raised in exile.

As a result of the political mobilization of nationalist sentiment, the conscious organization of language loyalty, and the new political structure of Catalonia, linguistic etiquette in Barcelona is in a process of change. While traditional norms are tenacious and fuel the fears of defenders of the Catalan language, conflicting new norms have begun to develop and are in use in certain segments of the population.

NORM 3. A new 'Bilingual Norm' is now explicitly espoused by many informants, especially adolescents. It is also the norm officially encouraged by the Catalan government during what it sees as an interim period in the normalization of the Catalan language (Generalitat de Catalunya 1980). By this norm, all members of the community have the right to express themselves in their native language; this implies that every member of the community has a duty to be at least passively bilingual. While it would seem to define a middle ground of mutual tolerance and respect and is deemed by many to be the ideal, this norm is rarely applied effectively. Bilingual conversations in which two participants use different languages are seen as anomolous, generate unease, and are rarely stable. They are susceptible to interpretations from the standpoint of other norms, whereby negative social or political intentions are attributed to the interlocutor, and it is often assumed that at least one party is being rude and presumptuous by refusing to accomodate to the other. Open conflict rarely results from these interpretations, but when it does it is most often seen in commercial settings such as restaurants where there is no lasting relation or background knowledge between client and service-provider to mitigate the tension. In more solidary two-person interaction, participants usually shift to a common language, although the tacit negotiation process may be lengthy when both are fluent in both languages. At present few are able to comfortably maintain the bilingual norm.

NORM 4. This 'Target Norm' is seen by language nationalists as the goal toward which linguistic change in Catalonia must be directed. It is the mirror image of the traditional norms. In this system, Castilian should be reserved for in-group use with co-members of the Castilian-speaking community; in all situations of communication in the larger public or when not all participants are known to be native Castilian-speakers, Catalan should be used.

In actual practice, it is impossible to distinguish Catalan speakers who are applying this norm from those who are attempting to operate according to the Bilingual Norm. Thus there is increased potential for Castilian speakers to assign negative meaning to an interlocutor's choice of Catalan and to believe it indicates not tolerance of the bilingual situation but an attempt to impose Catalan on all speakers. Among younger, intellectual, and politically progressive groups, however, there is growing acceptance of this norm, and accomodation to Catalan interlocutors by Castilian speakers is becoming frequent in these sectors.

The variability of linguistic etiquette sometimes leads to situations in which language choice must be specifically requested or negotiated, similar to those situations described for Montréal (Heller, this volume); that the request is usually made in terms of identity. — 'What are you?' — rather than language preference is a telling point. As seen, it also provides the potential for interpersonal conflict; this conflict is still most often resolved by all parties switching to Castilian and the security of the traditional norm. Choice of language in larger groups is even more complex and will not be treated fully here. Such choice often depends on critical mass; group language will usually follow the linguistic affiliation of the majority, with speakers of the second language continuing to address each other directly in their own language (Calsamiglia and Tuson, 1980). There is no embarrassment about the use of Catalan in front of Castilian speakers, such as is reported for Hungarian in Austria (Gal 1979). For example, Catalan families generally use Catalan in front of a Castilian-speaking son- or daughter-in-law, guest, or servant, although they employ Castilian to address that person directly. Because the key feature in code selection is the linguistic identity of the interlocutor rather than situation, the two languages have not acquired the connotations from their association with different domains that lead to metaphorical code-switching in other cases of language contact (Blom and Gumperz 1972). This form of language variation is not nearly as significant in Barcelona as has been claimed for other minority language situations.

Language Attitudes

The concerns of Catalan language nationalists are based on the tenacity of the traditional norms of language use. It is undeniable that Castilian pensisted as the dominant language in the information media and in literate uses as well as in interpersonal exchanges between members of the two linguistic groups. Catalans often see the traditional norms and patterns of language choice as reflecting a lack of prestige and respect for the Catalan language; the letters to the editor of the Catalan daily paper demonstrate this concern. As the general 'loser' in linguistic negotiations in both private and public domains, Catalan seems to have inferior status. This has led to dismal forecasts on the part of her defenders of the language (Argente et al. 1979) and to demands for strong policies of affirmative action for Catalan.

Few outside observers would deny the oppression the Catalan language has suffered. However, the inferior status of the language does not imply inferior status for its speakers. It must be remembered that unlike other areas, Catalan speakers have not been penalized socially or economically for their minority language affiliation. As has been seen, they dominate the upper occupational strata and attain relatively higher levels of education. At the University of Barcelona, Catalan speakers are somewhat over-represented, forming 60 percent of the student population (Junyent 1979). Although abusive and deprecatory attitudes toward the use of Catalan by schoolchildren existed during the Franco years, and in most schools no acknowledgment was given that Catalan children were being educated in a non-native language, almost no negative effects on school performance have been seen or claimed. Relatively secure social status appears to have counteracted the traumatic potential of linguistic policy.

Some American observers, seeing the official subordination of Catalan, have characterized it as a low prestige language (Ryan 1979). However, because of the predominance of Catalan speakers in positions of social, economic, and now even political power, this conclusion must be questioned. To further explore attitudes toward the two languages and expectations about speakers based on language choice, a matched-guise experiment modelled on the work of the Lambert team in Montréal (Lambert et al. 1960) was conducted among high school and college students in Barcelona and its suburbs.[4]

The 224 respondents to the test were asked to listen to eight female voices reading the same passage and to rate the speakers on fifteen personality traits. The passage was a short formal text, intended to be appropriate to the school domain, presented four times in Catalan and four times in Castilian. The respondents were unaware that only four speakers were heard, each reading the text once in each language. Speakers were chosen to represent the actual spectrum of accents in Barcelona rather than an ideal perfect bilingual; two were native Catalan speakers and two were of Castilian-speaking origin.

In the analysis of the ratings, three main factors were extracted statistically from the fifteen original traits. The first factor stressed affect or personal warmth ('likeable', 'open', 'sense of humor', etc.) and can be interpreted as a measure of solidarity (Ryan 1979; White 1980). The second stressed effectiveness or competence ('intelligent', 'cultured', 'leadership', etc.) and could be considered a measure of status (Ryan 1979) or power (White 1980; Brown and Gilman 1960). The third main factor extracted might be labelled 'egotism' since it loaded principally from the traits 'proud', 'ambitious', and 'ungenerous'. Each of these main factors was examined for the effect of change of language on the ratings given each speaker by the Catalan and Castilian-speaking respondent groups. A different pattern was found for each of the factors.

Solidarity

On the solidarity measure, each respondent group showed a preference for its own language. However, the picture is complex, indicating that judges are aware of cues to the underlying linguistic identity of speakers and that these identities enter into evaluations. Castilian respondents gave the highest solidarity ratings to native Castilian speakers when they used Castilian. These respondents gave the lowest ratings to the same speakers when they used Catalan, and they gave relatively neutral ratings to native Catalan speakers no matter which language they used. It appears that judges are indifferent to language choice on the part of members of the out-group, feel great solidarity with co-members who use the group's language, and penalize the use of the out-group language, or linguistic co-optation, on the part of co-members. Catalan respondents follow the same pattern although the evidence is weaker and the effects not as marked.

Power

Contrary to the expectations created by long-standing official policy and the traditional etiquette, there is no experimental evidence that Catalan is a low prestige language; in fact, there is noteworthy indication that Catalan gives higher status to speakers than does Castilian. Overall, the Catalan guises were evaluated significantly more positively than were the Castilian guises, although this effect was not significant for any individual speaker considered alone. This trend to regard Catalan more highly than Castilian is true of both Catalan and Castilian-speaking respondents. The two groups agreed in their ranking of speakers, and it was an immigrant from Andalucia whose speech was significantly stigmatized, regardless of the language she used.

Egotism

The results of the analysis of this factor are extremely complex. However, at base they indicate that each group views the other's language as more 'egotistical'. The effect was much stronger for Castilian respondents, indicating that they form stronger expectations about the egotism of a person on the basis of linguistic cues than do the Catalan respondents. Moreover, the Castilian respondents attributed much higher egotism ratings to the two native Catalan speakers than to the Castilians, no matter which language they used. This concurs with a prevalent stereotype in Spain of the Catalan as relatively cold, ambitious and selfish. Catalan respondents showed no evidence of holding the reciprocal view.

These results underline the irony that while the Catalan language may in fact be in a relatively powerless position, its speakers are not regarded as powerless by either linguistic group. Rather, Catalan may be the more personally prestigious language in Catalonia, reflecting the greater impact of socioeconomic factors on attitudes. Second, they show the important implications of language choice for group solidarity. Use of the out-group language may be perceived as a betrayal of solidarity and therefore negatively sanctioned. Contrary to what one might expect, Castilians seem even more concerned about this betrayal than do Catalans; Castilians in Barcelona may experience more insecurity about their identity than Catalans who have the weight of history and territory as well as socioeconomic status behind them. Lastly, the strong stereotypes which Castilian speakers seem to hold about Catalans as egotistical, in combination with their perceived power, may mean that they see the latter as personally threatening.

Such experimental results make sense of the behavior and attitudes of the respondents and other informants as elicited in interviews and observed in action. Many Castilian speakers express respect for Catalan, and surveys show that as many as 81 percent of immigrants believe that their children should learn Catalan (Subirats 1980). This follows logically from the perceived prestige of Catalan-speakers. However, few Castilian-speakers who are not embedded in Catalan social networks take the step of learning to speak the language, and even high-school students who must study Catalan are often reluctant to use it orally. When asked why, they cite the lack of necessity – '*Si no nos obligan . . .* ' ('if they don't make us . . . ') – or fear of ridicule. Yet it was pointed out by one student that it is most often fellow Castilian-speakers rather than Catalans who laugh at the mistakes of learners. At this time speaking Catalan is still largely viewed as a claim to being ethnically Catalan. Ethnographic evidence supports the experimental conclusion that social sanctions work against 'passing', or the betrayal of group solidarity which might be perceived in such linguistic shift.

The results also point out the quandary of language planners. While the language is powerless, its speakers are powerful. While active use of Catalan by Castilian speakers may only occur if it is made obligatory, obligation may exacerbate the sense of threat to individual and group. What then should be the goals and methods of the 'normalization' of Catalan?

Language Policy

There are two prevailing theories of the basis for language rights: the territorial and the individual (Ninyoles 1976). In the first, the territorial and historical integrity of the Catalan nation is posited as the basis of language policy. From this perspective, assimilation to Catalan should be encouraged so that ultimately Catalan may be the primary language of Catalonia. Furthermore, the strength of Castilian as a world language is such that 'equality' before the law is not believed to be sufficient to prevent the ultimate death of Catalan, and affirmative action measures are advocated to insure its survival.

The alternative position emphasizes the fact that half the population of Catalonia is undeniably Castilian-speaking. If linguistic policy is to be based on demographic reality, it is believed that peaceful co-existence of the two languages with full functions for both must be the goal. Moreover, since Catalan speakers generally enjoy higher socioeconomic status than Castilian speakers in Catalonia, efforts necessary to protect the language such as requiring it for jobs in government or industry are seen as discriminating against the already disadvantaged, those in most need of educational and economic assistance. Advocates of this viewpoint base their proposals on a belief in individual language rights.

That the Catalan language movement has garnered support from the immigrant population for so long is a testimony to their political unity against the harsh policies of the Franco state. But now that Catalan autonomy is a reality rather than a dream, and it is possible that the Catalan language may become a real prerequisite to a full life in Catalonia rather than simply an expressive symbol, there is danger of division in the community.

Indications of such divisiveness have already arisen. Until recently, those sympathetic with Catalan political demands have rarely expressed doubts about the defense of the Catalan language, since such expressions have traditionally been the weapon of strong anti-Catalanists and supporters of the central government. However, some immigrants express unease about the ambiguity of the *Generalitat*'s language goals and methods. Additionally, in early 1981 a manifesto signed by 2300 Castilian-speaking intellectuals and professionals residing in Catalonia protested perceived discrimination against the Castilian language. This move provoked angry response and denials from many intellectuals and government leaders (de Pedrolo et al 1981).

The disagreements stem mainly from different understandings of the balance of power in the current situation. These in turn are maintained by a difference in focus: Catalan defenders emphasize past events and external state-imposed injustices; Castilian-speaking leaders in Catalonia focus on future possibilities and internal inequalities. While Catalan speakers seek to protect their language, Castilian-speakers seek to protect themselves from economic and social disadvantage. Each interest group at least pays lip service to the respect of the rights and concerns of the other, but each sees the other's assurances as vague and unrealistic rhetoric. The positions taken are further complicated by their deep association with larger struggles over the political character of the Spanish state. At this time Catalonia as a whole has resisted polarization, but the unsettled and unsettling question remains of whether the nation or the individual should be the most important concern of language policy, and whether there can be a policy which does justice to both.

Notes

1. The research on which this report is based was carried out in 1979-1980 and supported by the Social Science Research Council Doctoral Fellowship Program. The opinions expressed here are not necessarily those of the Council.
2. Many Catalans reject the term 'region' and prefer 'nation' in reference to Catalonia. I have chosen 'region' because it better reflects the aspect I wish to stress, Catalonia's position within a larger political unit. No comment on the moral validity of that position or Catalonia's claim to nationhood is implied by this choice.
3. It may be objected that linguists do not agree on the criteria of a 'language' in contrast to a 'dialect'. Certainly it is true that the concept is as much political and historical as linguistic, and that the best definition of a language might be 'a dialect with an army'. However, Romance philologists concur in characterizing Catalan as an autonomous system (see Sanchis Guarner 1980 for a review); Kloss (1967) has called it an *abstand* language—i.e., a language by virtue of its linguistic distance from others. Catalan is not readily intelligible to the Castilian speaker. Sanchis Guarner documents the development of much of the Catalan lexicon from later and more popular forms of Latin than those that gave rise to Castilian. Finally, notable literary works in Catalan dating to the thirteenth century prose of Ramon Llull as well as administrative and religious texts from as early as the 12th century are testimony to the independent developmental trajectory of the language.
4. A more detailed report of the experimental design and statistical analysis appears in my doctoral dissertation prepared for the Department of Anthropology, University of California at Berkeley. I am greatly indebted to James Boster for his assistance in the analysis of the data, although all errors are my own.

Tables

Table 1: *Examples of Lexical Differences in Catalan and Castilian.*

	Castilian	Catalan
'to eat'	comer	menjar
'to carry, to wear'	llevar	portar
'to want'	querer	voler
'table'	mesa	taula
'bed'	cama	llit
'nothing'	nada	res
'dog'	perro	gos
'bad'	malo, -a	dolent, -a
'crazy'	loco, -a	boig, boja
'thin'	delgado, -a	prim, -a

Table 2: *Linguistic Profile of Population of the Barcelona Area.*

	Catalan	Castilian
A. Language in the home: (Adults over 18)	43 Percent	57 Percent
B. Native language of school children:		
1. Public schools	26.5 Percent	73.5 Percent
2. Private schools	48.2 Percent	51.8 Percent
C. Native language of primary school teachers:		
1. Public schools	29.4 Percent	70.6 Percent
2. Private schools	48.8 Percent	51.2 Percent
D. Native language of adults by level of education:		
1. Minimum education only	35 Percent	65 Percent
2. University	60 Percent	40 Percent

Sources:
A., D. Junyent 1979; data are for Catalonia
B. Arnau 1980; data are for the city of Barcelona
C. Arnau 1980; data are for the province of Barcelona

Table 3: *Distribution of Immigrants and Natives by Profession, Industrial Sector*

	Catalan-born	Immigrant	
Directors, upper management	74	26	Percent
Middle management and technical	75	25	Percent
Low management	56	44	Percent
Skilled labor	40	60	Percent
Semi-skilled and unskilled labor	18	82	Percent

Source: Sàez 1980.

References

Argente, Joan et al. 1979. Una Nació Sense Estat, Un Poble Sense Llengua? *Els Marges,* 15: 3-15.
Arnau, Joaquim. 1980. *Escola i Contacte de Llengües.* Barcelona: CEAC.
Azevedo, Milton. Forthcoming. The Reestablishment of Catalan as a Language of Culture. To appear in *Word.*
Blom, Jan-Peter and John J. Gumperz. 1972. Social Meaning in Linguistic Structures: Code-Switching in Norway. In J. Gumperz and D. Hymes (eds.), *Directions in Sociolinguistics.* New York: Holt, Rinehart and Winston. pp. 407-34.
Brown, R. and A. Gilman. 1960. The Pronouns of Power and Solidarity. In T.A. Sebeok, (ed.) *Style in Language.* Cambridge, Mass.: MIT Press. pp. 253-76.

Calsamiglia, Helena and Empar Tuson. 1980. Ús i Alternança de Llengües en Grups de Joves d'un Barri de Barcelona: Sant Andreu de Palomar. *Treballs de Sociolinquistica Catalana,* 3: 11-82.

de Pedrolo, Manual et al. 1981. *Quan Cal, Hi Som Tots!* Barcelona: Diàfora.

Fishman, Joshua. 1972. Impact of Nationalism on Language Planning. In J.A. Fishman, *Language in Sociocultural Change.* Stanford: Stanford University Press. pp. 224-43.

Gal, Susan. 1979. *Language Shift: Social Determinants of Linguistic Change in Bilingual Austria.* New York: Academic Press.

Generalitat de Catalunya. 1980. Declaració del Consell Executiu Sobre Normalització del Català. Barcelona.

Junyent, Rosa. 1979. L'Ús de la Llengua Catalana. *Avui* 2-18-89.

Kloss, Heinz. 1967. Bilingualism and Nationalism. *Journal of Social Issues* 23, 2: 39-47.

Lambert, Wallace E., R.C. Hodgson, R.C. Gardner and S. Fillenbaum. 1960. Evaluational Reactions to Spoken Languages. *Journal of Abnormal and Social Psychology* 60, 1: 44-51.

McDonogh, Gary. 1981. The Good Families: A Social History of Power in Industrial Barcelona. Unpublished Ph.D. dissertation. Department of Anthropology, Johns Hopkins University.

Medina, Manuel. 1975. Spain: Regional, Linguistic and Ideological Conflict. In: W. Veenhoven (ed.) *Case Studies in Human Rights and Fundamental Freedoms: A World Survey.* The Hague: Martinus Nijhoff.

Ninyoles, Rafael Ll. 1976. *Bases Per a Una Política Lingüística Democràtica a L'Estat Espanyol.* València: Quaderns Tres i Quatre.

Pinilla de las Heras, Esteban. 1979. *Estudios Sobre Cambio Social y Estructuras Sociales en Cataluña.* Madrid: Centro de Investigaciones Sociológicas.

Ryan, Ellen Bouchard. 1979. Why Do Low-Prestige Language Varieties Persist? In H. Giles and R. St. Clair (eds.), *Language and Social Psychology.* Oxford: Basil Blackwell.

Sàez, Armand. 1980. Catalunya, Gresol o Explotadora? Notes Sobre Immigració i Creixement. In *Immigració i Reconstrucció Nacional a Catalunya.* Barcelona: Editorial Blume. pp. 25-42.

Sanchis Guarner, Manuel. 1980. *Aproximació a la Història de la Llengua Catalana.* Barcelona: Salvat.

Strubell i Trueta, Miquel. 1978. Immigració i Assimilació Lingüística al Principat. *Quaderns d'Alliberament* 2-3: 241-57.

Subirats, Marina. 1980. La Utilització del Català; Entre la Precarietat i la Normalització. *Saber* 1: 34-50.

Vilar, Pierre. 1964. *Catalunya dins l'Espanya Moderna.* Barcelona: Edicions 62.

White, Geoffrey M. 1980. Conceptual Universals in Interpersonal Language. *American Anthropologist* 82, 4: 759-81.

Wooland, Kathryn A. 1974. The Politics of Language and Ethnicity in Barcelona, Spain. Unpublished doctoral dissertation. Department of Anthropology, University of California, Berkeley.

Joan Rubin

The Special Relation of Guarani and Spanish in Paraguay

The sociolinguistic situation in Paraguay, a country located in the center of South America, is unique in Latin America. Whereas, in all of the other Latin American countries, Indian languages take a secondary role, in Paraguay, the indigenous language, Guarani, is the paramount symbol of Paraguayan nationalism.

Every president of Paraguay has been able to speak Guarani and many have been known to use it to curry political favor. In contrast, in the rest of Latin America, presidential knowledge or use of the aboriginal language is rare. When educated Paraguayans go abroad, they are unique among Latin Americans because they often resort to using Guarani in speaking to each other. It is commonly held that Paraguayans should know and use Guarani— there are those who feel that one is not a true Paraguayan unless you can communicate with your friends in this language. The historian Perazzo typified this feeling in suggesting that "A Paraguayan who doesn't speak Guarani is like an Indian wearing clothes", that is, out of character.

In addition to the pride in and use of Guarani, another unique aspect of the Paraguayan sociolinguistic situation is the high percentage of the population who claim knowledge of the aboriginal language—some 92 percent of the population say they are capable of speaking Guarani.

It is unique in Latin America to find the aboriginal language given so much importance. Elsewhere in Latin America the Indian language has a secondary position; city people do not speak it at all or if they do, they may deny their language ability or the aboriginal language's importance. Indeed, one of the major criteria for becoming socially 'white' in most of Latin America is fluency in Spanish. Insofar as we can tell, bilingualism in the rest of Latin America is a transitional stage in the process of going from a *monolingual* aboriginal speaker to a *monolingual* Spanish or Portuguese speaker. This is in strong contrast to the Paraguayan situation where bilingualism has been and still is a permanent feature of the society. Such bilingualism presupposes that people continue to use the aboriginal language after learning Spanish. This is indeed the case.

Further, Guarani is known and used not only in the rural areas but also in the capital city. In contrast to the capital cities of Mexico where the number of inhabitants speaking both Spanish and an aboriginal language is below 10 percent and of Peru where the percentage is below 15 percent, the population of the capital of Paraguay, Asunción, is reported to be 76 percent bilingual.

Finally, it is important to note that in 1967, a new constitution was approved which named Guarani and Spanish as the 'national languages' of Paraguay with Spanish as the 'official language'. In no other country in Latin America has an aboriginal language been so recognized and so designated.

Nonetheless, most speakers are ambivalent in their feelings about the two languages. The *bilingual* speaker who prefers to use Spanish usually recognizes the importance of Guarani for most of the country. The *bilingual* speaker who prefers to use Guarani usually recognizes the international importance of Spanish, both economically and culturally.

Although there are positive attitudes associated with both languages. Spanish tends to be the language which is revered whereas Guarani is frequently belittled. The speaker who can control Spanish is *culto* (educated, civilized), *inteligente* (intelligent), *distinctivo* (distinctive), and *desarrollado* (cultured). The person who controls only Guarani is called a *Guarango* (ill-bred type) *menos inteligente* (less intelligent), *menos desarrollado* (less cultured), and *no tiene principios* (does not have [moral] principles). One sophisticated gentleman expressed surprise when he found that one of the most prolific writers of Guarani poetry was a man who had real principles and a well defined personality. Monolingual speakers of Guarani even refer to themselves as *tavi* (stupid) because they are unable to speak Spanish. This latter epithetic probably arises from the fact that a country person usually learns to speak Spanish in school, so hence, degree of education and ability to speak Spanish are closely linked in the minds of most rural people. Monolingual Guarani speakers consider those who can speak Spanish *iñarandu* (intelligent).

Still, the negative attitudes toward Guarani are minor in comparison with those toward the rest of the aboriginal languages in Latin America. In addition, there are many positive attitudes toward Guarani at all levels of society. Paraguayans who defend Guarani emphasize the social value of the language. It has been equated with 'the heart of the nation', and called 'the symbol of the true soul of the people'. It has also had certain special linguistic qualities attributed to it. One self-taught linguist Moises Bertoni (1914) suggested that Guarani has verb tenses unknown in Spanish. Decond Larrosa, dedicated student and promoter of Guarani, stated in a public lecture that Guarani has fourteen indicative tenses while Spanish has only ten. Several writers have praised the extensive vocabulary of Guarani particularly in the fields of botany, medicine, and agriculture. Guarani is also considered to be very melodious – full of onomatopeia. This quality is said to make Guarani especially suitable for declarations of love!!

On the other hand, despite the number of Spanish speakers in Paraguay, very little literature has been produced there. This contrasts with other Latin American countries where literary production in Spanish is more highly developed and its expressive values more frequently extolled.

Pro-hispanists attribute the limited literary production to the lack of a real market for books, a lack occasioned by the size of the country and its poor economy. For the Guarani supporter the explanation lies in the inferiority complex which many bilinguals acquire during schooling. They are forced to be silent until they can speak Spanish. This, say the critics, creates verbal inhibitions. The effects of bilingualism on Paraguayan literary production are frequently discussed by Paraguayan intellectuals. Hence, there is considerable debate about the values and problems associated with the effects of the kind of bilingualism Paraguayans acquire on the language abilities of its citizens.

Given the unusual recognition accorded the aboriginal language in Paraguay we can now ask how this came about. To answer this question, we should consider the historical as well as the current social features which contributed to this unique situation.

In looking at early Paraguayan history, we should start with three assumed preconditions:

(1) A relatively large area.
(2) A relatively homogenous population speaking one language before contact.
(3) The assignment of this area to one country at the time of independence.

As a result of this initial limitation, only five countries in Latin America fulfill the above conditions: Peru, Ecuador, Bolivia, Chile and Paraguay.

In Paraguay, the initial period of contact between the aboriginals and the Spanish was one of constant interaction. Collaboration between Indians and Spanish in Paraguay dated from the very beginning of Spanish colonization and continued through the initial years of Spanish occupation. This sort of mutual cooperation did not obtain in the other four countries. In Chile, although a small group of Picunche, who lived in the north were rapidly subjugated by the Spaniards, the Mapuche, who lived in the area south of the Bío-Bío River were not brought under control until sometime in the 1880s. In Peru, Ecuador and Bolivia, the general pattern was one of conquest and subjugation with little evidence of collaboration.

Paraguay was also noted for a high incidence of marital or concubinal unions which occurred on contact between the Spaniards and the aboriginals. This initial period provided many opportunities for the few Spanish men in Paraguay (very few Spanish women were attracted to isolated Paraguay) to learn Guarani from their wives. Further, since Paraguay did not offer many exploitable natural resources, unlike the west coast which was in constant contact with Spain throughout the colonial period, Paraguay was isolated from the mother country both economically and socially.

As a result of an extremely limited immigration and the high percentage of mestizo households, a really insulated upper-class – differentiated by language, education, and economic status–did not develop in Paraguay. Unknown was the rigid association which developed in Peru between those in the élite and use of only Spanish. Further, those Indians who came under the influence of the Jesuit missions (1604–1767) were taught only in Guarani. In most of the last quarter of the eighteenth century did schools begin to appear in some number.

It should be noted that, in contrast to the social and economic isolation of Paraguay, Peru, Ecuador and Bolivia were in extensive contact with Spain and as a result, an élite did develop with Spanish as an important feature of upper class status.

Guarani continued from the time of Independence into the twentieth century to be of great importance in Paraguay for three main reasons:

(1) a negative one, namely, the continuing isolation of the country;
(2) the positive association which developed between Guarani and Paraguayan nationalism during two major wars;
(3) the division of functional usage between the two languages which was maintained by the isolation.

Following Independence in 1811, Paraguayan leaders tried to establish relations, both economic and political, with their neighbors and some European countries. However, by 1823, difficulties encountered by Dr. Francia, then dictator of the country, caused him to close the country to all outside contact. Cultural contact with the outside appears to have declined or stopped during Francia's incumbency and the school system only functioned on a limited scale.

Between 1840 and 1862, during the dictatorship of Carlos Antonio López, Paraguay was once again open to the outside world with López' emphasis on commerce, diplomatic relations, immigration and schooling. Some schools are reported to have severely punished the use of Guarani, during class hours–though sanctions such as these were probably only effective in the better schools of Asunción, while in most rural schools Guarani probably remained the main language used.

In 1864, Paraguay fought the War of the Triple Alliance against Brazil, Argentina, and Uruguay. It is reported that one of the rallying forces for Paraguayans was the use of Guarani as a symbol of unity in the face of this terrible enemy. At the close of this war, Argentina and Brazil controlled Paraguay. They and the returning exiled Paraguayans introduced disdain for the aboriginal language since their major focus was on the international world. This rejection of Guarani probably continued until at least the beginning of the 1932 Chaco War.

Between the two wars, an ambivalent attitude toward Guarani appears to have prevailed. The urban upper classes, emulating the cultural values of the Argentinians, looked down on those who spoke only Guarani. Still, most people learned Guarani at home and continued to use it in many situations.

On the other hand, during the Chaco War of 1932—35, the government (for security reasons) prohibited the use of Spanish on the battlefield. Once again, Guarani came forward as a symbol of the uniqueness of Paraguay and a rallying force. After the Chaco War, contact with other nations increased and again use of Guarani was looked down upon by the urban élites.

It seems that the basic distinction to be made among supporters for greater use of and supporters for less use of Guarani is *not* along class lines but rather along party lines. Some political parties (such as the Colorado party) have strongly supported the status of Guarani while maintaining the importance of Spanish. The Colorado party sees an identification of Guarani with the national interest and national character. Naturally, among the Colorado party members some are in the ruling class today. In times past when the Liberal party was in power—after the Triple Alliance War—the focus was on greater use of Spanish with an attempt to reduce the status of Spanish. Hence, attitude toward the appropriate status for Guarani is *not* a class matter but rather more related to political philosophy. There is an association between the economic position of each party, self-sufficiency on the part of the Colorados, *laissez-faire* on the part of the Liberals, and the attitude toward language use.

With the rise of the Colorado party, from 1950 to today, the focus has once again been on the use of Guarani and the development of what is uniquely Paraguayan. As mentioned earlier, it was the Constitution of 1967 which named Guarani as national language along with Spanish. Today, the Ministry of Education no longer advises teachers to exercise sanctions against the use of Guarani; rather, it suggests a gradual transition from Guarani to Spanish.

One other factor has contributed to maintaining the status of Guarani, namely, the division of functional usage between the two languages. Both Spanish and Guarani are each largely used in different domains so that they are not in competition with one another. We describe this separation of functions below. We should further note that the powerful influence of the world language Spanish was reduced and kept from becoming a dominant language which is to be used in all domains because of the continuing isolation of the country. That is, if Paraguay hadn't been so isolated and closed at times, Spanish as a world language with high prestige might have led to more negative attitudes toward Guarani among the Paraguayan citizenry.

In fact, this did not happen and the functional allocation of Spanish and Guarani has remained largely intact.

A special feature of the Paraguayan sociolinguistic setting is the fact that use of the two major languages varies according to several dimensions. The interrelationship among these dimensions is best seen in Table 1.

We have isolated four dimensions (location, degree of formality, degree of intimacy, and seriousness of discourse) as the major determinants of language choice and three others (first language learned, predicted language proficiency and linguistic preference of speaker) which also affect the choice, though only after the other dimensions have been resolved.

What follows is a description of what these dimensions refer to in the Paraguayan setting.

(1) *Location.* The first and most important factor which influences language use in Paraguay is the location of the interaction. If it occurs in a rural area, Guarani is the rule. The great exception to this rule in 1960 was in speaking to one's school teacher. Due to past pressures of the Education Ministry, teachers and students were strongly encouraged to use Spanish at all times, even in remote rural areas. Since the 1967 Constitution with its recognition of Guarani and an increasing recognition of the children's need to use Guarani in early classes, this Spanish-only rule has been considerably relaxed, though teachers still use and expect students to use Spanish more than all other residents of the rural area.

Also, when talking to someone clearly from the country, Guarani is used. For example, since the *curandero* (herb-doctor) usually lives in the country, Guarani is the rule. Paraguayans who use Spanish in the rural area are said to be 'putting on the dog' (*odzedzapose*) if they did use Spanish.

Once outside the rural area, the rule of usage is not as clearly dependent on location. In a rural town, the rules of usage are more complex and each situation must be defined according to dimensions other than location. In Asunción, the capital, many people feel Spanish is in order although in fact they may use Guarani in accord with the other dimensions isolated.

(2) *Degree of Formality.* The second dimension which affects usage is the degree of formality of the situation. By formality is meant that there is a fairly limited range of expected behavior. The more formal the situation, the greater the probability that Spanish would be spoken. In Paraguay, formal behavior is evidenced by stiffness and reticence to talk; informal behavior often evokes animated discussions, manifest curiosity, and a great deal of joking. Formality may relate to a number of factors. Certain 'social identities' may require formal behavior and, consequently, use of Spanish. For example, a constitutent speaking to an authority uses a very limited range of behavior patterns. A patient speaking to a doctor also uses a very limited range of behavior patterns and will speak Spanish if he/she is bilingual. Formality may

also relate to certain occasions which require formal behavior, and when Spanish would be in order. In Paraguay, dances tend to be formal, however, there are a number of local criteria which dictate the degree of formality. Dances in the center of town are more formal than those held in the surrounding areas. Dances which take place on a brick floor are more formal than those which take place on packed earth.

Obviously, the degree of formality may shift if the two individuals are or become friends. In speaking to the mayor in his capacity as mayor, a friend will address him first in Spanish because he is the mayor, but then the mayor may choose to shift to Guarani. Although some Guarani may be used with the mayor when he is a friend, less is always used than when speaking to a friend occupying a less formidable role.

(3) *Degree of Intimacy*. A third dimension affecting linguistic choice is the degree of intimacy. With non-intimates, Spanish is the rule. On the other hand, for most Paraguayans Guarani is the language of intimacy indicating solidarity or identity with the addressee whereas Spanish indicates mere acquaintance. This is clearly indicated by the fact that when Paraguayans go abroad they tend to use more Guarani with other Paraguayans in order to establish their solidarity by the use of the more unusual and intimate language.

In making friends and in courting the normal progression is from the less intimate language, Spanish to greater use of Guarani as friendship progresses. For examples, when bilingual men and women first meet, they prefer to use Spanish because they don't know each other too well, but if they begin a courting process and intimacy grows, many switch to Guarani 'because it's sweeter and more intimate'.

(4) *Degree of Seriousness of Discourse*. A fourth dimension which enters into informal town-urban usage is the degree of seriousness of the discourse. The more humorous the conversation, the more Guarani is likely to be a part of it. Many bilinguals find jokes funnier in Guarani because they feel that it lends itself better to the expression of humor. If the conversation is serious then other factors seem to be important.

(5) *First Language Learned, Addressee's Estimated Linguistic Preference, and Speaker's Linguistic Preference*. Three personal traits—first language learned, addressee's linguistic preference and speaker's linguistic preference — resolve the question of which language to use in non-rural informal, intimate but serious discourse. For example, angry discourse, i.e., when you are angry with someone, is usually conducted in the first language acquired. Those whose first language was Guarani felt that '*se rete mejor*' (one scolds someone better) in Guarani whereas those whose mother tongue was Spanish preferred Spanish to indicate the seriousness of the matter. In addressing a woman wearing a long skirt and smoking a big black cigar most speakers said they

would use Guarani because it was thought that such an addressee was probably from the country or was probably monolingual.

Information for the above analysis was gathered in Paraguay in 1960–61 (for further details, see Rubin 1968b). Readers may wonder whether any changes have occurred since that time in the functional distribution of the two languages. A restudy conducted in 1965 and 1967 (Rubin 1969) showed that some changes were indeed occurring in the rural area. This was probably due to the fact that roads had been paved between the rural area and the rural town so that regular bus service permitted a much higher frequency of contact with the rural town and even with Asuncion, the capital city. (In 1960, there was no bus to the rural area.) This access to the rural town made it possible for many more students to attend higher level schools–the school in the area goes to the fifth grade – which led to an increase in knowledge of Spanish as well as providing other opportunities to use this language. In addition, the advent of the transistor radio and its mass production at very low costs had by 1965 invaded the usual silence of the rural area. Everyone became an avid listener to the radio. For many, this was their first real contact 'with the outside world', i.e., both Asuncion and abroad. It is hard to assess the effect of the radio on the linguistic ability and usage of the people of Itapuami because although most of the programs were in Spanish and not Guarani, a large percentage of those living in the rural area only listened to music.

The decision of the 1967 Paraguayan Constitutional Congress to make Spanish the official language and Spanish and Guarani the national languages, may have encouraged people to use more Guarani. In fact, in 1967, Paraguayans seemed less defensive about Guarani and many respondents when indicating use of Guarani in a particular situation said: 'Es mi nación' (It's my nation) or 'Es mi raza' (It's my race).

The results of the restudy did not show a spectacular change in the model or dimensions isolated in 1960. Yet the data were suggestive of some change trends. Indeed, it would have been surprising if such changes were readily evident in the short period of seven years.

The change observed in this restudy was not in the *dimensions* identified in the above model. Rather, there is some indication that the dimension, *degree of formality* is now taking precedence over that of *location*. Whereas, in 1960, the only person regularly addressed in Spanish in the rural areas was the school teacher, in 1965–67, young people in the rural area reported that they more frequently addressed each other during courting situations in Spanish, i.e., for them, a formal situation. This indication of greater use of Spanish and both languages in courting situations in the rural area appears to be a consequence of the increased bilingual ability of younger females and the sharing with the rural town of the feeling that courting is a very formal relationship (at least in the initial stages) and great respect should be shown. In the past, since many girls were monolingual Guarani speakers such niceties were inaccessible. In 1965–67 even young men who were not fully bilingual said they made an effort to use what Spanish they knew in initiating courting.

The greater use of Spanish in more formal situations by younger rural inhabitants was also seen in other now formal occasions such as in 'confessing' and 'in speaking to a medical doctor who is a friend'. These increases do not require a change in dimensions but rather show the intensification of the model. If rural inhabitants continue to use Spanish in more formal situations, then we would suggest that the degree of formality should be the first dimension to be considered in choice of language.

Despite this apparent shift of usage, one should not forget that there continues to be a functional differentiation between the appropriate social situations for use of each language—with each language having an important role to play for bilinguals.

In summary, we have shown how and why the relation between the aboriginal language, Guarani and Spanish is so unique. This is due to a combination of historical and geographic factors as well as the positive association and role which has developed for the aboriginal language.

Table 1: Ordered dimensions in the choice of Language.

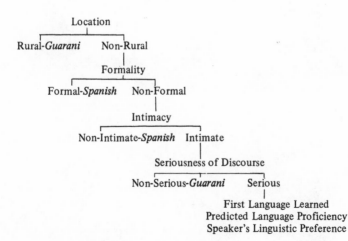

References

Bertoni, Moises Santiago, Ortografía Guarani Sobre la Base de la Ortografía Internacional Adoptada, por los Congresos, de Zoología Botánica, con Arreglo á la Ortografía Lingüística Adoptada por el Congreso Científica International de Buenos Aires (1910) y á la Generalmente Seguida por los Lingüistas Norteamericanos ... (Asunción, M. Brossa, 1914).

Rhodes, Nancy C. 1979. Attitudes Toward Guarani and Spanish: A Pilot Study in Paraguay. (Long paper for M.S. degree.) Georgetown University.

Rubin, Joan. 1968a. Language and Education in Paraguay. In: *Language Problems in Developing Languages*, edited by J. A. Fishman, C. Ferguson, J. Das Gupta. New York: Wiley.

– 1968b. *National Bilingualism in Paraguay*. The Hague: Mouton.

– 1969. Toward the Use of Formal Methods in the Detection of Culture Change. *Suplemento Antropológico* (de la Revista del Ateneo Paraguayo) vol. 4:1.

– 1978. Toward Bilingual Education for Paraguay. In *International Dimensions of Bilingual Education* edited by James E. Alatis. Georgetown University Round-Table on Languages and Linguistics 1978. Washington, D.C.: Georgetown University Press.

LANGUAGE ATTITUDES IN THE COMMUNITY

Benji Wald

Vernacular and Standard Swahili as Seen by Members
of the Mombasa Swahili Speech Community

The issue discussed below is the impact that the standardization of Swahili
has been having on the perceptions and attitudes of members of the Swahili-
speaking community of Mombasa, Kenya. It will be shown that the changing
evaluations of different varieties of Swahili by Mombasa Swahili (MS
hereafter) speakers themselves reflect larger changes in Mombasa's integration
into the larger unit of Kenya as a developing nation.

It is the universal experience of linguists and anthropologists to discover
that, in every speech community, there is general agreement among its
members that certain forms of language are poitively valued as 'good', or
words to that effect, and other forms of the same language are 'bad'. In
Euro-American (Western) communities, where standard languages through the
agencies of larger socio-political units, such as the nation-state, have long
imposed their standards, especially through the schools, and impressed their
power as a means to both greater economic and academic achievement, it is
usually the case that 'good' is overtly associated with 'standard', or other
words referring to the standard, e.g. 'school language', 'written language', and
so on, and 'bad' is associated with local speech, where it contrasts with the
standard and marks the speaker as 'nonstandard'. The situation is quite close
to the reverse among members of the Swahili speech community of Mombasa.
For many, 'good' is closer to 'local' (Mombasa) than to 'standard', and 'bad'
the reverse. It should be clear that this is an oversimplifying point of departure for a discussion of the attitudes and terminology used by Mombasa
Swahili speakers in characterizing different kinds of Swahili. In the following
exposition I will clarify to what extent a reversal of Euro-American expectations is accurate. Of particular interest is that there are signs of disagreement
among Mombasa Swahili community members indicating that there is
currently conflict between the Euro-American situation and its reverse. These
signs may indicate that social forces are developing, which are already firmly
established in the Western world. They reflect the sociolinguistic side of the
term 'developing nation' as applied to Kenya, the nation of which Mombasa is
a part.

Standard and vernacular in Mombasa

A basic distinction made by linguists is between *standard* and *vernacular*
languages. A standard language is a language which has been overtly codified
in its vocabulary, grammatical structure, and to a lesser extent in its pronunciation. It is closely associated with literacy, a written form. Although
it may be historically based on a particular local dialect, it is a reflection of
the amalgamation of a number of speech communities into a larger sociopolitical unit, such as a state or nation. While each speech community in the
larger unit may have distinctive local dialect for everyday use among
members of the community, each also shares with other communities in its
unit, a standard which is the same across communities. This standard acts as a
symbol of unity within the larger unit, and as a convenience for carrying on
whatever business is required by the larger unit. Ideally, standard speech does
not identify the local origin of the speaker, as the standard written language
does not identify the origin of the writer, although, in practice, sometimes
one can detect features of pronunciation which are not covered by the
standard, and thus identify some more specific social attribute of the speaker.

On the other hand, a vernacular language is associated with a local dialect.
The key word is *local*, rather than *dialect*, since a linguist would consider any
coherent form of language a dialect, including the standard language. A
vernacular is the set of language conventions of a specified localized speech
community. It is the first learned language of members of that community. It
is primarily associated with speech, although it may also be represented in
writing. The speaker of a vernacular is immediately recognizable, to those
familiar with the particular dialect, as coming from a particular community.

Using these terms, standard Swahili is an example of a standard language.
MS is a dialect containing a vernacular and other forms of speech, as discussed
in more detail below.

The sociolinguistic context of Mombasa

Throughout East Africa, including the nations of Kenya and Tanzania, and
adjacent parts of Uganda, Zaire, Mozambique and Somalia, some form of
Swahili is widely spoken as a language of contact (*lingua franca*) across groups
of speakers, who use different non-Swahili vernaculars (first languages) in
speaking to people within their own group. The sharing of Swahili as a *lingua
franca* throughout East Africa allows people to communicate, even if they do
not know a single word or phrase of each other's vernaculars. This use of
Swahili as a solution to the communicative needs of the highly multilingual

East African area is no less true of Mombasa than elsewhere. However, like many traditional Swahili cities, Mombasa also has groups of people for whom varieties of Swahili are also their vernacular, not only a *lingua franca* for use across groups. These people are the members of the MS speech community.

Mombasa is an extremely multilingual city on the coast of Kenya. As Kenya's port city, it has developed into a large and ethnically diverse urban area, attracting sizeable populations from all parts of East Africa, especially the Kenyan interior and adjacent Northern Tanzania, Southern Arabia and Western India. There is a strong tradition of associating language with ethnicity in Mombasa, as in most areas of East Africa. Both the ethnic structure of many neighborhoods in Mombasa, and the tendency of many ethnic groups to maintain contact with members of their family in ancestral areas, whether in other parts of East Africa or in Asia, contribute to the maintenance and vitality of multilingualism in the city. The glue that maintains the lines of communication among the diverse ethnic groups in the city, and between the city and the rest of East Africa, is Swahili. People who have grown up in Mombasa and speak Swahili as their first language are members of the *MS speech community*. They are ethnically diverse. Many indicate one or more ancestral languages other than Swahili. Many others, but fewer, identify only Swahili as their ancestral language. Even among these latter people, as among speakers of all known languages in East Africa, there is a general belief that the ancestral language (Swahili) was different from the language (still Swahili) that they now speak, as discussed below. Quite apart from the beliefs of the Mombasa Swahili community, there are features of their variety of Swahili which they hold in common, and which distinguish them from speakers of other varieties of Swahili, whether as a first or non-first language. Some of these will be discussed later.

Both the tradition of Swahili and of multilingualism no doubt predate the colonial period and recent great expansion of Mombasa as an important international port city.

Multilingualism in Mombasa

The multilingual tradition of Mombasa City is undoubtedly quite old, given the role Mombasa, among other traditional Swahili cities, has long played in the Indian Ocean trading area, linking East Africa with Arabia, India and points east.

Southern Arabians, speaking forms of Arabic, have continually settled in Mombasa. More recent and temporary migrants maintain Arabic, but a great number of MS speakers claim Arab ancestry and have assimilated to the Swahili language.

(1) Sijui lugha isipokuwa ni kiSwahili, na kiArabu cha kujua manake kuombea
     jambo la kusaidiana au nini katika upande wa kiArabu. Lakini zaidi ni ki-
     Swahili kabisa, lugha ambayo ninayoelewa kutoka mwanzo nilipoanza kusema
     ni kiSwahili mpaka hivi sasa. . .

     "I don't know any language beside Swahili, and Arabic to know, I mean, to ask
     for some help or what-not in an Arabic place. But more is Swahili only; the lan-
     guage I have learned since I first started to speak is Swahili, right up to now. . ."

                                                                    (AY 23m, Msa)

It is quite clear that Arabic has long been spoken in Mombasa, and indeed
many of the same Arabic words are common to most dialects of Swahili.

Many MS speakers claim Arab ancestry, either through recent immigration
of parents or grandparents, or through more distant tracing of lineage to clans
of Arabian origin. Indeed, many scholars have conjectured that the Swahili
language owes its origin to an ancient fusion of early Arab settlers and East
African coastal Bantu speakers, as explanation for the large contribution of
Arabic to Swahili vocabulary (similar to the contribution of French to English
starting with the Norman French takeover of England).

Other languages which must have been long spoken in Mombasa are Bantu
languages, historically and structurally related to Swahili but not mutually
intelligible. Among these, those still spoken closest to Mombasa are the rural
Miji Kenda languages, especially Digo to the south, and Giriama and Rabai to
the north and west. Contact between some members of these groups and MS
speakers has long been intimate, and many have moved into the city or its
suburbs, and speak a form of Swahili closely resembling MS, as well as their
ethnic languages. Through intermarriage the MS community is increased at
the expense of the Miji Kenda peoples, according to lineage traditions.

During the colonial period of the late nineteenth and early twentieth
centuries, in which many groups from other parts of the British Empire
settled in Mombasa, the multilingual nature of the city greatly increased,
reflecting the attraction of Mombasa as an international port.

From Interior Kenya came other Bantu speaking peoples, each with their
own languages. Most numerous in Mombasa are the Kamba and Gikuyu.
From Tanzania, smaller numbers of other Bantu speakers, traditionally
familiar to Mombasans, are found permanently or temporarily settled. Luos,
speaking a Nilotic language of western Kenya, have a sizeable and well
established community in Mombasa, as well. Finally, from the North, in the
Horn area of East Africa, many Kushitic speaking peoples have arrived, of
which the Somali are prominent by language, dress and physical appearance.

For many generations, Indo-European speakers from Western India and
more western parts of southern Asia have lived in Mombasa. To a large extent
the Afghan-origin Baluchis have become Swahilicized while maintaining their
ethnic identity. Among the diverse Indian groups, the Gujerati speakers
(Bombay area) are the most numerous in Mombasa and have largely

maintained their language. In Mombasa, Hindi is widely spoken among Indians of various ethnic and linguistic backgrounds in the same way that Swahili is among all groups (cf. Neale, 1974).

Though the schools and other colonial-initiated structures, English has become a visible written language, among the western-educated, in which MS community participation has so far been small although increasing. English is also spoken in public among the western-educated. English words have penetrated the Swahili spoken in Mombasa in both vocabulary associated with Western technology and institutions, and in the slang of MS speaking teenagers. Some of the more enterprising MS speakers have accomodated not only to English, but more recently also to German and Swiss-German in order to participate in the considerable tourist trade centering around the beaches near the city. It is not unusual for MS speakers who have dealings outside of their home neighborhood to have knowledge of a large variety of languages, at least to the point of being able to ask for and give 'help', as AY put it above (1).

According to the 1969 census, only 38 percent of the residents of Mombasa were born there. This puts an upper limit on the number of MS-speakers living in the city. It also shows the remarkable growth of the city over the course of a generation, not unusual among many African cities in the late and post-colonial period (see Table 1).

It is not possible, on the basis of current information, to specify exactly what proportion of the population speaks MS. While it is commonly observed by all inhabitants that some variety of Swahili is known by everyone, the association of ethnicity and vernacular in actual practice can only be estimated. People born in Mombasa, of all ethnic backgrounds, usually speak a variety of Swahili closely related to MS, especially if they were raised in the less affluent multiethnic neighborhoods in which the majority of the population dwell. Communication among kin and other co-ethnics tends to use the ethnic vernacular. Otherwise, Swahili is used both among adults and children. In the case of mixed families, with parents of different first language, in many cases Swahili is the language used by children addressing their parents, even in response to parents' use of the ethnic language. As discussed in more detail below, this is one way that MS expands to incorporate more recent immigrants, assimilating them into the MS community. The census figures do not distinguish mixed ethnicity from claimed ethnicity, and make it difficult to estimate the proportion of ethnic groups traditionally associated with a non-Swahili vernacular, who actually speak the MS vernacular.

Standard Swahili and its relation to Mombasa

Standard Swahili is the form of Swahili developed in East Africa for printed literature, education and official government business, both written and oral. In Tanzania it is the only national language. In Kenya it shares that status with English.

Its external history has been described in some detail by Whiteley (1969). Briefly, in pre-colonial times, the coastal speakers of Swahili vernaculars acted as intermediaries in commerce between Indian Ocean Asians, particularly Southern Arabians and Persians, but also Indians and Chinese, and interior East African peoples. In this commerce, Swahili spread into the interior of current Tanzania and further westward into Zaire in a variety of forms resembling the Southern varieties of Swahili of Zanzibar City and the traditional Swahili cities of the Tanzanian coast. The Germans and British made further use of this already established pattern of Swahili as a trade *lingua franca*, extending it to further areas of East Africa whose economies they linked by building more extensive trade networks. The varieties of Swahili which are spoken in interior Kenya, as a *lingua franca*, are more similar to southern (Tanzanian) than to coastal Kenyan (e.g. Mombasa) Swahili.

The shaping of trade networks into administrative units during colonialism continued the tradition of using Swahili as East Africans were integrated into the administrative system, usually at lower civil service and submanagerial levels. As a function of European economic and administrative organization, the need for literacy in Swahili became an objective of the colonial system of education.

Standard Swahili arose to meet the needs of the British, who administered the East African territories of Tanganyika, Zanzibar, Kenya and Uganda until the early 1960s. In the early twentieth century, educational concerns had been carried out by various Christian missionary groups on populations, particularly in Tanzania, whose first language was not Swahili. A Southern form of Swahili emanating from Zanzibar had already begun to spread throughout the Tanzanian interior due to trade between the East African interior and the trading centers of the Indian Ocean, through the mediation of members of coastal Swahili communities cooperating with Southern Arabians.

Local Swahili communities, who are virtually totally Muslim (Sunni) by religion, tended to avoid Western-style schools, which they associated with conflicting religious norms (cf. Mazrui, 1978). Thus, the mechanisms for introducing Swahili into the Western-style schools was the transference of a form of urban Zanzibari Swahili through the mediation of European colonial and missionary authorities to non-Swahili populations.

In order to standardize the Swahili used for Western educational purposes throughout the colonial territories, particularly for preparing and publishing school textbooks, an interterritorial conference was held in Mombasa in 1928. The two candidates considered for service as the base for developing a standard Swahili were the dialects of Zanzibar City and Mombasa. Given the already widespread use of Southern forms of Swahili similar to Zanzibari in Tanzania, the decision was made in favor of Zanzibar City (cf. Gorman, 1974).

Although historically standard Swahili is based on Zanzibari Swahili, MS speakers do not associate the two as the same. Rather they associate standard Swahili with the language of the mass media and the schools. Many MS speakers consider this language to be a fabrication of 'missionaries' and other Europeans. One middle-aged speaker expressed the common point of view by saying:

(2) Swahili Standad khaswa si lugha ya kienyeji bali mimi nasema ni lugha iliyokusanywa na watu.

"Standard Swahili is not an indigenous language, but rather, I would say, it is a language which was gathered together by people."

(AH 53m, Msa)

AH was personally a victim of language standardization. A genteel speaker of MS, highly respected in his community, able to quote the poetic verses of Muyaka, the late eighteenth century Mombasan poet, he had taught at the former Arab Boys Primary School in Mombasa. At one time he had hoped to obtain a position teaching Swahili, rather than written Arabic, but failed because his language was 'old fashioned' (*ya kizamani*):

(3) Basi, nlipokuwa nkisomesha yaani saa nyingine nikatarajia mimi kuwafundisha watoto lugha, lugha hii ya kiSwahili. Lakini kwa lugha yangu ambavyo ni lugha ya kizamani. Yule prinsipali wangu na wale walimu ambao wao wamesoma wankwenda katika zile yaani Teacher Training College zile waliofundishwa Swahili Standad . . .

"Well, while I was teaching, sometimes I had hopes of teaching the children the language, the Swahili language. But using my language, which is the old-fashioned (or ancient) one. The principal and the teachers who had gone and studied at the teacher training colleges were taught Standard Swahili . . ."

(AH 53m, Msa)

It is evident that AH would have found it galling to learn Standard Swahili, an 'artificial' language, in order to teach Swahili to Mombasan children. It is also evident that he did not want to teach the standard language, but rather the most cultivated forms of Mombasan Swahili, the language of his community.

His attitude toward Standard Swahili was the predominant one in the MS community, especially in Old Town, the site of the most concentrated number of MS speakers, and the center of Mombasa in precolonial times. Adolescents there, who had generally not completed more than primary school and were engaged in local occupations such as diving, fishing, sailoring and cargo handling, had a negative view of Standard Swahili, and a highly positive view of the local Swahili, although they would defer to the older generation as the best representatives of the local language, associated with 'old times' (*zamani*).

The issue of Swahili, both as a language and as an ethnic identification, is emotionally charged in Mombasa. On one occasion, a heated argument broke out concerning the meaning of *mSwahili* 'a Swahili (person)' between an MS speaker and several non-MS speakers, all adolescents. The argument started when one speaker, a non-Swahili, asserted that Swahili were people without an ethnic background (*kabila* = ethnic group). An MS speaker vehemently protested that, although Swahili is not an ethnic label, the people who speak Swahili as a first language have specific ethnic backgrounds, i.e. they are not a people without their own ethnic identities. The issue of being a Swahili and having an ethnic identity is pursued further below.

The origin of kiSwahili (the language) is a welcome topic to MS speakers, and I have witnessed many spontaneous occurences of this topic in conversation, among male adult hangout groups.

One particularly revealing argument between two MS speakers represents the conflict now taking place within the community as economic forces favoring Western education and Standard Swahili conflict with local pride and identity.

YI, 20m, an MS speaker of Arabic background, expressed admiration for the technological accomplishments of the Europeans (*wazungu*) and professed faith in whatever technological principles were involved in the construction of Standard Swahili. His argument was essentially that while the indigenous Swahili speakers *speak* the language, the inventors of Standard Swahili *studied* the language (according to scientific principles). YI was currently a Swahili teacher at a Goan school, a private school supported by the Goan community (originating in Goa, a former Portuguese colony of Western India, whose members have adopted Portuguese names and the Roman Catholic religion while maintaining their own language, Konkomi). YI reported that the salary was much lower than in the government schools, and not sufficient to support his wife and child, who had to live with her parents in a Digo village about 15 miles south of Mombasa. YI intended to save some money and gain admittance to the Teachers Training College in Nairobi (Kenya's capital and largest city, in the interior) in the hope of obtaining a better paying teaching job.

BL, 20m, an MS speaker of Baluchi ancestry, and an actor by profession, vehemently disputed YI's argument about the scientific basis of Standard Swahili. He insisted, to the approval of gathered listeners, that:

(4)   ijapo wazungu wao wenyee waingereza wana—wametengeneza mabuku yao ya gramma, ya Swahili grammar, lakini sioni kwa kuwa wao mahodari zaidi kuliko wenyeji.

"Even though the Europeans—the English—have written the textbooks of Swahili grammar, I still don't see that they are more competent/skilled (in Swahili) than the speakers themselves (i.e. the indigenous)."

(BL 20m, Msa)

This is the same opinion as expressed in the rhetorical question of a younger speaker, AK 16m, in discussing Standard Swahili under the label 'book Swahili' (*kiSwahili cha vitabu*):

(5)   ki tofauti kabisa. Unaelewa lakini ni kitabu kile pengine kimetungwa na mtu ambaye kiSwahili si lugha yake. Sasa itakuwaje?

"It (i.e. book Swahili) is completely different (i.e. from spoken Swahili). You understand it but maybe the book was written by somebody whose language is not Swahili. Now, how (do you suppose) it will be?"

(AK 16m, MS)

BL went on to express his irritation at value judgments favoring Standard over Mombasa:

(6)   ndio hata wakaandika mabuku yao kwa kuonesha kwa kuwa kiSwahili neno kama hili latamkwa hivi badili ya hivi hilo si jambo vizuri manake . . .

"and they (the originators of Standard Swahili) even wrote their books to show that a word like this is pronounced like this instead of like this; that is not a good thing . . ."

(BL 20m, Msa)

The likely source of his annoyance concerning judgments of good and bad pronunciation according to the standard norms will be discussed later.

Of course, there was no resolution to this argument, and it is no doubt being repeated daily among proponents of each point of view in the streets, houses, and hangouts (*maskani*) of Mombasa.

On the one hand, Standard Swahili is seen as a vehicle of economic opportunity. On the other hand, the Swahili of the MS community is the symbol of local identity and means of mutual identification of members. Members of the MS speech community identify their traditional form of Swahili as kiMvita, after the ancient name of Mombasa City (Mvita):

(7)   Kuna Standad Swahili na kuna kile kiSwahili cha kiMvita, wajua Mvita ni hapa. Basi kile kiSwahili cha kiMvita ndo hichi tusemacho hapa. Na kile Standad Swahili kama le tumiwa kwenve vitabu, gazeti . . .

"There's standard Swahili and there's the Swahili of kiMvita. You know Mvita is here. Now, the Swahili of kiMvita is the one we speak here. And the standard Swahili is like (the one) used in books, magazines . . .

(FM 18m, Msa)

FM's concept of KiMvita is similar to the concept of MS that I identified at the beginning of this article. However, when we compare the various concepts of kiMvita held by MS speakers, it is necessary to distinguish the two.

kiMvita

As a holistic term without specific linguistic content, kiMvita refers to the language associated with the traditions of the MS speech community. The highest tradition MS speakers associate with kiMvita is the poetic language of the Mombasan nationalist poet, Muyaka, who lived in the late eighteenth and early nineteenth centuries. Muyaka is a culture hero to most MS speakers. Commonly, kiMvita is exemplified by speakers by means of lexical items (words) which are poetic, archaic, or otherwise not in common use either in the standard or in MS, e.g. *matembezi* 'legs' (literally, 'walkers'-inanimate) or *kenda* 'nine' (as opposed to the usual MS word *tisia*, standard *tisa*, but still used in the Miji Kenda—i.e. nine cities—languages surrounding Mombasa).

Although, as we will soon see, there is disagreement among MS speakers about which features of Swahili are to be identified with kiMvita, no MS speaker identifies kiMvita or any feature he associates with it as 'bad', 'wrong', 'incorrect', etc. On the contrary, speakers generally claim that they are 'bad' speakers of kiMvita, and that better speakers are older than they. Inevitably, most MS speakers are convinced that the best speakers of kiMvita are all dead, and that better speakers than those living have recently died.

For these reasons, kiMvita cannot be equated with MS. KiMvita is the symbol of ethnic pride and unity for the MS community, but it is not a language whose features are agreed upon, or known and used by all members of the community.

In the following section, we will see that kiMvita, as a positively evaluated label, is included in the more general folk-term, *kiSwahili cha ndani, 'inside-Swahili'*. Inside-Swahili approaches the concept of the vernacular more closely than kiMvita.

Inside and Outside Swahili

A basic distinction made in Swahili speech communities is inside-Swahili (kiSwahili cha ndani) and outside-Swahili (kiSwahili cha nde). Neither of these terms is tied to any particular locale.

(8)   KiSwahili (cha nde) ni ile lugha ambayo kila mtu anaisema, lakini *kiSwahili cha ndani* ni le lugha ambayo waSwahili wenyewe wanaijua.

"Swahili (outside) is the language that everybody speaks. But *inside Swahili* is the language that (only) the Swahilis themselves know."

(BF 21m)

Built into BF's statement is the common MS perception that "everybody" in Mombasa can speak some variety of Swahili. However, he further asserts that there is a special group of people, called Swahilis, who speak a special kind of Swahili, called *inside* Swahili.

In order to appreciate more fully, what the speaker means, we must consider more closely Swahili speakers' perceptions of the linguistic situation on the East African coast.

a. Outside-Swahili. Swahili, in some form or other, is spoken throughout East Africa, from Somalia to Mozambique and from the coast to Uganda and Zaire. For most speakers, Swahili is not their first language. The first language, or vernacular, if it is not a form of Swahili, is generally referred to in Tanzania as *kilugha* (*ki* 'the class prefix for languages among other things' + *lugha* 'language'). In Kenya, the terms most commonly used are *kikwetu* (*ki* + *kwetu* 'our place') or *kinyumbani* (*ki* + *nyumbani* 'at home'). Those are the words used by speakers when referring to their first language in Swahili. These terms are more commonly used by such speakers than the actual name of the language, e.g. *kiDigo* (the Digo language) or *kiZaramo* (the Zaramo language).

The type of Swahili spoken by non-first speakers varies according to area and education. Generally, in Kenya, the Swahili spoken by non-educated speakers either closely resembles the Swahili of first Swahili speakers in their vicinity, if coastal, or more closely resembles a Swahili-based pidgin, which is quite different in grammatical structure from other forms of Swahili, and is called *kiBara, ki* + *Bara* 'interior (of East Africa)', by MS speakers. Non-first speakers, educated at least through primary school, generally speak a form of Swahili similar to Standard Swahili. In Tanzania, even uneducated non-first speakers tend to speak a Southern form similar to the standard.

The pidgin-like kiBara is held in low regard by MS speakers, as is the case for most speakers of any pidgin's base language. Attitudes toward Southern, and, as we have seen, Standard Swahili are more complex. Tanzanian standard Swahili is associated with radio broadcasts, and is highly regarded. AK (cited in (5) above) said of the Tanzanian radio broadcasters, "when they speak their Swahili even you would find it pleasing", although he quickly added, "but they don't speak Swahili better than us" (wale wakisema kiSwahili yao (sic) wewe mwenyewe unaona raha . . . lakini hawasemi kiSwahili kutushinda sisi).

MS speakers are generally aware of the national and international prestige that Tanzanian standard Swahili has. They also recognize a similar form of Swahili used by Kenyan Swahili radio broadcasts, but in the early and mid 1970s, the Kenyan radio broadcasters tended to have accents attributable to their first languages, usually interior Bantu languages, recognizable to MS speakers. MS speakers preferred Tanzanian broadcasters. They associated the Kenya accent with Bara, although the grammatical structure of the Swahili used was standard rather than pidgin.

With regard to Tanzanians, MS speakers distinguished the Swahili of the Tanzanian radio from the Swahili of the lower and working class Tanzanians with whom they had contact in Mombasa. They did not consider the Swahili of those Tanzanians to be prestigious although it was not pidgin-like.

In general, then, pronunciation, like grammatical structure, is used as a basis to identify and evaluate different varieties of Swahili by MS speakers. Non-first varieties of Swahili are identified by MS according to pronunciation, as well as grammar, and are referred to, if recognized, by the first language of the speaker, e.g. *kiSwahili cha kiChagga*, Chagga Swahili (a Northern Tanzanian group), *kiSwahili cha kiJaluo*, Luo Swahili (an interior Kenyan Nilotic group), *kiS cha kiHindi*, Indian Swahili (referring to any Indian ethnic group with a recognizable Indic accent).

All non-first and standard forms of Swahili are outside-Swahili to first Swahili speakers.

b. Inside-Swahili. If inside-Swahili is the Swahili that only Swahilis know, who are the Swahilis?

MS speakers respond to the question *mSwahili ina maana gani* (what does mSwahili mean?) or *mSwahili ni nani* (who is a Swahili?) with the answer *mSwahili ni lugha tu* (literally, a Swahili is just a language). The response is so regular for MS speakers that it is inferred that it is a cliché in the MS community. Further questioning indicates that a Swahili is usually associated with certain ethnic groups, particularly those which claim historic kinship affinities with the Arab, but the term Arab is not understood in the same way by all MS speakers. The features of the term common to all appears to be someone whose ancestors come from Southern Arabia or some point on the East African coast between Southern Arabia and Mombasa (cf. Prins, 1967). A few MS speakers identify their ancestors as the original inhabitants of Mombasa and include among such people the Tangana and Kilindini. These people account for a very small number of the total population of MS speakers, and while most MS speakers have heard of the Tangana and the Kilindini, few know any of them. Most people who claim such ancestry also admit to other ancestors as well, such as the Ajemi (claiming Persian ancestry) and Baluchi (Asians from Baluchistan). However, following the logic of their original response to the term mSwahili, MS speakers admit the possibility that a member of any ethnic group can be a Swahili if Swahili is his first language. In Mombasa, this usually only happens through intermarriage with people who are already Swahilis, and thus language and lineage are preserved together.

This use of mSwahili contrasts with that of non-MS speakers in Mombasa. For example, many lower class second language speakers of Swahili in Mombasa define the term as appertaining to coastal people of mixed ancestry, occasionally claiming that they are people 'without a tribe' (*bila kabila*). An MS speaker would not identify himself ethnically as a Swahili, nor hear mSwahili as an ethnic identification when spoken by anyone else.

The Swahili people are ethnically diverse. Probably the majority claims Southern Arabian ancestry, and identify themselves as Arabs, a cover term which includes many specific clans. Specific local groups are recognized by each other as Swahilis according to the areas, usually urban, which they consider their ancestral home. Thus, in Mombasa and its suburbs the Tangana, Kilindini, Jomvu and Changamwe are mutually recognized as Swahilis. Incorporated into these and other Swahili groups are more recent immigrants from Arabia and Baluchistan, who have given up their ancestral languages and intermarried with the earlier Swahilis for several generations.

Outside of the Mombasa area the Amu and the Bajuni (commonly called waGunya by Mombasans) are considered Swahilis, as are various groups from Pemba and Zanzibar and other areas of coastal Kenya and Tanzania, and the waNgazija of the Comoro Islands off Mozambique. The forms of Swahili spoken as a first language by these speakers are called *inside-Swahili*. The particular names of inside-Swahili dialects are the same as the ethnic labels attached to the people who speak them. Thus, kiAmu refers to the Swahili traditional to Lamu, and kiUnguja refers to that of Zanzibar (Unguja).

This is the primary meaning of inside-Swahili. More specialized groups have their own inside-Swahili. Thus, Mombasan adolescents often refer to the slang vocabulary used by their age groups by the same term. For example, a word like *fiti* 'good, great' (from English 'fit') was often offered to me as the adolescents' inside Swahili. Another example involves metaphor; *ngao*, literally 'shield', is used for 'sunglasses' by MS adolescents, instead of the more circumlocutive *miwani ya jua* ('eyeglasses for the sun').

There is a generalization that can be made to include all uses of the term *kiSwahili cha ndani*. That is, that *inside* refers to inside a specific social group, where there is a maximum of shared knowledge based on membership in a local culture, whether by ethnicity or age.

c. Mafumbo. The most intimate characterization of inside-Swahili by Swahili communities both within and outside of Mombasa is called talking *mafumbo* (literally, 'riddles', singular *fumbo*, pl. *mafumbo*).

A *fumbo* is an utterance with more than one meaning. On the surface a speaker seems to be saying one thing, but there is a hidden meaning in what is being said. Talking in *mafumbo* may mean talking indirectly, when direct expression is socially sensitive. For example, one speaker exemplified a fumbo by saying:

(9)   . . . fumbo ni kitu ambacho unasema, yaani, unasema ambacho mtu yule unam-
unamsemea kwa kinyume . . . humwambii kwa wazi kabisa kuwa nakwambia
kitu fulani. Kwa mfano, fumbo naweza kutoa . . . tuseme huyu hapa amenibia
pensil yangu. Naeza kusema a! lakini watu wengine humu ndani humu (clicks
tongue) tunaoneana sana. Mi nlipotewa na kitu hapa, lakini mtu mwenyee
anakufahamu wewe ajitokeze toa hii pensil yangu, lete. Hiyo unaweza kusema
kuwa ni fumbo, yaani namfumbia . . . namjua ni yule ambaye ameiba pensili
yangu lakini sitaki kumwambia, nasema kinyume. Ye mwenyewe ajijua kuwa
mimi namfahamu, lakini ananirudishia ile pensili yangu. Ile tunaita fumbo.

"... a *fumbo* is something that you say, I mean, that you say to tell somebody
indirectly (lit. backwards) . . . you don't tell him completely openly that you're
telling him a particular thing. For example, I can give you a *fumbo* . . . let's say
this guy here stole my pencil. I can say a! some of us in here (clicks tongue as
signal of complaint) we really don't get along very well. I lost something here.
But the guy (who took my pencil) recognizes (that I'm saying) give me back my
pencil. This (example) you can say is a *fumbo* because (I'm telling him) in a
closed way . . . I know he's the one who stole my pencil but I don't want to tell
him directly. I speak indirectly. He knows that I know (it's him), so he returns
my pencil. We call that a *fumbo*."

(JN 19m, DSM)

In this example, JN clearly equates a *fumbo* with an indirect accusation. The essence of the term is that the speaker of the *fumbo* appears to be saying one thing, when in reality he is saying something else. In the citation JN refers to the etymology of the word *fumbo* when he says, "I'm telling him in a *closed way*". The Swahili verb used, *fumbia*, is a verbal form of *fumbo*, meaning 'close', as in '*close* your eyes' or 'hide something from ordinary vision'.

In this case, a fumbo is used to avoid direct confrontation. However, the meaning of fumbo is more general. Many MS speakers consider kiAmu, the Swahili of Lamu, to be difficult to understand when spoken among Amu speakers. These MS speakers say that Amu speakers talk in *mafumbo*. This seems to mean that they use words with different meanings, rather than that the words themselves are unfamiliar. It is, in fact, the basis of much Swahili interdialectal humor that words having a particular meaning in one dialect have a quite different meaning in another. A common stereotype of Lamu Mombasa is that an Amu speaker may come up to you and say, *mbwa nyani*. In Mombasa this sounds like an insult, *mbwa* 'dog' + *nyani* 'ape'. However, as MS speakers know, the Amu interpretation is: *mb* (copula) + *wa* 'of' + *nyani* 'who', i.e. 'whose (child) are you?' equivalent to MS *n(i) wa nani?* This example is conventionally amusing in Mombasa and evokes laughter.

The meaning of *fumbo* to describe homophonous expressions also extends to other Bantu languages:

(10)   watu kutoka bara waweza kusema naye kiSwahili akafikiri we wamtukana.

"you can talk Swahili to people from the interior and they might think you're insulting them."

(FM 18m, Msa)

FM gave the example *kinu*, the Swahili word for 'mill' but homophonous with the Gikuyu curse-word for 'vagina'.

Finally, the following citation from an MS speaker illustrates the use of a *fumbo* to relate the terms *inside-Swahili* and *kiMvita*, as the specific type of inside-Swahili of the MS community.

(11)   *kiMvita* ni lugha ambayo wewe mwenyewe umezaliwa nayo bila ya kufun-dishwa na mtu . . . Standad mana ni lugha ambayo ni lugha ya kila mtu. Swahili standad ni lugha ambayo kila moja unaposema anaelewa we unasema nini . . . ile lugha ya kiMvita tunageuza kitu kukifanya mtu, tunageuza mtu kumfanya kitu . . . *nikitaka kusema ile lugha ya kiMvita, ile ya kindani haswa ambayo si wengi wanayoielewa*, sasa hivi wewe mi naweza kukugeuza ukawa jiwe. nikazungumza kitu jiwe mi na A. tutazungumza jiwe. tunalisema jiwe lakini si jiwe. tunazungumza habari zako.

"*kiMvita* is the language that you yourself were born with without being taught it . . . standard is that language of everybody. Standard Swahili is the language that if you speak it, everybody understands what you're saying . . . in kiMvita we change a thing into a person and a person into a thing . . . *if I want to talk kiMvita, the really inside kind, that not many people understand*, right now I can change you into a stone. I'm talking about something called 'stone', me and A (another participant in the conversation), we talk about a stone. We say 'stone' but it's not a stone. We're talking about you."

(MK 25m, Msa)

Given such an example, it's not difficult to see why East Africans express desirable competence in a second language as the level at which one cannot be talked (badly) about (*kusengenya* 'to talk "behind someone's back" ') in one's own presence.

In the example, MK's discussion of kiMvita, as the inside-Swahili of Mombasa, starts out similar to FM's in (7) above. But he goes on to emphasize the fumbo aspect of kiMvita, i.e. that it sounds like one thing when it means another. In his example, homophony is characterized as intentional by the deliberate change in the conventional reference of words.

By drawing a linguistic boundary between insiders and outsiders, MS community members use the Swahili language to help maintain their distinctive identity. In this way they behave like most other East Africans, who consider their ethnic language to be an inalienable part of their ethnic identity and distinctiveness. It is widely believed by East Africans that every ethnic group has its own language. As mentioned above, the notion that MS speakers do not have an identity, complete with its own language, was considered offensive by members of the community, and was vehemently denied. That notion only arises among East Africans who do not realize the distinction made by Swahilis between inside and outside Swahili. Fascination with the origin of their language, and pride in its history and distinctive characteristics characterizes the general attitude of the MS community.

Attitudes and speech in the MS community

So far we have considered the attitudes, opinions and folk-beliefs of MS speakers about Swahili without considering, for the most part, the substantive features that distinguish the different types of Swahili believed to exist by MS speakers. In point of fact, since the polarization of different forms of a language is motivated by sociopolitical concerns rather than linguistic ones, it is not necessarily the case that the substantive linguistic differences between opposed varieties of a language, held by a population to be antithetical, are very large. For example, it is reported that the difference between Serbian and Croatian in Yugoslavia was mainly a difference of which alphabet is used, the Catholic Serbians using the Roman alphabet and the Eastern Orthodox Croats using the Cyrillic. Similarly, the difference between Hindi and Urdu in Northern India is mainly registered in the use of the devanagri (Sanskrit) alphabet and preference for incorporating Sanskrit words by the Hindu Hindi speakers, while the Muslim Urdu speakers use the Arabic alphabet and prefer using words of Arabic origin (cf. Fishman at al., 1968).

The Swahili situation in Mombasa is perhaps substantively somewhat more complex. There are differences in phonology, grammatical structure and vocabulary between MS and the standard language. Nevertheless, it is in the attitudes toward particular linguistic features, rather than attitudes toward labelled language varieties, that change and conflict between local and national norms is most detectable. One revealing case is based on a linguistic self-stereotype of MS-speakers (cf. Wald, 1981b for further discussion of stereotype).

The most commonly used self-stereotype used by MS speakers to characterize the difference between their own inside-Swahili and other varieties of Swahili is the imperative of the verb 'come' (infinitive *kuja*). MS speakers report that they use the pronunciation *nDoo* 'come!', while other Swahili speakers (meaning Southern or standard speakers) say *njoo*. The speaker may even gratuitously offer a third possibility used by Bara (pidgin) speakers, *kuja*, a form which is infinitive in both MS and other inside-Swahili varieties, but is used in all grammatical contexts by pidgin speakers. The form nDoo in MS has the same self-stereotypical value for MS speakers that *joual* [žwal] for 'horse' has for Montreal French speakers (as distinct from the standard French *cheval* [š(ɔ)val], cf. Laberge and Chiassen-Lavoie, 1971).

Most MS speakers characterized MS nDoo as *kiSwahili cha ndani*, or kiMvita, a subtype of inside-Swahili, as opposed to njoo, *kiSwahili cha nde* (outside-Swahili) or *kiSwahili cha kila mtu* (everybody's Swahili).

By association with kiMvita such a pronunciation is highly valued. Because the standard norms in this case are also the same as the Southern norms, including the first Swahili community of Zanzibar City, the *njoo* pronunciation was not seen as 'bad' or humorous by most speakers, who were aware they occasionally used the pronunciation themselves, but simply as not inside-Swahili or kiMvita. Atypical of the reactions of MS speakers was a Jomvu speaker who considered the palatal pronunciations to be Bara, and thus incorrect. The Jomvu community is suburban and relatively isolated from the social factors affecting the judgments of MS speakers in the city.

However, a few adolescent speakers did not characterize *nDoo* as kiMvita. Instead they said it was 'ungrammatical' (*si gramma*). One speaker, using the example Tupa 'bottle' contrasted the standard and MS pronunciations, and said:

(12) hiyo Tupa makosa. Sawasawa ni Tupa hiyo chupa . . . hiyo si Swahili ya
 sawasawa manake hiyo ni kiSwahili cha kuzungumza tu.

 "That *Tupa* is a mistake. The correct (way) is *chupa* . . . that (Tupa) isn't
 correct Swahili. It's just Swahili for conversation."

 (BD 18m, Msa)

BD is a first speaker of MS of Somali ethnicity. He dropped out of school after six years, but maintains the school norm as the correct one. He does not associate the MS norm with kiMvita, but simply with 'conversational (everyday) Swahili'.

Another speaker, CM 20m, of Barawa ethnicity, raised in the Old Town section of Mombasa completed secondary school and obtained a job as a clerical worker at the docks of the main harbor (Kilindini Harbour). He characterized the standard pronunciation as *swafi* 'correct' (literally, 'clean') and expressed his desire to follow the standard norm in his own speech:

(13) . . . ninajitahidi sana kusema kiSwahili swafi. Badili ya kusema nDoo nasema
 njoo. Lakini mara nyingi huja nikasahau nikambia ah! Ee, bwana, nDoo.
 twende zetu.

 " . . . I try very hard to speak correct Swahili. Instead of saying nDoo I say
 njoo. But often I forget and I say, hey, man, nDoo (i.e. come on) let's go."

 (CM 20m, Msa)

In this passage CM seems unaware of the social forces which would favor his use of the MS norm among his MS peers, but only aware of the standard norm which he consciously seeks to follow. He goes on to give a rationalization common among those who share his admiration for the standard at the expense of the vernacular form.

(14)   . . . nDoo ni kama ile ndoo ya chooni, wewe unayo chooni kule.

"*nDoo* is like that *ndoo* (pail) in the toilet, that you have in the toilet."

(CM 20m, Msa)

Underlying this rationalization of his overt preference for the standard pronunciation is an argument based on orthography. Rationalization for correctness based on orthographic conventions is commonplace in many Western language communities. Thus, New Yorkers often argue that in English *February* is correctly pronounced with an *r* immediately following the *b*, as in the spelling, although it is near universal in American English colloquial to pronounce the word as *Febyuary*. Similarly, in Manchester a number of words spelled with *oo*, e.g. *book, look, took* are commonly pronounced either to rhyme with *luke* or *luck*. When I asked one Manncunian teenager which pronunciation of *book* he thought was correct, he chose the rhyme with *luke* (the more usual form for older speakers according to my observations). When I asked him why, he shrugged and said, "I guess because of the spelling." This response strikes Americans and Southern British speakers as amusing, since it would never occur to them to pronounce a word such as *book* either as a rhyme for *luke* or *luck*, even though *oo* is often pronounced like the *u* in *luke* as in the words *school, loop, boot, soon* (but there is variation for words such as *room, root, roof,* in some areas, including Los Angeles).

Ironically, in CM's example, *nDoo* 'come' is not pronounced identically to *ndoo* 'pail'. MS speakers pronounce *nDoo* with the tip of the tongue touching the upper teeth, as in English *though*. But *ndoo* is pronounced with the tongue touching the alveolar ridge well behind the upper teeth. This distinction is not made in the conventional spelling of Swahili using Roman letters. The distinction is not needed to spell standard Swahili. Even though CM himself distinguishes the pronunciations, he argues on the basis of the *written* (standard) language. Rather than find fault with the orthography of standard Swahili as inadequate to represent the vernacular, CM and likeminded youth, criticize the vernacular for not fitting the standard orthography. This rationalization of the 'correctness' of the standard orthography appears to derive from exposure to an educational system modelled on the British system, which, like other European and American systems, advances such rationalizations in support of the standard at the expense of the vernaculars.

In any case, those speakers who accepted this judgment of the MS pronunciation would not associate *nDoo* with kiMvita, but rather with Swahili 'slang' or some other term included in inside-Swahili which does not refer directly to traditional local identity. While the vernacular may come under attack in the school system using standard reference points, kiMvita is inviolable. It is always the 'good' traditional speech of Mvita (ancient Mombasa). In this way, MS speakers' perceptions of what is included in kiMvita may change, but kiMvita as a concept and symbol of local pride cannot be negatively appraised.

KiMvita itself shows no signs of losing its high prestige in the community, although the content of what is considered kiMvita shows instability, while rationalization of correctness compounds the traditional MS respect for the ancient and no longer usual forms of Swahili in Mombasa.

Conclusions

The change in attitudes toward the relative value of the vernacular and the standard is seen in particular forms, not in the labels applied to holistic varieties. KiMvita is a symbol which may remain constant by reference to a traditional set of norms exemplified in the poetry of Muyaka. However, both kiMvita and the more encompassing *inside* Swahili are interchangeable labels used by community members to refer to the positively valued aspects of what they actually speak, but which is different from the standard language. A form like *nDoo* (contra standard *njoo*) shows division in the community. Older and/or minimally educated speakers associate this form with inside Swahili, and with kiMvita. The form is indeed commonly used, although the standard *njoo* is not unheard. The form *nDoo* is traditionally used in reciting Muyaka's poetry, an oral event which is highly respected in the MS community.

(15)   Tujapoyambia *"NDoo!"* haitujii tambuu!

'Even though we tell it *"come!"* the betelnut doesn't come to us!'
(Muyaka, ca. 1830, in Hichens, p95)

However, the process of standardization excluded *nDoo* in favor of *njoo*. The use of the educational system to teach the national standard reflects the practice in both other developing and developed nations of using education to integrate local community members, especially non-adults, into the national system. What is more interesting to us here, is that the effect of this process on attitudes toward standard and nonstandard languages in Mombasa shows a great similarity to the effect already well established in developed nations.

These include the use of the standard values 'correct', 'right', 'good', opposed to the opposite values for local vernaculars. In addition, rationalizations supporting those values arise, e.g. use of orthography arguments that the same spelling for two different words is inferior to separate spellings.

As community members come to accept those standards and arguments, their attitudes toward the vernacular necessarily change. While kiMvita is safe in the abstract as a symbol of local identity, the details of the vernacular, as acutally spoken, are fit into a national system of values as well as a local one. Older speakers, like AH, indicate that they see the use of the standard as a threat to local identity. However, the youth are more divided. Some, like CM, express acceptance of the standard values to the point of trying to substitute standard forms for vernacular forms on all occasions. However, the pull of the vernacular among community members is still felt, even by CM.

Sociolinguistic studies of local speech communities in developed nations show that acceptance of standard values has little effect on many aspects of everyday speech (e.g. Labov, 1972, Trudgill, 1972). The vernacular continues to evolve in its own separate way. This will undoubtedly remain the case for the MS vernacular. This is partly because many of the vernacular features of MS are unnoticed even though they are different from the standard. For example, in the standard, as in Southern Swahili, *andika* 'write' has the same *nd* sound as *ndoo* 'pail'. However, in MS, *anDika* 'write' has the same *nD* sound as *nDoo* 'come', and is distinct from *ndoo* 'pail'.

The question of how attitudes and perceptions of MS speakers toward the vernacular will change is more difficult to predict. This will depend on how local and national communities adjust to each other, how local and national identity come to a mutually acceptable resolution.

Tables

Table 1: Adaptation of 1969 Census of Kenya to the percentage of residence of Mombasa City by Ethnic and Linguistic Origin.

	Swahili	Arab	Coastal Asian	Interior Bantu	Bantu	Nilotic	Other
% of total population	04	06	10	24	30	09	17
N: (in 1000s)	(9)	(14)	(24)	(61)	(76)	(22)	(4.4)

References

Fishman, J., C.A. Ferguson and J. Das Gupta. 1968. *Language problems of developing nations.* New York: Wiley.

Gorman, Thomas P. 1974. The development of language policy in Kenya with particular reference to the educational system. pp. 397-454 in Whiteley, 1974.

Hichens, W. 1940. Diwani ya Muyaka bin Haji al-Ghassaniy. Johannesburg: University of Witwatersrand Press.

Kenya Population Census, 1969. Statistic Division. Ministry of Finance and Economic Planning. Republic of Kenya. 3 Vols.

Laberge, Suzanne and Michele Chiasson-Lavoie. 1971. Attitudes face au francais parle a Montreal et degres de conscience de variable linguistique. pp. 89-126. In: R. Darnell, ed. *Linguistic diversity in Canadian society.* Edmonton: Linguistic Research Inc.

Labov, William. 1972. *Sociolinguistic patterns.* Philadelphia: University of Pennsylvania Press.

Mazrui, Ali A. 1978. The religious factor in language nationalism—the case of kiSwahili in Kenya. *Studies in African Linguistics.* 9:2, 223-232.

Neale, Barbara. 1974. Language use among the Asian communities. pp. 263-318, in Whiteley, 1974.

Prins, A.H.J. 1967. *The Swahili-speaking people of Zanzibar and the East African Coast* London: International Africa Institute.

Trudgill, Peter. 1972. Sex, covert prestige and linguistic change in the urban British English of Norwich. *Language in Society* 1:2, 179-196.

Wald, Benji. 1981a. Swahili pre-pidgin, pidgin and depidginization in Coastal Kenya: a systematic discontinuity in non-first varieties of Swahili. pp. 7-26 in A. Highfield and A. Valdman, eds. *Historicity and variation in creole studies.* Ann Arbor: Karoma Press.

– 1981b. English in Los Angeles: searching for a speech community. pp. 250-272. In T. Shopen and J.M. Williams, eds. *Style and variable in English.* Cambridge: Winthrop.

Whiteley, W.H. 1969. *Swahili: the rise of a national language.* London: Methuen.

– 1974. ed. *Language in Kenya.* Nairobi: Oxford University Press.

John R. Rickford

Standard and Non-Standard Language
Attitudes in a Creole Continuum

I. Introduction

I.1: The significance of language attitudes

The study of language attitudes—how people feel about the language varieties
in their speech community—may be important to the linguist from several
perspectives. In language planning, it may provide indispensable data on
which to base decisions about which variety to use in education or which
variety to standardize for use as the official language of government (cf.
Ferguson 1966). In the study of synchronic variation, it may explain patterns
of style-shifting and interference (cf. Weinreich 1953). In the study of
diachronic processes (change within one language, borrowing and shift from
one language to another, pidginization, creolization, decreolization, language
death) it may be critical for explaining the occurrence and direction of
language change (cf. Labov 1963). In the study of second language acquisition, it may predict the degree of competence which is likely to be developed
in the second language (cf. Lambert 1967).

I have deliberately chosen the references included in the opening paragraph
to demonstrate that the significance of language attitudes has been recognized
for at least twenty to thirty years (of course there are references which go
back further than these). During this period, and in particular within the past
fifteen to twenty years, the study of pidgin and creole languages has increased
by leaps and bounds, but the systematic study of language attitudes where
such languages are spoken has generally been neglected.[1]

This neglect has been particularly acute in the study of creole continua,
where a spectrum of varieties (or mesolects) is found between the most
non-standard Creole variety (the basilect) and the standard variety (the
acrolect), as shown by this example of different ways of saying 'I told him' in
the Guyanese Creole continuum:[2]

1. me tell am (basilect)
2. me tell e
3. a tell e (mesolects)

4. a tell im
5. I told him (acrolect)

While we have made progress in the technical description of variability in Creole continua, we still do not have satisfactory answers to such fundamental questions as why and how this variability continues to exist. What I will refer to as the standard view of language attitudes in Creole continua is too shallow to constitute viable explanation.

I.2: The standard view of language attitudes in creole continua

The standard view of language attitudes in creole continua is that the standard variety is good, and the non-standard varieties (including the 'Creole') are bad. This view may be referred to as the standard one, not only because it is the orthodox one—the one usually reported in the academic literature and the local press—but also because it assumes a positive orientation toward the standard variety alone. Examples abound. Stewart (1962), summarizing attitudes to Creole varieties throughout the Caribbean, noted that they included the belief that the Creole is not a language, has no grammar, and is either a made-up form of speech, or a corruption of the lexically related standard.

As a native Guyanese, I have encountered this derogatory view countless times. One recent example is contained in a report in the Guyanese *Sunday Chronicle* newspaper of Feb. 15, 1981 (p. 4):

(1) Home Affairs Minister Stanley Moore said that too many Guyanese used Creole so as to escape proper English: He dubbed Creolese as a vulgar, rough and ready mode of expression.

Finally, we have the particularly trenchant views expressed by Oxford, a retired chauffeur and taxi-driver, and a member of the Non-Estate or lower-middle class in Cane-Walk, Guyana. In a recent interview with me, he had this to say about Guayanese Creole:

(2) It don't take you nowhere. It don't do good to a person . . . . There is no good in it at all, whatsoever. It don't carry you nowhere. If—if one can pick up, you know, good English, you know, you see, he can spread it among his children them . . . . But if you start with the different kind of Creole language on them, you know, you'll make them go out in the wrong side . . . . Well, they might get, you know, the bottom job. They *will* get, you know, bottom job, but not top job! (Spontaneous Interview 30).

One of the attractions of the standard view is that it fits in naturally with the theory of decreolization by which such continua are thought to have come about (DeCamp 1971a: 29–30; Bickerton 1975: 16–17). The places which now have creole continua are usually assumed to have been essentially bilingual situations, involving only a highly divergent Creole and a standard variety, at some earlier point in the past.[3] Then, with the breakdown of social barriers between Creole and standard language speakers, and with increased opportunities for socioeconomic mobility, the Creole speakers are assumed to have had increased opportunity and motivation to modify their speech in the direction of the standard variety, thus beginning the decreolization process which has continued up to the present day. Without some acknowledgement that the standard language is considered better or more useful in social advance (Weinreich's 1953: 78 definition of 'prestige') the creation of creole continua could equally be attributed to destandarization as to decreolization, and it would be difficult to explain why the general direction of change in such continua over the past century has been towards the standard language rather than the Creole.[4]

Although the standard view of language attitudes in a creole continuum is theoretically useful, and obviously has some basis in reality, it is limited in at least the following respects:

(i) In the presentation of this view, the social class and language use of the people whose attitudes are reported are typically not taken into account, and these may themselves be significant variables. If we look again at the negative attitudes reported above, we note, for instance, that they are almost all from middle-class or highly privileged sections of the community.

(ii) This view is invariably based on anecdotal rather than systematically assembled evidence.

(iii) This view leaves us with the irresolvable paradox: if everyone agrees that the non-standard or Creole varieties are bad and the standard language good, why hasn't more progress been seen in the elimination of the former? In Guyana, as in most Caribbean creole continua, the official language is standard English, and this is the language of government and education, and the language used most often in the media. But the everyday language of the mass of the population continues to be some variety of Creole despite this, and despite the fact that decreolization may be assumed to have been taking place for the past 150 years or more.[5]

II. Matched Guise Evidence on Language Attitudes in the Guyanese Continuum

II.1: Description of the Matched Guise test

In an effort to overcome the preceding limitations of the standard view, I used a Matched Guise experiment and other means of eliciting language attitudes in a systematic way in recent research in the Guyanese Creole continuum. The respondents in my investigation were twenty-four members of the Cane Walk community whose speech I had sampled extensively in two prior years of fieldwork involving spontaneous interviews, peer-group recordings and participant observation—techniques designed to overcome the constraints of the recording situation and encourage the emergence of vernacular speech (Labov 1972a).[6] The Matched-Guise experiment was part of a controlled interview which I conducted after all the spontaneous or naturalistic, recordings had been completed.[7]

The respondents themselves represented equally the two major social classes in the community: the Estate Class (EC), whese members worked as cane-cutters, weeders, and in other field-work capacities on the sugar-estate around which the community was organized, and the Non-Estate class (NEC), whose members held jobs as clerks, contractors, book-keepers and shopowners.[8] The unifying characteristic of the NEC group is that its members have escaped the backbreaking labor, oppressive working conditions, and poor pay of the menial estate laborer role which the members of this community inherited from their forebears. (East Indians were brought to Guyana as indentured servants between 1838—1917, initially as a replacement for African slaves after emancipation). The EC/NEC distinction is an ethnographic, community-based one, involving cultural and psychological factors in addition to purely socio-economic ones, but it may be thought of in broader sociological terms as equivalent to the Working Class/Lower Middle Class distinction in Western metropolitan societies.

The Matched Guise experiment which I conducted, consisted, like its predecessors in Canada (Lambert 1967, d'Angelan and Tucker 1973), the USA (Tucker and Lambert 1969, Williams et al. 1976, Ryan and Carranza 1975). and Britain (Bourhis et al. 1975, Romaine 1980), of samples of speech from the same speaker(s) recurring in the guise of different language varieties. The respondents hearing the sample believe that they are hearing different speakers, and are asked to evaluate each 'speaker' on a number of dimensions. The different ratings which they give to each sample are then interpreted as subtle indicators of their attitudes towards the language variety represented in that sample, and/or their social perceptions of the people stereotypically associated with that language variety.[9]

In my Cane Walk experiment, respondents were asked to evaluate three 'speakers' via tape recorded samples of them conversing with me individually about how they had met their spouses—a question which the respondents had been asked in their own interviews and so found quite natural and familiar. In fact, the three 'speakers' were one speaker performing in the guise of basilectal, mesolectal, and acrolectal language variets.[10] The *opening* lines of each narratives are reprinted here to represent the character of the different guises:

Matched Guise Speaker 1 (Basilectal)

... Well hear how de ting, de ting bin happen. *Me* frien dem did passin' me house wan Saturday aftanoon. Me an' me lil brudda—awe bin deh upstairs by de window. Well, dem call awe fuh come out and ta-tek wan walk wid dem ...

Matched Guise Speaker 2 (Mesolectal)

Well, actually how uh meet me wife is like, dis. Yuh see, my modda had a good frien' who used to come an' visit she regular. An' *my* modda used to go around by de, you know, by de odda one steady too. Dey was frien's from long, you know ...

Matched Guise Speaker 3 (Acrolectal)

... I'm a pretty shy type by nature, and I never had much to do with girls. But one day, my friends invited me to go with them to a party, and I went along, you know, just for the fun of it ...

After hearing each of the samples in its entirety, each respondent was asked to rate the speaker in terms of the kind of job he probably held, and how likely he would be to fit in with the respondent's own circle of friends.

II.2 : Results on the job scale

The results on the job scale are indicated in Figure 1.

FIGURE 1
MEAN RATINGS OF THE MATCHED GUISE (MG) SAMPLES, JOB SCALE

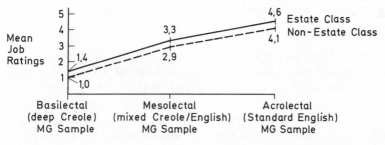

Note: 5 = Field Manager/Headmaster; 4 = Field Foreman/Book-keeper; 3 = Shop-owner; 2 = Security Guard; 1 = Canecutter. (Highest to lowest socioeconomic status.)

Two points are particularly noteworthy: the fact that the EC and NEC ratings run parallel to each other even though there is a slight consistent difference between them, and the fact that the relative prestige of the jobs with which each sample is associated is directly proportional to the relative standardness of the speech in that sample. EC and NEC respondents agree in associating basilectal speech with the lowest jobs in the prestige hierarchy, acrolectal speech with the highest, and mesolectal speech in-between, just as the standard view of language attitudes in a creole continuum would have predicted. These results also point in the same direction as earlier reports of language attitudes in almost every community where prestige and non-prestige varieties have been compared.

II.3: Results on the friend scale

When we turn to the results of our Matched Guise experiment on the *friena* scale, as shown in Figure 2, we get a very different picture, however, and one which requires more extensive interpretation.

FIGURE 2
MEAN RATINGS OF THE MATCHED GUISE (MG) SAMPLES, FRIEND SCALE

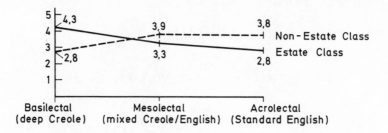

Here the NEC respondents appear to be behaving in accord with the standard view again, at least insofar as they rate the basilectal 'speaker' most negatively (least likely to fit in with their circle of friends) and the mesolectal and acrolectal 'speakers' more positively. The ratings of the EC respondents, however, are no longer *parallel* to those of the NEC, but almost diametrically *opposed*. On this scale, it is the basilectal 'speaker' who is rated most favorably by the EC, and the mesolectal and acrolectal speakers less so – quite contrary to what the standard view of language attitudes in creole continuum would have predicted.

In attempting to make sense of this striking reversal of the expected situation, it seems appropriate to begin by considering the results of Labov et al. (1968)—one of the only other studies to have elicited respondent ratings on *both* a job scale *and* a friend scale. Labov and his colleagues reported very similar results: agreement among respondents of all social levels in rating the standard language speaker higher than the vernacular speaker on the job scale, but a difference between one group of Northern Black adults and the other respondents insofar as the Northern Black group rated the vernacular speaker most likely to become a friend. The authors suggested that the differences between the ratings of the respondents on the two scales might be attributed to the fact that the job scale elicited overt social norms about language and the social order while the friend scale elicited more covert attitudes having to do with values of identity, solidarity, and community.

This analysis receives support from other Matched Guise studies which, utilizing a variety of other scales, indicate that: (i) language attitudes frequently have a multidimensional character (Ryan 1979), and (ii) standard language varieties tend to be favourably evaluated along the status or power dimension, and non-standard varieties along the solidarity or friendship dimension.[11] Cheyne (1970), for instance, reported 'accent loyalty' among Scottish respondents who rated Scottish speakers as more generous, friendly, likeable, and attractive in other social/personality respects than English speakers.

The distinction between status-related and solidarity-related language attitudes will certainly help to explain the friend-scale results of the EC (if not those of the NEC) represented in figure 2. But we can go beyond the analysis of Labov et al (1968) and the Matched Guise studies cited above in two respects: (i) relating the language attitudes which are revealed in the Matched Guise test to the *actual linguistic usage* of our respondents, and (ii) attending to attitudes about language and the social order which emerged from other questions and on other occasions over the two-year fieldwork period. Both of these reflect the advantage of conducting Matched Guise studies with respondents who are well-known from independent fieldwork rather than with respondents who are encountered for the first (and last) time when they take the Matched Guise test.

II.3.1: Language of respondents in relation to friend-scale ratings

With respect to the language of the respondents, Table 1 uses evidence from their usage in two pronoun subcategories in the spontaneous recordings to illustrate what could be shown from almost any other area of their linguistic behavior: that the everyday speech of the EC respondents is more basilectal (including a mix of basilectal and mesolectal elements), while that of the NEC respondents is upper mesolectal (including a mix of mesolectal and acrolectal elements).[12]

Table 1: Relative frequencies of pronoun variants in the speech of Case Walk respondents by pronoun subcategory and social class.

SOC. CLASS	N	FIRST SING. SUBJECT		N	THIRD SINGULAR FEMIN. POSSESSIVE		
		Bas. 'me'	Acr. 'I'		Bas. 'he'	Mes. 'she'	Acr. 'her'
EC	(2309)	.89	.11	(120)	.46	.53	.01
NEC	(3012)	.11	.89	(142)	.04	.38	.58

Note: Numbers in parentheses represent total number of pronoun tokens or occurrences considered in each category.

If we compare Table 1 now with Table 2, which shows the relative frequencies of the pronouns in these very two subcategories in the Matched Guise samples, the sense in which the friend scale elicits values of solidarity or identity can be made clearer: *The respondents in each group are essentially warming to the Matched Guise 'speaker' who sounds most like themselves.*

This is as true for the EC respondents, who favour the basilectal MG1, as it is for the NEC, who favour the upper mesolectal MG2 (whose usage matches theirs more closely than any of the other Matched Guise 'speakers' does).[13]

Table 2: Relative frequencies of pronoun variants in the matched guise samples.

MG SAMPLE	N	FIRST SING. SUBJECT		N	THIRD SINGULAR FEMIN. POSSESSIVE		
		Bas. 'me'	Acr. 'I'		Bas. 'he'	Mcs. 'she'	Acr. 'her'
MG 1	(31)	.90	.10	(3)	.33	.67	.00
MG 2	(22)	.00	1.00	(3)	.00	.33	.67
MG 3	(15)	.00	1.00	(3)	.00	.00	1.00

Note: As in table 1, numbers in parentheses represent total number of tokens or occurrences per subcategory.

This principle is implicit in the solidarity results reported in Labov et al. (1968), Cheyne (1970), Milroy and McCleanaghan (1977), and Romaine (1980). But because we have access to the actual language usage of our respondents, the principle can be stated and validated more explicitly here.

The pattern of the NEC responses on the friend scale is particularly significant because, on closer examination, it is adequately explained *neither* by the standard view of language attitudes in a creole continuum *nor* by the assumption that 'the vernacular' always elicits favourable solidarity reactions. The problem with the standard view is that, if more standard speech were always evaluated more positively, it is the speaker in the MG3 sample who should have been rated *most* likely to fit in with the NEC respondents' circle of friends. Instead, MG3 is rated on the *same* level as MG2 (in fact, *lower* than the latter by a decimal point). For the fact of the matter is that, although many of the NEC respondents aspire to be like the headmasters and the field managers above them in social status, they are not yet in that class, and their speech is actually more like that of MG2 than MG3. The problem with the vernacular principle is that it is frequently interpreted to refer to a *single* uniform variety, typically the one most deviant from the standard. In our case, this would be the basilect, as spoken by MG1, who is the *least* positively evaluated by the NEC, rather than the most. What we need instead is a principle which can allow for vernaculars rather than a monolithic vernacular—the notion vernacular varying across social groups to refer to the variety which each group speaks most naturally and most fluently, its 'primary mode of interaction' (Hymes 1971).[14] This principle works perfectly for both groups of respondents in this study, as Tables 1 and 2 together illustrate.

II.3.2.: Friend-scale ratings in relation to perception of language and the social order.

There is more to it than this, however. The principle that covert solidarity values attach to vernacular varieties is only part of the explanation for the EC respondents' highly 'non-standard' language attitudes as these are revealed on the friend scale. For some of the EC members, the endorsement of the basilect or deep Creole variety on this scale is part of a more general reaction against the dominant society, an assertion that it is the society which must change to accomodate them rather than vice-versa.

The first evidence we might consider on this point is the response to an interview question about whether speaking 'good English' (a common term for the acrolect in Guyana) would help one to get a better job and get ahead. Eleven of the twelve NEC respondents (92 percent) said yes, but only five of the twelve EC respondents (42 percent) agreed. This might seem paradoxical at first in view of the evidence of the job-scale responses that both groups agree in associating occupational status and level of language use. On closer examination, it is clear that what they disagree on is the *nature* of this association, with the NEC members seeing more acrolectal usage as *contributing* to more prestigious occupational and social class status, while the EC members see language use as merely *reflecting* socioeconomic status.

Both groups are right from their own perspectives. For the NEC members, the next step on the socioeconomic ladder is that of the teachers, managers, and senior civil servants in the capital city of Georgetown, whose positions seem to demand command of the acrolectal or English end of the continuum. Increasing one's command and use of this end of the continuum is therefore seen as a means of preparing for future socioeconomic mobility, in much the same way that fraternizing with these higher status outsiders (and their children) is. For the EC members, however, possibilities for socioeconomic mobility—insofar as they exist—may involve learning a trade like carpentry or getting a job in a shop, and there are examples of skilled tradesmen and shopowners in the community who appear to have achieved financial success *without* speaking 'proper English'.

More to the point is that the opportunities for socioeconomic mobility are extremely limited for the EC members. Seymour, an NEC member, once described the sugar-workers as "marking time . . . One spot, and they can't move."[15] And in an even more expressive vein, Mani, herself a sugar-worker, exclaimed:

(3) Yuh a throw down yuhself a de bank an' yuh seh, "Lawd, a when dis cutlass a go come out a me han?!" (Spontaneous Int. 13)

You throw down yourself on the bank and you say, "Lord, when will this cutlass (machete) come out of my hand?!"

In this situation, society's cards are perceived as being too firmly stacked against the sugar-worker for individual efforts at self-improvement to succeed, whether these involve using 'good English', or trying to secure a Non-Estate job. It is the *social order* itself which is perceived as in need of change, and it is instructive to note that the cane-cutters in our EC sample frequently serve as workers' representatives in labour disputes with the sugar-estate management (these often involving strikes, go-slows and other forms of industrial protest in support demands for better pay and working conditions).[16]

One final point requires making. The skepticism which the majority of the EC respondents express about the value of speaking 'good English' does *not* appear to be simply a defense mechanism, a way of compensating for the fact that they are themselves limited to the deep Creole or basilectal level. This may be true for some of the respondents, but not for most of them, as the results of a formal Creole to English correction test which we conducted in this community demonstrated. In this test, we presented each individual with tape-recorded Creole sentences like the following one:

(4) E thief me book

and asked how they would say it in 'good English'. Restricting our attention to the possessive pronoun in this sentence, note that nine of the eleven EC individuals who responded produced the correct acrolectal equivalent, 'my', even though three of the nine had *never* used a single 'my' in their spontaneous recordings, and even though the overall frequency of 'my' in the EC recordings prior to this had only been *I percent* (only 7 'my') tokens contrasted with 496 'me' tokens in this subcategory).

A particularly striking example in this regard was Irene, a vigorous and hard-working member of the weeding-gang. In hours and hours of spontaneous recordings, she had not produced a single token of first possessive 'my' (over 82 subcategory tokens), a single first subject 'I' (over 395 tokens), a single 'him', 'his' or 'her' (over 114 occurences of the relevant third-person subcategories). But any impression we might have had that she was confined to the basilectal or deep Creole level was dispelled by the fact that she rattled off all of the previously unattested forms where required in the correction test.[17] For her, the use of basilectal Creole in everyday life appears to be a language choice in and of itself, a matter of choice rather than necessity.

And so too for Reefer, leader of a tight and militant cane-cutters' group, who suggested that language use was imbricated in a larger process of sociocultural re-evaluation and revolution:

> (5) ... yuh gat to larn fuh larn yuh, yuh own language, yuh know .... Abee na waan dem Englishman teachin an ting da no mo, man. Dem ting da mus' done .... Yuh see, dem a write dem own book fuh suit dem own self, and abee mus' larn from dem and *subdue* under dem! (Spontaneous Int. 44)
>
> ... you have to learn to learn your, your own language, you know ... We don't want those English people's teaching and so on any more, man. Those things must end .... You see, they write their own books to suit themselves, and we learn from them and *be subdued* under them!

III. Conclusion

To summarize: although previous reports of language attitudes in Creole continua emphasize the positiveness of orientations towards the standard variety and the negativeness of orientations toward the non-standard "Creole" varieties, the situation in Cane Walk is more complex. One intervening variable is the *dimension* on which the language attitudes are tapped—the dimension of occupational stratification and socioeconomic prestige appearing to elicit the standard view, and the dimension of friendship, identity, or solidarity eliciting 'non-standard' responses to the extent that the vernacular of the respondents is itself non-standard. Another intervening variable is *social class*: the NEC members appearing to have accepted the Georgetown middle-class assertion that 'good English' helps to guarantee upward socioeconomic mobility, while the EC members are more skeptical about the nature and value of this association.

Although we have to recognize social class as a significant variable, however, it would be insufficient to say that there are two types of language attitude now, each linked to a different social class. Although Chauffeur expresses the view in (2) that there is no good in the Creole whatsoever, and although Reefer sees the English language and culture as instruments of subjugation (see (5) above), the attitudes of the average member of each class are less dogmatic and more ambiguous. We have already noted that the NEC members see equal value in their mesolectal Creole variety where solidarity and friendship are concerned, and when we asked when it was appropriate to talk 'good English', only two out of ten NEC respondents suggested that it *always* was. Similarly, although we have noted that the EC members display a more positive orientation toward basilectal Creole with respect to friendship or solidarity, only three out of eleven EC respondents, in answer to the preceding question, suggested that 'good English' *never* was appropriate. Regardless of class, respondents seemed to agree that appropriateness of language choice depended to some extent on who the addressee was, English being more appropriate with interlocutors who usually spoke English and didn't understand Creole ('dem correct person who educated'), and Creole with those who usually spoke in Creole ('There are times when you ought to break down into Creole, like when you're with people who speak Creolese all the time'). There is a shared recognition, then, that there is place for standard *and* Creole varieties.

If we look closely in the literature, too, we can detect some traces of the positive attitude to Creole which is usually overshadowed in the standard view. Thus despite its definition as 'bad' or 'brokop' language, Reisman (1970: 40) notes that in Antigua:

(6) Creole occurs in contexts of relaxation, expressiveness, involvement, letting go . . . . Creole is intrinsically felt to be the code of the genuine.

Hall (1966: 133—quoted in Hymes 1971: 87) reports the identical sentiment

(7) For the normal, unpretentious Haitian, use of Creole is the symbol of truth and reality, and French is the language of bluff and mystification and duplicity. . .

In conclusion, what we have to recognize is the existence of language attitudes which are multidimensional, and more complex and ambiguous than earlier assumed. The ambiguities extend to other cultural elements too—like the 'Creole' tomato, considered less attractive in Guyana than the 'English' tomato, in terms of symmetry of shape and general appearance, but also considered sweeter, and more resistent to wilt and other garden diseases. Or the Creole egg, ranker in smell than the English egg, but also tastier, and richer in vitamins and minerals. Or the association between Creole and 'making noise' in Antiguan arguments, which violates 'English' standards of "order, decorum, quietness, and authority", but in which people in fact "take great joy" (Reisman, 1970: 141).

Reisman's paper on linguistic and cultural ambiguity in Antigua (op. cit.) is in fact one of the best existing works on the duality which pervades Caribbean societies, and creole communities more generally.[18] We have some distance to go in terms of trying to specify the nature and intensity of the factors which impel speakers in these communities forward toward the acrolect and backwards toward the basilect in a seemingly endless dialectic. Social class has to be taken into account, and occasion, and relevant dimension, and undoubtedly even other factors. But it seems clear that only an approach to linguistic and cultural attitudes which is infinitely more sensitive than the 'standard' view is can serve to explain the unsettled and dynamic character of creole continua. It will also be undoubtedly relevant to the many other situations where standard and non-standard varieties coexist, and where these are associated with social inequalities and differences.

This is an expanded and revised version of a paper presented at the annual meeting of the Linguistic Society of America in San Antonio, Texas, in December 1980. The research reported in this paper was made possible through a grant from the National Science Foundation (GS-42475) and a grant from the University of Guyana Research and Publications Fund. It is a pleasure to acknowledge the assistance of these agencies, as well as the guidance provided by Dell Hymes, William Labov, and Richard Tucker, who read and commented on the original report of the Matched Guise test in Rickford (1979). As usual, my wife Angela has offered every encouragement, and made it possible for me to get this written.

1. Agheyisi and Fishman (1970) list only one reference (Samarin 1966) on language attitudes for 'Creoles, Pidgins, and Trade languages', and note that this was one of two substantive areas which "provide the major gaps in the systematic study of language attitudes" (p. 144).
2. This example is based on the nine ways of saying 'I told him' in Allsopp (1958).
3. See Alleyne (1980) for the claim that most of the intermediate varieties in Creole continua may have existed from the beginning of European/African contact. And see Rickford (1983) for models of decreolization which take both possibilities into account.
4. The evidence for this is the fact that texts from earlier periods contain basilectal forms which are rare or non-existent today.
5. This figure takes us back to the approximate date on which the slaves were emancipated in several Caribbean territories. This may well have been a significant factor in the weakening of rigid class barriers which DeCamp (1971b) lists as one of the prerequisites for decreolization.
6. Cane Walk is a pseudonym for a village on the East Coast, Demerera, within half an hour's drive of Georgetown, the capital. Its population is almost entirely East Indian – the descendants of indentured labourers from India.
7. The data collection methods mentioned in this paragraph are discussed in detail in Labov (1972a, 1972b), but will be briefly explained here. In *spontaneous interviews* topics like the danger of death and childhood games are introduced to involve the speaker intensely and encourage spontaneous or casual speech. *Peer-group recordings* aim for the same end, but use different means: here it is not the topic, but the influence of the participants (everyday peers) which encourages the emergence of casual speech despite the presence of an outside observer. In *participant observation*, the linguist participates in the ongoing activity of the individual or group, and informally observes their language use at the same time, but tape-recordings are not normally employed (see Rickford 1975). Finally, *controlled/formal interviews* have a

different *aim* from the preceding interviews: they are designed to tap the careful end of the stylistic continuum, and achieve this in part by focusing directly on language.

8. The term 'Estate Class' follows the term 'Estate people' (sometimes 'field worker' or 'sugar worker') which occurs natively. There is no single native term for the people who are not members of this class: the term 'Non-Estate Class' captures their most salient characteristics. The social/psychological reality of this division is increased by the fact that it parallels the distinction between 'labourers' and 'junior staff' in the traditional occupational hierarchy of the sugar estate. The estate has a third category – 'senior staff' – for the top-level managers and technical personnel who are housed in a fenced compound near to the factory, away from the housing schemes in which the other workers live. Cane Walk was developed originally as an estate housing scheme, and does not include representatives of the 'senior staff', nor – in more general terms – of the upper middle class.

9. The advantage of Matched Guise tests over alternative methods in which *different* speakers are used for each sample on the test tape is that the effect of individual voice quality is controlled. See Hudson (1980: 204).

10. In preparing the test tape, I was able to benefit from the linguistic and dramatic virtuosity of a Guyanese amateur actor, who like the respondents, was East Indian. I prepared the three Matched Guise samples myself, controlling the forms carefully to represent basilectal, mesolectal, and acrolectal levels of usage. The actor's 'script' as we sat about making the test tape was these three passages; but he 'read' them as if involved in a live interview/conversation, with appropriate interlocuter vocalizations and responses provided by me throughout.

11. The distinction between power and solidarity as key dimensions affecting linguistic usage received its earliest and most extensive examination within the sociolinguistics literature in Brown and Gilman's (1960) analysis of the variation between T and V pronouns (e.g. French *tu* and *vous)* in several languages.

12. In the third feminine possessive, as in other pronoun subcategories with a basilectal, mesolectal, *and* acrolectal variant, speakers tend to use either the former two or the latter two, but rarely all three. This datum lends some support to the position sometimes expressed by native speakers that there are only two systems involved: Creole (sometimes referred to as 'Patois' and by other names) and English. For speakers using the basilectal and mesolectal forms, the former is Creole and the latter is English; for speakers using the mesolectal and acrolectal forms, the former is Creole and the latter English. (See Rickford 1979 for more discussion.) The existence of this pattern makes it possible for a hearer to make certain deductions about a speaker even on the basis of a single basilectal or acrolectal token in this subcategory (a single basilectal token suggesting that the speaker is basically basilectal/lower mesolectal, a single acrolectal token suggesting that he or she is acrolectal/upper mesolectal). This is what allows the feminine possessive pronouns in the Matched Guise samples to have significance even though they occur only three times in each sample (see Table 2).

13. The status of the second Matched Guise sample as upper mesolectal rather than acrolectal is not obvious in the first singular subject subcategory, but it is clear from the three-variant subcategories (like the third feminine possessive), and from other areas of the grammar.

14. In this view, the vernacular is not the property of any single social group, but something which (in different forms) every social group possesses. Note the classification of RP ('Received Pronounciation') as the vernacular of the British elite in Labov (1980), contradicting the assumption that 'vernaculars' are ipso facto 'non-standard'.

15. Seymour narrated a telling anecdote about the son of a sugar worker who had passed the high school entrance examination but could not take up the opportunity because of his family's poor financial straits: "And the parent could not send the boy, because they were not seeing their way to send the boy to school. That boy now, today, he's married, *and he's working in the fields*" (Emphasis added).
fields. (Emphasis added.)

16. Raj gave this example of the way in which he usually talks to estate management on these occasions, suggesting that effective articulation of the workers' cause might depend more on appropriate content and rhetorical style than on the use of 'good English: "Yuh a cry out, 'Man look, well me na know wuh go happen today. Yesterday me barely get lil daal an rice an lil mango curry fuh eat. Well me na know wuh go happen to morrow . . . Allyuh *do* wid me wife and pickney, man!'" ("You would cry out, 'Man, look, well I don't know what will happen today. Yesterday I barely got a lil dhal and rice and a little mango curry to eat. Well I don't know what will happen tomorrow . . . You have done bad things to my wife and children, man!'")

17. There was only one exception to this: in one of three sentences where 'him' was the correct acrolectal form, Irene gave 'he' instead. In the other sentences she used the correct forms, including 'her' and 'his' where appropriate.

18. Reisman in turn pays tribute to earlier discussions of the duality in Caribbean and Afro-American communities in Herskovits (1941) and other sources. For a recent reference to conflicting 'push-pull' pressures experienced by Black Americans in relation to White American language and culture, see Smitherman (1977).

References

Agheyisi, Rebecca, and Fishman, Joshua A. 1970. Language attitude studies: a brief survey of methodological approaches. *Anthropological Linguistics* 12 (5): 137-57.

Alleyne, Mervyn. 1980. *Comparative Afro-American.* Ann Arbor: Karoma.

Allsoff, R. 1958. "The British Language in British Guinea." *British Language Teaching* 12 (2): 59-66.

Bickerton, Derek. 1975. *Dynamics of a creole system.* Cambridge: Cambridge University Press.

Bourhis, R.Y., Glies, H., and Lambert, W.E. 1975. Some consequences of accommodating one's style of speech: a cross-national investigation. *International Journal of the Sociology of Language* 6:55-72.

Brown, Roger, and Gilman, Albert. 1960. The pronouns of power and solidarity. In *Style in language,* ed. by T.A. Sebeok. Cambridge, Mass.: MIT Press, 253-276.

Cheyne, W. 1970. Stereotyped reactions to speakers with Scottish and regional accents. *British Journal of Social and Clinical Psychology,* 9: 77-79.

d'Angelan, A. and Tucker, G.R. 1973. Sociolinguistic correlates of speech style in Quebec. In *Language attitudes: trends and prospects,* ed. by R.W. Shuy and R.W. Fasold. Washington, D.C.: Georgetown University Press.

DeCamp, David. 1971a. Introduction: the study of pidgin and creole languages. In *Pidginization and creolization of languages,* ed. by Dell Hymes. Cambridge: Cambridge University Press, 13-39.

— 1971b. Toward a generative analysis of a post-creole speech continuum. In *Pidginization and creolization of languages,* ed. by Dell Hymes. Cambridge: Cambridge University Press, 349-370.

Ferguson, Charles A. 1966. On sociolinguistically oriented language surveys. *The Linguistic Reporter* 8(4): 1-3. (Reprinted in *Language structure and language use,* ed. by A. Dil, Stanford University Press, 1971).

Hall, Robert A. Jr. 1966. *Pidgin and creole languages.* Ithaca: Cornell University Press.

Herskovits, Melville G. 1941. *The myth of the Negro past.* New York: Harper.

Hudson, R.A. 1980. *Sociolinguistics.* Cambridge: Cambridge University Press.

Hymes, Dell. 1971. Introduction. In *Pidginization and creolization of languages,* ed. by D. Hymes. Cambridge: Cambridge University Press: 65-90.

Labov, William. 1963. The social motivation of a sound change. *Word* 19: 273-309.

— 1972a. Some principles of linguistic methodology. *Language in Society* 1: 97-120.

-   1972b. The design of a sociolinguistic research project. (mimeo.) Chapter II of the report of the sociolinguistics workshop held by the Central Institute of Indian Languages in Mysore, India.
-   1980. Is there a creole speech community? In *Theoretical orientations in creole studies*, ed. by A. Valdman and A. Highfield. New York: Academic Press: 369-388.
-   Cohen, R. Robins, C. and Lewis, J. 1968. A study of the non-standard English of Negro and Puerto Rican speakers in New York City. Final Report, Cooperative Research Project 3288. Vols. I and II. Philadelphia: U.S. Regional Survey.
Lambert, Wallace. 1967. A social psychology of bilingualism. *The Journal of Social Issues* 23 (2): 91-109. (Special issue on problems of multilingualism, ed. by John Macnamara.)
Milroy, L., and McClenaghan, P. 1977. Stereotyped reactions to four educated accents in Ulster. *Belfast Working Papers in Language and Linguistics* 2 (4): 1-10.
Reisman, Karl. 1970. Cultural and linguistic ambiguity in a West Indian village. In *Afro-American anthropology*. New York: Free Press, 129-144.
Rickford, John R. 1975. Carrying the new wave into syntax. In *Analyzing variation in language*, ed. by R.W. Fasold and R.W. Shuy. Washington, D.C.: Georgetown University Press: 162-183.
-   1979. Variation and change in a Creole continuum: quantitative and implicational approaches. Ph.D. dissertation, University of Pennsylvania, Philadelphia.
-   1981. A variable rule for a Creole continuum. In *Variation omnibus*, ed. by D. Sankoff and H. Cedergren. Edmonton, Canada: Linguistic Research, Inc.: 201-208.
-   1983. What happens in decreolization. In *Pidginization and creolization as language acquisition*, ed. by R.W. Andersen. Rowley, Mass.: Newbury House.
Romaine, Suzanne. 1980. Stylistic variation and evaluative reactions to speech: problems in the investigation of linguistic attitudes in Scotland. *Language and Speech* 23 (3): 213-232.
Ryan, Ellen Bouchard. 1979. Why do low-prestige varieties persist? In *Language and social psychology*, ed. by Howard Giles and Robert M. St. Clair. Oxford: Basil Blackwell, 145-157.
-   and Carranza, M.A. 1975. Evaluative reactions towards speakers of standard English and Mexican-American accented English *Journal of Personality and Social Psychology* 31 (5): 855-863.
Samarin, William J. 1966. Self-annulling prestige factors among speakers of a creole language. In *Sociolinguistics*, ed. by William Bright. The Hague: Mouton, 188-213.
Smitherman, Geneva. 1977. *Talkin and testifyin: the language of Black America*. Boston: Houghton Mifflin.
Stewart, William A. 1962. Creole languages in the Caribbean. In *Study of the role of second languages in Asia, Africa and Latin America*, ed. by W.A. Rice. Washington, D.C.: Center for Applied Linguistics, 34-53.
Tucker, G. Richard and Lambert, Wallace E. 1969. White and Negro listeners' reactions to various American English dialects. *Social Forces* 47: 463-68.
Weinreich, Uriel. 1953. *Languages in contact*. N.Y.: Linguistic Circle of New York.
Williams, Frederic, Hewett, N., Miller L.M., Naremore, R.C. and Whitehead, J.L. 1976. *Explorations of the linguistic attitudes of teachers*. Rowley, Massachusetts: Newbury House.

PATTERNS OF SHIFT AND MAINTENANCE:
A QUESTION OF LIFE AND DEATH

Richard R. Day

The Ultimate Inequality: Linguistic Genocide*

Introduction

In this chapter I explore a form of language death which I call linguistic genocide. I seek to demonstrate how linguistic genocide is the result of cultural contact between two unequal societies — unequal in terms of economic resources, military strength, and international prestige. I explain how this process occurs—how one language replaces another—by looking in depth at what happened to the Hawaiian language and what is happening to Chamorro, a language indigenous to the Mariana Islands, as used on Guam, the largest island in this western Pacific island chain.

Language death may be regarded as an extreme case of language contact with the victorious language slowly replacing the dying language (Dressler 1972: 448). This phenomenon has been referred to by many names: language suicide (Denison 1977; Andersen 1980); an obsolescent language (Swadesh 1948); a disintegrating language, a decaying language, a dying language (Dressler 1972); and linguistic genocide (Day 1981). By whatever name it is called, language death involves a language shift—the switch from one language to another by the people in a given culture. This may take a long time—witness the switch from Irish to English—or it may take only a few generations, as in the case of Chamorro. However long it takes, the result is that a group of people ends up using a different language as their first language. In this sense the first language is dead—it lacks native speakers; it is no longer the language learned first by children. In another sense, it may be preserved in much the same fashion other artifacts from a previous period in a culture's history are preserved in a museum. There may be a written record if the language has a writing system. Or certain religious or art forms might still require or allow the ex-native language to be used. In Hawaii, for example, chanting and prayers are still done in Hawaiian by Hawaiians on certain occasions. Also, adults may learn their ancestral language as one would a foreign language (e.g., enrolling in an introductory language course in a school or a college).

Language death is not necessarily the fate of all languages. Languages which are viable, which have an active network of speakers who learn them as their first language, are not static; they change, evolve over time. Old English, for example, is almost unrecognizable to speakers of present-day English. Not only do languages change slowly, they may evolve into different languages, as Latin became French, Spanish, Italian, and Portuguese.

Gal (1978: 23) links language change to social change. As changes in society occur, the linguistic needs of its members may change, which results in a change in linguistic patterns. This may be done voluntary, as in the situation which Gal describes in a town in Austria. The residents for centuries were bilingual, speaking Hungarian and German. However, in recent years the pattern began to change, with German being used more often than Hungarian. Age was found to be a factor in determining the amount of Hungarian an individual used, but it was not sufficient to explain language choice. A key factor was what Gal terms a speaker's social networks and the peasant or non-peasant nature of these networks. To the extent that an individual had a high degree of peasantness of social network, Hungarian was more often used. As life in the village changed, as people began to become workers rather than peasants, German was used to signify the newly acquired status. Thus the choice of language, in this village at least, can be seen as part of a speaker's presentation of self.

In this Austrian village, the shift from Hungarian to German will not result in language death. Hungarian will continue to be spoken in Hungary. In addition, as described above, this is a voluntary shift. There are situations where the language shift does result in language death and where the shift, although aided and abetted by some of the language's speakers, was not voluntary. When American Indians shifted from their languages to English, their languages died, since if the Indians did not speak them, no one else would. These deaths were not voluntary in a sense, since the Indians were not willing recipients of the largess of Western culture.

It is to characterize this phenomenon that the term linguistic genocide is employed. It is the systematic replacement of an indigenous language with the language of an outside, dominant group, resulting in a permanent language shift and the death of the indigenous language. As we learn from examining policies and practices in Hawaii and Guam, the use of the outside language was at first restricted to a limited number of domains (e.g., trade) but this use gradually increased until the outside language was widely used in domains previously restricted to the native language (e.g., government, religion). The new language gains in prestige and status among the speakers of the old language while the old language loses its usefulness (and, in some cases, prestige); children no longer learn it as their first language. Without native speakers, the indigenous language faces extinction.

Generally, the policy- and decision-makers do not announce as a goal the death of the native language. They may claim that they seek the use of the outside language only in certain domains such as education, using to support their plans such reasons as, 'It will help the children to receive a better education.' 'Learning the new language is important for life in the twentieth century. The old language is inadequate for the science and technology of today's world.' 'They will get better jobs speaking the new language.' As we see in this chapter, one result of such thinking and planning may be and has been linguistic genocide.

We examine policies and practices in business, government, religion, and education to account for linguistic genocide. We look first at Hawaii, and then at Chamorro. The parallels are obvious. Chamorro is doomed for extinction, if present trends continue, much as Hawaiian was in the nineteenth century. Chamorro could very well take its place alongside Hawaiian in the linguistic museum of dead languages.

Hawaiian and English

The Hawaiian language is an example of linguistic genocide. Hawaiian culture came into extensive and, as it developed, lasting contact with Western culture, primarily American and English. As a result, Hawaiians shifted first languages, changing from their indigenous language to English or a creolized variety, Hawaii Creole English. As mentioned earlier, the use of Hawaiian is restricted to a limited number of domains (e.g., prayers, chants, songs) which may be shared with English. Children generally do not learn it as their first language.

The death of Hawaiian has been a gradual process, starting first with commerce. Although the British sea captain, James Cook, landed in Hawaii in 1778, it was not until the first part of the nineteenth century that there was any extensive contact with foreigners. During the early 1800s, a large sandalwood trade was established with the West, resulting in a number of trading vessels making regularly scheduled stops in the Hawaiian Islands and groups of foreigners taking up residence in the Islands. Although insightful records of linguistic usage are not available, we may reasonably assume that Hawaiians and non-Hawaiians communicated with one another during this initial period of contact through interpreters (either Hawaiians who learned a Western language, or Westerners who learned Hawaiian) or through the use of Maritime Pidgin Hawaiian (MPH). For our purposes, a pidgin may be thought of as a form of communication used in limited circumstances (e.g., for trading) by different groups of people who have no common language. It is generally regarded as a simplified linguistic system, based on the native tongues of its users. The pidgin which arose in Hawaii during this period was used mainly by traders and, later, by whalers, to communicate with Hawaiians.

As the supply of sandalwood gave out in the 1820s, the whaling industry became important, further increasing the exposure of the Hawaiian Islands to the Western world. It is important to note that the primary reason for the culture contact between Hawaiians and foreigners was economic. Once outsiders realized the economic importance of Hawaii, other trappings of Western civilization (e.g., religion, education) followed.

We should further note that from the beginning outsiders were welcomed. Although Captain Cook was killed during his visit because of a classic case of cultural misunderstanding, foreigners were generally regarded as privileged guests. Hawaiian society at that time had a sharp class distinction between rulers and ruled; foreigners were usually placed somewhere in between, if not with the rulers. As a result, things foreign were also welcomed and, in many cases, prized. Language, as a symbol of the outsiders, was no exception. And since the majority of the foreigners during this early period spoke English, the English language acquired prestige.

This early period set the stage for the remainder of the nineteenth century: increasing trade with foreigners, mainly English-speaking; an increasing number of foreign residents, again, mostly English-speaking; the growth of a contact language (MPH); and increasing prestige of artifacts of the Western world, including the English language.

It was not until the 1820s that a foreign language became a serious threat to the survival of Hawaiian. Missionaries from New England arrived to save the Hawaiians from such heathen practices as the hula; whaling became an important industry, bringing to Hawaii sailors from many parts of the world. As the number of foreigners increased, conditions changed. Many foreigners did not always understand the customs of the Hawaiians and did not bother to learn them. If they did learn them, many showed little respect for them. Only a few foreigners bothered to learn Hawaiian, relying on Hawaiians to learn their language, which was generally English.

Among those few foreigners who bothered to learn Hawaiian were the missionaries. They figured out that the best way to convert the natives was to learn their language. Indeed, a printing press was brought to the Islands, and the Bible was printed in Hawaiian. However, missionaries played an important role in the death of Hawaiian for, in a change from their earlier position of advocating public education in Hawaiian, in 1854 they switched and voted that the government should make "immediate and strenuous efforts to import a knowledge of English language to the natives of these islands" (Minutes of the Hawaiian Evangelical Association, 1854, p. 6).

The missionaries changed because of what they saw happening to the Hawaiians. The missionaries believed the Hawaiians were losing their vitality as a culture and that in order to survive, the Hawaiians had to deal with the outside world on its terms. And that meant, among other things, learning

English. Without English, many missionaries believed that the Hawaiians would not survive.

The missionaries were not alone in their belief. Reinecke (1969: 45) claimed that Kings Kamehameha III and Kamehameha IV were in favor of English education for Hawaiians. He offered the following quotation made by Kamehameha IV in an opening address to the Legislature in 1855 (from Lydecker, *Speeches of Sovereigns and Presidents*, p. 58, cited by G. A. Odgers, 'Educational Legislation in Hawaii, 1845–1892', M.A. thesis, University of Hawaii, p. 125):

> It is of the highest importance, in my opinion, that education in the English language should become more general, for it is my firm conviction that unless my subjects become educated in this tongue, their hope of intellectual progress, and of meeting the foreigners on terms of equality, is a vain one.

In 1854, a law was enacted which established government schools in which English was the medium of instruction. These schools were supported in part by the Hawaiian government and by charging a small tuition. One of the major historians of Hawaii, Kuykendall, observes, "This was the beginning of a movement which ended many years later with the complete abandonment of the Hawaiian language as the medium of instruction in the public schools of Hawaii" (1926: 362).

There was some resistance to this policy. The president of the Board of Education, Mr. Kekuanaoa (a Hawaiian), in his 1864 report to the Legislature, warned that educating Hawaiian children in English was dangerous. He said that the preservation of the Kingdom of Hawaii for Hawaiians depended on educating its people in the Hawaiian language. Apparently his report did not change policy.

It is perhaps not too surprising that governmental policy favored the use of English over Hawaiian. Recall that foreigners were not only welcomed, but were regarded with favor. It did not take long before some of the King's advisers were foreigners. As contacts with foreign governments increased, their influence grew. Gradually the administration of governmental institutions was in the hands of English-speaking advisers. For a short time, legislative enactments and other governmental policies were printed in both English and Hawaiian. By the 1870s, however, English had replaced Hawaiian as the original language of government papers. The Hawaiian versions were translated from English, which was referred to for meaning. It should also be noted that the major newspaper in the 1840s was published in English, establishing a tradition for the remainder of the lief of the Kingdom of Hawaii.

The years 1876–1893 saw the final victory of English over Hawaiian in the speres of education, government, and business. It is not perhaps coincidental that these eighteen years were the final years of the Kingdom of

Hawaii. The plantation economy, which began in the 1850s, had to import labor from abroad in order to expand. The indigenous labor force—the Hawaiians—had proven to be too small and reportedly unreliable. We read reports which disapprovingly claim that the Hawaiians would rather fish and farm for themselves on a subsistance basis instead of working in the sugar cane fields 12 hours a day for the foreigners. Portuguese and Chinese, at first, and later Japanese were brought to the Islands to work on the large plantations. These plantations were owned by English-speaking foreigners, mainly Americans.

The Portuguese, as part of the enticements to get them to come to Hawaii, were promised free schooling for their children. When they discovered that free schooling meant education in Hawaiian, they protested. They wanted their children educated in a European language. They refused to pay the small tuition which was required to attend English schools since their labor contracts called for free education. The sugar barons, rather than paying the tuition for the Portuguese, went to the Legislature and got the tuition rescinded for the Portuguese.

The fact that the Portuguese did not have to pay tuition to attend the English schools did not strike the Hawaiians as the most equitable situation. They protested to their government, claiming they were being treated unfairly in their own country. As a result, the government removed tuition charges from the English schools in 1888, driving the final nail in the coffin of the Hawaiian schools. Within a few years of that decision, there were only a handful of schools which used Hawaiian as the medium of instruction. Later, of course, there were none.

In looking over the period when Western civilization first made recorded contact with the Hawaiians—1778—to the end of the rule of the Hawaiian Islands by Hawaiians—1893—we see how gradual was the decline of the Hawaiian language and the rise of the English language. There is no one turning point, no one piece of legislation, no royal decree that we can point to and say with confidence that it marked the time when Hawaiian lost to English. There was no policy which had as its stated goal the death of Hawaiian. There was, however, a series of incidents in which policy was formulated declaring, first, that governmental matters were to be translated from Hawaiian to English, then that government business could be in both Hawaiian and English. In public education, the policy was not to eradicate Hawaiian as a medium of instruction, but with the government sponsorship of English schools, the inevitable result was the closing of Hawaiian public schools. The English-speaking foreigners were aided and abetted in their efforts by the Hawaiian elite, much to their detriment, as we see what finally happened when the foreigners seized control of the government in 1893.

In 1893, a group of foreigners, primarily businessmen, overthrew the Hawaiian government, then headed by Queen Liliuokalani, and expected the United States to annex the Islands immediately. When this was not forthcoming, they established a republic and drew up a new constitution. This constitution contained a clause which had the effect of requiring voters to be able to read, write, and speak English. In 1898, the Republic of Hawaii was indeed annexed by the United States. Hawaii's *Organic Act* of 1900, which served as the governing document of the Islands, directed legislators to do their business in English.

In 1900, then, legislation made official what had been happening since the 1820s. The Hawaiian language, in competition with English and, to a lesser extent, Hawaii Creole English, was relegated to a secondary role in its own homeland. Business, religion, education, and governmental policies played a role. They helped to create a climate in which English became the preferred language, gaining prestige in the eyes of Hawaiians and non-Hawaiians at the expense of the Hawaiian language.

We do know that there were profound changes in the social and economic life of the Hawaiians during the 1800s. Not only was their language dying, but the Hawaiians themselves were also dying, primarily because of diseases brought to the Islands against which they had no natural immunity. Reinecke (1969: 30) claimed that the decline of the Hawaiian people "deepened the feeling of hopeless discouragement in the face of Western culture. The people were dying, the language was dying with the people – such was the feeling of many."

Reinecke also claimed that the creation of a part-Hawaiian group—in 1866, 2.8 percent of all Hawaiians were of mixed parentage—was a factor in the decline of the Hawaiians and, subsequently, their language (1969: 30–31):

> It is obvious that many of the mixed bloods would be thrown within the English-speaking circles of Honolulu and other ports, and that they would not have the same traditions, and therefore not the same incentives to perpetuate those traditions in carefully chosen Hawaiian, that an unmixed native population would have. As the mixed-blood group increased it drove the wedge of bilingualism, of language dualism, deeper and deeper.

Implicit in Reinecke's thinking about bilingualism is that it resulted in the Hawaiians losing their language—that Hawaiian-English bilingualism led to English monolingualism.

A reflection of the low esteem to which the Hawaiian language had fallen may be seen in the quality of the schools in the late 1800s where Hawaiian was the medium of instruction. Reinecke (1969: 48–49) quotes from various *Reports of the President of the Board of Education to the Hawaiian Legislature:*

> Why worry over the quality of teachers in Hawaiian? We shan't need them much longer, anyway. (1884: 11)

The teaching in these schools . . . is very poor. This result may be attributed to several causes. In the first place, Hawaiians who have any ability and aptitude for teaching generally drift into other more lucrative (sic) occupations; and secondly, those who do teach prefer to teach in English, thus leaving the more incompetent for the Board of Education to select from. (1886: 12)

Another factor in the decline of Hawaiian may have been the missionaries' literacy efforts. Creating an alphabet and making Hawaiian a literary language may have undermined its uniqueness, its distinctness from other languages. Reinecke (1969: 29) observed that the influence of English was particularly evident in essays in Hawaiian newspapers, since the Hawaiian writers "had no tradition of style for this particular type of composition". Thus, while the creation of a writing system has helped to preserve the Hawaiian language, it may have helped to kill it as a spoken language.

Thus, by 1900, attitudes toward Hawaiian and English, brought about by policies and practices in business, religion, government, and education, left Hawaiian as a dying language, and English as the official language of the Hawaiian Islands. We might claim that 1900, since it is an easy date to remember and since a significant policy was formulated then, marks the official date of the shift from Hawaiian to English, the date when Hawaiian was declared the loser and English the winner, when Hawaiian became a victim of linguistic genocide. Whether the English-speaking foreigners could have killed Hawaiian alone, without help from the Hawaiians themselves, is an open question with no conclusive answer. However, it is a moot point. Most, if not all, Hawaiians and part-Hawaiians learn another language as their first language. Its uses, as I mentioned earlier, are restricted.

There have been attempts to breathe life into the language. It is offered as a language by the state university system the same way French, Japanese, and other foreign languages are taught. In 1978, the voters of the state approved a constitutional amendment which established Hawaiian as a required subject in public schools, with all students receiving fifty minutes per week of Hawaiian. These efforts are classic examples, of too little, too late. Hawaiian is a victim of Western civilization and progress.

Was it worth it? Has the death of Hawaiian brought financial, social, academic and political success to Hawaiians? Unfortunately and tragically, it has not. It is a well known and documented fact of the Hawaiian Islands that Hawaiians in general are at the bottom of the social, economic and political scale. Although there are exceptions, Hawaiians are usually employed in the bluest of blue collar jobs; they have the highest rate of unemployment, of juvenile delinquency, of school dropouts; and they have lost political control of their islands. The problem, obviously, is not merely a linguistic one; it is a social and racial and economic one.

Before leaving Hawaii for Guam, we should consider the role of Maritime Pidgin Hawaiian and Hawaii Creole English, mentioned earlier, in the linguistic history of the nineteenth century. I claim that MPH was a contact language, used at first in trading and whaling deals by both Hawaiians and foreigners. As the whaling trade declined and the sugar plantation economy in the Islands became stronger, Maritime Pidgin Hawaiian evolved into Plantation Pidgin Hawaiian. This pidgin was influenced and used by the first generation of immigrants who were brought to the Islands to work on the plantations. Those immigrants who came later learned this pidgin in order to communicate with those from different language backgrounds. The children of the immigrants learned Plantation Pidgin Hawaiian as a first language and, since it was their first language and not a second (unlike their parents), it changed from a simplified, limited form of communication into a full-blown language. In linguistics this new language is called a creole. Hawaii Creole English was based on Plantation Pidgin Hawaiian, Hawaiian, English and other immigrant languages, such as Portuguese. Hawaii Creole English, which is called Pidgin today in Hawaii, is spoken by a large segment of the population (cf. the chapter in this volume by Sato).

It is difficult to determine what role these linguistic systems played in the downfall of Hawaiian. It does not seem too unreasonable to suppose that they were a factor, since the linguistic resources of a community are usually defined functionally, although the symbolic value of a language cannot be underestimated. In any event, Hawaii Creole English is widely-used in the Islands today and is learned as a first language by a segment of the population.

Chamorro and Spanish

In looking at the policies and practices of both the foreigners and the Chamorros, we can see a picture similar to the one painted for Hawaii. Business, religion, education, government—all are playing leading roles in the genocide of Chamorro.

The Portuguese explorer, Ferdinand Magellan, made the first Western contact with Guam on March 6, 1521, and claimed Guam and its neighbor Rota for Spain. Magellan's contact was brief and disastrous. After restocking his ships' almost depleted provisions, Magellan prepared to sail when he discovered that a small boat was missing. He blamed the Chamorros and set about to teach them a lesson. Magellan and forty of his men went ashore, torched about fifty homes, and killed seven Chamorros. He than sailed for the Philippines and named the two islands Las Islas Ladrones — the Islands of Thieves.

Several other Spanish expeditions visited Guam after Magellan, including one by Miguel Lopez de Legazpi in 1565. His expedition also resulted in the death of some Chamorros, which seems to have anticipated the behavior of later Spanish soldiers. This expedition discovered a return route to Mexico through what is now the Northern Marianas, which resulted in making the Marianas, as they were later named in honor of the Spanish queen Mariana, a port of call in Spanish trading between Mexico and the Philippines.

We should note the similarity between Guam and Hawaii on this point: Western contact, bloodshed, return visits, and a realization that the island might be useful economically. On Hawaii, after trading was established, the missionaries arrived. On Guam, the situation was similar. In 1668, a Catholic priest named Diego Luis de Sanvitores, fulfilling a vision he had as a child, arrived on Guam to save the natives and convert them to Catholicism. Although it is beyond the scope of this chapter to discuss the life and times of Padre Sanvitores on Guam, I must mention the tremendous impact his coming to Guam had. To begin with, it set the stage for turning Guam from a mere way station in the lucrative Manila Galleon trade to a Spanish colony. In addition, he introduced Chamorros to the Catholic religion. An understanding of these two factors is necessary to understand contemporary Chamorro society and language.

Initially, the colonialization of the Chamorros was brutal. After a ruthless and successful campaign of genocide, the surviving Chamorros intermarried with Spanish, Mexicans, Filipinos, and other Pacific Islanders (Manchester 1980). The Spanish developed a new class system based on both birth and merit which resulted in a new Chamorro elite. This new elite justified itself on Spanish lineage, which affects life on Guam today. Those Chamorros who successfully claimed Spanish lineage have come to occupy high positions in the political and socioeconomic fabric of the island.

This creation of a new Chamorro elite and a class system, while vital to an understanding of today's Chamorro identity, is perhaps secondary to the impact Catholicism has had on Chamorro society and culture. We can only explore the perimeter of the complexity of Chamorro identity and Catholicism here. Approximately 90 percent of Chamorros today are Catholic. From this we can catch a glimpse of the socializing role which the Church has played on Guam. It was not just a religion; as Underwood (1980: 11) notes, "It provided a framework through which all important forms of social and cultural interaction could be played out. As such, it became a symbol of culture as well as religion and to separate the two would rip the process from a context in which its true meaning can manifest itself." Catholicism and Chamorro merged, in such a way that both changed. Not only did the Chamorros change their ways and adopt the Church, but the Church adopted certain Chamorro patterns. For example, we find that today every notable political or social event has an obligatory mass which must be celebrated. This merging of the Chamorro identity with the Catholic Church has an important implication for the maintenance of the Chamorro language, as we discuss below.

Given the enormous influence of the Church on Chamorro culture, it is not surprising to learn that the first formal school on Guam was established as a seminary for Chamorro boys. This school evolved into an institution for the children of the new Chamorro elite. Spanish, of course, was the language of instruction. Although the Spanish did not have a policy of universal, compulsory education, eventually the priests set up schools in most villages in which literacy was emphasized as were such practical skills as carpentry. Underwood (1980: 23) claims that these schools functioned primarily to reinforce the new class system.

The use of Chamorro in the new class system and in the religious schools was not even an issue. The Spanish did not attempt to regulate the use of Chamorro or offer their language in place of Chamorro, as happened under American rule (see next section). Rather, there was a belief that the elite would, of course, learn Spanish, as all educated people should do. And since educated people controlled the government, in the 1790s and the nineteenth century one of the requirements for government employment was knowledge of Spanish (Underwood 1980: 8). It is not too difficult to imagine the effect this thinking had on the Chamorro language. It aided in the development of a negative attitude by Chamorros toward their language. Not only was it not the language of the Church, but it was not even fit to be used in the governing of the island.

Another factor which contributed to a negative attitude by Chamorros toward their language was the borrowing of words from Spanish and incorporating them into Chamorro. We learn from history that this is not an uncommon phenomenon in conquest situations. For example, English borrowed heavily from Norman French after the successful conquest of England by William the Conqueror in 1066. Generally it is only the vocabulary or lexicon which is affected. Chamorro in terms of its sounds, syntax and semantics remained Chamorro. But the heavy Hispanicization of the Chamorro lexicon has left many Chamorros with the mistaken impression that presentday Chamorro is not really Chamorro, that it is merely a mixture of 'true' Chamorro and Spanish.

We note that this is similar, although not identical, to what happened to Hawaiian. Written Hawaiian was apparently influenced by English, which served to undermine its vitality as a language. The impact of Western religion on Hawaiian and Chamorro was also similar. Both cultures came under strong religious influence in which missionaries used the native languages to educate and convert the island populations, and they also promoted their native tongues–Spanish and English–as the language of the educated elite. A major difference was education for the common people, pushed by missionaries on Hawaii but not by those on Guam. Governmental practices by the Spanish resemble those advocated by the English-speaking foreigners acting as advisers to the Hawaiian kings: use the outsider's language whenever possible. The affairs of the state had to be conducted in the foreigner's language.

Thus, under Spanish rule, Chamorro began to lose ground. A Chamorro ruling class developed which not only spoke Spanish but tried to trace ancestry to the Spanish. The Chamorro language borrowed extensively from Spanish. As a result, many Chamorros came to hold negative attitudes toward their language. The Spanish laid an excellent foundation for the death of Chamorro on which the Americans were to build, even though Chamorro remained the dominant language of the Chamorro people during the Spanish occupation, which lasted until the end of the nineteenth century.

Chamorro and English

The status of Chamorro on Guam was to change even more when control of the island passed from Spain to the United States in 1898 as a result of the Spanish-American War. From then until 1950, except for a brief period of Japanese occupation during World War II, Guam was ruled by an American governor appointed in Washington. One observer claims that these governors ruled the island in the manner of a battleship or a naval base (Kloss 1977: 251). The Chamorros had virtually no control over their island during this period.

Under American rule, the practice of using the dominant, foreign language in governmental affairs begun by the Spanish was continued and extended. The American governor in 1906, for example, made English the official language for court proceedings, land registration, and so on. Other administrative restrictions and laws included a ban on Chamorro in government buildings and in the presence of American military personnel. This latter restriction was rather sweeping, since the American military controls approximately one-third of Guam (Betances 1980).

Unlike the Spanish, the Americans established a public school system on the island, calling for compulsory education for children between the ages of eight and fourteen. Not too surprisingly, English was the medium of instruction and the use of Chamorro was restricted. In fact, *restricted* might be too tame an adjective. In 1922, for example, Chamorro was prohibited on school grounds and Chamorro dictionaries were collected and burned. In an editorial in the February 1925 issue of the *Guam Recorder*, a magazine written by Americans, we find the following:

The basis of progress in Guam must be the English language. The limitations of the Chamorro language must restrict the progress that could be made with that as the only medium of communication . . . . It is beyond question that a fluent knowledge of the English language, written and spoken would be the greatest possible aid to progress in Guam—agricultural, social, business, and in all other ways . . . .

This is American territory. It is American to have public schools where only English is taught. Americans have an obligation and such they have never shirked.

This same article also claimed that if Chamorros learned English they would acquire a knowledge of sanitation and hygiene, in addition to being able to improve their economic condition and their sense of fair play and honor.

The attitudes displayed by the Americans in Guam are strikingly similar to those held by Americans in Hawaii. They believed firmly that English was the key to salvation—economic, political, and social. We might wonder why a nation of immigrants could be so single minded. An explanation might be found in the unshakable conviction held by most Americans that the American way of life is the only way. Part of the American way of life is speaking English. Our immigrant ancestors had to learn English to succeed, and they did. Thus not only is it possible to learn English, if you can, you will succeed. This belief expressed in Hawaii in the nineteenth century and in Guam fifty years ago in one language—one America is still held by many Americans today.

There was one major flaw in the American plan for linguistic domination of the Chamorros in the first fifty years of American rule: It was difficult to recruit enough English-speaking teachers to staff the schools. The American military, while controlling the island, had not yet come to regard Guam as a key to the defense of the country. This was to come later. Until the 1950s, Guam remained relatively undisturbed economically, a forgotten colony of America in the Pacific Ocean.

In 1950, Guam was changed to an organized territory by the Organic Act. This allowed residents of Guam to control island affairs; it also declared Chamorros to be American citizens. The governorship of Guam became an elective office in 1968. A locally elected unicameral legislature has jurisdiction over island matters, with the United States Congress maintaining control over foreign policy and all other matters.

The casual observer might expect that, with the Chamorros in control of the internal affairs of their island, the policies and practices of the outsiders toward their language would be reversed. To expect this would be to forget the Hawaiian experience, in which the Hawaiian rulers aided and abetted in the genocide of their language. The Chamorros continued to kill their language. In governmental affairs, for example, Section 3000 of the Government Code of Guam, one of the first laws passed by the all-Chamorro legislature, established English as the official language and did not allow government employees to speak other languages at work (Underwood 1980: 17). This law had an important effect on the use of Chamorro in the public schools. Since the school system was operated by the Government of Guam, the use of Chamorro in the public schools was illegal. It could not even be taught as a subject, much less used as a medium of instruction.

In the 1970s, there was a change in policy. In 1974, for example, an amendment to the Government Code of Guam established Chamorro, along with English, as an official language of Guam. However, English remains 'more official' since Chamorro is not required for official recordings, as is English.

Since most all Chamorros were Christians when the Americans took control, the missionaries did not flock to Guam as they did to Hawaii in the 1800s. Religion, as described above, had already undermined Chamorro. But when the Americans came, religion may have been a factor in the maintenance of Chamorro. Underwood (1980: 15) claims that the Spanish priests, when Spain turned over control of Guam to the United States, began using Chamorro in catechism and sermons. They began to use Chamorro because Spanish apparently lost its social and economic utility, once the Spanish rulers left the island. Apparently the Spanish priests were either unable or unwilling to use English, so they made Chamorro the language of the Church on Guam. Since most Chamorros are Catholic, the Church became a factor in the maintenance of Chamorro. Today, church services are held in both Chamorro and English, which shows the inroads English has made into Chamorro society.

There is one major difference between the linguistic genocide of Hawaiian in the nineteenth century and the possible death of Chamorro in the twentieth century: the mass media. The use of English most of the time in the major newspaper and magazine, on radio, and on television on Guam must be taken into account. Although I am aware of no research on this topic, it is reasonable to assume that the mass media have played a crucial role in the shift from Chamorro to English. We might expect to find, when this matter is investigated, that the use of English in the mass media has helped to undermine the Chamorros' confidence in their own language and has helped them to learn English. Given the lack of empirical evidence on this topic, we can do no more than mention it here, and point out the urgent need for research not only on Guam but in other areas of cultural contact as well.

As on Hawaii, business has played a role in the demise of Chamorro on Guam. As contact with the outside world increased, English-speaking businessmen found their way to Guam, making the use of English more desirable. In addition, as in Hawaii, Guam's leaders claim that there has arisen a need for a large work force; as a result there is a large number of immigrants on Guam.[1] Perhaps the largest group of outsiders is those from the United States, often referred to as *statesiders*. Statesiders come to Guam as part of the military, as teachers, as business people, lawyers or other professional or technical occupations, and as missionaries. This large block of English-speaking immigrants has undoubtedly reinforced existing policies for education in English. A move to have public school education in Chamorro would most likely meet with stiff opposition from them. They would also most likely oppose any moves to use Chamorro in other phases of government or business.

In addition to statesiders, a large number of people from the Philippines, Korea, Vietnam, Taiwan, and other Pacific Islands have come to Guam in search of work. Generally they have been able to find employment in the construction industry, which receives contracts from the US military, among others. The *lingua franca*—or common language—which is used on Guam by most all immigrants is English. They can see little need for learning Chamorro, since it would be of no use outside of the Marianas, whereas English will be of use to them throughout the United States. To the extent that these immigrants have families, they will also expect that their children will be instructed in English in the public school. This expectation by immigrants that their children be educated in English and not Chamorro is also related to the usefulness and prestige of English around the world—it is the leading *lingua franca* in the world today.

In spite of the large number of immigrants, Guam, unlike Hawaii, has not experienced any pidginization or creolization. However, this matter has not been researched to the extent that it has been in Hawaii, so we should regard the issue as unresolved. Whatever turns out to be the case, it would not change the basic pattern formulated in this chapter.

Americans and things American have been highly regarded by Chamorros, much as the Hawaiians valued foreigners and their products in the 1800s. On Guam, the American life style, values and belief systems are considered desirable. Betances (1980: 75) believes that the American military is regarded by the Chamorros as a good friend of Guam. Americans freed Guam from the brutal Japanese control during World War II and, as a result, the Chamorros are exceptionally grateful. Betances believes that many Chamorros look upon American citizenship as "a guarantee to maintaining Chamorro identity; in essence, the American flag and other US symbols are identified with the Chamorro's finest hour in their struggle to survive as a people" (1980: 75). The English language, as a symbol of the United States, has come to occupy a privileged status in the minds of many Chamorros.

As a result of this favorable attitude towards the United States, governmental policies and practices, the influence of Western religion and business, Chamorro is dying. In assessing the status of the Chamorro language, Underwood, a Chamorro, believed that as the 1960s ended it was apparent that Chamorro was showing signs of loss: "The local elite had raised their children using English and the rest of the population was following suit. Despite these linguistic imperialist policies, little opposition was ever in evidence" (Underwood 1980: 18–19). Again, the similarity to the Hawaiian situation is striking. Somewhere during the early twentieth century, bilingual Hawaiian parents began teaching their children English instead of Hawaiian. By the 1940s, at least, there was a generation of Hawaiians who did not speak Hawaiian as a first language, and perhaps not even as a second language. On Guam, apparently the same phenomenon has begun. Since the late 1960s and early 1970s, bilingual Chamorro parents have been teaching their children English at home.

The are doing this because they believe that English is the key to academic and economic success. If their children do not speak English, then they will not do well in school. If their children do not speak English, then they will not be able to obtain desirable jobs. Odo, in an investigation into the use of Chamorro, found that the majority of Chamorro parents surveyed did not speak Chamorro to their preschool children, and that they wanted their children to learn English, not Chamorro (Odo 1972). We might wonder where Chamorro children will learn Chamorro if they do not learn it at home. If Hawaii's experience can serve as a model, Chamorro children will not learn Chamorro outside the home; Chamorro as an active language will not be available to succeeding generations on Guam.

Recall that identical reasons for Hawaiians acquiring English were advanced but that Hawaiians have not fared well economically, politically, and academically. Are the Chamorros any different? Has the acquisition of English been beneficial? Apparently not, even though they have political control of their internal affairs. Betances (1980: 81) reports an estimate which given the real unemployment rate for Chamorros as close to forty percent. While Chamorros are unemployed, immigrants, particularly Filipinos, are working. Outsiders account for 90 percent of the jobs in the construction industry. So much for economic benefits as an excuse for linguistic genocide.

Four hundred years of cultural and linguistic subjugation have taken their toll on the Chamorro people. The view that the outsider's language is to be preferred and that their language is somehow second-rate has now become part of the fabric of society. As I explained earlier, the heavy borrowing from Spanish has led many Chamorros to view their language as not really a language. As a result of such thinking, Underwood (1977: 12) notes that if Chamorros speak Chamorro at a public meeting, they inevitably excuse themselves. Topping (1973), in a discussion of the positive attitudes towards English and the negative attitudes towards Chamorro, says the linguistic future is clear: Within two generations, Topping predicts, Chamorro will cease to be spoken on Guam; English will be the language which everyone born on Guam learns and speaks.

As in Hawaii, there has been an attempt to revive the indigenous language on Guam. Recent legislation requires that Chamorro be taught in the public schools for approximately fifty minutes each week. In addition, there is a bilingual-bicultural program teaching young children both English and Chamorro. These are welcomed trends for those interested in saving the Chamorro language and culture. We must wait to see if these attempts will be successful.

Chamorro and the Northern Marianas

As described earlier in this chapter, Chamorro is not restricted to Guam; it is also spoken in the Northern Marianas. The Northern Marianas has a distinct political existence from Guam, and has a different relationship with the United States. Given this, we might hope that Chamorro, which may become a victim of linguistic genocide on Guam, could survive in the Northern Marianas. This does not appear to be likely. Underwood (1980: 9) writes:

> However, upon closer examination, we find that whatever route Guam has taken in its development, the rest of her sister islands in the chain seem insistent on doing the same. Moreover, the speed at which changes are made in the Northern Marianas appear (sic) to exceed Guam's rate of change when it was undergoing the 'boom' of the late 60s and early 70s.

This is rather discouraging, for Chamorro had received different treatment from the United States military in the Northern Marianas. It was used as a language of instruction in the public schools after World War II. Granted that this use of Chamorro was only to aid Chamorro-speaking children learn English, it was better treatment than it received on Guam. However, in the late 1960s, there was a change in policy, and English became the medium of instruction. Thus it would appear as though the stage is set for Chamorro to disappear from the Marianas altogether and, consequently, cease to be an active language—another victim of linguistic genocide.

Conclusion

In this chapter I have described linguistic genocide—a type of language death which occurs when two unequal societies come into lasting contact. I examined in detail two cases of linguistic genocide: Hawaiian, which is *in extremis*; and Chamorro, which is in progress. The causes are found in the practices and policies of government, education, religion, and business.

The outsiders play the major role in the death of the native languages. But it could not be accomplished without cooperation from the indigenous elite. We must question if linguistic genocide is voluntary, perhaps a type of linguistic suicide (see Denison 1977). The answer must be no, since suicide generally involves committing an act knowing the outcome. In linguistic genocide, the native speakers of the language apparently do not believe that their language will die; they only see benefits which might accrue from learning the outsider's language.

It is much too late to stop the linguistic genocide of Hawaiian. The Hawaiian Islands became the fiftieth state, firmly wedded to America and the English language. For Guam and the Northern Marianas, perhaps it is not too late. There are signs that Chamorros are becoming aware of the predicted fate of their language. The writings of Underwood, for example, are receiving attention (1977; 1980). However, I believe the situation is bleak. As long as the Marianas remain under the control of the United States, the English language will continue to replace Chamorro until there are no native speakers left. This has been American policy and practice elsewhere, and there is no reason to believe that Guam and the Northern Marianas will be an exception.

Notes

* I would like to thank Joan Manes for her helpful comments.
1. For an interesting discussion of immigration and ethnic conflict on Guam, see Betances 1980.

References

Andersen, R.W. 1980. Determining the linguistic attributes of language attrition. Paper delivered at the Language Skill Attrition Conference, University of Pennsylvania.

Betances, S. 1980. Cross cultural education and ethnic conflict in Guam. *NABE Journal* V: 1. 71-91.

Day, R.R. 1981. ESL: A factor in linguistic genocide? *On TESOL '80 Building Bridges: Research and Practice in Teaching English as a Second Language.* J.C. Fisher, M.A. Clarke and J. Schachter (eds.), Washington, D.C.: TESOL. 73-78.

Denison, N. 1977. Language death or language suicide. *International Journal of the Sociology of Language.* 12. 13-22.

Dressler, W. 1972. On the phonology of language death. *Papers from the Eighth Regional Meeting Chicago Linguistic Society.* P.M. Peranteau, J.N. Levi and G.C. Phares (eds.). Chicago; Chicago Linguistic Society. 448-457.

Gal, S. 1978. *Language Shift: Social Determinants of Linguistic Change in Bilingual Austria.* New York: Academic Press.

Kloss, H. 1977. *The American Bilingual Tradition.* Rowley, Massachusetts: Newbury House.

Kuykendall, R.S. 1926. *A History of Hawaii.* New York: Macmillan.

Manchester, W. 1980. *Goodbye, Darkness.* Boston: Little, Brown.

Odo, C. 1972. *A Survey of Language Use and Attitudes on Guam.* Agana, Guam: Guam Department of Education.

Reinecke, J.E. 1969. *Language and Dialect in Hawaii.* Honolulu: University of Hawaii Press.

Swadesh, M. 1948. Sociologic notes on obsolescent languages. *International Journal of American Linguistics 14.* 226-35.

Topping, D.M. 1973. Spoken Chamorro tomorrow. *Guam Recorder.* January-March. 45-48.

Underwood, R. 1977. A Chamorro challenge to 'statesiders'. *Islander.* October 23. 8-13.

– 1980. Untitled manuscript.

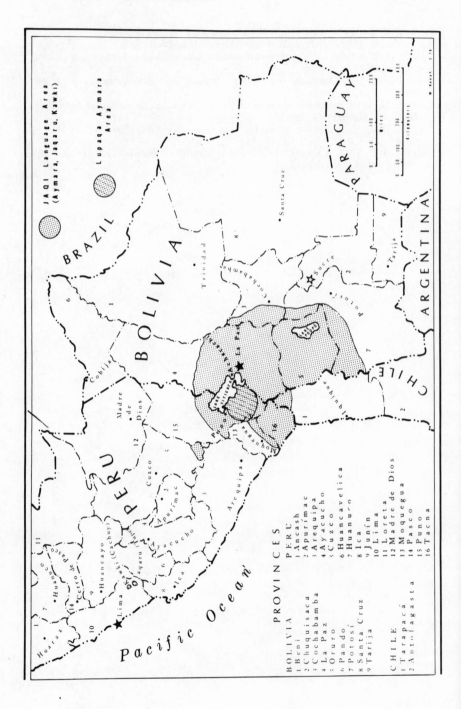

Martha Hardman de Bautista

The Imperial Languages of the Andes

The Andes mountains, reaching from Ecuador down through Peru and Bolivia and including the northern parts of Chile and Argentina, form a rugged terrain. The peaks rise so abruptly that in places the continental divide is only 50 miles from the Pacific Coast. Walking from one valley to the next can appear a journey of major proportions to one unaccustomed to such imposing grandeur. 'Just over the hill' may involve a climb of some 5000 feet and an equal drop back down again. It is the kind of terrain that one might imagine either uninhabited or one in which each small group would exist isolated from all others, living and dying within the confines of the natal village — much as in old Europe.

However, the case for the Andes is different, very different indeed. The Andes have been so continuously and heavily populated that, when walking over that rugged terrain, it would appear, close-up, that these mountains are sculpted by human hand. Very little remains that has not been, at some time, now or far in the past, reformed by the work of people cultivating or traveling over what would seen to a European impossible terrain. Obviously, Andean people have handled physical obstacles in their own unique fashion, in a style that has prehistoric roots and that has continued through to today.

In the Andes of today, in spite of 400 years of strenuous imposition of the European pattern of oneness—one farmer on one plot of land in one house—people regularly own numerous little fields. Furthermore, these fields are scattered up and down the mountains such that a single farmer has access to many ecological niches. It is also the common pattern to have houses at more than one of these locations. For example, one farmer I know has a house not far from the high areas where she herds cows and some sheep and goats. She also has a house down further where the corn grows. She has a third house in the lower valley where she has her plantations of citrus. And she has a fourth house in the large town where she does most of her trading and where her children study. Marriage typically increases access to ecological niches through joint cultivation (though never joint ownership) of lands belonging to each partner.

This pattern of land tenure means that farmers—virtually every adult in a native community—travel large distances both in miles and in altitude on a regular basis simply for cultivation. They travel additionally for the trading of goods and to visit kinfolk, real and spiritual, residing, working or studying in other areas. Though one member of a family group may be the principal trader—usually a mature woman—the Andean people all travel a great deal by European standards, from their earliest years. By their own standards this is not so. Anything short of international travel is just 'staying right here'.

Modern travel, where it is feasible, is via motor roads. These are relatively recent—1925 was the first big push for roads in the highlands. There is still in use an extensive road system consisting of 'large roads', i.e. passable by pack animal, and 'small roads' passable only on foot (and by, e.g., goats). These roads, largely unmapped even today, date from prehistoric times, and are maintained even today by communal labor. They bear place names (toponyms) at frequent intervals, at landmarks, at places where something memorable happened, at spots believed to hold power, at meeting or trading places. These toponyms are so frequent along the way that one can often specify one's journey to within ten yards. These toponyms are heavily Jaqi. That is, they have their ultimate origin from a language of the Jaqi family of languages. A large proportion of the toponyms are also Quechua; in some areas (but not all) the Quechua is of Inca origin. These latter are less frequent than one might think, given the fame of the Inca Empire. There are also some toponyms that are today unidentifiable, that presumably came from language families other than Quechua or Jaqi.

Some essential definitions:

JAQI LANGUAGE FAMILY: today spoken by around three million people. Three extant languages:
KAWKI: 20 speakers, a dying language, in the Yauyos valley southeast of Lima;
JAQARU: 3000 speakers, in Tupe, Yauyos, and in migrant groups in several cities;
AYMARA: close to 3 million; native language of one-third of the population of Bolivia, spoken by more than half a million in Southern Peru, and by some 20,000 in Northern Chile.

Also Jaqi languages were still spoken in this century in Canta (north of Lima) and in Huarochiri (between Canta and Yauyos).
QUECHUA LANGUAGE FAMILY: today spoken by upwards of 20 million people in Ecuador, Colombia, Peru, Bolivia, Argentina. At least 6 different languages. Best know is the CUZCO VARIETY, used by the Incas as a conquest language.

The toponymic situation in the Andes is more complicated than outlined above. Many places have more than one name—an imposed conquest name and a local name (which may in its turn have been an earlier conquest imposition—but that we cannot always reconstruct). For example, one town near Tupe where Jaqaru is spoken is called, today, Catahuasi. This is obviously a Quechua term although the local people believe it to be Spanish. Jaqaru speakers call the town Watxuqu. Catahuasi may have been imposed by the Inca, or more likely, by a Quechua speaking guide for Spanish conquerors surveying their new territory. Thus, a toponym may itself carry the history of the meeting of two conquerors in an area which was not, in some senses, ever completely conquered, even today.

The Andean situation is then, that, after 400 years of strenuous attempts by outsiders to impose the European pattern of staidness for farmers on the farmers of the Andes, the people are far from it. They travel, often and far, for cultivation, for trade, and to maintain personal links.

These monumental human efforts to render Andean geography manageable do not reduce the Andes to the equivalent of a flat plain. It is not easy to maintain close contacts with rapidity across long distances—horizontal and vertical. In fact it is extremely difficult even today; the motor roads do not improve matters that much. As we look back over the historical and prehistorical periods, what we do see is a tension between the pull to unify and the pull to diversify. These take alternate ascendency without the other ever fully losing force. Thus we have an alternation between widespread unifying 'empires' or expansions, and their dissolution into local control and separatist cultural development. The localist developments are so numerous and so complex that there is no way we could even list them. For example, each stream valley up and down the coast has its own history. At the time of the conquest, chroniclers would often simply state that each group had its own language. We can guess that each highland valley had its own individual history—each one investigated so far has shown such, although less has been done in the highlands than on the coast. We can speak, however, of the pan-Andean periods and of the localist periods.

The periods we will look at are:

I.   Chavin pan-Andean
   A. localist—Puquina, Jaqi, Chinchay developments
II.   Tiwanaku pan-Andean
   B. localist—Chinchay, Mochica, Puquina developments
III.   Inca pan-Andean
   C. localist—Quechua, Spanish, Aymara developments
IV.   Spanish (republic) pan-Andean

Looking back as far as we can with current knowledge, the first pan-Andean period appears to be the Chavin, starting around 900 B.C. with its center at

Chavin de Huantar in the North Central Highlands with expansion most intensively in the direction of the North Coast, but establishing trading patterns northward to connect with Central America and southward toward the area that became Jaqi. It is indeed possible that many of the unknown toponyms came from the language(s) used in this first (as far as we know) expansionist Andean culture. The name 'Chavin' itself is a common toponym throughout the Andes—one must always specify *which* Chavin (e.g. Kawki is spoken in Chavin de Yauyos). However, there are not, to our knowledge, any remaining languages from this expansion, although it is possible that the Mochica/Chimu of the later North Coast cultures were direct descendants (linguistically/culturally speaking) of this first expansion. The language(s) these people spoke is (are) also now extinct, leaving only a few word lists, surnames, and toponyms. If the Chimu/Mochica of the northern Peruvian Coast did indeed speak languages carried there during the Chavin expansion, then this would be also an early example of language imposition by a dominant group. This is by no means certain; nor can it be ascertained by the data at our command today. More certain is that the last group to occupy the area, with the center at Chan-Chan near Trujillo did indeed impose themselves linguistically and otherwise, on local populations, leaving behind the many surnames and toponyms typical of the north Coast of Peru today (surnames like Llontop and Neciosup).

Following the Chavin expansion there was a long period of local developments, for a period of several hundred years. Three of these local developments will concern us here: Paracas/Nazca, Chincha, and Tiwanaku.

On the South Coast there was the development of the Paracas culture on the coast itself, which we know through its textiles primarily, and later, further inland, of the Nazca, a resurgency of those we project to be the descendants of the Paracas. These people were, by all we can reconstruct, Jaqi speakers, moving further and further inland, without losing all contact with the coast. Even today there are networks of the road system I described earlier leading from modern Jaqi speaking areas into Nazca—used by contemporary peoples for herding as well as other purposes. In this early expansion of the Jaqi we may hypothesize that smaller local languages were replaced as they went. This is most evident in the extreme diversity found in the Yauyos valley even today, where obviously a number of original languages were once spoken, but are now unrecoverable. It may, indeed, be the case that Jaqaru and Kawki, as well as the other Jaqi languages spoken in this area before the Inca and Spanish intrusions, moved into the valley at the time of the Nazca pre-Wari Jaqi expansion.

Also on the coast, but a bit further to the north, in the area known as South Central Coast, was a group known as the Chincha who were building themselves a flourishing naval trading industry, mainly towards the north, particularly up into Ecuador. They were speakers of what came to be the mother tongue of all the modern Quechuas. To them we will return a bit later in more detail. What is important to note is that they were already by this time establishing a Chinchay (Quechua) speaking outpost in Ecuador.

Meanwhile, another, quite different group, was building a complex civilization on the southern shores of Lake Titicaca—the people who built Tiwanaku. These people developed widely appreciated trade goods and a distinctive style that gave renown to their name even in our day. These people were most probably Puquina speakers.

Following this very long period of localist development the also long and extensive expansion of the Jaqi speakers began—the Wari/Tiwanaku horizon, which lasted for some 400 years at least. Today there are only three of the Jaqi languages left, but at one time Jaqi was spoken the length and breadth of the Andes, if not as a first language then as a second, or trade language. The center for the Jaqi expansion was Wari, near modern Ayacucho, but by the time that capital was built the Jaqi people already had heavy contacts with many other areas. In particular they had apparently established intense trading relations with the Puquina of Tiwanaku, and with the coastal Chincha, spreading their goods from one end to the other, building roads—and giving them Jaqi toponyms—building trading centers, and, as a practical matter (we assume), imposing the necessity of learning Jaqi. Even so famous an Inca outpost as Cajamarca, for example, bears a Jaqi place name: q'aja marka 'town in the valley'. One result of this expansion was that in the area around Ayacucho and to the south and coastward, the local languages, of which we now have only the faintest traces, largely disappeared, so that the area inland back of what is today Lima and south around what is today Cuzco became dotted with Jaqi speaking populations, eventually becoming, in some cases, different Jaqi languages. A second result was massive borrowing from Jaqi into the other languages which did not disappear, for example into the language spoken by the Chincha—the ancestor of modern Quechua. Some of the words borrowed at that time from Jaqi are

Quechua:	chunka	cf. Jaqaru cxunhka	'10'
	pachak	pacxaka	'100'
	qucha	qucxa	'lake'

This period of Jaqi expansion lasted for nearly 500 years before it eventually gave way to the localist and separatist tendencies always present in the Andes. But we have here, easily documented, a case of widespread language imposition and influence, largely, apparently, through trade. That is, the motivation for giving up one's own language would appear to have been primarily cultural and economic, including access to and the enjoyment of the variety that goes with the multiplicity of ecological niches on the Andean vertical scale. Some evidence does indicate that trade was at times imposed in a military fashion, so that not all of the expansion can be assumed to have been peaceful. Some of the languages may have disappeared because the population did, replaced by the conquering forces.

The period of localist development that followed the Jaqi expansion lasted some 400 years. During this period there were, again, three that merit our attention here, remembering always that the actual number was at least in the hundreds.

First, the Chincha continued expanding and intensifying their naval power, such that they became an important power to be reckoned with and their language became an important one not only in the South Central Coast and in the North Central Highlands, but also in Ecuador. The trade with Ecuador appears to have been particularly vigorous; indeed they apparently transhipped goods even during the Wari period up north into Central America, and continued even more so during the localist period which followed. We can presume that some local languages were displaced in the process. It is probable that some of the descendants of these earlier settlers from the South Central Peruvian Coast interacted with and became part of the wide-traveling traders of Otavalo.

On the Northern Coast the Chimu were also developing intensely their own rather locally contained expansion that took in most of the North Coast. They also traded, by sea, with the Chinchay group further south.

The Puquina, meanwhile, having suffered numerous reverses in their original environment, among which were apparently mud slides, began a northern trek for more favorable territory, crossing Lake Titicaca (preserved in the tale of Mama Oclla and Manco Capac) and eventually settling in the Cuzco valley.

This Puquina group, then, began their expansion at the end of this localist period, in time (according to their accounts) for there to be fourteen Incas—ruling emperors—before the arrival of the Spanish.

The situation, then, at the dawn of the Puquina/Inca expansion is: a flourishing trade with skillful navigators using advanced large reed boats plying their trade and culture up and down the coast, using Chinchay as the trading language, in contact with at least one other large flourishing culture (Chimu) and numerous smaller ones. These navigators have also invaded the interior of the northern Andes establishing their language in the area over so long a period that it has begun to develop local varieties. There were no other large unified competitors, but only the remnants of the earlier Jaqi all around them.

If we pause for a moment, at the dawn of what became the Inca empire, we can see that up to this time there has been no period of staidness for the Andean population. They were ever a mobile people, traveling, even in times of the most localistic and individualistic tendencies, interacting with others, imposing themselves on others, by trade primarily, but also by force (weapons are among the artifacts) and by religions (the large ceremonial centers).

The Puquina then, began to expand. The specific royal family of the specific group of Puquina speakers which undertook this empire building were the Inca. There remained other groups of Puquina speakers until after the conquest that were known as 'poor relations' of the royal family. Unlike the Jaqi, who used their own language in expansion, the Inca immediately ran into the existence of a widely known trade language that was also the native language of many of the populated areas into which they were expanding. This *lingua franca* was the remnant of the formerly dominant Jaqi, now in its version as proto-Aymara. Faced with this, the Inca elected to keep their own language for internal court purposes, and take advantage of the already existing language for conquest purposes (not unlike the Vandals in Spain who accepted the Latin varieties then in use by the populace, or the Normans in England). During the reign of some nine of the Incas (if the list can be considered historical) the language of conquest was Jaqi, i.e., proto-Aymara, which meant that Cuzco was, in reality, a bilingual city; certainly all of the ruling Incas themselves became fluent in the tongue. Thus the earlier Incas spread Jaqi further that the Wari themselves.

During the reign of the grandfather of Huayna Capac, the Inca to die of smallpox before ever setting eyes on a Spaniard, the expansion began to gather steam and began rolling across the peaks and valleys under the direction of this famed Pachacutic. It rather rapidly bumped into the enormous power of the Chincha on the coast with their enormous sea power and with a most powerful oracle located in Pachacamac, near modern Lima. Clash would appear inevitable, but the Inca, with what has come to be recognized as a sheer genius for avoiding conflict in conquering, took another tack. The Inca's son Tupac Inca Yupanqui married a woman of Chincha, said to be much beloved, and the mother of Huayna Capac. It was under the command of Tupac Inca Yupanqui that the empire reached its great expansion. Sometime during the reign of Pachacutic and/or Tupac Inca Yupanqui, but less than 100 years before the Spanish, the official conquest language was switched to the language of the Chincha—Chincha was, after all, more powerful than the Jaqi. They thus joined forces with the Chincha as the 'conquered' becoming subjects of the Inca empire, but enjoying a privileged status.

Thus it became the task of the bureaucrats in Cuzco to learn another language. For the space of at least one generation, the city was, in reality, trilingual. In fact, it remained so even at the arrival of the Spaniards, although the Jaqi, by then being less useful than the new 'general language', was dropping out. Because the entire court already spoke Jaqi, it is not surprising to discover that the Cuzco version of Chincha became heavily influenced by the first imperial language, to the extent of borrowing even some phonological features. The famous glottalization of Cuzco Quechua, for example, is an importation from this period. There was also a very large second wave of borrowings into Imperial Quechua from Jaqi as proto-Aymara, such as

Quechua:	jamp'atu	cf. Aymara	jamp'atu	'frog'
	k"itu		k"it"u	'scrape e.g. wood'
	suti		suti	'name'

During this period and into the Spanish conquest period, the Cuzco variety was considered inferior to the Chinchay variety, a fact often commented on in the early documents, especially since a good many of the interpreters came from the Ecuadorian area.

The Inca expansion wiped out many local languages, but not as an absolute policy. If there was resistance, then the residents were scattered and others brought in (the mitimaes) which resulted in loss of one language and the introduction of some variety of the 'general language' (Quechua) which policy explains some apparent anomalies in language distribution today. Some localities decided it was in their best interest to switch, for whatever reason. Huarochiri appears to have been one such place. They had apparently almost completed the switch from Jaqi to Quechua when the Spaniards arrived, at which point they switched to Spanish. However, even into the early part of this century natives of the area have reported older people still speaking Jaqi. I have not been able to document this personally.

Another policy of the Incas was to send the children of community leaders to Cuzco for a four-year higher education program, of which one year was devoted to language learning. This was high incentive (not unlike our bringing foreigners to the US for graduate training) for spreading Quechua when they returned as leaders themselves.

The accounts we have given so far of imposition have been relatively speaking rather benign, leaving intact most local languages at least initially, even if the community leaders were required to become bilingual. Not all takeovers were so peaceful. The flourishing Chimu on the North Coast were bloodily subdued, leaving only remnants of the language to disappear when the Spanish arrived not too many years later.

The process of spreading use of the 'general language' was far from complete at the arrival of the Spaniards. Population decrease was rapid, from plagues, abuse, and massacre. From estimates as high as 30 million, the population dropped within 25 years to only one million. That drop is difficult even to imagine—reading the account of visits by colonial officials to the towns, seeing the numbers spelling out the populations drops, it still seems stunningly impossible. Twenty five years after Pizarro first met Atahuallpa Inca less than one of 25 individuals in the Andes still survived. Many of the local languages simply died out with all speakers. Others were extinguished in more brutal ways. One of the victims was Chinchay itself, spoken too close to the Spanish capital of Lima. Some documents, however, have been preserved: all early writings were in this more prestigious variety. Its demise was rapid enough, however, and the prestige of the city of Cuzco was great enough, that the Spanish conquerors took the Cuzco variety to be the one and only language, the 'pure', 'true' Quechua. Another victim was Puquina, largely because the royal family was almost entirely killed, and the poor relations to the south died off with the plagues or eventually melted into the southward moving Aymara speaking groups.

The Spaniards then, like the Incas with Jaqi before them, began a far more thorough implantation of what is today known as Cuzco Quechua, or simply Quechua, than had been ever accomplished by the Incas. Cuzco, which at the moment of conquest was trilingual, became bilingual, only Quechua tying the two periods together. The priests proselytized in Quechua. Landholders, in spite of orders to the contrary, feared knowledge of Spanish on the part of the serfs and thus learned Quechua themselves—in some cases thus obligating people who spoke other languages to abandon these in favor of Quechua. Spanish was a privileged language of the ruling class. One of the results of this Spanish-inspired Quechua expansion was another wave of borrowing, but this time from Quechua into Aymara, for example:

| Aymara: | ancha | cf. Quechua | ancha | 'much' |
| | qincha | | qincha | 'fence' |

Thus only a few of the Andean population came to learn Spanish. Rather, there began another period of localist development, in which the imposed Inca Conquest Language followed individual paths to great dialect diversity, separating ever further the original varieties and those based on the Jaqi-influenced Cuzco variety. Aymara, during this period, was pushed ever further away from the Cuzco area, south into the area it occupies today, developing as the second major language of the Andes.

The result, as of today, is that, except for a few Jaqi languages and Chipaya in southern Bolivia, *all* other languages have been erased from the Andean highlands.

Independence, the republican period, and the construction of east/west motor roads have brought the beginnings of a new expansionist period, Spanish in language, but a Spanish born of the intense interaction between conquered and conqueror. This Spanish has adopted, as did the conquering Quechua before it, many of the elements from the earlier conquering

Jaqi. We may never know what elements Jaqi adopted from those it overtook. The current rapid expansion of Spanish follows the earlier patterns of the expansions of Jaqi and Quechua: there is some imposition by force (not very successful), but far more so by the motives of trade, culture, variety, schooling, work, education. Thus loss of local languages continues and/or bilingualism becomes again the norm.

Language and culture are intricately tied together, but neither is immutable. Both change; both carry on through the change elements from the previous identity. The history of the Andes, over three thousand years, is at once the history of continuity and of disruption. And the search for the ideal balance between unity and diversity continues.

Sources

Most of the pre-historical outline presented in this paper is the result of my own work in proto-Jaqi reconstruction and comparisons with Quechua (with which I worked for two years in the Urubamba valley and at Cornell) (Hardman 1966, 1975, 1976, 1978a, 1978b, 1979, 1981, forthcoming). The other primary source is the work of Alfredo Torero, both published (1964, 1972, 1974) and that which he has shared with me in many personal conversations over some 20 years of friendship. Also, my student Lawrence Carpenter has been building on this base, and has added some important refinements to the Ecuadorian phase of the Chinchay expansion (in preparation). Another student, building on the published materials cited above, has called to my attention some references in the chronicles (Mannheim 1981). It would be impossible to cite all of the chronicles, works written by persons present during the conquest and early colonial years, on which I draw to supplement and flesh out the work done in reconstruction. Obviously Garcilaso de la Vega, son of a member of the royal Inca family and a Spanish conqueror (1615/1929) is an important source, but only one. A good overview of the chronicles is Valcarcel (1964). I also wish to acknowledge the contributions made by the work of Collins (1981) and Painter (1981) in researching colonial documents in southern Peru and in their confirmations of the contemporary existence of prehistoric cultural patterns, as reported in their dissertations and in forthcoming publications.

References

Carpenter, Lawrence. In preparation. Ecuadorian Quichua and the Implications for Development. Dissertation, University of Florida.

Collins, Jane. 1981. Kinship and Seasonal Migration among the Aymara of Southern Peru: Human Adaptation to Energy Scarcity. Dissertation. University of Florida.

Garcilaso de la Vega, el Inca. 1615/1929. Antología de los comentarios reales. Madrid: M. Aguilar. (Critical edition by José de la Riva-Agüero.)

Hardman, M. J. 1966. *Jaqaru: Outline of Phonological and Morphological Structure.* The Hague: Mouton.

— 1975. El Jaqaru, el Kawki y el Aymara. Actas, El Simposio de Montevideo (1969). Mexico City, Mexico: PILEI.

— 1976. Proto-Jaqi: reconstrucción del sistema de personas gramaticales. *Revista del Museo Nacional*, vol. XLI. Lima, Peru.

— 1978a. Jaqi: The Linguistic Family. *International Journal of American Linguistics.* 44:2.

— 1978b. La familia lingüística andina jaqi: Jaqaru, Kawki, Aymara. *Vicus Cuadernos, Lingüística ii Amsterdam.*

— 1979. Quechua y Aymara: lenguas en contacto. *Antropología I-1* (Revista del Instituto Nacional de Antropología). La Paz, Bolivia.

— 1981. *Aymara Language in its Cultural and Social Context.* Social Science Monograph Series, University of Florida.

— Forthcoming. Aymara and Quechua: A Case of Language Contact. In *South American Indian languages, retrospect and prospect*, ed. Louisa Stark and Harriet E. Manelis Klein.

Hardman, M. J., Juana Vasquez and Juan de Dios Yapita Moya. 1975. *Aymar ar yatiqañataki* (To Learn Aymara). 3 vols. Ann Arbor: University Microfilms.

Mannheim, Bruce. 1981. Ethnohistory and Historical Linguistics in the Southern Peruvian Andes: on Quechua-External Genetic Relationships and Contact. Unpublished paper.

Painter, Michael. 1981. Political Economy of Food Production: an Example from an Aymara-speaking Region of Peru. Dissertation. University of Florida.

Torero, Alfredo. 1964. Los dialectos quechuas. *Anales Científicos de la Universidad Agraria* 2: 447-78. Lima.

— 1972. Lingüística e historia de la sociedad andina. In *El Reto del Multilingüismo en el Perú*, ed. Alberto Escobar. Lima: IEP.

— 1974. *El quechua y la historia social andina.* Lima: Universidad Ricardo Palma, Dirección Universitaria de Investigación.

Valcarcel, Luis E. 1964. *Historia del Perú Antiguo a través de la fuente escrita.* 3 vols. Lima: Editorial Mejía Baca.

Michael Clyne

Language Maintenance and Language Shift:
Some Data from Australia*

Mass immigration has turned Australia into a kind of sociolinguistic laboratory. This paper attempts to account for the maintenance of immigrant
languages other than English and the shift to English in Australia, on the basis
of data from the 1976 Australian Census, the first to elicit information on
language. This census asked respondents to list all languages regularly used by
each person over the age of 5. Owing to errors in processing, data on some
languages (e.g., Serbo-Croatian, Arabic) were distorted, and due to storage
restrictions, some information is not as exhaustive as it could be (Clyne
1979). It is recognized, of course, that there are limitations to the application
of self-reporting in censuses for conclusions on anything as personal as
language usage. Some people do not report the use of their language other
than English because they think Australian society expects them to assimilate. Others mention English only because they consider the use of other
languages to be a private matter. Still others report the use of one language
other than English but not another, or give their language 'another name'
because they consider it of low prestige. Many Macedonian speakers in
Melbourne reported the use of English and Greek, Serbo-Croatian, or
Bulgarian (which is closely related to Macedonian), but not Macedonian, their
normal home language, or called it 'Yugoslav' or 'Serbian'.[1] Also, language
shift is too complex a process to be gauged by responses to a single question.

Of the total population, 12.3 percent (including 4.2 percent of the
Australian-born) reported *regularly* using a language other than English. In
Melbourne, the proportion is 20.7 percent, including 7.1 percent of the
Australian-born persons there.

The most widely spoken languages other than English throughout Australia
are, according to the census: Italian (444, 672), Greek (262, 177), German
(170, 644)[2] Serbo-Croatian (142,407),[2] French (64,851),[2] Dutch (64,768),
Polish (62,945), Arabic (51,284),[2] Spanish (48,343), Maltese (45,939),[2]
followed by Chinese, Hungarian, Turkish, and Macedonian.

Within the metropolitan areas, the use of Turkish and Macedonian is
highly concentrated in particular districts.[3] There are medium concentrations
for (in order of concentration): Maltese, Greek, Spanish, Arabic, Ukrainian,

Dutch, and Hungarian, while German is generally the most dispersed language. Almost invariably, high concentration goes hand in hand with adjacency of concentration area.

The comparative rate of first generation shift to the regular use of 'English only' in seven groups based on birthplace follows the same rank-ordering in practically all parts of Australia, as can be deduced from Table 1: Greek-born, Italian-born, Yugoslav-born, Polish-born, German-born, Dutch-born. The only major fluctuation is for the Maltese, whose rate of language shift is either high (as for the Dutch) or medium (as for the Germans), depending on the size of their community.

Among second generation Australians from intra-ethnic marriages, language shift is considerably higher in all groups, but the order is *almost* the same, however, with Maltese-Australians shifting slightly less than German-Australians. The shift (see Table 2) from Greek and Italian is still fairly low, but that from Maltese, German and Dutch represents the majority of this population.

Where one of the parents is Australian-, British-, or Irish-born, the maintenance of the language other than English is negligible (along the same continuum as the second generation from intra-ethnic marriages) with a range from 68.4 percent shift for children with one Greek parent to 99.09 percent for children with one Dutch parent (Table 3). Where the parents speak different ethnic languages, it is unusual for either of these to be used regularly in the second generation. The exception to this is Australians of mixed Italian-Greek parentage, the majority of whom use Italian regularly and a large minority of whom maintain Greek as well.

As can be seen in the first table, there are distinct differences between first generation language shift rates of the same groups in different states of Australia. A similar pattern is continued in the second generation (Table 2)–with South Australia showing the lowest shift in most groups, and Queensland and Western Australia the highest (discounting the very small immigrant population of the Northern Territory).

Why do some ethnic groups and some states face a far greater language shift than others? Let us test a number of possible determining factors: *Similarity of language and culture* to that of the dominant group is one of the variables which Kloss (1966) regards as 'ambivalent' in that it can promote language maintenance or language shift. Of the languages under consideration, Dutch, German and Italian are those closest to English (the latter being a Germanic language, strongly influenced by Romance languages). In both the first and second generations, Dutch-Australians experience the highest shift, German-Australians are in the medium bracket, and Italian-Australians have a low language shift. The language typologically most distant from English is Maltese (a Semitic language) from which there is a medium shift. Greek,

Polish, and the Yugoslav languages are in an 'in-between' position as to language typology, being Indo-European languages like English, but more distant in grammar and lexicon than Dutch, German and Italian. However, Greek-born immigrants rarely shift exclusively to English, and the Yugoslav-born do not frequently do so, while the Polish-born shift almost as much as the German-born.

The Maltese have undergone considerable Italian and British influence (something reflected in the lexicon of the language). At the time when most Maltese immigrants came to Australia in the 1950s, Malta was still a British colony. Though the normal means of interaction between the people was Maltese, the language of the 'high' domains (Ferguson 1959) such as administration, newspapers, and many schools was English. The main language of the church was Italian, and there was little literature in Maltese. The high status of English in Malta at the time also contributes to the linguistic behaviour of the group.[4]

Generally, our data confirm the impression of a 'geographical-cultural continuum' of language maintenance—Southern Europeans maintain L1 (first language) better than Northern Europeans, and Eastern Europeans better than Western Europeans. Those ethnic groups whose cultural value systems and patterns of speech behaviour ('doing things with words') deviate most from those of Anglo-Australians (e.g., Greeks, Italians) maintain L1 most. Those whose cultural value systems and speech behaviour are most similar to Anglo-Australian norms (e.g., Dutch, Germans, Maltese) are more likely to shift to English as this does not involve such a marked behavioural change. Neustupný (1971) has shown that common rules for *communication* (e.g., politeness, irony, disagreeing) do not necessarily overlap with linguistic relationship or common *grammatical* rules. Geographical proximity (as between Austrians and Hungarians) and historical contact (as between the Maltese and the British) are likely to lead to common communication rules. The Greeks (South-Eastern Europeans) experience the lowest shift while the Dutch, the group geographically and culturally closest to the British, shift to English the most. It seems that cultural similarity (including common communication rules) is more important than linguistic (grammatical) similarity, and a clearcut factor, not an ambivalent one.

Numerical strength is another of Kloss's ambivalent factors. Large groups can afford extensive language maintenance efforts but cannot avoid multiple contacts with the dominant group. The three largest birthplace groups (Italians, Greeks, Yugoslavs) show the lowest language shift. However, the Greeks' language shift in even the lowest in parts of Australia where they the Greeks' language shift is even the lowest in parts of Australia where they are also outnumbered by other groups (e.g., Germans, 'Yugoslavs', Dutch). There are far more Dutch than Maltese in South Australia, yet the latter have a smaller language shift. A similar relationship occurs between Germans and Poles in Western Australia, and Dutch and Poles in the Australian Capital Territory. The only fairly clear picture of correspondence between absolute numerical strength and language maintenance is among the Maltese. On the other hand, the Polish-born shift to English most in Victoria, the state where they have the largest numbers and represent the highest population ratio. Correspondence between relative numerical strength and relative language shift of the ethnic groups is borne out in first generation comparison between New South Wales and South Australia, but not, for example, in comparisons between Victoria and New South Wales, and between Victoria and South Australia.

Almost universally, language shift is greater outside the metropolitan areas than in the capital cities of New South Wales, Victoria and Queensland. This is in spite of the lesser degree of urbanization in Queensland than in the two more populous states. But in postwar Australia, non-metropolitan use of languages other than English tended to mean dispersion (except for Italian in some rural areas).

Relatively low language shift in a city or ethnic group corresponds to a higher concentration of the appropriate language *only* insofar as this agrees with the rank ordering of language shift indicated earlier. Comparatively high shift goes hand in hand with relatively low concentration *only* where this corresponds to the language shift rank ordering.

From the above, it can be deduced that absolute and relative numerical strength and dispersion of the language community are only of marginal significance to language ecology, though urbanization can promote language maintenance. It is possible that such variables can have some explanatory power, together with other factors, such as government policies. For instance, South Australia has a tradition of multilingualism, due to the presence, from the earliest years of white settlement, of a large non-English-speaking minority (the Germans).[5] Thus the speaking of languages other than English may have been accepted more widely in South Australia than elsewhere (except during the war and inter-war periods)—and, in fact, that state has pioneered many developments in Australian multilingual and multicultural education.

Taking Australia as a whole, the rank ordering of birthplace groups according to the percentage of non-English users stands in inverse proportion to the percentage first generation shift. The sex (female) and groups (Greeks, Italians, 'Yugoslavs') with the highest percentage of monolingual non-English speakers also show the greatest language maintenance. The exception is the Maltese, who have a higher percentage of non-English users than the Polish- and German-born, but also a higher shift. However, if we compare the states: The Victorian ethnic groups have a higher proportion of non-English users than their counterparts in South Australia, but most of them experience a higher language shift. On the other hand, the percentage of non-English-using Italians and 'Yugoslavs' is lowest in Tasmania, the state where their language shift is highest. The group in Western Australia and the Australian Capital Territory with the smallest proportion of non-English users has experienced the highest shift.

Numerous studies (e.g., Smolicz and Harris 1976, Harvey 1974, Zubrzycki 1964, Johnston 1973, Clyne 1977a) have commented on differing attitudes and efforts towards language maintenance in ethnic groups. Poles and Greeks are depicted as maintaining their L1 more than Germans or Dutch, Germans as shifting less than Dutch, and Balts and Ukrainians as maintaining their L1 best. The consistent rank-ordering of language shift in the first generation for six of the seven groups for which such census data are available, and in the second generation for four of the five for which we have the necessary information, supports the evidence of smaller surveys. They back up the theory, which Smolicz (1979) has developed and tested by means of attitudinal studies, that some cultures attach more emphasis on language as a symbol of ethnicity than do others, i.e. language may or may not be a cultural *core value*. If a culture regards language as central to ethnicity, it is likely to be maintained as a matter of policy rather than merely in an instrumental way (for communicative purposes). So functions will be found for its use. On the one end of the scale we have the Greeks as a language-centered culture, on the other the Dutch as a non-language-centered culture (see also Pauwels 1980). The Poles are also often portrayed as a language-centered culture (Smolicz 1979). However, it is necessary to see core values as interdependent. While the Italians are depicted as a family cohesion-centered culture, they, unlike the Dutch, who share this value, seem to require their language as a basis for family cohesion. Undoubtedly it is a fusion of the religious, linguistic and other cultural core values that has led to the low language shift among Greek-Australians. This is accentuated in the high percentage of Greek-background children enrolled at part-time ethnic schools as opposed to children from the other groups under discussion.

Owing to incomplete census statistics on period of residence, it has been impossible to gauge the importance of this factor. The census does not help us either with the effect on language maintenance of factors such as income or educational level. On the whole, the Poles, Dutch, Germans and Maltese (those with a medium to high language shift in the first generation) have been in Australia the longest of the groups under investigation, and the Greeks (those with the lowest shift) as well as some of the Yugoslav-born the shortest period. The *main* wave of Italian immigration (rather low shift) took place between the two other clusters.

It is not easy to generalize on the income brackets of immigrant groups, since there are rich and poor sub-groups within many of them. (There is no census cross-tabulation between income and actual languages used.) Of the groups under consideration, the Polish-born, for instance, have the highest percentage of high income earners and one of the highest proportions of low income earners. It should also be taken into account that political emigrants from Poland, Yugoslavia, Germany and other countries were often *déclassé* and present income levels are no indication of class. This applies especially in the many ethnic groups with aging populations where low income are largely pensions. On the other hand, some economic immigrants (from the Netherlands, Germany, Italy and elsewhere) have raised their socioeconomic status since their arrival in Australia as young people. For many immigrants, aspirations are vested in the children. If we were to hypothesize that first generation language maintenance is related to present socioeconomic disadvantage, this hypothesis would not stand up to the *collective* data available. The three most 'disadvantaged' and least 'advantaged' groups ('Yugoslavs', Greeks and Maltese) all exhibit different rates and patterns of language shift (see Table 1).

In the first generation, males have a greater tendency than females to shift from L1 (see Table 4). The two groups with the most marked differences between male and female language shift in the first generation are the Dutch- and Polish-born. A contributing factor may be a high degree of exogamy (with English speakers in the case of Dutch-born men and with other Europeans in the case of Polish-born men), in contrast with Italians or Greeks (Price 1975: 39), and the less international function of the language in comparison with, say, German (i.e., the wife is unlikely to learn, or have learned, the husband's L1). The Australian-born speakers reveal a fairly even distribution of language shift between the sexes (except for Maltese-Australians, where 4.21 percent more females than males shift to English only).

We have mentioned the effects of exogamy on second generation shift from the various ethnic languages. Such shift is greater, in Anglo-ethnic marriages, if the language other than English is the father's language than if it is the mother's language. The difference is only small for Dutch, German and Maltese, and medium for Italian, but much greater for Greek. This all applies to both sons and daughters of mixed marriages.

In the family of an inter-ethnic marriage, Italian appears to survive most (cf. the greater vitality of Greek in other situations) and, even if the *father's* language is Italian or Greek, that language is maintained the most, regardless of which is the mother's language. This may reflect a patriarchal family structure in families of Greek and Italian background. The number of Australian-born offspring of certain inter-ethnic combinations is too small to make generalizations.

In the first generation, language shift tends to be lowest in the 50+ age group and highest in the under 30 age groups. This is probably due to a combination of factors: younger people tend to acquire languages better than older people, and they tend to be socially more flexible and motivated (cf. e.g. Schumann 1978), and older people often revert to their L1 and lose some of their competence in later acquired languages (Clyne 1977b). On the other hand, for the five second generation groups under consideration, language shift increases with age. A sharp increase in the 50+ age group may be due to death of the parents, who are the main (or last remaining) agents of language maintenance for people in this age group. It may also be attributed to the anglo-conformist phase in Australian history which people of this vintage had to live through.

In summary: Of the factors discussed, those most influential in determining the rates of language maintenance and shift appear to be: cultural core values, degree of cultural similarity to the dominant group (including common rules of communication), and extent of intermarriage. Other factors that may play some part in governing language maintenance or shift in ethnic groups or states are (in order of importance):

Group factors

1. Multicultural history and language policy
2. Urbanization
3. Number of non-English speakers using the language
4. (Of marginal significance) Absolute and relative numerical strength

Group and personal factor

Period of residence(?)

Personal factors

1. Age
2. Sex

No single factor is powerful enough to achieve language shift, and relative language maintenance or shift is determined by a combination of factors.

Notes

* An earlier version of this paper was presented at the International Congress of Applied Linguistics, Lund, August 1981. I thank Nessa Wolfson, Joan Manes, Wilfried Stölting and Monty Wilkinson for helpful comments. This research has been supported by Monash University and an ARGC grant.
1. Personal communication, Prof. Peter Hill, who believes that the use of Macedonian in Melbourne has been severely underreported.
2. Estimates based on cross-tabulation of census data.
3. Concentration is calculated according to the formula:

$$\frac{\text{No. of users of language district}}{\text{Population of district over 5 years of age}} \quad \frac{\text{Population over 5 throughout metropolitan area}}{\text{X No. of users of language throughout metropolitan area}}$$

4. Even now, English is a co-official language in Malta. (Fishman, Cooper and Conrad, 1977:10).
5. Cf. Kloss (1966) who regards early immigration as a L.M. (language maintenance) factor in the U.S.

References

Clyne, M.G. 1977a. Nieuw Hollands or Double Dutch. *Dutch Studies* 3: 1-20.
- 1977b. Bilingualism of the Elderly. *Talanya* 4: 45-56.
- 1979. Community languages in Australia – What the 1976 Census will (and will not) tell us. Paper presented to the Society for Linguistics in Education.
Ferguson, C.A. 1959. Diglossia. *Word* 15: 325-40.
Fishman, J.A., R.L. Cooper and A.W. Conrad. 1977. *The Spread of English.* Rowley, Mass.: Newburg House.
Harvey, S. 1974. National language usage among Dutch and Polish immigrant children. In: D. Edgar (ed.), *Social Change in Australia.* Melbourne; 131-44.
Johnston, R. 1973. *Future Australians.* Canberra.
Kloss, H. 1966. German-American Language Maintenance Efforts. In: J.A. Fishman (ed.), *Language Loyalty in the United States.* The Hague: Mouton. 206-52.
Neustupný, J.V. 1971. A Model of Linguistic Distance. *Linguistic Communications* 5: 115-32.
Pauwels, A.F. 1980. The effects of mixed marriages on language shift in the Dutch community in Australia. M.A. thesis, Monash University.
Price. C.A. 1975. *Australian Immigration.* Canberra.
Schumann, J.H. 1978. *The Pidginization Process: A model of second language acquisition.* Rowley, Mass.: Newbury House.
Smolicz, J.J. 1979. *Culture and Education in a Plural Society.* Canberra.
- and Harris, R.Mc D. 1976. Ethnic Languages and Immigrant Youth. In: M. Clyne (ed.), *Australia Talks.* Canberra; 131-76.
Zubrzycki, J. 1964. *Settlers in the La Trobe Valley.* Canberra.

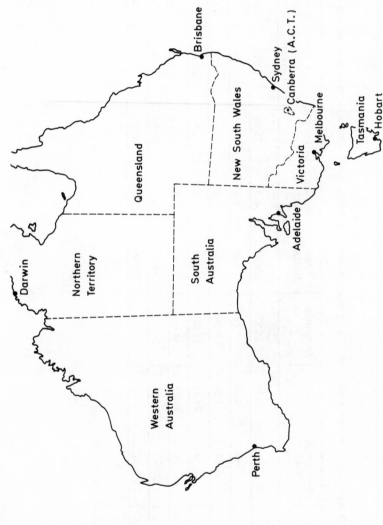

Map 1: Australia

Tables

Table 1: Language shift in first generation. (Based on cross-tabulation 'Birthplace by languages regularly used'–and expressed in percent).

Birthplace	New South Wales	Victoria	Queensland	South Australia	Western Australia	Tasmania	Australian Capital Territory	Northern Territory	Average for Australia
Germany	27.94	26.48	35.97	24.82	36.93	29.69	27.70	30.13	27.79
Greece	3.49	2.56	6.22	2.09	5.13	3.54	3.66	2.06	3.00
Italy	7.44	5.26	8.06	4.99	6.25	13.99	6.68	8.89	6.26
Malta	29.29	28.31	46.68	33.91	52.26	—*	41.50	—*	30.49
Netherlands	43.71	44.18	44.90	39.50	42.83	43.32	48.96	52.17	43.55
Poland	20.63	21.64	20.81	14.94	20.39	16.44	16.36	29.13	20.18
Yugoslavia	9.24	8.37	16.66	10.69	11.44	20.29	10.37	14.46	9.54

* Total number less than 100.

Table 2: Percentage language Shift in the second generation—children of intra-ethnic marriages in five birthplace groups. *(This information not available for children of Poles and Yugoslavs).*

Birthplace of parents	New South Wales	Victoria	Queensland	South Australia	Western Australia	Tasmania	Australian Capital Territory	Northern Territory	Average for Australia
Germany	57.93	57.23	84.09	52.16	65.04	53.77	42.80	58.73	62.28
Greece	8.69	9.72	11.73	3.62	41.92	12.47	24.94	0.46	10.08
Italy	21.02	14.56	26.95	16.23	22.61	28.70	21.82	23.11	18.56
Malta	56.77	49.51	64.96	54.34	33.46	*	53.84	*	53.68
Netherlands	80.69	83.66	80.65	79.91	73.87	77.30	88.17	*	80.79

* Total number less than 100.

Table 3: Percentage Language Shift in the second generation Australian-born of whom one parent was born in one of five selected countries and the other in Australia, Britain or Eire. *(This information not available for children of Poles and Yugoslavs).*

Birthplace of ethnic parent	New South Wales	Victoria	Queensland	South Australia	Western Australia	Tasmania	Australian Capital Territory	Northern Territory	Average for Australia
Germany	95.77	96.08	97.18	95.00	96.79	95.30	95.64	96.61	96.16
Greece	68.60	72.25	61.55	57.65	71.88	86.99	81.59	76.61	68.40
Italy	80.58	78.64	74.74	79.09	76.12	93.76	87.90	81.77	78.51
Malta	94.72	95.00	94.92	92.93	92.19	*	90.90	*	94.58
Netherlands	99.17	98.87	99.06	99.43	99.03	98.90	100.00	*	99.09

* Total number under 100.

206   *Michael Clyne*

Table 4: Percentage language shift to English only: males and females.

Birthplace	Males	Females	Difference
Germany	30.0	26.6	3.4
Greece	3.6	3.1	0.5
Italy	6.6	5.1	1.5
Malta	30.4	28.2	2.2
Netherlands	46.8	39.8	7.0
Poland	21.4	14.6	6.8
Yugoslavia	10.9	8.0	2.9
All the above	16.7	14.1	2.6

Figure 1: Language Shift by Age.

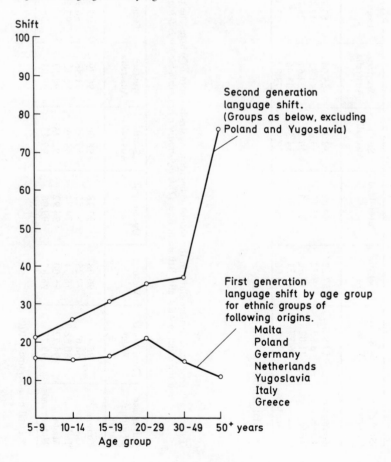

Joshua A. Fishman

The Lively Life of a "Dead" Language
(or "Everyone Knows that Yiddish Died Long Ago")*

An unlikely scenario

Let us imagine a highly unlikely scenario. A small people is forced to leave its
homeland, partially as a result of repeated military debacles and partially as a
result of severely and recurringly unfavorable economic conditions. It scatters
initially, primarily throughout the Euro-Mediterranean world, and, subsequently, over a period of milennia, even further afield. Over the centuries,
many of its sons and daughters are lost to it, due to persecution, forced
conversion and quiet 'passing'; nevertheless, a huge proportion remain identified with their ethnocultural heritage. Notwithstanding the adverse circumstances of its bearers, the heritage continues to evolve and to attain marvelous
heights of religious, philosophical and literary creativity throughout the
centuries and in various parts of the globe, indeed, wherever its bearers
succeed in maintaining their own daily lifestyle, social institutions and social
boundaries. The people whom we are imagining are therefore triply miraculous. Its conquerors perish and pass into oblivion while it itself somehow
'muddles through' one cataclysmic reversal after another. In its dispersion, its
non-communicating branches become greatly dissimilar and, for periods, even
unaware of each other, and yet they do not lose their sense of ultimate
unity. Its culture changes drastically (and differently in its various branches)
and yet it loses neither its creative élan nor its sense of ultimate continuity
vis-à-vis its original mainsprings.

The ethnolinguistic counterpart to the above highly improbable scenario is
equally miraculous. The people loses its original vernacular and creates
literally dozens of new ones while maintaining the original in sanctified and
textual functions. Several of its new vernaculars become subtle vehicles of
literary and philosophical expression and works of truly enduring value are
created in them. During the past milennium, one such vernacular in particular
was associated with exceptional heights. It was not only used as the language
of popular translation and of learned discourse with respect to hallowed texts
in the sanctified original language (all of its many new vernaculars were used
in this way and this use, therefore, drastically influenced all of their grammars

and their lexicons; Fishman 1981a), but it became the vehicle of their controlled modernization as well. Through this vehicle (let us call it New Vernacular), this people began to modernize in its own way, according to its
own lights, often with a sense of continuity with its own eternal values and
unique history. Modernization was a terribly dislocating ordeal for this people
(if it was such for peoples with governments, economies and armies of their
own, how much more so was it for a people that lacked all of the foregoing?),
splitting it apart into contentious splinters which finally undercut the
vernacular's own vitality. Yet all of these warring splinters not only initially
used this particular New Vernacular to reach and teach their constituencies
but they were themselves ultimately united by it, elevated by it and softened
by its links with intergenerational authenticity. Accordingly, this New
Vernacular became the vehicle for more modern schools for a huge branch of
this people, for a modern press of its own, for a theater of its own, for a
modern belleteristic literature of its own and for a modern art-and-song
repertoire of its own. Its major writers became names recognized and prized
the world over.

But the winds of change were too strong for this New Vernacular. Massive
exterminations, externally controlled modernization movements (benevolent
ones and malevolent ones) and an internal movement to return to its ancient
homeland and its ancient vernacular, all of them tore huge proportions of its
speakers away from it. Yet, just as the people has miraculously recovered
from its recent travail, so has the New Vernacular begun to get to its feet.
Bloodied but unbowed it has begun to peek forth again from the ultra-tradi-
tional and the ultra-modern circles which alone gave it a haven during its
worst tribulations. But in doing so, what does it find? It is greeted by many
of its own kin, by the children and grandchildren of its erstwhile speakers,
with a strange greeting. 'We thought you were dead,' they say to it. 'Why do
you return to disturb our peace? We owe you nothing. You have nothing to
give us any longer. The languages we now use relate us either to our
neighbors, to our jobs or to the world at large, on the one hand, and
(referentially at least, because we have not relearned our ancient tongue) to
our new-old land and its inhabitants. Be gone! Return to the dead where you
belong!' The New Vernacular—now old and struggling—weeps, but it continues to create. It is surrounded by a chorus proclaiming it to be dead, yet it
lives. Its widespread rejection only serves to make it some how more Jewish,
more worthy of rediscovery. It waits to be reclaimed, remembered,
rejuvenated.

Language death: objective and subjective

Setting metaphor aside, it is important to realize that the view that 'Yiddish is dead' (or 'should die') has quite a history behind it and is related to *much more general* intellectual and sociopolitical trends as well as to corresponding developments within the Jewish fold per se. Thus, from the very beginning of the 19th century, spokesmen for Western European capitalist political establishments trumpeted the death of Welsh and Irish, the passing of Breton and Occitan, and the demise of Flemish and of Frisian. When champions of all the above languages arose not only to deny their death but to foster their growth, these champions were attacked not only as debasers of civility and as plotters against public peace, but as necromancers as well! Communist spokesmen of the middle and latter nineteenth century were no better. They too had an incorporative, supra-ethnic goal in mind that, although it differed from that of Lord Acton or John Stuart Mill, was equally impatient of 'special pleading' on behalf of small languages and small peoples (see, e.g., Engels 1866). 'Remnants of peoples long gone by', 'never had a history nor the energy required to have one', 'absurdity', 'intermingled ruins . . . which even now the ethonoligst can scarcely disentangle', and 'intermixed in interminable confusion' are among the choice epithets hurled by self-serving 'internationalists' on the right and on the left at language communities seeking either political recognition or cultural democracy. 'Beauty is in the eyes of the beholder', but so is ugliness and death. The death-wish toward obstreperous minorities was barely disguised in the pronouncements of nineteenth century spokesmen for self-aggrandizing capitalism and proletarianism. It is only slightly better disguised today, even among liberals and co-ethnics, 'some of whose best friends' still speak minority languages and implement minority identities in one part or other of their total speech and identity repertoire. It is true, of course, that some languages do die away as a result of the dislocation of their speech communities (Dorian 1981), but many others have death wished upon them, projected unto them, diagnosed and predicted for them far in advance of, unrelated to and in objective disagreement with any objective change in the variety of their functions or in the numbers of their users. Yiddish is certainly a case in point.

When did Yiddish die?

The death of Yiddish begins to be announced (predicted, desired) in Germany in the late eighteenth and early nineteenth century. The major proponents of this death-wish were advocates of 'enlightenment' (Westernization, Euro-

peanization) within the ranks of German Jewry proper (e.g., Mendelssohn
1783), i.e. Jewish intellectuals who were most familiar with fashionable
non-Jewish thinking at the time. Indeed, non-Jews, too, derided the language
as uncounth, corrupt, ungrammatical and utterly laughable (Low 1979). Such
a 'jargon' was 'obviously' not long for this world, since, on the one hand, such
'jibberish' 'obviously' contributed to anti-Semitism, and, on the other hand,
'Germans of Moses' persuasion' required 'pure German' in order to discharge
their prospective roles as full-fledged citizens. As Western 'enlightenment'
(*haskole*) spread from Germany into Slavic Eastern Europe in mid-nineteenth
century, its views of Yiddish and of 'pure German' followed. Once more, the
demise of the language was both predicted and desired, by purveyors of elitist
controlled modernization (e.g. Feder 1853 [1816]), by Hebraists (Ahad
Ha-'Am 1910), by Zionists (see, e.g., Malakhi 1961 about N. Sokolov), by
socialists (see Tobias 1972 about the early Bund) and by out-and-out assimilationists (see Heller 1977). Nevertheless, the language did not die as was hoped
or predicted and all of its nineteenth century detractors finally needed to
apologetically make use of it in order to propogate their programmatic vies
among 'the masses', who really knew no other tongue well. Finally, Yiddish
also began to attract its overt champions and ideologists – both in traditional
(Bik 1833 [1815]) and secular (Lifshits 1863) circles – something no post-
exilic vernacular since Aramaic has succeeded in doing. While the holocaust
and Israel have displaced Yiddish from the center of the Jewish stage, it
continues as a sidestream that nourishes the tempest-tossed seas of Jewish
eternity.

Yiddish *did* ultimately fade away among most German Jews, but is was a
slow process, indeed, and its initial replacement was more often 'Ashkenazi
German' than 'pure German' (Wexler 1981, Freimark 1979, Lowenstein
1976). To the very end of the nineteenth century, many German Jews
continued to speak Yiddish informally with each other and it was not until
the rise of Hitlerism and the genocidal dislocations of the Second World War
that the last pockets of German Yiddish were uprooted in Alsace, Germany
proper and parts of Austria and Hungary. And if Yiddish did any dying in
Eastern Europe prior to being burnt alive in Nazi crematoria, it was only
because Soviet Communism began to suppress it ruthlessly in public life in
the mid-thirties. Otherwise, it continued to be massively spoken, written, read
and taught there with literally thousands of periodical publications (see e.g.,
Shavn 1963 and Fishman 1981a [pp. 29-31]), libraries (Meyer 1922), schools
(Kazhdan 1947, Parker 1981) and theaters (Zilbertsvayg 1931–1967) functioning in it throughout Poland, the Baltic states and Rumania and with well
over ten thousand writers and journalists all told! Nevertheless, the predic-
tions of doom continued throughout the entire pre-Hitler period, both among
those who envisaged holocausts from without as well as those who foretold
sociocultural change from within.

In America, the death theme repeated itself. The death of Yiddish was foretold by Leo Wiener (1972 [1899]), professor of Slavic and Germanic literatures at Harvard University, even prior to its major flowering on these shores (1910–1930). The theme was taken up by German Yahudim and by Jewish socialists fresh from the pale of settlement. Ultimately, it became a self-fulfilling prophecy. As was the case with nineteenth century German Jewry, Yiddish was drastically weakened in America by Jewish involvement in rapid urban-industrial-commercial-cultural mobility, on the one hand, and by 'progressive'/'liberal' studied assimilation on the other. While the myth of its death in the USA is vastly exaggerated, its general ill health cannot be denied. However, as I.B. Singer has pointed out, death and ill health are not the same thing and the motives of analysts who actually refer the former to the latter must be suspect, indeed.

How does Yiddish live today?

At this moment, there are slightly more than three million mother tongue claimants of Yiddish throughout the world, the bulk of whom reside either in the USA (roughly a million and a half), the Soviet Union (roughly half a million) or Israel (roughly half a million). Among those whose mother tongue is Yiddish, that language continues to be the major spoken language for some 100,000 individuals and a frequent auxiliary or secondary language for roughly twice as many. Obviously, the number of active *speakers* of the language is much smaller than the number who claim it as their *mother tongue*, but the ranks of the speakers will probably begin to increase again in another decade or two (Oxford et al. 1982). This last prediction is based on the fact that the bulk of its most active speakers are now restricted to ultra-Orthodox circles (non-Hasidic and Hasidic) and these—in contrast to those of the secular Yiddishists—are constantly growing in numbers, primarily due to natural increase (early marriage of the young and large families). Thus, barring further unpredictable world events (note the concentration of Yiddish speakers in high risk areas from the point of view of possible conventional and nuclear warfare), the number of Yiddish speakers may stabilize in the vicinity of a quarter million by the end of the 20th century and begin to expand again thereafter. This is the same order of magnitude that Yiddish possessed in early modern times, although, obviously enough, the historical context is far different now than it was then.

To the ranks of speakers of Yiddish there should also be added those who are learning Yiddish (outside of ultra-Orthodox and secular Yiddishist circles, whose ranks have already been counted above). Some 50–60 colleges and universities in the USA and a dozen or more in other countries (including Canada, France, Holland, Germany as well as all four of the major Israeli universities) now offer instruction in Yiddish. Yiddish is also part of the curriculum in some 1000 Jewish elementary and secondary schools, primarily in the USA (Pollack 1981), but also in Canada, Mexico, Argentina and Australia (indeed, the most intensive programs are in the latter four countries). In addition, instruction in Yiddish is also offered at over a dozen secular high schools in Israel. Although few students master Yiddish as a result of all of the above mentioned courses at various levels (not to mention the adult education Yiddish courses that are quite popular in the USA), their considerable numbers bespeak a lively interest, which increasingly spills out of the classroom per se into theaters, song recitals, open-air concerts and, lo and behold, even into book stores and lecture series.

Yiddish theater and Yiddish literature are still very much alive today and indeed, may be the two most visible representatives of ethnic America in both of these cultural arenas. Although the theater is neither quantitatively nor qualitatively anywhere near its mid-twenties to mid-thirties peak (Sandrow 1977), it has experienced some unanticipated growth in both respects in the past decade. This past season, three Yiddish plays were running for months in New York, two of which also toured the country. Yiddish theaters are also active in Montreal and Israel. State supported theaters are constantly playing in Warsaw and in Bucharest. Intermittent performances are reported from various Soviet cities, Paris, Brussels, Toronto, Buenos Aires and Mexico City. Usually overlooked on the theatrical front are the traditional efforts of the ultra-Orthodox, e.g., Purim plays (often for extremely large audiences) and morality plays for women and children, which are repeatedly advertised in the Orthodox press in New York, Antwerp, Jerusalem, Bnai Brak and elsewhere.

Yiddish literary efforts are still proceeding at a substantial pace. Well over a hundred books are published annually (see the annual listings in the Jewish Welfare Board's *Jewish Book Annual*) and first-rate talents of a calibre meriting world-wide attention (Issac Bashevis Singer, Avrohom Sutskever) are still creatively active, as are a host of smaller figures. Yiddish literature has always reached its public primarily via the Yiddish periodical press. This press today boasts five dailies, half a dozen weeklies and literally scores of monthlies and quarterlies, a total of 35 in the USA alone.

In each of the foregoing areas, some 'new blood' has recently been infused via the appearance on the scene of young, primarily secular, post-holocaust writers, teachers, actors, researchers and cultural activists. Their numbers are small (far too small to safeguard the continuity of all that currently exists, meager though even *that* may be relative to what *was* before the holocaust). Nevertheless, it is clear that there are heirs and that each of the above areas of cultural efforts will continue intergenerationally, albeit in more meager fashion and with *proportionately* greater ultra-Orthodox representation in the future than has been the case during the past century of superb secular creativity. The world of native speakers and writers is still there to be used as resources and informants for schools and theaters, for adults and youngsters who are willing to do more than 'bemoan' or even 'admire' Yiddish from a distance. We can still make Yiddish our own again. It is here. We are here. An active connection in terms of daily life is all that is needed to secure its role. Such an active personal connection at the level of daily life is more important than all of the 'institutions' that Yiddish still boasts, for even if there were no Yiddish schools today, no theaters and no periodicals at all, that would not necessarily be the end if the 'connection' in daily life was implemented.

Most languages of the world today exist without formal institutional supports and many of the languages that *do* have such institutions have fewer of them than Yiddish does. Whereas no one trumpets *their* demise, the demise of Yiddish has not only been predicted for nearly two centuries but in many quarters it has already been declared to have occurred. Its mysterious, miraculous élan vital, however, has been strangely ignored. It was this untold story that motivated me to put together my *Never Say Die!Loy omes ki ekhe!* (1981a). Jews continue to treat Yiddish (even after the holocaust and rebirth) the way the Christian and Moslem worlds have become accustomed to treat Jews: with denial, with death expectations, with death wishes.

Death: an unsatisfactory and unsavory metaphor

The recent difficulties encountered by physicians, lawyers and clerics with respect to defining life and death in *biological* terms (vis-à-vis abortion and/or 'right to life' legislation and rulings) should prepare us to suspect the utility of such metaphors for sociocultural systems such as languages and speech communities (Gallaher and Padfield 1980). Even for animal and plant life, the exact limits of life and death are hard to find and this is all-the-more so for sociocultural systems. However, the difficulties encountered are not merely with respect to limits (i.e. 'would Yiddish be dead if no one spoke, read, wrote or understood it, but if lots of people still loved it?') but with respect to the concepts of life and death themselves as applied to languages and sociocultural systems more generally. Animal and plant life are developmentally programmed to constantly approach an irrevocable and inevitable endpoint: death. Sociocultural systems have no such irrevocable and inevitable pre-programmed linear endpoint. Presumably 'dead' cultures/languages can become revived and rejuvenated. Presumably strong cultures/languages nevertheless change, amalgamate or fuse with others. Cultures/languages move backward as well as forward, experiencing nativization and purification movements. Languages and cultures not only detach themselves and separate from one another but also interpenetrate one another via pidginization and sycretism. All of these are alternatives that apply to the future of Yiddish as much as they do to the future of English or Swahili. Jewish culture has outlived Babylonian and Roman culture. Yiddish has outlived the international ascendancy of German and French. It may yet outlive other major languages that are even more exposed to the forefront of modern warfare and modern industry.

Languages gain and lose functions/speakers/readers/understanders/ admirers. At the same time they are changing differentially as to their lexical, semantic, grammatical and phonological characteristics. Indeed, language change is much more common than language death: the former being ubiquitous and the latter being merely indeterminately final. It is, indeed, a trite (and wicked) stereotype to speak of Yiddish in terms of death alone: (When did it die? When will it die? Why did it die? Why will it die?), an ethnopaulism every bit as much as 'dumb Pollacks', 'lazy niggers', 'promiscuous French girls', 'money-mad Jews' and 'thieving gypsies'. Little wonder, then, that Yiddish poets like Avrohm Zak have railed against the voodooistic conspiracy that proclaims the death of a language that is still alive and creative.

> *O neyn! mir zenen nit di letste,*
> *undzer yidish loshn vet ibergeyn*
> *nokh lang fun dor tsu dor*
> *Bekhinem di baveyners un umzist der kadish*
> *vos s'zingen oys kabronim in a khor.*

> (Oh no! we are not the last ones,
> Our Yiddish language will yet long be handed
> on from generation to generation
> For naught the lamentations and prayers for the dead
> That gravediggers sing forth in recitation!)

Obviously, the 'death of Yiddish' (and of other weak languages) has been vastly exaggerated, but why? Why is that death still proclaimed today, even by those who unconsciously enjoy its humor, its melody, its ethos, or at least by those who have no systematic ideological bias (e.g., Zionist, Hebraist, Communist, 'Progressive Thinker', Americanizer, social climber, 'Orthodoxy-too-can-be-modern') against it? Would its death free some from a sense of guilt due to responsibilities unmet?, loyalties betrayed?, identify undefended?, aggressors joined?, underdog unbefriended?, kith and kin denied? There is more here than meets the eye. 'Death' is not an idle phrase, an empty metaphor. As the rabbis have long taught: 'Language creates and destroys

worlds. Life and death depend on language.' When Yiddish is killed, more
than Yiddish is killed.

When culture-systems shatter

When culture-systems prosper, their members identify with each other. If the
systems are numerically large ones, their members must, of necessity, interact
more often at a purely referential level than in actuality, at a face to face
level. Their members must have the sense of being together, the impression of
acting in unison, more than is objectively the case. In any large community,
the number of 'others' that anyone actually interacts with overtly must be far
less than the total number of possible 'others'. Nevertheless, members believe
that they are in touch, in tune, in accord with one another, and a common
language fosters this impression. A common language preserves the *myth* of
interaction because it preserves the *possibility* of interaction via shared texts,
metaphors, songs, jokes, slogans, proverbs and other forms of linguistic
bonding. Without a common language, the various branches of the joint
ethno-community are cut off from each other referentially as well as
interactionally. Just as they were originally more *alive* to each other than
their actual experience confirmed, so they are subsequently more *dead* to
each other than is objectively true. Much of the claim that Yiddish is dead
merely reflects how dead it is to the claimants and how dead *they are* to its
continued speakers. As in the case of the 'God is dead' movement, the
'Yiddish is dead' chorus merely proclaims that it is dead for those who have
cut themselves off from 'the source', i.e. it is dead for those who are dead to
it.

The progression from Gemeinschaft to Gesellschaft, from intimate community to megalopolis, had deadened us all in part. It is not only no longer
possible to feel each neighbor's pain, but we steel ourselves neither to feel the
pain of those whose pain we *could* still feel nor, indeed, to feel *our own* pain
overly much. Gesellschaft makes us more superficially aware of more others,
but it also makes us fundamentally 'more deeply dead' to more others and
makes more of them 'more deeply dead' to us. No wonder, when we do not see
the agony and misery that shouts out to us from the poverty pockets that we
pass *every day*, that Yiddish, too, is dead, since most of us encounter secular
or Hasidic Yiddish so rarely if at all. We cannot understand it. We do not
hear it. We do not interact with those who speak it ('They all know English
now, you know', we console ourselves irrelevantly and inaccurately). We
have lost or forgotten what we have in common with them. The very fast that
Yiddish *lives* amongst 'them' becomes a confirmatory sign of how *dead* it is

for us; in our fantasy it is dead. However, the world of Yiddish, shrunken through ist is, continues at its own rate and its own direction. It has schools (for children), it has periodical and book publications (even periodical publications for children, and several new adult periodical publications have been added in the past few years), it has movies (even several new movies made in the past few years), it has radio and television programs in large cities throughout the country (15 to be exact), it has courses at the college and university levels, it has several smallish but innovative foundations supporting and cultivating it. Nevertheless, the imagery of death surrounds it for 'progressive thinkers', for socially mobile Jews (afraid of unleashing in themselves their parents' sarcasm and their grandparents' humor), for Gentiles who have been brainwashed by 'some of their best friends' who seek nothing more than the anonymity of full assimilation, for Jews who have gone on to more stylish and more successful Jewish causes, for Jews who cannot speak (and for many who cannot pray in) Hebrew but who are convinced that if Jews *do* need a language of their own nowadays it should be Hebrew ('because of Israel, you know'). Yes, it is dead to them, but it is hard to know whose tragedy is greater: that of the language that has been robbed of its children or that of the children whose ties to their roots have been sundered. Yes, Ashkenazi Jews can live without Yiddish, but I fail to see what the benefits thereof might be. (May God preserve us from having to live without all the things we *could* live without). At best, proclaiming Yiddish to be dead is a kind of 'sour grapes' existence; at worst, it is a kind of self isolation from a rich area of potential feeling, identity and creativity. It is similar to the behavior of the rich recluse who never touches his money. It is a case of living death but not for Yiddish as much as for those who deny themselves of its riches. Indeed, Yiddish and those who still live with it can withstand adversity ever so much better than can mainstream American Jewry (Bertrand 1980). Yiddish itself is symbolic of both Jewish adversity and Jewish triumph over adversity. The struggle against adversity is its self-renewing essence.

What is 'archaic' and why?

Yiddish, like other presumably dead languages is often proclaimed to be linguistically archaic (vis-à-vis German or Hebrew) This judgment is passed with a smug, self-satisfied ignorance that always typifies the top-dog relative to the underdog. 'My language is strong; therefore it is not archaic. That language is weakening; therefore it is archaic.' The underlying syllogism runs as follows: Old organisms die. Weak organisms die. Therefore, weak organisms must be old (archaic). The argument is clinched by citing various examples of lexical items that are still present in Yiddish but are no longer present in modern German or Hebrew. However, the 'archaic' argument is as fallacious as the 'dead' argument and is as self-serving to boot.

Languages change at approximately equal rates if exposed to approximately the same influences. The relative rate of change of two languages cannot be gauged by comparing the number of *unchanged* elements (archaisms) in one with the number of *changed* elements (modernisms) in the other. In order to compare Yiddish and Hebrew (or German) as to their archaism they might both be examined relative to their lexical base 400–500 years ago. What proportion of the 'elements' in a modern Yiddish novel were present in the *Shmuel-bukh* or in the *Rovo-bukh* of the fifteenth and sixteenth centuries? What proportion of the 'elements' of a modern English novel were present in Shakespeare's plays? What proportion of the 'elements' of a modern Hebrew novel were present in the *Shulkhan-aroch* or another such popular work of the sixteenth century? I don't know what the results of such comparisons would be because no such empirical comparisons have ever been attempted. My impression is that Yiddish may have changed every bit as much as English in the intervening 400 years and that Hebrew, having been largely in bookish hibernation during most of this period will have changed least of all. If my impression is correct, then obviously the state of health of a language and its 'relative archaism' would be totally unrelated to each other. Indeed, change in a language is related to change in functions and to increase in rate of interaction with other languages. However, both of the foregoing processes can also serve to weaken a language.

Impressions of 'archaicity' (to coin a term and to add to the innovativeness of English) are often derived from locating 'elements' in language/dialect A which were once also present in (indeed borrowed from) language/dialect B but which are no longer encountered in the latter. However, such impressions are misleading since they do not inquire as to how many of the once-shared elements in A and B are *still* shared; nor do they inquire as to how many of the once-shared elements are now present only in B and are no longer present in A. Obviously, attending to shared elements alone (once-shared vis-à-vis now-shared) is *not* a good overall measure of archaicity. The once-shared elements may belong disproportionately to a traditional (i.e. relatively unchanging) facet of life in one or another of the two languages and, accordingly they would change relatively little in that particular language. Nevertheless, the language as a whole, outside of that traditional facet might be changing at quite a different rate. Nevertheless, unsatisfactory though this approach might be as a reflection of overall change, it would be a better empirical check on 'impressions of relative archaicity' than no empirical checks at all.

Unfortunately, unsupported impressions, based on purposively selected examples of unknown representativeness, are all that are usually offered in pronouncements as to the purported archaicity of weaker or less prestigeful languages/dialects. As my mother used to say: *Af an avngefalenem ployt shpringen ale tsign* ('All the goats jump upon a fence that has fallen down'). It is easy to pick on weak languages. They have few defenders. However, *accusing* them of archaicity (or of being dead) and *proving* it are two quite different things. Proof takes more time and effort and most accusers are of the hit-and-run variety. They are accustomed to immediate gratification rather than to the perils of study design, data collection, data analysis and data interpretation. In the absence of data, the archaic features of generally modernized and vibrant languages and the modernized features of generally traditional and weakening languages both remain conveniently unnoticed. The entire stereotypic charge of relative archaicity, therefore, remains unproven and, very much like the stereotype 'dead' or 'dying', is often little more than a self-aggrandizing or self-protective view based more upon ignorance and bias than upon evidence and discipline.

Concluding sentiments

The natural life sequence of an individual is completed when he or she dies. The natural life sequence of a culture, on the other hand, is completed when the culture proves itself *intergenerationally continuous*. It is as unnatural for a culture to die as for an individual never to die. Cultures and their accompanying languages never die naturally; they *are* killed (by uncontrolled sociocultural change). Indeed, no Jewish cultural features have ever 'just died'; they have been dispersed, murdered, gassed, burnt and buried alive but they have never 'just died'. This applies as much to Yiddish as it does to all other aspects of Jewish life.

A century ago it seemed that it was necessary for Jews to choose either modernity or tradition, either secularism or religion, either their Jewish vernacular or the co-territorial vernacular, either the diaspora or Zion, either social mobility or social justice. Each choice inevitably involved a corresponding rejection. Jews identified themselves as much by what they rejected as by what they selected. But after a century of terrible suffering, at our own hands only slightly less than at the hands of murderers, the time for ingathering and integration has surely come. We now know we can combine both modernism and tradition, secularism and religion, diaspora-positiveness and Israel-positiveness, mobility aspirations and justice aspirations. Surely, then, the time has come to admit Yiddish back into the parlor where all other

Jewish verities are gathered. If we cannot learn it ourselves, our children or grandchildren can do so. If we cannot understand it, we can at least cherish it. If we cannot laugh and cry and sing with it, we can at least long for it.[1] Yiddish will contribute handsomely to all the other Jewish commitments that we espouse. I say this as an observant Orthodox Jew whose Jewishness encompasses ever so much more than Yiddish alone but, also, ever so much more than Gemora-and-halakha as the be-all and end-all for the intellectual, ideological, aesthetic and daily life needs of modern Jewry. Was there ever an elementary truth more generally overlooked than the following: With Yiddish our Jewish experiences will be fuller, more throbbing, more colorful, more varied, more continuous, more authentic than they will be without Yiddish. *Aza yor of mir, aza yor af aykh, aza yor af undz alemen!*

Notes

* Preparation of this paper was made possible by NSF Grant BNS 79–06055 (Division of Linguistics) on behalf of 'A Study of the Minority Language Resources of the United States'. This article first appeared in 1982–83. *Judaica Book News*, vol. 13, no. 1.

1. American Jewry's disinterest in Yiddish is in some ways a reflection of its American rather than its Jewish heritage. It is an expression of mainstream America's lack of language loyalty, language consciousness, language sentiment, even insofar as English is concerned. Language advocacy–particularly non-English language advocacy–is plain silliness as far as most Americans (and by extension most American Jews) are concerned. But our shallow, lumpen-Americanism impoverishes us Jewishly in this respect as in many others.

References

Ahad ha-'Am. 1910. Riv leshonot [Language struggle]. *Ha-Shiloah*, 22, 159-164.
Bertrand, Alvin L. 1980. Ethnic and social class minorities in the dying small community. In Gallaher, Art, Jr. and Harland Padfield (eds.), The *Dying Community*. Albuquerque: University of New Mexico Press, 187-206.
Bik, Yankev Shmuel. 1833. [Letter to Tuvye Feder in defense of Mendl Lefin-Santanover and the Yiddish language] [1815]. *Kerem Hemed*, 1, 96-99.
Dorian, Nancy C. 1981. *Language Death*. Philadelphia: University of Pennsylvania Press.
Engels, F. 1866. What have the working classes to do with Poland? *Commonwealth*, March 24, March 31 and May 5.
Feder, Tuvye. 1853. *Kol Mehazezim* [Cry of the Archers]. [1816]. Lemberg.
Fishman, Joshua A. (ed.). 1981a. *Never Say Die! A Thousand Years of Yiddish in Jewish Life and Letters*. The Hague-Paris-New York: Mouton.
1981b. The sociology of Jewish languages from the perspective of the general sociology of language. *International Journal of the Sociology of Language*, 30, 5-18.
Freimark, Peter. 1979. Language behavior and assimilation: the situation of the Jews in Northern Germany in the first half of the nineteenth century. *Leo Baeck Institute Year Book*, 24, 157-177.

Gallaher, Art Jr. and Harland Padfield (eds.). 1980. *The Dying Community*. Albuquerque: University of New Mexico Press.

Heller, Celia. 1977. Assimilationists: Poles in culture and self-identity; in her *On the Edge of Destruction*. New York: Columbia University Press, 183-210.

Kazhdan, Kh. Sh. 1947. *Di geshikhte fun yidishn shulvezn in umophengikn polyn* [The History of Jewish School Systems in Independent Poland]. Mexico City, Kultur un Hilf. (See the table on p. 549 for the statistical distribution of Yiddish schools in 1934-35.)

Lifshits, Y.M. 1863. Di fir klasn [The four classes]. *Kol mevaser*, 323-328, 364-366, 375-380.

Low, Alfred D. 1979. *Jews in the Eyes of the Germans*. Philadelphia, ISHI.

Lowenstein, Steven. 1976. The pace of modernization of German Jewry in the nineteenth century. *Leo Baeck Institute Year Book*, 21, 41-56.

Malakhi, A.R. 1961. Nokhem sokolov un di yidishe shprakh [Nokhem Sokolov and the Yiddish language]. *Ikuf-alamakh*, 466-493.

Mendelssohn, Moses. 1783. *Or la-netiva* [Light on the Path]. Berlin.

Meyer, D. 1922. Yidishe bibliotekn in poyln [Jewish libraries in Poland]. *Bikhervelt* 1922, 1, nos. 4-5, 467-475. Also see his initial study: Bibliotekvezn: di bibliotekn af der provints. [Library World: libraries in the provinces]. *Bikhervelt*, 1, no. 3, 331-335.

Mill, John Stuart. 1910 [1859]. *Utilitarianism, Liberty and Representative Government*. New York: Dutton.

Oxford, Rebecca, Louis Pol, David Lopez, Paul Stupp, Murray Gendell and Samuel Peng. 1981. Projections of non-English language background and limited English proficient persons in the United States to the year 2000: Educational planning in the demographic context. *NABE Journal*, 5, no. 3, 1-30.

Parker, Sandra. 1981. An educational assessment of the Yiddish secular school movements in the United States, in J.A. Fishman (ed.), *Never Say Die! A Thousand Years of Yiddish in Jewish Life and Letters*. The Hague: Mouton, 495-512.

Pollack, George. 1981. Teaching Yiddish in Jewish schools, June 1981. *Better Personnel Practices* (American Association for Jewish Education), no. 50.

Sandrow, Nahma. 1977. *Vagabond Stars: A World History of Yiddish Theatre*. New York: Harper and Row.

Shayn, Yisroel. 1963. Materialn tsu a bibliografye fun yidisher periodike in poyln, 1918-1939 [Toward a bibliography of Yiddish periodica in Poland, 1918-1939], in J.A. Fishman (ed.), *Shtudyes vegn yidn in poyln, 1919-1939* [Studies on Polish Jewry, 1919-1939]. New York, YIVO Institute for Jewish Research, 1974, 422-483. (Also see his earlier *Bibliografye fun oysgabes aroysgegebn durkh di arbeter parteyen in poyln in di yom 1918-1939* [Bibliography of Publications Issued by the Workers' Parties in Poland in the Years 1918-1939]. Warsaw: Yidishbukh.

Tobias, Henry J. 1972. *The Jewish Bund in Russia from its Origin to 1905*. Stanford: Stanford University Press.

Wexler, Paul. 1981. Ashkenazic German, 1760-1895. *International Journal of the Sociology of Language*, 30, 119-132.

Wiener, Leo. 1972 [1899]. *The History of Yiddish Literature in the Nineteenth Century*. New York, Hermon Press (Introduction by Elias Schulman).

Zilbertsvayg, Zalmen. 1931-1967. *Teater entsiklopedye* [Theater Encyclopedia]. Six volumes. Warsaw-Mexico City.

Glossary

Ashkenazi, adjectival form derived from Ashkenazim, Jews who trace their ancestry back to Central or Eastern European Jewish communities, as contrasted with Sephardi, adjectival from derived from Sephardim, Jews who trace their ancestry back to Spanish or Portuguese Jewish communities. Each of these Jewish cultures has its own rite and its own vernacular (Yiddish and Judezmo).

Purim plays are amateur performances that occur on or near the celebration of Purim, the holiday (end of February/beginning of March) commemorating the deliverance of the Jews in accord with the account in the Old Testament Book of Esther. Purim plays constitute indigenous Jewish folk art that began in early medieval times. They are traditionally performed by male actors and deal with such themes as the story of Purim, the selling of Joseph into slavery in Egypt, etc.

Hasidic, adjectival form derived from Hasidism, a movement founded in eighteenth century Poland which encourages joyous religious expression through music and dance (in contrast to the more academic formalism of rabbinic Judaism). Originally considered a heresy, Hasidism is today one of the major mainstays of Orthodox Jewry.

Tables

Table 1: *Estimated Yiddish mother tongue incidence, 1980.*

Country	Total Jewish Population (TJP)*	Yiddish Mother Tongue (YMT)	Approximate *Ratio* YMT/TJP
1. *Europe*			
Austria	13,000	2,600	.20
Belgium	41,000	8,200	.20
Czechoslovakia	13,000	2,600	.20
Denmark	7,500	1,500	.20
Finland	1,320	265	.20
France	650,000	97,500	.15
Germany (East Germany, West Germany and both sections of Berlin)	34,000	6,800	.20
Great Britain	410,000	61,500	.15
Hungary	80,000	24,000	.30
Ireland	4,000	800	.20
Italy	39,000	7,800	.20
Netherlands	30,000	6,000	.20
Poland	6,000	1,800	.30
Rumania	60,000	18,000	.30
Sweden	16,000	3,200	.20
Switzerland	21,000	4,200	.20
U.S.S.R.	2,678,000	535,600	.20
Other Europe	–	2,000	–

2. *America*

Canada	305,000	91,500	.30
Mexico	37,500	11,250	.30
United States	5,781,000	1,500,000	.25
Argentina	300,000	90,000	.30
Bolivia	2,000	600	.30
Brazil	150,000	50,000	.30
Chile	35,000	10,500	.30
Colombia	12,000	3,600	.30
Ecuador	1,000	300	.30
Peru	5,200	1,550	.30
Uruguay	50,000	15,000	.30
Venezuela	15,000	4,500	.30
Other America	–	2,000	–

3. *Asia*

Israel	3,076,000	450,000	.15
Other Asia	–	500	–

4. *Australia and New Zealand*

Australia	70,000	21,000	.30
New Zealand	5,000	1,500	.30

5. *Africa*

Republic of South Africa	118,000	35,400	.30
Other Africa	–	1,000	–
Worldwide Total:	14,286,620	3,072,065	.22

* *American Jewish Yearbook* 1979, Estimated Jewish Population 1977.

SECTION TWO: LANGUAGE PLANNING AND DEVELOPMENT

LANGUAGE STANDARDIZATION AND EDUCATIONAL PLANNING: OVERT AND COVERT INFLUENCES

Franklin C. Southworth

The Social Context of Language Standardization in India

In the last chapter of his book *Language*, Leonard Bloomfield suggests a relationship between language and social status, and implies that the acquisition of the latter can be assisted by the manipulation of the former (or that this is at least a common belief):

> The background of our popular ideas about language is the fanciful doctrine of the eighteenth-century "grammarians" .... It is no accident that the "grammarians" arose when they did. During the eighteenth and nineteenth centuries our society went through great changes; many persons and families rose into relatively privileged positions and had to change from non-standard to standard speech (Bloomfield 1933: 496-7).

What may not be clear from Bloomfield's discussion of this point is that the very idea of a 'standard' language—a single, uniform variety which serves as a model of usage for everyone in a society, and which everyone is supposed to be able to learn—was a very new idea at that time. Up until the mid-eighteenth century or so, such an idea would have been meaningless, since the class structure was quite rigid, the speech habits (as well as other social customs) of different social classes were often sharply different, and there was in general no reason to expect a member of one class to learn the speech of another. The speech of each group was considered appropriate to that group and its activities: thus, for example, upper-class speech was the language of education, since only the upper classes were educated.

The changes which Bloomfield discusses did not come about merely as the result of changes in the fortunes of particular families. Rather, it was the result of changes in the mode of production, as western Europe moved from a feudal to a capitalist stage, which brought greater economic—and ultimately political—power to the emerging bourgeoisie. During the late eighteenth and early nineteenth centuries there was a partial lessening of the rigidity of class barriers in England, as the rising business class attempted to gain social prestige which had long been denied them. In this context the new democratic ideology, encouraged by the revolutions of the late eighteenth century, justified the members of the mercantile class in aspiring to membership in a class to which they had not been born. (This is not to say that nobody ever had such an idea previously, but rather that in earlier periods it was mostly restricted to isolated individuals.) The re-organization of the power structure, and the drastic changes in social relations that resulted from the full-fledged development of capitalism and the emergence of democratic ideals (whether realised or not), must have played a major part in the growth of the idea of a single 'standard' which could be adopted by all members of the society.

Traditionally, language was one of a number of forms of social behavior which kept people 'in their place'. The new democratic ideology holds that this kind of difference can and should be eliminated by universal education. It is merely(?) a matter of selecting, or if necessary creating, an appropriate standard language, and then plugging it into a system of mass education. In many of the new nations of the world, particularly the ex-colonial countries which have recently attained independence, this is precisely what has been attempted. These nations have tried to go from a stage comparable to that of pre-eighteenth-century England, in which there was no idea of a standard language (in the sense defined above), directly to a new 'democratic' stage, by means of mass education and adult literacy campaigns. If we look at the results now, for example in India (independent since 1947), we may ask how much movement there has been in the desired direction. What I will attempt to show in the remainder of this essay is not only that the amount of movement has been disappointingly small, but that the reasons for this result are not primarily (or at least not exclusively) lack of resources, or governmental inefficiency, or any such convenient factors. The result is, in a sense, intentional—in that, in spite of a democratic ideology which upholds the principle of equality through education, other ideological principles (derived from other sources) conflict with this ideal to such an extent as to nearly nullify it.[1] First, however, it will be useful to look at the main types of linguistic variability found in India, and the attitudes toward them, in earlier periods as well as the present.

Linguistic variation

India has long been a rich source of data on all kinds of linguistic variation. *Regional* variation (local 'dialects') is mentioned in the earliest grammatical treatises, and is shown to exist by the inscriptions of King Ashoka (mid-third century B.C.), written in different local forms of Prakrit.[2] In the modern scene, there are regional variants of all the major languages,[3] and in some cases there is wide divergence between forms of speech which are regarded as 'dialects' of the same language. Local forms of eastern and western Hindi, as well as northern and southern forms of Tamil, for example, are different enough from each other to make communication between them quite difficult.[4] *Social* variation (differences in speech correlating with socio-economic class, caste, occupation, sex, age, etc., within the same geographic region) has been widely documented in India.[5] In rural areas, particularly in south India, it is still possible to see remnants of the earlier situation. In many parts of the south, the speech of both the highest (Brahman) and the lowest (untouchable)[6] castes is still sharply distinct from that of the intermediate castes, which tend to be more like each other because of frequent interaction.[7] The Tamil spoken in Brahman homes, for example, is different in its phonology and verbal morphology from that of other castes, and also (because of the Brahmans' association with Sanskrit ritual) tends to use many Sanskrit-derived terms.[8]

Stylistic variation (the use of different linguistic varieties by the same individual in different social contexts) is, like the other types of variation discussed above, also referred to in ancient sources. Patanjali, a Sanskrit grammarian of the first century *B.C.* notes that a learned man is expected to use one form of speech in addressing another learned man, and a different form in talking to women and children who have no knowledge of Sanskrit. The grammatical tradition also distinguishes sharply between the language of worldly affairs and that of the Vedic sacrifices—which was of course a rigidly codified ritual language, and was in fact a 'dead' language in Patanjali's time (i.e., it was no longer anyone's native language). Stylistic variation is found in most languages of the world and is found in very marked form in a number of Indian languages. Perhaps the most extreme cases are Tamil and Bengali, in which the variety used for formal writing and discourse is as different from that of ordinary conversation as, say, Shakespearean English is from modern spoken English.[9] Other cases are less extreme, but in most of the major languages of India the differences between conversational and formal styles of language is probably more marked than it is, say, in most modern European languages.

Attitudes toward linguistic variation

Though from the point of view of linguistic science all varieties (regional, social, or stylistic) of a language have equal status and are all equally worthy of study, such a view is clearly not shared by most members of any society. In fact, there is usually one variety which is widely regarded as the 'best' form of the language, and which is used to the exclusion of others for most public or formal purposes. The extent of agreement on the standard variety (including its official name, and at least some of its identifying characteristics) is high in most contemporary societies. This is impressive because (if for no other reason) this consensus is shared by many people who do not really know the standard form, not only by those fortunate enough to have learned it at home or in school. Most individuals also accept without question the general principle that there can only be *one* standard—just as there can be only one king in a monarchy, one president or prime minister in a democracy, and only one seat of government in each political entity. A related principle, also accepted implicitly, is that the 'standard' form of a language must be defined within very rigid limits. Some usages are 'correct', others are 'incorrect'.

If we look at the actual *behavior* of people in contemporary stratified societies, we see a different picture. Whatever people's expressed or unexpressed views toward 'correct' language may be, when they *use* language they tend to use a variety which is *appropriate to the context*. The choice of the appropriate variety is often made without much conscious thought, but analysis of stylistic variation shows that people respond to a complex array of situational cues in making these choices. For example, a formal speech or lecture requires a different style of speech than, say, an informal conversation about a football game. (Apart from differences in the *content*, there would be many linguistic differences such as the length and complexity of sentences, the use of formal words (such as *therefore* or *consequently*) in the one case, and informal expressions like *Hey... or y'know...* in the other.)[10] The usual view of language, including the official view of educational and other governmental institutions, has no place for this notion of appropriateness. There is, in the usual conception, a variety of language which is 'proper' or 'pure' or 'correct'; all others are either 'incorrect' or 'colloquial' or 'slang' or 'corrupt' or 'low-class' or 'local' or something of the sort.

Even among educated Indians, in spite of the great amount of contextual variability which almost all participate in, this type of 'one-standard' notion tends to prevail. The fact that different varieties may be used in different situations is commonly explained in terms of 'not needing' to use a formal variety in a particular context: for example, a businessman does not "need" to use *šuddh hindii* in an informal discussion with colleagues. The notion that it would be *inappropriate* to use it in this situation (because it would create an undesirable social distance between the participants), though perhaps understandable when explained, is not the explanation that first occurs to people.

Over the past twenty-odd years, I have talked with Indians from many different backgrounds about this question of appropriate language, especially about the use of language in *new* contexts. For Indians in many regions, even the idea of printed matter in their own language—magazines, newspapers, books, billboards—is only two or three generations old. Every schoolchild who is the first in his or her family to go to school is meeting language in new contexts. The idea of a monthly magazine aimed at agricultural workers, for example, is totally new, since in the past there were no literate agricultural workers. The tendency in India today, however, is to consider all uses of written language to be the same, and to require the most formal and 'correct' variety of language for all of them; the same is true to a large extent of material broadcast over the radio, since this is considered a public use of language.[11] The suggestion that written language could be made closer to ordinary spoken language is almost universally rejected by educated people.

Here, briefly, are some of the major arguments I have encountered in support of this trend. The argument heard most often is, on the surface, an esthetic one: formal or public language should look or sound 'right'. This attitude is hard to escape for anyone who has received a formal education (in *any* society), where teachers are primarily concerned with the *form* of language and hardly at all with *content*. (Students who express themselves spontaneously. and originally, but in somewhat 'incorrect' language, are regarded as poorer students than those who write dull and unoriginal sentences in "correct' form).[12] Thus one implication of this argument is that 'correct' language serves, among others, the purpose of showing that one is educated. And after all, if one has taken the trouble to get an education—especially in a society where the majority are uneducated—one would like it to show. Thus we find schoolchildren in Hindi-speaking villages introducing highflown words like *parantu* 'but' (instead of normal *lekin*) or *tathaa* 'and' (instead of the usual *aur*) into their conversation when talking in public places. Another very common reaction I have met, in response to the suggestion that written language could be made closer to ordinary spoken languages, is the following: 'Do you want us all to talk like taxi drivers?' (Taxi drivers in India, as a matter of fact, are usually at least literate, and I have met some who are moderately knowledgeable and articulate. The point of this argument, however, is clearly that people of high social status should speak in such a way that no one could possibly mistake them for taxi drivers).

The notion that a more colloquial variety of language could be used in adult literacy programs is sometimes regarded as implying that one should 'talk down' to people: 'Shouldn't we bring them up to the standard, instead of bringing the standard down to them?' The result of this line of thinking is that uneducated laborers are given the task of learning a totally new vocabulary at the same time that they are facing the difficult task of learning to read and write. Another argument encountered in this connection is that, since spoken language differs according to region, caste and class, only the regional standard language can reach all the people. How, then, we may ask, has the movie industry managed to solve this problem? (See below for more on this point).

Two other arguments, both of a political nature, should be mentioned. All modern Indian languages contain words of English, Persian, and other origins, largely as a result of the centuries of foreign rule. It is the fashion nowadays to replace many of these words, even those in common use, by Sanskrit-derived words (many of them newly coined for the purpose).[13] Of course, if new technical terms are being introduced, the source is immaterial since in any case they are new words, but when words in general use are replaced, the result is to make the language less accessible to those who have no formal education.[14] Such a policy is defended, first of all, the basis of nationalistic feeling, which demands the removal of these linguistic leftovers of the colonial period—even at the cost of making the language more difficult for the majority of people. A related argument is that the use of Sanskritic vocabulary unites the different regional languages, since the earlier (pre-British) written forms of most languages contained many Sanskrit-derived words. This again is a politically interesting argument, since in fact it was only the *elite* class dialects which contained large amounts of Sanskritic vocabulary. Thus, while this argument might be valid in the long term (i.e., after universal mass education has been in effect for at least a generation), the immediate effect can only be to reinforce the unity of the elite groups all over the country (who are in fact already united by their knowledge of English), while at the same time increasing the gulf between elite and non-elite in each region.

Traditional views of language

The Sanskrit grammatical tradition, of whom Panini (fifth century *B.C.*) was the most famous exponent is widely credited with being the first scientific study of grammar. Modern linguists often speak admiringly of this tradition, but few have considered the social context in which it was created. According to Patanjali, the study of grammar has as its motive the preservation of the Vedas, the learning of proper language for use in the sacrifice, the avoidance of barbaric speech, the preservation of one's proper status, and related purposes. The use of proper grammar leads to heaven, whereas improper grammar can lead to defeat, can nullify (or even reverse) the effects of a sacrifice, and even in some circumstances cause the death of the speaker. Tradition tells us that the Brahman grammarians taught Sanskrit to the sons (not the daughters) of upper-caste families, in circumstances which prevented even accidental hearing by low-caste people (usually in the home of the Brahmaan *guru*, which could not be approached by members of lower castes). Drastic penalties were prescribed for members of lower castes who either heard or spoke any words of the Vedas. Thus the Vedic sacrifice and the associated ritual language, both symbols of elite status, were effectively monopolized by the highest class and the upper castes. There appears to have been, then, in that early period of Indian history, a social motivation behind the establishment of a grammatical tradition, of a type similar to that described by Bloomfield in the passage quoted above.

The linguistic empire of the Brahman *gurus* was first seriously challenged by the Buddhists, Jains, and other social reformers, beginning around the sixth century *B.C.* Wishing to reach the widest possible audience, they used popular forms of language both in speaking and writing. But orthodox Hinduism ultimately triumphed over all these reformist sects, and Sanskrit re-established itself as the main language of literature, ritual, and administration.[15] Around the tenth century *A.D.*, another wave of religious reform was responsible for the creation of literary forms of modern Indian languages such as Bengali and Marathi. With the coming of the Moghuls, Persian became the main administrative language in most of the country, as well as a widely-used medium of court literature and wider oral communication (especially in army camps and bazaars). By the time British rule was consolidated in the nineteenth century, English had become the predominant language of administration. Formal education, and law, as well as an important commercial and journalistic medium.

The British educational system created an English-speaking elite to man the colonial civil service, and the traditional Sanskrit-based elite faded into the background (except for those, such as many Tamil Brahmans, who took to the new English education). Only people who had the means, of course, could get this education, and so it led to no major changes in the make-up of the elite group. English education has remained, up to the present day, as an important means of acquiring or maintaining high socioeconomic status in India.

Contemporary India

Beginning before Indian Independence in 1947, and with great rapidity since that time, the regional vernacular languages have been replacing English in the administrative, educational, journalistic, and (to some extent) legal spheres— apart from their importance as languages of literature and oral communication (including the radio and the cinema, and recently television). The home languages of the urban-based elite in each region have now become official state languages, as well as media of formal education up through the college level (though English is still an alternative at all levels, at least in some urban areas). Even before their promotion to official status, these elite varieties were substantially different from the various colloquial forms used by the majority of speakers in each region.[16] The process of 'standardization' has removed them even further from normal conversational speech, primarily by the introduction of huge doses of new vocabulary (see above). The following paragraphs describe the situation in three important linguistic regions of the country.

Hindi. The current 'standard' Hindi is the official language of the Hindi-speaking states,[17] as well as the official national language of India.[18] This language, as used in government documents, textbooks, newspapers, and radio programs, is probably not comprehensible to the majority of inhabitants of the Hindi area.[19] Das Gupta and Gumperz have discussed the socio-political background of the creation of the new Hindi, showing that in the conflict between liberal national leaders, like M.K. Gandhi and Pandit Jawaharlal Nehru, and conservative politicians from the Hindi region, it was the latter's view of how the new language should be shaped which ultimately triumphed.[20] From the point of view of education in this new language. Das Gupta and Gumperz make the following statement:

> . . . the new grammatical differences between colloquial and literary Hindi resulting from recent language reform materially add to the ordinary speaker's task of learning literary Hindi. Many of the new rules are irregular. . . . Considerable exposure time is required before such rules can be mastered . . . those who have been exposed to the present form of literary Hindi as part of their family background have considerable advantage in the educational system (Das Gupta and Gumperz 1968: 163).

The new Hindi as developed by pandits and politicians, is one of the most important tools in the struggle to oust English from its position of importance in government, commerce, and elsewhere. Hindi-speaking politicians have been able to use this issue to strengthen their local political base, since the replacement of English by Hindi means more jobs (both in the state and central administrations) for Hindi-knowing people.[21] The policy of Sanskritizing Hindi is also popular with many because it shows that an Indian language can be independent of English and other international languages in terms of its vocabulary.

The irony of this situation is that there exists a fairly widely-understood form of Hindi, namely that which is used in the cinema and in the armed services. This is basically identical with what Gandhi called 'Hindustani'. It is a *lingua franca* which grew in a fairly natural way starting in army camps, bazaars, and other places where people from different regions had to communicate with each other. The popularity of the Hindi cinema does not, of course, guarantee that the language is completely understood by everyone who goes to the movies, since the plots of most movies can be understood, and the songs enjoyed, with a minimum knowledge of the language. Nevertheless, this widely-used variety would have provided a more viabl? basis for mass communication and universal education than the current Sanskritised Hindi. Apart from the fact that colloquial Hindi has borrowed a significant proportion of its vocabulary from non-Indian sources (as most cosmopolitan languages have done throughout history), the very fact that it *is* a popular language used by people of different social and regional background seems to have worked against its candidacy for official status.

Marathi. Outside of the Hindi area, which has long included the seats of national power and has therefore been more strongly exposed than other areas to the influence of foreign invaders, the regional language situations all present somewhat similar features. The case of Marathi may be considered more or less typical. Here, the Sanskritized 'standard' form is quite close to the home language of urban Brahmans and a few other high castes, and presents no special difficulties in learning for those brought up in a high-caste household. As Apte (1962) has pointed out, the Brahman variety is the most distinct variety of Marathi—all others are more similar to each other than any of them is to the Brahman dialect.[22] Until very recently, this area has been strongly dominated by Brahmans in political and intellectual life, though they constitute well under 10 percent of the population. Clearly, the perpetuation and development of elite Marathi as an official 'standard' language helps to make it more difficult for others to enter these fields. This is particularly true of rural people from the lowest castes, who (here as elsewhere) have traditionally lived in separate areas of villages, or even in separate hamlets.

Tamil. The situation in Tamil, until comparatively recently, was similar to that in the Marathi area. The 'Brahman standard' form of Tamil is highly Sanskritized (even though Tamil is not a Sanskrit-derived language). Since the early part of this century, as certain high non-Brahman castes gained political and economic power (Hardgrave 1965), the Sanskritized form of Tamil was replaced, as an official and literary language, by a form known as 'pure' Tamil (*sen tamiẓ*), which derives its morphology, and much of its vocabulary, from the Classical Tamil of the early centuries *A.D.* This language, while politically acceptable to many Tamilians as an expression of their rejection both of the Brahmans and of the Indo-Aryan north of India, nevertheless leaves many Tamil speakers (especially those from illiterate, low-caste backgrounds) in as bad a situation as before. When village children start school, they are expected to learn every subject through a medium substantially different from their own home language, or any language they have heard. The headmistress of a school in Madras City pointed out to met that when 'servant-class children' (by which she meant poor children of low-caste background) first enter the school, their language is so different even from the common colloquial language that they often do not understand simple Tamil instructions like *ukkaaru* 'sit down' or *peeca maaTTe* 'don't talk' (because of differences in vocabulary). For higher-caste children from educated families, this is less of a burden. For others, it is often too great to be overcome. They are not even considered educable until they show the capacity to perform in this difficult language. They are expected to fail this test by the time they reach high school, and the large majority of them do (if they do not drop out of school for economic reasons).

An experiment in comprehensibility

As pointed out above, very few actual tests of the comprehensibility of Indian languages have been carried out. In 1976, I had an opportunity to carry out a small-scale test in Malayalam (the language of the state of Kerala, in southwest India). The purpose of the experiment was to test the hypothesis that written materials, even when ostensibly intended for mass consumption, are not fully comprehensible except to the highly educated. That is, even writers who sincerely intend to communicate with a mass audience cannot, because of their education and their class backgrounds, write in a language which their intended audience can understand.

Kerala is a good area for such a test, since the rate of literacy is higher here than elsewhere in India. In addition, many educated Malayalis claim that even illiterate laborers are familiar with many of the Sanskrit words found in literary Malayalam. This would seem to imply that there is less distance between elite and non-elite forms of Malayalam than is the case for other Indian languages. Malayalam, then, is a good test case for our hypothesis, since if the hypothesis turns out to be applicable to this language, it is likely to be more true for others.

The experiment was carried out on the outskirts of Trivandrum (the state capital) using a text selected from a leftist magazine intended for agricultural workers. A short initial portion of an article was selected, and questions were formulated which would yield a comprehension score of 0–5. This brief text (Text A) was shown to five subjects, all literate male agricultural laborers with an average age of 37 years and an average of 8 years of school, who were allowed to read it as many times as they wished, and were then asked questions about it. Only one subject (who had completed 10 years of school) scored as high as 4 out of 5; the average for the group was 1.6 out of 5. A simpler version (Text B) was prepared, and tried with 9 subjects of a somewhat lower educational level (average 4.4 years of school; average age

39).[23] The average score on Text B was 0.77 (out of 5) for the 9 subjects, and it was therefore considered inconclusive. A third, more simplified version (Text C), was tried with a group of ten subjects similar to the group exposed to Text B (average age 40, average education 3.3 years). The average score for this third group was 2.0, which though not startling, was at least an indication that the modifications introduced in Text C were in the right direction.

While we cannot claim to have adequately tested the hypothesis with such small samples, the results certainly are suggestive. But perhaps the most significant outcome of the study was the reaction of the investigators and others associated with the experiment, as well as other educated people with whom it was discussed. All were extremely surprised to find the levels of comprehension so low, and to observe that many words which they considered quite 'simple' were unfamiliar to the subjects. One colleague, an active political worker, used our texts for some informal testing of his own, with laborers of his acquaintance. He reported that he was 'dumbfounded' to find that even members of his party who had had several years of school and had regularly attended party meetings, were unable to make any sense out of either Text A or Text B. This reaction on the part of Malayali intellectuals, particularly those who have a sincere desire to communicate with their less educated brethren, is the most convincing evidence I have seen of the linguistic gap discussed here.

Conclusions

Social variation in language is a manifestation of social structural barriers in a society. In many older societies, such as those of India and nearby countries, it is not uncommon to find that people have 'language loyalty' to forms of language which are quite distinct from the vernacular. This situation arises from a long tradition of using the local languages, which show great regional and social diversity, as the main media for in-group communication, whereas they are replaced with 'superposed' varieties for wider communication (Gumperz 1962: 108–9). When such societies enter the ranks of modern democratic nations, and attempt to broaden their bases of political participation, formal education and mass communication become powerful tools for influencing linguistic norms, as well as linguistic attitudes. These tools can be used either to reduce socio-economic barriers, or to legitimize them.

In the cases discussed above, it is clear that traditional attitudes have triumphed over egalitarian ideology, with the result that language education continues to function as an exclusive mechanism. This effect has been achieved by defining much of normal spoken language as 'non-standard', legitimizing this claim by various intellectual and pseudo-nationalistic arguments, and then refusing to look at the results. Thus the ruling groups in each region, however much they may appear to support the principle of equality, have in fact given higher priorities to social status, economic self-interest, and political expediency.[24]

Notes

1. In an earlier paper (Southworth 1972), I attempted a preliminary discussion of this subject. I wish to thank Dr. Joan P. Mencher for a number of helpful comments on the present paper.
2. *Prakrit* is a term used to denote a group of languages which evolved from Sanskrit by the first half of the first millenium *B.C.*, and which were later used for religious and secular literature, as well as administrative purposes, alongside Sanskrit.
3. India recognizes 16 official languages, of which those in italics are also official state languages: *Assamese, Bengali,* English, *Gujarati, Hindi, Kannada,* Kashmiri, *Malayalam, Marathi, Oriya, Panjabi,* Sanskrit, Sindhi, *Tamil, Telugu, Urdu.* (Kannada, Malayalam, Tamil, and Telugu are Dravidian languages; the rest (except for English) are Indo-Aryan—i.e., derived from Sanskrit, and distantly related to the Germanic and Romance families and other languages of Europe.)
4. It is difficult to find scientific criteria to determine whether two forms of speech should be considered as dialects of the same language, or as distinct languages. To circumvent this terminological problem, linguists use the term (linguistic) *variety* to denote any form of speech with definable characteristics which is used in a particular region or by a particular population.
5. See, for example, Ferguson and Gumperz 1960, Gumperz 1958, Berntsen 1975, Pandit 1972, Ramanujan 1967, Southworth 1976a, 1976b, 1977. Social dialects in India have often been referred to as 'caste dialects', a misleading term. (See Bean 1974 for a discussion of this point.) The existence of social dialects in ancient India is perhaps implied by the form of the classical Sanskrit dramas, in which the higher-ranking characters speak Sanskrit and the lower ones speak various Prakrits.
6. 'Untouchability' refers to a set of provisions in traditional Hindu law which specified harsh penalties for members of the lowest castes who approached within certain distances (varying from region to region) of higher-caste people, their dwellings, etc. Although legally abolished (untouchables are now referred to as 'ex-untouchables' or by various other euphemisms, see Southworth 1974), the practice of untouchability has not yet been eradicated, especially in rural areas. In many parts of the country, for example, the ex-untouchables still live in separate hamlets, away from the villages of caste Hindus, and 'atrocities' against them are frequently reported in the press.
7. Gumperz (1958) has suggested that such dialect differences arise, and are maintained, because linguistic usage is strongly influenced by peer groups, and in particular by male friendship groups. In rural India, these groups rarely include both Brahmans and non-Brahmans, or touchables and untouchables, though may include members of different touchable castes. This suggestion ignores the possibility that female friendship groups might have an equal importance in maintaining dialect differences. Even though in this area wives often come from distant villages, and occasionally speak different dialects from their husbands at the time of marriage, they learn the dialect of the husband's village readily—because they are usually married in their early teens, and there are great pressures on them to conform to local custom. Fur-

thermore, the influence of female members of the household on the dialect acquired by children cannot be denied.

8. For example, the word for '(cooked) rice' for most Tamilians is *cooRu*, but for most Brahmans is *saatam* (derived from Sanskrit *prasaadam* 'food given to temple worshippers after being offered to the deity'–so-called because of the Brahman custom of offering the food to the household deity before the meal). (See Ramanujan 1967, also Southworth 1977.)

9. These special formal varieties actually have separate names, e.g., *sen tamiz* 'pure Tamil' as opposed to *peeccu tamiz* 'spoken Tamil', and Bengali *s̆adhu bha̋s̆a* 'proper language' as opposed to *colit bha̋s̆a* 'current language'. The two varieties not only differ extensively in vocabulary, but also use very different sets of morphological forms. (Exx. for Tamil in Southworth 1977, Shanmugam Pillai 1968.)

10. A person who uses an inappropriate variety is likely to be accused either of ignorance (if too informal a variety is chosen), or of snobbishness and pretentiousness (if the variety used is regarded as too formal). Blom and Gumperz (1972) describe, for example, the criticisms which residents of a small Norwegian town made of certain individuals who used an urban variety of the language where the local variety was expected. It is claimed that Tamil-speaking Brahmans modify their speech in the direction of 'general colloquial Tamil' when interacting with people of other castes in public places. Not to do so would be considered standoffish.

11. There are, however, in most areas, a few programs (dramas, interviews, etc.) in which a more colloquial form of language is used.

12. Labov (1969) has given some very apt illustrations of this point for contemporary American society.

13. The main exceptions to this are Tamil (which takes its formal vocabulary from the Classical Tamil of the early centuries *A.D.*) and Urdu (which derives its higher-level vocabulary from Persian and Arabic).

14. For example, the most common word for 'anger' in Hindi is *gussaa*, which happens to be derived from Arabic. This has been replaced in official Hindi by the Sanskrit *krodh*, a totally unfamiliar word to most people. A child who writes *gussaa* instead of *krodh* in a school essay will be marked down. This is the case with hundreds of words in Hindi and other modern Indian languages.

15. Prakrits remained in use in inscriptions, and Tamil was used in the south both in inscriptions and for literary purposes, but in most areas the prestige of Sanskrit remained high.

16. There are still a number of languages which are not official languages and have never become 'standardized': e.g. Tulu, Konkani, Bhojpuri, Maithili. In these cases, the traditional type of variation still exists, with different classes having their distinct 'class dialects' (see above).

17. Uttar Pradesh, Bihar, Haryana, Madhya Pradesh, Rajasthan, Himachal Pradesh.

18. English is still frequently used for official purposes, both in the central government and some of the state governments, as well as in the higher courts.

19. The evidence for this statement comes from several sources, though none of them are as reliable as we might like. The only actual test of the comprehensibility of Hindi which I know of was carried out by a political scientist, Melnick (1974). His test indicated that only about 32 percent of people could understand 'many' of the words in his sample (of political vocabulary). Since this test was carried out in Uttar Pradesh, in the core Hindi area, it is likely that people in peripheral areas would score even lower. (A more detailed discussion of Melnick's results is given in Southworth 1978.) A second source of data on this point comes from statements made by speakers of Hindi, of which two will have to suffice here. A colleague of mine, a native speaker of Hindi who has an M.A. in Hindi and currently holds a high position in a government language institute, once commented to me that it was difficult to understand the Hindi news without great concentration. Another well-known comment on this question was made by the late Pandit Nehru, India's first prime minister, who spoke

fluent Hindi (though it was not his first language). Nehru alienated the Hindi pardits on several occasions by remarking that he could not understand the *śuddh hindii* versions of his own speeches which were broadcast over All India Radio. Another source of data is the high levels of failure in Hindi in the statewide examinations at the end of high school throughout the Hindi region, particularly in rural areas. Against this evidence, inadequate though it may be, those who disagree with the statement made above have offered nothing but their opinions. (The fact that proponents of *śuddh hindii* have not attempted any practical tests of its comprehensibility is perhaps significant in itself.)

20. Gandhi was an advocate of Hindustani, a widely-used colloquial variety, for official status. This is a term hardly used nowadays, and I have even been told by highly-educated Indians that there never was any such language 'except in Gandhiji's imagination'–though Indira Gandhi, Nehru's daughter and currently Prime Minister of India, recently (mid-1981) used the term to refer to the language she herself used in a televised speech. What Gandhi was referring to is essentially the same variety which is used in the Hindi films, the armed forces, and as a *lingua franca* in urban areas all over India.

21. On the other hand, it is frequently reported in the press that even some politicians who strongly support this policy send their own children to English-medium schools.

22. Here Apte is referring primarily to phonology, but there are also substantial differences in vocabulary. Kinship terms, for example, are strikingly different (Orenstein 1965) and non-Brahman children are said to have difficulties in learning to use the kin terms used in school texts.

23. The notion of 'simplification' is an ill-defined one, which requires a good deal of ' practical testing before it can be made precise. For Text B, our first 'simplified' text, we merely replaced words which seemed highly literary with more familiar synonyms. For the second 'simplification' (Text C) we broke long sentences down into shorter, simpler ones, and used a much more colloquial type of language.

24. In discussing this question with colleagues in the field of Indian studies, I have often been accused of ethnocentrism. The viewpoint expressed in this paper is said to be a peculiarly 'American' one, for two reasons: first, it proposes that social differences in language should be eliminated; secondly, it ignores the importance of *ritual* in Indian society, especially where public uses of language are concerned. The answer to the first claim is that I do not propose to eliminate differences in language, but to encourage the use of forms of language which are *appropriate* (to the participants, the subject matter, and the situation). To the second point, the only answer is that it is not unusual for elite groups to use ritualistic or nationalistic arguments to justify policies which further their own selfish interests. (See Mencher 1974 for a discussion of the ways in which traditional caste differences have served to maintain the status of elites in Indian society.) I would add that similar situations exist in many other parts of the world, including the 'developed' as well as the 'developing' countries.

References

Apte, M. L. 1962. Linguistic acculturation and its relation to urbanization and socio-economic factors. *Indian Linguistics* 23: 5-25.

Bean, S. S. 1974. Linguistic variation and the caste system in South Asia. *Indian Linguistics* 35: 277-93.

Berntsen, M. 1975. The invariant model of language: Some data from a study of Marathi speech. *Indian Linguistics* 36: 227-33.

Blom, J-P., and J. J. Gumperz. 1972. Social meaning in linguistic structures: Code-switching in Norway. In *Directions in sociolinguistics*, ed. by J. J. Gumperz and D. H. Hymes, New York: Holt, Rinehart and Winston.

Bloomfield, L. 1933. *Language*. New York: Holt, Rinehart and Winston.

Das Gupta, J. 1970. *Language conflict and national development: Group politics and national language policy in India*. Bombay: Oxford University Press.

— and J. J. Gumperz. 1968. Language, communication and control in North India. In *Language problems of developing nations*, ed. by J. A. Fishman, C. A. Ferguson & J. Das Gupta. New York: John Wiley.

Ferguson, C.A. 1964. Diglossia. In *Language in culture and society*, ed. by D.H. Hymes. New York: Harper & Row.

—, & J. J. Gumperz (eds.). 1960. Linguistic diversity in South Asia. Bloomington, Illinois.

Gumperz, J. J. 1958. Dialect differences and social stratification in a North Indian village. American Anthropologist 60.668-82.

— 1962. Types of linguistic communities. Anthropological Linguistics 4.1.28-40. Reprinted in Language in social groups: Essays by John J. Gumperz, ed. by A. S. Dil. Stanford University Press, 1971, pp. 97-113. (Page references to this article refer to the reprinted version.)

Hardgrave, R. 1965. The Dravidian movement. Bombay, Popular Prakashan.

Labov, W. 1969. The logic of non-standard English. In Language and social context, ed. by P. Giglioli. London, Penguin Books.

Mencher, J. P. 1974. The caste system upside down, or the not so mysterious east. Current Anthropology 15.469-94.

Melnick, D. 1974. The political argot of the Hindi region: Survey data from a North Indian district. Ms.

Orenstein, Henry. 1965. Gaon: Conflict and cohesion in an Indian village. Princeton University Press.

Pandit, P. B. 1972. India as a sociolinguistic area. Gune Memorial Lectures. University of Poona.

Ramanujan, A. K. 1967. The structure of variation: A study in caste dialects. In *Social structure and change in Indian society*, ed. by B. Cohn & M. Singer. New York, Viking Fund Publications in Anthropology.

Rubin, J. 1970. *National bilingualism in Paraguay*. The Hague: Mouton.

Shanmugam Pillai, M. 1968. Merger of literary and colloquial Tamil. *Anthropological Linguistics* 7.4.1-10.

Southworth, F. C. 1972. Problems in defining "standard" languages in India, England and the United States. *International Journal of Dravidian Linguistics* 1.2.29-37.

— 1974. Linguistic masks for power: Some relationships between semantic and social change. *Anthropological Linguistics* 16.5.177-91.

— 1976a. Sociolinguistic research in South India. In *Essays on South India*, ed. by B. Stein. Honolulu, University of Hawaii Press.

— 1976b. Review of Pandit 1972. *Indian Linguistics* 37: 60-68.

— 1977. Sociolinguistic variation and semantic structure: The case of Tamil *kaRi*. In *Approaches to language: Anthropological issues*, ed. by W. McCormack & S. Wurm. The Hague, Mouton.

— 1978. On the need for qualitative data to supplement census language statistics: Some proposals based on the Indian census. *Indian Linguistics* 39: 136-54.

Jane Zuengler

English, Swahili, or Other Languages?
The Relationship of Educational Development Goals
to Language of Instruction in Kenya and Tanzania*

Introduction

It is difficult for Westerners to fully appreciate the language dilemmas existing in many Third World countries which, by American standards at least, are minute both in terms of total population and total geographical area. Tanzania, for example, with its 18 million people, and Kenya, with 15 million, together contain less than 15 percent of the American population. Yet each consists of dozens of ethnic and linguistic groups. Decisions to be made concerning language policy, and in particular the choice of educational language, are neither simple nor universally acceptable. The purpose of this paper is to suggest that a country's educational language policy can be best understood within the broad context of the relationship of education to that society. By comparing post-colonial Kenya and Tanzania, two countries which have developed contrasting educational language policies, this writer will argue that dissimilar policies can largely be a result of differing educational development goals.

Language policy is a topic of obvious interest and concern, for decisions regarding the structure and use of language have tremendous sociocultural ramifications (see, e.g., Fishman 1972, 1977). Within the area of African educational language policy, there is a growing literature. It is written through the auspices of international organizations (see, e.g., UNESCO's 1974 *Education in a Rural Environment* and 1976 *Education in Africa*, as well as the World Bank's 1974 *Education: Sector Working Paper*), or independently (e.g., Ansre n.d., 1976; Bagunywa 1970; Gachukia 1970; Kunene 1978; Scotton 1978). The majority of writers argue for a change in educational language policy, frequently advocating, from a psychological, sociocultural, or linguistic perspective, the mother tongue as educational medium. Or they assess the linguistic effects of a present policy. Few of their discussions, however, focus on educational language policy as a reflection of the society's educational development goals—a link which is important to see in order to understand present, and predict future, language policy.

Kenya and Tanzania: the Current Role of Languages in Education

For the reader not conversant with East African education or language, brief descriptions of the general educational structure and language situation will be provided. More detailed treatment of the structure as well as the administration of Kenya and Tanzania's educational systems can be found in Cameron (1970), King (1974), Komba (1979), Muncie (1973), and Raju (1973), among others. The linguistic composition of Kenya is discussed extensively in Whiteley (1974b); other sources on Kenyan and/or Tanzanian languages include Abdulaziz (1971), Harries (1968), Heine (1970), and Kihore (1976).

At the time of independence (Tanzania's in 1961 and Kenya's in 1963), both countries inherited a four-tiered, British system of formal education. While Tanzania and Kenya have made very different decisions regarding curricular emphases, allocation of educational resources, etc., the basic structure has remained the same. Educational innovations have either been superimposed on or placed into the existing structure (Court and Kinyanjui 1978: 65). 'Primary' school, the first level of public education, comprises seven 'standards' (i.e., grades). Normally, Standard One is the pupil's first year of education; in Nairobi, however, children now receive a pre-primary year, which gives them an advantage over the others.[1] The seven standards are free for all pupils in both countries. In the last year of primary school, the pupils take a standardized, written examination to determine selection for the four-year secondary level. The percentage admitted to government socondary schools is very low: 14 percent in Kenya and less than 5 percent in Tanzania (Court and Kinyanjui 1978: 18, and Sheffield 1979: 105, respectively). 'Secondary' school has four 'forms' (i.e., grades). Rural secondary schools are normally boarding schools, as are the 'higher' schools, which comprise the next, two-year level. Selection to higher school is also achieved by means of a written examination. In Forms Five and Six of the higher school, pupils concentrate their studies in an area of arts or science. Then, another examination is taken for admittance to the fourth, and highest, level of education, which is the three-year university. To date, there is only one university in Kenya,[2] the University of Nairobi, and one in Tanzania, the University of Dar es Salaam.

Tanzania's linguistic composition is complex, for there are today over one hundred vernacular[3] language groups. This is, however, only a rough estimate, since little analysis has been done as to what objectively constitutes a dialect, and what a language. One suggestion is to view the situation in Tanzania as a linguistic continuum (Abdulaziz 1971: 161). The vernaculars fall into three language families (Bantu, Nilotic, and Cushitic). Over 90 percent of the population speak a Bantu language as first language, and of this proportion, 10 percent are native speakers of Swahili.[4] They are mainly people living along the coastal area and in Zanzibar (Abdulaziz 1971: 161; Kihore 1976: 4). For the rest of the population, Swahili is a second language that has become very widespread, due to its societal and educational roles (which will be illustrated shortly). It is both the national and official language of Tanzania.

In Kenya, Swahili is also the national and official language. But in reality, it does not have as many domains of use as in Tanzania. That is because it is not the medium of Kenya's power structure. Swahili is used as a symbol of nationalism and unification (when the President delivers a public address, for example, he speaks in Swahili), but English is the language of Kenya's economic and legal spheres. Due to this, and to its prominence in the educational system (which will be discussed below), English has become the channel of socioeconomic mobility in Kenya. (For a discussion of the consequences, see Scotten 1978; for a description of Kenyan English, see Zuengler 1981).

The vernacular languages in Kenya have been placed in four major groups (although this is not universally accepted; see Whiteley 1974a: 13). One of these is the Bantu language group, which accounts for 65 to 70 percent Kenyans (Abdulaziz 1971: 161; Whiteley 1974a: 60). As in Tanzania, Swahili is spoken as a first language by only a small percentage. A national survey, however, indicated that 75 percent of Kenyan Bantu speakers claimed some competence in Swahili. Among the 30 percent of Kenyans who are non-Bantu speakers, though, only 10 percent claimed competence in Swahili (Whiteley 1974a: 59–60).

As stated earlier, Kenya and Tanzania have contrasting educational language policies. A difference is apparent beginning the first day of primary instruction. A Tanzanian pupil, whether in an urban or rural school, will hear and speak only Swahili for all but one period a day.[5] That one period is when English is taught as a subject. Every other subject will be taught in Swahili. The language his Kenyan counterpart will be exposed to as initial medium of instruction will be more difficult to predict, for it will be the 'predominant' language of the community in which the school is situated. Two examples— one in Nairobi and one in a rural area—will be used as illustrations.[6] If the pupil attends school in Nairobi, he will have English as medium of instruction from Standard One onward. English will be used to teach all subjects except Swahili, which the pupil will study one period a day. In the rural schools of Kitui, on the other hand, the instruction will begin in languages other than English. At Central Primary School in the town of Kitui, most of the instruction is in Swahili from Standards One through Three. The teachers also use a bit of Kikamba. In schools outside the town, Kikamba is the sole medium for the first three years, except for one period a day of English.

The Tanzanian pupil will continue to use Swahili six out of seven periods a day through Standard Seven, his last primary year. All of his textbooks (except for English class) are written in Swahili. He will study English for one period a day through the final, seventh year. Though a majority of Tanzanians speak a vernacular as first language, there is no use of the vernaculars in the Tanzanian primary system.

Meanwhile, beginning with Standard Four, the Kenyan rural and urban schools' curricula will become uniform. That means that every Kenyan pupil in Standard Four and above has English as the medium of instruction, with Swahili taught as a subject. The language of the Kenyan pupil's textbooks is just the reverse of the Tanzanian's—all of the materials are written in English except for the books he uses one period a day in his Swahili class. While the Tanzanian uses Swahili on the playground, his Kenyan counterpart will be strongly encouraged to use only English.[7]

At the end of Standard Seven, both the Kenyan and the Tanzanian sit for the examination which will determine whether they will be among the lucky minority admitted to secondary school. The Kenyan's examination is entirely in English, except for one section testing Swahili as a subject. For the Tanzanian, it is just the opposite. All of his examination is written in Swahili, except for the section on English as a subject. Since only a minority in each country are selected for government secondary schools (14 percent in Kenya and less than 5 percent in Tanzania, as mentioned above), there is tremendous pressure to do well on the examination. It has effects on the syllabus; in some Kenyan schools, the pupils and their parents have successfully urged the teacher to drop Swahili completely from the syllabus, so as to spend more time studying English (King 1974: 128).

The Kenyan pupil who goes to secondary school and beyond will have all of his instruction in English, except for Swahili as a subject. The post-secondary examination is written in English, and Swahili is an optional subject on the exam. The succeeding examinations, at the higher school and university levels, are in English.

The Tanzanian who is admitted to secondary school will see Swahili used increasingly as the medium of instruction. It has, in the last several years, become the medium of instruction in subjects such as geography, history, arithmetic, and domestic science at Form One level (*Africa Contemporary Record* 1978–79: B403). Ideally, according to national guidelines, every secondary-level subject will be taught in Swahili by 1983. There is also some talk of changing the university to Swahili-medium.[8]

The Link Between Educational Goals and Language of Instruction

At the time of independence in both Tanzania and Kenya, the languages used as media of instruction in the primary schools reflected the racial segregation existing in the larger society (Cameron and Dodd 1970: 175). Swahili was the initial medium of instruction, followed by English, in Tanzanian African schools. In schools for Africans in Kenya, the vernaculars or Swahili were used for the first few standards, and beyond that, English became the instructional medium. English was the sole medium used in European schools in both countries. In the Asian schools, languages such as Gujerati, Hindi, and Urdu were used in the first few standards, followed by English. With the advent of an African-run government in each country, both Kenya and Tanzania outlawed racial segregation. They also issued their first national development plans, which included projections for education.

Newly-independent Kenya and Tanzania both formulated dual goals of increased economic output and eventual mass education. And both placed priority, at the outset of independence, on the former goal. The Kenyan Ministry of Education Annual Summary of 1965 stated that

> education was to be considered less of a service to individuals and more of a service to the state through the production of engineers and teachers, doctors and agronomists, etc., and all the other skilled people in short supply. (Introduction: first page)

Tanzania also clearly declared that "the supply of trained manpower is the first priority in the development of Education Training" (*Annual Report of 1964*: 6).

In order to produce skilled workers for increased production, Kenya and Tanzania expanded the number of schools at all levels, but particularly the secondary and higher levels. Basically, the languages in the schools remained much the same as they had been before in the African schools. That meant that in Tanzania, Swahili was the only initial medium in the primary schools. It was used until Standard Six, when English became the medium and continued as such. English or the vernaculars were the media of instruction in the first two years in Kenyan primary schools. From the third standard onward, English was the medium.

By the time each country issued its second development plan (in 1969), their educational development goals had begun to diverge. Kenya still gave priority to the meeting of manpower needs, which it stated very explicitly:

> the first and most important goal for education is to produce sufficient numbers of people with the skills and knowledge required to support a high economic growth. (*Planning for Progress* 1969: 23)

Other goals, including the achievement of universal education and the fostering of cultural values, were secondary. There were no changes in educational language policy.

In Tanzania, however, goals were changing. President Nyerere argued for a re-orientation of the educational system in a 1967 'post-Arusha'[9] policy statement entitled 'Education for Self-Reliance'. In it, he criticized primary education in particular for being geared to the minority. Education was too academic and irrelevant in content for the masses of terminal students. Priorities must shift, Nyerere argued, to meeting the needs of that majority who would be going no further through the educational system. Each level must be complete in itself, and should prepare pupils not for possible further education, but for going back to assist development in the rural areas. The development of socialist attitudes had become the primary aim of education (Court and Kinyanjui 1978: 52).

Nyerere declared that the needs of the majority included the ability to read and write fluently in Swahili. At the same time, he conceded that an introduction to English was important, "especially so that the people who wish may be able to learn more by themselves in later life" (Nyerere 1967: 289). It was to remain secondary, however, to Swahili.

As one of the results of 'Education for Self-Reliance', Swahili was to become, beginning in 1968, the medium of instruction in *all* standards of all primary schools. That is, the previous shift within the later primary years to English as a medium of instruction was discontinued. Formerly, English was begun as a subject in Standard Three. Beginning in 1968, English was to be introduced even earlier, in Standard One. It would remain a subject, though, rather than a medium of instruction, through the seven primary years.

The paramount importance that Swahili was granted over English as primary educational medium was thus a reflection of Tanzania's re-directing of educational goals. The emphasis on high-level manpower needs had changed to an emphasis on mass needs. The primary level was to serve as preparation for a life engaged in rural labor, rather than as preparation for going further in the educational system. The emphasis on mass needs was articulated within a socialist framework, and Swahili was selected as its conveyor:

> Swahili has not simply been used as a medium of instruction but has developed itself for the purpose of conveying certain political concepts which are central to the task of socialist education. (Court and Kinyanjui 1978: 51)

In 1969, Tanzania's *Second Five Year Plan* expressed concern over the implementation of Swahili medium as set forth in 'Education for Self-Reliance'. By this time, there had energed a system of levels differentiated by language—the primary level with instruction entirely in Swahili, and the secondary and higher levels in English only. The Plan mentioned two unsatisfactory results of the new language policy. One of these was educational. Problems were occurring because the children beginning secondary school were confronted with instruction through a new language (i.e., English) at the same time as they began taking a more difficult set of courses. To alleviate the difficulty, it was proposed that those pupils who were recruited to secondary schools be provided with an intensive, basically remedial English course, to combat the effects of having been taught the language as an isolated subject by teachers whose grasp of English was often inadequate. The aims of the remedial course were

> to give pupils intensive exposure to the kind of English they need to use as a tool of learning all subjects in secondary schools, and to boost the pupil's confidence in his ability to succeed in secondary studies. (*Second Five Year Plan* 1969: 152)

The second unsatisfactory result of the language policy was considered more serious than the educational problem just discussed. A linguistic gap was being created between the masses and those going further through the educational system. The Plan expressed concern that the use of English would alienate higher education from the problems of the Tanzanian masses. While not outlining new policy, it indicated future policy *direction*:

> as government moves over to the complete use of Swahili, it will become more and more inappropriate to have the secondary and higher educational systems operate in English. (*Second Five Year Plan* 1969: 152)

Since 1969, Tanzania has continued to commit itself to an educational system oriented toward socialism and rural development. The *Third Five-Year Plan*, for example, reiterates what Nyerere said in his 1967 'Education for Self-Reliance':

> The Party's policy is to emphasize education as a tool for preparing Tanzanians to fulfill their responsibility in national development under the policy of socialism and self-reliance.... Educational plans in the Third Five Year Plan will be guided by the Party's policy of providing social services in the rural areas. (*Third Five Year Plan* 1976: 79)

The use of Swahili as medium of instruction has become an integral part of Tanzania's educational development goals. Tanzania's aim, as mentioned earlier, is to teach every secondary-level subject in Swahili by 1983. It may become a medium of instruction at the university level as well. While Swahili has taken on a more and more important role in the Tanzanian educational system, English has been relegated to a minor position with policy unclear as to its use. Recently, it was noted that comprehension of English had fallen at all levels, including the university. This was attributed to the lack of a clear policy in the teaching of English (*Africa Contemporary Record* 1978–79: B403). Concern about the decline in English ability had led the Ministry of

National Education to direct one of its colleges of education to devote itself exclusively to the improvement of English language teaching (Court and Kinyanjui 1978: 50).

In Kenya, on the other hand, English retained an important role in education. As mentioned earlier, newly-independent Kenya emphasized goals of economic growth; the educational system was given the task of producing high-level manpower. English was the sole medium of instruction in urban primary schools, and became the medium of instruction by Standard Three of the rural primary schools. In fact, because of the role of English as examination medium, many of the rural schools were using English, rather than the vernaculars, as initial medium of instruction.[10] As in Tanzania, only a minority (14 percent) went on to secondary school. The orientation of Kenya's educational system was toward the minority who would succeed.

By 1974, though, there was concern expressed about this minority orientation. Kenya's 1974–78 *Development Plan* acknowledged that the educational system was producing large numbers of people, all of whom were competing for relatively few jobs in the urban sector. Educational expansion, which had taken place on all levels since independence, had exacerbated rather than alleviated the problem:

> This expansion, in the final analysis, has merely heightened the competition among the products of the system for individual social and economic advancement within the modern sector of the economy. (*Development Plan 1974–78*: 405)

While there was concern over the practical effects of a minority-oriented education, the educational goal which had brought this about was not fundamentally questioned. This was the goal of expansion of educational opportunity (see the *Development Plan 1974–78*: 404). Around this time, educational policy rationale began to de-emphasize education's manpower contribution and emphasize the philosophy of expanded educational opportunity instead (Court and Kinyanjui 1978: 26). Where Tanzania had formed an educational system which socialized its pupils toward rural employment after finishing primary school, Kenya was building a system which at least had the illusion of offering every pupil an equal opportunity to compete for higher educational selection, and ultimately, high-level employment.

The effect of equal opportunity to compete for scarce rewards conflicted, however, with other stated values:

> Its [education's] highly selective nature and exclusive orientation towards the modern urban sector are in fundamental contradiction to the social and cultural values upheld by the Government. (*Development Plan 1974–78*: 404)

This, and the awareness of unequal development in the rural and urban areas, led the policy makers to announce the establishment of a 'National Commission on Educational Objectives and Policies', which would evaluate the educational system. In addition, the Commission's tasks were to draw up a new set of educational goals and determine means by which these goals could be implemented (*Development Plan 1974–78*: 406).

The 'Gachathi Report' (the National Commission's unofficial title, after the name of its chairman) was completed in 1976, but wasn't published until 1978. What caused the delay was apparent disagreement among senior education officials over some of the report's 340 recommendations (*Africa Contemporary Record* 1978–79: B274–5). Comprising over 200 pages, the Gachathi Report made recommendations relevant to every aspect of education in Kenya. Prior to stating its recommendations for educational reform, the Report pointed out what it considered to be two main sources of educational problems. One was the belief, by the public, that the educational system was the individual's best channel of advancement. Most of the economic rewards existed within the modern, formal sector of the country, which was largely open only to those who had completed higher levels of education. The second problem source was related to this. The educational system was highly selective, because its aim was to produce those relatively few individuals equipped for employment in that small, concentrated sector (p. ix). The overall effect was to waste an increasing proportion of the country's human resources (p. x).

With this in mind, the Gachathi Report recommended that the primary level be changed from seven years to a nine-year, 'basic' education which would orient itself to the needs of the majority to whom it would be terminal (pp. 52–3). This would end the present focus on the minority who succeed, and as a consequence, make Kenya's educational system much more similar to Tanzania's. The syllabus and content would be more relevant to the pupil's future (rural) social and economic environment (p. 55).

The Gachathi Report made several recommendations regarding languages of instruction in primary schools. It was felt that the educational system should make better use of the 'local languages' in early primary education, because most of the rural children "can only speak their vernacular language at the time of starting primary education" (p. 54). Consequently, Recommendation 101 was

> To use as a language of instruction the predominant language spoken in the schools' catchment area for the first three years of primary education. (p. 54)

According to Recommendation 102, English was not to become the medium of instruction (unless it was the predominant language spoken) until standard Four. Prior to that, it was to be taught as a subject only (p. 55).

Kenya's current (1979–83) *Development Plan* was formulated a year after the release of the Gachathi Report's recommendations. The current Plan gives evidence of a basic needs strategy regarding education, which was predicted earlier (see Court and Kiyanjui 1978: 67). That is, educational development goals in this planning period are to emphasize 'basic technologies' which will increase the individual's income-earning opportunities (*Development Plan 1979–83*: 152). While there seems to be a new focus on the rural sector, the modern sector still merits emphasis:

> Education and training will continue to be the means through which people become more economically productive in the modern sector of the economy as well as in the rural and the informal sector. (*Development Plan 1979–83:* 152)

The Plan then states that those recommendations in the Gachathi Report "which are acceptable and consistent with the strategies contained in this Plan" have been incorporated (*Development Plan 1979–83*: 154).

Though not explicitly stated in the Plan, the recommendations regarding languages of primary instruction are being carried out.[11] Consequently, the initial (and continuing) medium of instruction in Nairobi primary schools is English. But in the rest of Kenya, where English is not the 'predominant language', the initial medium of instruction is one of the vernaculars or Swahili. Then, in Standard Four, instruction through English begins, and continues through the final, seventh year.

The recommendation to extend the primary level to nine years, with a 'basic' education emphasis, was not accepted. Its failure was attributed to both political and financial reasons.[12] The result is that the Kenyan formal educational system has not undergone the radical changes in emphasis and orientation that the Tanzanian system has. Though Kenya's policy makers have indicated their concern over the problems which result from the present system of education, and expressed the need for rural development, the educational goals have not fundamentally changed:

The development of education and expansion of educational opportunities continue to be the major policy objectives of the Government. (Kenya's *Economic Survey 1980*: 178)

It is a selective school system geared primarily to manpower requirements, which emphasizes the concept of equal educational opportunity to achieve in it (Court and Kinyanjui 1978: 70). Education is still perceived to be the prime allocator of socioeconomic rewards, just as the Gachathi Report pointed out when it drew up its recommendations.

While the specification that the area's 'predominant language' be the medium of instruction in the first three primary standards has resulted in greater use of the vernaculars and Swahili, English has retained its role as medium in all succeeding instructional levels. The dominance of English in the schools parallels its dominance within the higher socioeconomic strata that every Kenyan pupil is striving to enter. The whole educational system in Kenya clearly continues to be focused on the minority who succed.

Conclusion

At the time of their independence in the 1960s, Kenya and Tanzania inherited similar systems of formal education. Since then, the two countries have formulated very different goals regarding educational development. In Tanzania, the educational system is now oriented to the majority for whom primary school will be terminal. Pupils are prepared for lives engaged in rural occupations. In Kenya, on the other hand, the focus is on providing equal opportunity to compete for the relatively few positions in the modern, urban sector. Each country has corresponding differences in the languages selected as educational media. Tanzania uses Swahili, the dominant language of the majority, while Kenya uses English, which is the language of its socioeconomic elite. It has been argued that educational language policy in these countries reflects their educational development goals. Consequently, it is unlikely that Swahili will change its dominant position in Tanzanian schools, or English its dominance in Kenyan schools, unless there is a fundamental change in their goals for educational development.

Notes

* The author would like to thank the following for their assistance in obtaining information about current educational language policy in Kenya and Tanzania: Dr. David Court, the Rockefeller Foundation, Nairobi, Kenya; Dr. Jeffrey Fine, the International Development Research Centre, Ottawa, Canada; Mary Mwinzi, Kitui High School, Kitui, Kenya; Said Bilal and Raphy Tobing, Teachers College, Columbia University.

1. Personal communication from Dr. Jeffrey Fine, who was involved in writing the educational section of Kenya's 1974-78 *Development Plan.*
2. Recently, there has been talk of building a second Kenyan university (*Africa Contemporary Record* 1978-79: B274).
3. The term 'vernacular' refers to indigenous African languages, such as Kikamba, Kisukuma, and Dholuo. According to this definition, Swahili is also a vernacular, but for ease of discussion, 'vernacular' will here refer to indigenous languages *excluding* Swahili. Since 'vernacular' was sometimes used derogatorily during the colonial period, some researchers prefer the term 'mother tongue' (see, e.g., Ansre n.d., 1976). 'Mother tongue', however, is a problematic term, because the language *first* acquired is not necessarily the child's *dominant* language. This distinction becomes particularly important in urban areas as well as in Tanzania's *Ujamaa* (i.e., communal) villages, where there is a great mixing of language groups. It is obvious that new terms are needed to describe the complexities of language acquisition and use among multilingual speakers.
4. The Bantu prefix *Ki-* (meaning 'language') is sometimes attached, so the reader will find both 'Swahili' and 'Kiswahili' in the literature. In terms of common usage, there seems to be a preference for 'Swahili'. 'Swahili' can also refer to the people who speak Swahili as a first language.
5. Information concerning the implementation of Tanzanian educational language policy was given by Said Bilal, a Tanzanian who recently chaired a committee organized to translate primary level mathematics textbooks into Swahili.

6. Information about language in Nairobi primary schools was provided by Dr. Jeffrey Fine (see note 1 above). Mary Mwinzi, an English language teacher at Kitui Eoys' High School, provided information on the primary schools in Kitui, a rural area about one hundred miles east of Nairobi.
7. 'Encourage' is a euphemism. While teaching at Kenya's Kenyatta University College, this writer had students who related various punishments they were given, when they were primary pupils, for not speaking English. They assured this writer that even today, physical punishment is still being meted out for use of 'inappropriate' languages.
8. Personal communication, Said Bilal.
9. 'Education for Self-Reliance' was issued in March of 1967. It followed the 'Arusha Declaration', which was a document issued by TANU (Tanzanian African National Union, the ruling political party) in January, 1967. The 'Arusha Declaration' set forth a new orientation toward socialist policy. See 'The Arusha Declaration' 1967: 231-50.
10. A survey carried out by Hemphill (1974) between 1968 and 1965 found that 60 percent of the Kenyan primary schools surveyed nationally used English as initial medium of instruction.
11. Personal communication, David Court and Jeffrey Fine.
12. Personal communication, David Court.

References

Abdulaziz, M. H. 1971. Tanzania's national language policy and the rise of Swahili political culture. In Whiteley, W. H. (ed.), *Language Use and Social Change*, 160-77. London: Oxford University Press.
Africa Contemporary Record. 1976-77, 1977-78, 1978-79. Annual Survey and Documents. Legum, C., ed. New York and London: Africana Publishing Co.
Ansre, G. 1976. Four retionalisations[sic] for maintaining the European languages in education in Africa. Paper presented at the International Seminar on African Languages in Education, Kinshasa, Zaire, 1976.
– n.d. The use of indigenous languages in education in sub-saharan Africa: presuppositions, lessons and prospects. Mimeo.
The Arusha Declaration: socialism and self-reliance. 1967. In Nyerere, J. K., *Freedom and Socialism: Uhuru na Ujamaa*, 231-50. Dar es Salaam and London: Oxford University Press, 1968.
Bagunywa, A. M. K. 1970. The teaching of vernacular languages in primary schools. In Gorman, T. P. (ed.), *Language in Education in Eastern Africa*, 25-9. Nairobi: Oxford University Press.
Cameron, J. 1970. *The Development of Education in East Africa.* New York: Teachers College Press.
– and W.A. Dodd. 1970. *Society, Schools & Progress in Tanzania.* Oxford and New York: Pergamon Press.
Court, D., and K. Kinyanjui. 1978. *Development Policy and Educational Opportunity: the experience of Kenya and Tanzania.* International Institute for Educational Planning Working Paper. Paris: UNESCO.
Education in Africa in the Light of the Lagos Conference. 1976. Paris: UNESCO Educational Studies and Documents No. 25.
Education in a Rural Environment. 1974. Paris: UNESCO.
Education: Sector Working Paper. World Bank. December 1974.
Fishman, J. A. 1972. *Language and Nationalism: Two Integrative Essays.* Rowley, Mass.: Newbury House.
– 1977. Language and ethnicity. In Gilas, H. (ed.), *Language, Ethnicity and Intergroup Relations*, 15-57. London and New York: Academic Press.

Gachukia, E. 1970. The teaching of vernacular languages in Kenya primary schools, In Gorman, T. P. (ed.), *Language in Education in Eastern Africa*, 18-24. Nairobi: Oxford University Press.

Harries, L. 1968. Swahili in modern East Africa. In Fishman, J. A., C. A. Ferguson, and J. Das Gupta (eds.), *Language Problems of Developing Nations*, 415-29. New York: Wiley.

Hazlewood, A. 1979. *The Economy of Kenya: the Kenyatta Era*. Oxford: Oxford University Press.

Heine, B. 1970. *Status and Use of African Lingua Francas*. Ifo-Institut für Wirtschaftsforschung München, Afrika-Studienstella. Munich: Weltform Verlag.

Hemphill, R. J. 1974. Language use and language teaching in the primary schools of Kenya. In Whiteley, W. H. (ed.), *Language in Kenya*, 455-79. Nairobi: Oxford University Press.

Kihore, Y. M. 1976. Tanzania's language policy and Kiswahili's historical background. African and Asian Studies Seminar Series No. 25, University of Khartoum: Institute of African and Asian Studies, February 1976.

King, K. 1974. Primary schools in Kenya: some critical constraints on their effectiveness. In Court, D., and D. P. Ghai (eds.), *Education, Society and Development: New Perspectives from Kenya*, 123-48. Nairobi: Oxford University Press.

Komba, D. A. 1979. The integration of education and work in Tanzania. Unpublished Ph. D. dissertation, Columbia University.

Kunene, D. P. 1978. Mother tongue education: a necessity or luxury? Paper presented at the Symposium on African Language Policies, LSA Summer Institute, University of Illinois-Urbana, July 6-8.

Morrison, D. R. 1976. *Education and Politics in Africa: the Tanzanian Case*. Montreal: McGill-Queen's University Press.

Muncie, P. C. 1973. *Torches in the Night: Educational Experiences in Tanzania and the Ivory Coast*. Washington, D. C.: World Bank Group.

Nyerere, J. K. 1967. Education for self-reliance. In Nyerere, J. K., *Freedom and Socialism: Uhuru na Ujamaa*, 267-90. Dar es Salaam and London: Oxford University Press.

Raju, B. M. 1973. *Education in Kenya: Problems and Perspectives in Educational Planning and Administration*. Nairobi: Heinemann.

– 1969. *Planning for Progress: Our Second Development Plan, A Short Version of the Development Plan 1970-1974*, Nairobi: Government Printer.

Republic of Kenya. 1974. *Development Plan 1974-1978*. Part I. Nairobi: Government Printer.

– 1976. *Report of the National Committee on Educational Objectives and Policies*. (the "Gachathi Report") Nairobi: Government Printer. First released in 1978.

– 1979. *Development Plan 1979-1983*. Part I. Nairobi: Government Printer.

– *Economic Survey 1980*. Nairobi: Central Bureau of Statistics, Ministry of Economic Planning and Development.

Scotton, C. M. 1978. 'Elite closure' and language policy in Africa. Paper presented at the Symposium on African Language Policies, LSA Summer Institute, University of Illinois-Urbana, July 6-8.

Sheffield, J. R. 1979. Basic education for the rural poor: the Tanzanian case. *The Journal of Developing Areas* 14.1.99-110.

– 1964. *Five-Year Plan for Economic and Social Development. 1st July 1964-30th June 1969*. Vol. I. Dar es Salaam: National Printing Co.

United Republic of Tanzania. 1967. *Annual Report of the Ministry of Education 1964*. Dar es Salaam: Government Printer.

– 1976. *Third Five-Year Plan for Economic and Social Development. 1st July 1976-30th June 1981*. First volume. Dar es Salaam: National Printing Co.

– 1969. *Second Five-Year Plan for Economic and Social Development. 1st July 1969-30th June 1974*. Vol. I. Dar es Salaam: National Printing Co.

Whiteley, W. H. 1974a. The classification and distribution of Kenya's African languages. In Whiteley, W. H. (ed.), *Language in Kenya,* 13-68. Nairobi: Oxford University Press.
— ed. 1974b. *Language in Kenya.* Nairobi: Oxford University Press.
Zuengler, J. 1981. Kenyan English. In Kachru, B. (ed.), *The Other Tongue: English Across Cultures.* Urbana: University of Illinois Press.

Charlene J. Sato

Linguistic Inequality in Hawaii:
The Post-Creole Dilemma*

Introduction

Kauai, Niihau, Oahu, Maui, Molokai, Lanai, and Hawaii, the inhabited islands of the Hawaiian archipelago, are located 3850 miles west of Japan and 2390 miles east of California. Roughly 865,000 people live in these islands, a disproportionate 82 percent of them in and around Honolulu, the state capital on Oahu (Nordyke 1977). The economy depends primarily on the US military-industrial complex, tourism, and agriculture. Although the state maintains a relatively high standard of living, the cost of living is also one of the highest in the nation.

The people of Hawaii form one of the most ethnically diverse communities in the US. Hawaii is, in fact, the only American state where no single ethnic group comprises a majority and where most of the people come from Asia and a myriad of Pacific Islands rather than from Europe or Africa (Nordyke 1977). Although about 39 percent of the population is now Caucasian, they are outnumbered by the combined Asian and Pacific contingent: Japanese, Filipinos, Hawaiians, Chinese, Koreans, and others. This cosmopolitan make-up has resulted from a complex history of immigration to the islands, with each group arriving at different times and under varying circumstances.[1]

Present-day native Hawaiians descend from Polynesian settlers who crossed the Pacific to the islands as early as the eighth century *A.D.* and flourished in isolation until the arrival in 1778 of Captain James Cook, an English explorer. Cook's visit having opened the door to Western contact, it was not long before the feudal economy of the Hawaiian kingdom crumbled under the force of the capitalist enterprises of *haole* traders, merchants, and missionaries.[2] The development of a plantation economy followed during the second half of the nineteenth century and, thereafter, the importation of thousands of laborers from around the world to work the plantations. Increased economic ties with the US bolstered the political stance of the *haole* planter oligarchy, which eventually overthrew the Hawaiian monarchy in 1893 and secured US annexation of the islands in 1898. In little more than a century, the Hawaiian people had come to be politically subjugated by

Westerners and numerically dominated by Asians and other immigrant groups. By the start of the twentieth century, pure native Hawaiians accounted for a mere 19 percent of the total population of roughly 154,000.

How these sweeping changes in the economic, political, and social life of the islands restructured language choice and language use among Hawaii's people is the focus of this paper. We will first look at the historical context of multilingual contact in Hawaii, with special reference to the linguistic processes of pidginization, creolization, and decreolization. In detailing this background, we will see how the linguistic imperialism which suppressed the Hawaiian language in the late 1800s still manifests itself a century later with respect to Hawaii Creole English.[3]

First, some terms need to be defined. Throughout the paper we will refer to Hawaii Pidgin English (HPE) and Hawaii Creole English (HCE). They will be distinguished from each other on the basis of the following definitions current in the field of pidgin and creole linguistics:

1.   A *pidgin* is "a contact vernacular, normally not the native language of any of its speakers. It is used in trading or in any situation requiring communication between persons who do not speak each other's native languages. It is characterized by a limited vocabulary, an elimination of many grammatical devices such as number and gender, and a drastic reduction of redundant features" (DeCamp, 1971: 15).

A pidgin "always arises . . . from a situation involving a target language and *two or more* substrate languages", where that socially superior target language is sufficiently inaccessible to the substrate speakers that there is little motivation to improve performance and where a "defective language can be functionally adequate" (Whinnom, 1971: 106).

In other words, a pidgin is developed by speakers of different languages for use among themselves. There is an alternative view, which holds that a pidgin results from attempts by speakers of the socially dominant language to simplify their speech to non-speakers of their language. This 'foreigner talk' view is not supported by the facts of the Hawaiian situation and must therefore be distinguished from the *multi*lingual contact said to characterize pidgin development.

2.   A *creole* is a language spoken by the native-born children of pidgin-speaking parents. It functions as the mother tongue of its speakers, *not* as a functionally restricted, structurally reduced second language.

While many scholars claim that a creole develops out of its antecedent pidgin through large-scale lexical and grammatical expansion and diversification, some features seem totally new and unrelated either to the earlier pidgin or to the donor languages. In any case, a creole's basic vocabulary is usually taken from the standard or colonial language of the community, while its grammatical structure derives from its antecedent pidgin, the donor languages to the pidgin, and from innovations by creole speakers.

E komo mai[4]

Prior to the growth of the sandalwood and whaling industries during the first half of the nineteenth century, contact between the Hawaiian and English languages was largely restricted to communication between the Hawaiians and foreign, mostly American, traders and sailors during their brief stopovers. Day (this volume) uses the term Maritime Pidgin Hawaiian to describe their speech. With the expansion of the sandalwood trade, whaling, and related commercial enterprises came an increase in the resident English-speaking population in ports such as Honolulu and Lahaina on Maui. While this may have motivated some of the foreigners to learn Hawaiian, the move toward bilingualism was apparently not reciprocated by many Hawaiians (Reinecke, 1969). There was no need then for the numerically dominant and socially secure Hawaiian population to learn English, the outsider's language.

The arrival and settlement of Protestant missionaries from New England in 1820 and thereafter changed the picture considerably. Not only did the missionaries devise an orthography for the Hawaiian language for Bible translation purposes, but they also opened schools in which the Hawaiian language was, at first, the medium of instruction.[5] Enrollment, however, was reserved for the elite segment of Hawaiian society during the first half of the nineteenth century, and the majority of the Hawaiian people remained monolingual. Reinecke (1969: 32) remarks, "apparently the genuinely English-speaking natives were very few and were mostly confined to Honolulu, Hilo, and Lahaina prior to the late 1800s."

As it happened, Christianity was soon associated with capitalism, as the missionaries were rewarded for their efforts at educating the *ali'i* ('chiefs') and their children with an entré into elite diplomatic and social circles and, more importantly, with gifts of land. They became political advisors to the Hawaiian royalty and thus steered the island kingdom toward a capitalist economy, the basis of which was the sugar plantation.

Communication between the *haoles* and the Hawaiian commoners, especially during the early years of the plantations when the latter constituted the bulk of the labor force, was apparently conducted in *hapa-haole* ('half-foreign'). Bickerton (Bickerton and Odo 1976: 14) describes this talk as "a 'foreigner's English' continuum rather than a pidgin language in the sense in which the latter term is normally understood." Reinecke (1969: 35) characterizes this speech as one which "never attained any sort of fixity in either grammatical structure or vocabulary. Each Hawaiian spoke the best English he could."

Very early on the harsh, exploitative working conditions on the plantations discouraged the Hawaiian workers. Between 1872 and 1890, the proportion of Hawaiians in the labor force dropped from 85 percent to a mere 11 percent (Beechert, 1977). To compensate for the steady loss of workers, the planters brought in small groups of Chinese and Micronesian men, roughly 4000 in all, between 1852 and 1885. Neither group had much effect on the plantation language, as quite a few Micronesians returned home, and many Chinese left the plantations for the towns. Those who remained often married Hawaiian women and learned to speak Hawaiian.

The plantations and pidginization

The sugar industry received a major boost from the 1876 Reciprocal Trade Treaty with the US, which guaranteed a market for Hawaiian sugar, and the planters wasted no time in launching a massive recruitment effort. The amazingly diverse work force that subsequently arrived in the islands included, chiefly, Chinese, Portuguese, Japanese, Puerto Ricans, Spanish, Koreans, and Filipinos. Although smaller groups of Germans, Galicians, Micronesians, Russians, and Scandinavians were also brought in, they did not influence the development of HPE nearly as much as the Portuguese, Japanese, and Filipinos did.

The crucial period for HPE formation seems to have been the period between 1890 and 1910 when most of the Chinese, Portuguese, and Japanese arrived. Bickerton and Givón (1976: 11) assert that "a recognizable Hawaiian Pidgin English probably did not develop until the last decade of that [the nineteenth] century or the first of the twentieth", and Reinecke (1969: 35) reports: "All *Kamaaina* (old time) Islanders whom I have asked have said that a 'pidgin English' did not arise until after the Chinese and Portuguese immigration."

Scholars agree that the pidgin was probably highly unstable and that it varied widely among the different ethnic groups and from locality to locality. Basically, HPE consisted of Hawaiian and English vocabulary embedded in the grammatical structure of a speaker's native language. Even today, the ethnic background of the few remaining pidgin speakers can be accurately determined from features of their speech such as pronunciation and word order. The following examples come from a Filipino pidgin speaker and a Japanese pidgin speaker, respectively:

(i) *mo plæni da ilokano en da tagalog* (MF64M)[6]
more-plenty-the-Ilokano-than-the-Tagalog
'[There were] more Ilokano [speakers] than Tagalog [speakers]'

(ii) *samtaim gud rod get, samtaim, olsem ben get, enguru get, no? enikain sem, Olsem hyumen life, olsem. gud rodu get, enguru get, mauntin get – no?* (MJ66H)[7]
sometimes-good-road-get, sometimes, all same-bend-get, angle get, no? any kind-same. all same-human-life, all same.
'Sometimes there's a good road, sometimes there's something like a bend, an angle, right? Everything's like that. Human life is the same. There are good roads, there are angles, there are mountains – right?'

The great structural variability in HPE, both within and across individual speakers, is understandable in view of the demographic circumstances. Each plantation was relatively self-contained, which meant that people dealt with each other on a regular basis and somewhat conventionalized their own 'local' HPE. Within each plantation, the different ethnic groups were usually housed in separate camps or separate areas in the same camp. On the one hand, this proved to the workers' liking, since it helped them to maintain ethnic boundaries. On the other, such physical separation served the planters' interests, as it discouraged collective organization among the different groups against the plantation management. In any case, intergroup contact was mainly limited to the workplace—the fields and the mills. HPE functioned, then, as a secondary mode of communication for speakers who conducted the bulk of their interactions in their native tongues. Neither the immigrants nor the planter oligarchy saw fluency in English as desirable or necessary. It was certainly not very likely, given the sparse input available to the workers.

Here, it is important to point out that, while all of the immigrant groups were subject to roughly the same kind of plantation environment, each arrived at a different time and settled under unique circumstances. Their roles in the development of HPE and, later, HCE therefore vary somewhat. As this aspect of our understanding of pidgin-creole communities is most easily overlooked, let us more closely examine the sociolinguistic impact of the serial migration of the Portuguese, Japanese, and Filipinos on the Hawaiian situation.

The Portuguese seem to have played a major role in extending HPE use. Roughly 10,000 of them arrived and settled in the islands during the 1880s, many with wives and families. Not only were they given better jobs than were the Chinese who had arrived before them (Adams 1933: 14), but the Portuguese were also offered homestead land and free schooling for their children. As Europeans, they occupied a socioeconomic position between that of the *haole* plantation owners and the Asian laborers. They held what might be called 'middle management' positions; they served as *lunas* (overseers), along with some Hawaiians. Because they came into close contact with both their English-speaking bosses and the non-English-speaking workers, the Portuguese were forced to reconcile whatever English they could pick up with the plantation Hawaiian then in use—all without the benefit of intensive language courses.

The fact that the Portuguese, unlike the other immigrant groups, came with their families had an important effect on the use of English in Hawaii. They did not want their children taught in Hawaiian, as was then the practice in most of the schools. Portuguese parents demanded, and got, instruction in English for their children. By this time, the Hawaiian language was already losing its battle with English in the business and governmental arenas (see

Day, this volume), and the influx of Portuguese children made it even more difficult for Hawaiian language advocates to hold their ground. The issue of English schooling will be more fully discussed in conjunction with the development of HCE. For the moment, the point is simply that, by the turn of the century, Portuguese children were being exposed to English in the school context at the same time that their parents were using an untaught variety of it in their plantation networks. As Reinecke (1969: 92–93) has observed, the Portuguese "were much less isolated culturally and in social relations than the Oriental groups were, and had more reason to learn English than had the latter". In sum, both occupational and educational circumstances favored Portuguese assimilation and their adoption of a new language.

The next and largest group recruited by the planters were the Japanese, the first handful arriving in 1898. By 1920 roughly 109,000 lived in the islands, 43 percent of the total population. The Japanese remained the largest ethnic group here until the 1960s, when the Caucasians came to outnumber them. As "the most widely and evenly distributed of the immigrant groups" (Reinecke 1969: 53), they must be credited with expanding HPE use considerably. However, their exposure to English was at first much more limited than that of the Portuguese, primarily because of their maintenance of Japanese culture.

The Japanese also differed from the Portuguese in that they did not originally intend to settle in the islands. Many of the men who arrived in the earlier groups planned to work only long enough to save some money to take back to Japan. Nonetheless, they were a cohesive group who married—many sent for picture brides from Japan—and raised families early on. Thus it was not long before there were thriving Japanese enclaves in many plantation areas, with Japanese language newspapers and an extensive system of language schools. The Japanese language naturally retained its vitality in such a supportive environment. No doubt this mother tongue retention had the effect of increasing the amount of Japanese features that became conventionalized in HPE because there were so many of these speakers around.

By the time some 18,000 Filipino recruits were brought in between 1907 and 1915, HPE had been used for some time among their predecessors. The Filipinos were mainly single men who remained on the plantations for a long time and, unlike the Portuguese and Japanese, were slow to marry and start families. They associated most regularly with their own countrymen and less often with other co-workers. Because of their late appearance on the scene, the Filipinos heard a lot of HCE, in addition to HPE, being spoken around them. As a result, their variety of HPE contains many creole forms, although it sounds distincty Filipino. Some linguists have described this situation as 'repidginization'.

The Filipino experience is important in clarifying an issue in pidgin-creole linguistics, since it shows that pidgin languages do not always or only arise out of *simultaneous* contact among several different language groups. In this case, as a result of the serial importation of the various groups of workers, HPE became, not a stable, monolithic entity, but a conglomerate of Hawaiian- and English-related varieties which strongly reflected the native languages of their speakers. Recent research analyzing the speech of survivors of the plantation era (Bickerton and Odo 1976; Peet 1978; Perlman 1973; Sato 1978) documents the highly variable nature of their HPE.

Stabilization did take place, however, though the development of HCE after the turn of the century. Hawaii Creole English served as the mother tongue of the children of the pidgin-speaking immigrants. According to our definition of creole languages, the earliest Hawaii-born children of immigrant parentage were, technically, HCE speakers. However, most of them tended to be bilingual in their ancestral tongues as well as in the creole, as they received considerable input from members of their own ethnic groups. It was not until the mid-1930s or so, when HCE usage was at its peak—judging from the greater proportion of locally-born to immigrants in the population—that significantly more of the second and third generation offspring approached monolingualism in the creole. It was often the case that these HCE speakers could understand but not speak their ancestral languages, so a kind of 'dual-lingualism' arose in many households, with parents speaking the ancestral language and children, the creole.[8]

The fact that the earliest HCE speakers were often bilingual provides evidence against a view that attributes creolization exclusively to children's innate language creation abilities. While it is probably true that the HPE input the Hawaii children received was scanty, it is difficult to imagine their not relying heavily on their ancestral languages in developing the creole. On the other hand, there are unquestionably some HCE features, such as the system of marking tense, aspect, and modality, which bear such a striking resemblance to those of other creole languages in the world, that we must acknowledge the role of universal tendencies in language development (see Bickerton 1981). The point to note here is that in the HCE case, there was some carryover of forms from HPE, Hawaiian, English, and the various immigrant languages. The convergence of features was systematized and elaborated by the creole speakers, who contributed innovations of their own. The result was a unique mother tongue common to the majority of Hawaii-born children of various ethnic backgrounds.

An example of HCE should help clarify some of its differences from HPE. The following excerpt comes from a 45-year-old HCE-speaking man from the island of Kauai, one of the least decreolized islands:

(iii)   *luk nau, a bin go si Toni abaut go spansa da kidz, ae, da bæskitbawl tim, da wan ai ste koch fo — ai tel, e, Toni, hauz abaut, a, spansa da kidz, boi, yu no æfta awl iz awl Puhi kidz, yu no — æen awl as gaiz awl y unyen membaz, ae?* a tel am yu — yu gaiz kæn spansa ada gaiz — ai no si wai yu gaiz no kæn spansa da kidz. (MF45 K)[9]

look-now, I-been-go-see-Tony-about-go-sponsor-the-kids, eh, the-basketball-team, the-one-I-stay-coach-for-I-tell, hey, Tony, how's-about, uh, sponsor-the-kids, boi.   you-know-after-all-it's-all-Puhi-kids-you-know—and-all-us-guys-all-union-members, eh? I-tell-him-you—you-guys-can-sponsor-other-guys—I-no-see-why-you-guys-no-can-sponsor-the-kids.

'Look now, I went to see Tony about [their] sponsoring the kids, eh, the basket-ball team that I'm coaching — I said, "Hey, Tony, how about sponsoring the kids, boy. You know after all they're all Puhi [name of a town] kids, you know — and all of us [parents] are union members, eh?" I told him. "You — you guys can sponsor other guys — I don't see why you can't sponsor the kids."'

An important point to note here is that this speaker's ethnic background—he is Filipino—is *not* determinable from his speech, as is true of all 'true' creole speakers. Other characteristically HCE features include the speaker's preverbal tense/aspect markers—*bin, ste*—his negative modal—*no kæn*—and his unmarked past tense in *tel* ('said' or 'told').

Creolization and schooling

Normally, the introduction of mass education in the colonial language in an incipient pidgin-creole community undermines stabilization of the creole in that community. It either sets in motion or accelerates decreolization, the process through which the creole language loses its functional and structural integrity in merging with the colonial language. Although this is what eventually happened in the Hawaiian situation, nearly a century ago quite the opposite resulted from the elitist, separatist langue policies of the English-speaking oligarchy.

Prior to the influx of the plantation workers' children, the schools originally set up by the New England missionaries had only to deal with Hawaiian- and English-speaking children. In the 1830s, there were 'select' schools for the children of Hawaiian royalty and 'common' schools for all others, both taught in Hawaiian (Stueber 1965). Then there were the English schools reserved for missionary and other privileged *haole* children. This dual system worked well at the time, as Hawaii was still a kingdom ruled by Hawaiians, and the *haoles* were, in a sense, their guests.

It was missionary zeal for educating the unconverted that led to the establishment, in the 1880s, of a public school system whose target population was the Hawaiians and part-Hawaiians. English was adopted experimentally as the language of instruction in a few of these public schools beginning in 1854 (Stueber 1965). By the time Chinese, Portuguese, and Japanese children arrived on the scene in the 1880s, over 84 percent of the 8770 students in island schools were being taught in English. Within the next decade, in 1894, English was declared the official medium of instruction in all of Hawaii's schools.

Given this institutional shift to English, the claim that creolization was fostered rather than suppressed might seem questionable. The facts of the situation, however, provide strong evidence for just such a claim. If we look beyond the official adoption of English to its use in the day-to-day context, it becomes clear that there was, in fact, no substantial increase in the amount of English input and interaction made available to HCE-speaking children. In the first place, the classroom constituted an English as a second language, if not an English as a *foreign* language, setting, serving as it did Hawaiian, part-Hawaiian, Portuguese, Chinese, Japanese, and virtually no *haole* children. Moreover, pedagogical practices of the time resulted in teachers more often than not speaking English *at* rather than with the students. There was, no doubt, considerable variability in the 'standardness' of their English as well, since many of the teachers were Hawaiians and part-Hawaiians who were themselves non-native speakers of English.

More important was the absence of a primary source of target input from native English-speaking peers with whom the non-*haole* population could interact. Recall that almost all *haole* children attended the private schools and were therefore not available either as play partners or as language models in the classroom. In such a setting, HCE naturally came to serve as the primary channel of communication for the children, one that was conventionalized as social networks crossed ethnic boundaries.

Also critical to the maintenance of HCE in the face of institutional pressure from English was the climate in the multilingual community outside the schools, where English dominance was tolerated or accepted rather than actively supported. While some Hawaiians and, particularly, part-*haole* Hawaiians sought to become English speakers, the Asian groups, in passive resistance to Americanization, remained culturally homogeneous during this period. Ultimately, it was their traditional quest for education rather than any particular passion for English that led to consistently high enrollment figures for Chinese, Japanese, and, later, Koreans in Hawaii's public schools. Their home languages remained viable through constant use with family and community members as well as through daily attendance at language schools. In sum, English acquisition was, for the most part, a peripheral phenomenon in the language socialization of these children.

The *haole* elitism that had motivated private schooling early on led to agitation in the 1920s for segregated public schooling. By this time, a sizable non-planter class *haole* population, mainly from the southern and western US, lived in Honolulu. It was now this group that objected to contact between their children and the 'pidgin-speaking' non-*haole* children. Because these parents could not afford private school tuition, their only alternative was to call for segregation in the public school system. However, racial segregation was unconscionable in an American territory such as Hawaii had become, and more to the point, impracticable in light of the extensive intermarriage across the various ethnic groups.

A solution emerged in the report of a team of federal investigators who had conducted a study of Hawaii's educational system in 1919. One of their recommendations was to group children in different schools according to their proficiency in English. Such a policy was directed at the Asians, mainly the Japanese, who accounted for just over 44 percent of the total 57,502 enrollment in 1922 (Reinecke 1969: 76–77). The segregationists claimed that the admission of the Japanese to the English Standard schools, as they would be called, "was blocked, not because of prejudice, but because their attendance at foreign language schools before and after their attendance each day at the public school was responsible for keeping their English sub-standard" (Stueber 1965: 31).

Despite considerable protest from the Asian community and some progressive educators, the English Standard (ES) system was implemented in 1924, with a few of the islands' schools designated ES schools for those children who could pass the English test. The major effect of this system was the further stratification of Hawaiian society along ethnic lines by means of discrimination along linguistic ones. By institutionalizing linguistic inequality in this way, the ES schools legitimized the negative stereotyping of HCE speakers, very few of whom ever benefited from the academic advantages provided in these schools. In fact, the ES system never accommodated more than 10 percent of the total school population in Hawaii during its 25-year life span; the overwhelming majority of its students were *haole* (Stueber 1965).

The system's abolition was eventually brought about by World War II, when roughly 2000 *haole* children were withdrawn from the schools at the war's outbreak. At this time, less than 7 percent of all the school-aged children were enrolled in ES schools, and the departure of the *haole* children effectively removed the bulk of the ES population (Fuchs 1961: 279). In 1948, the system was abolished and in 1960, the last ES class was graduated from high school. The vacuum was shortly filled, however, by the establishment of English sections (classes) in individual schools. The practice remained the same, to foster academic success in those who made a conscious effort to adopt English at the expense of those who either could not or would not do so.

Paradoxically, the ES schools played a crucial role in the development of HCE, simply because they helped maintain the distance between HCE speakers and English speakers for another twenty years. Stueber (1965: 31) notes that, as late as 1940, "the great bulk of non-haoles completed their schooling without making intimate contact with Standard English speakers, mainly the haole population". In such circumstances, it is understandable that HCE remained a functional means of communication.

In summary, while the groundwork for English adoption in Hawaii's schools was laid in the late nineteenth century, the extensive contact with native speakers vital to such a shift in language use was not readily available to the non-*haole* children of Hawaii for three or four decades thereafter. In current bilingual education terms, had 'mainstreaming' of the non-*haole* children into schools primarily composed of English speakers been practicable, English would have taken root much sooner than it did.

Decreolization and the post-creole dilemma

Mass education eventually became a strong force promoting decreolization, the linguistic convergence of HCE with Standard English (SE) at the societal, although not necessarily at the individual, level. During the 1930s and 1940s, decreolization accelerated, reflecting the islands' rapid economic and political incorporation into the US, which resulted from the plantation oligarchy's channeling of sugar and pineapple industry profits into other interests: transportation, banking, public utilities, merchandising, and tourism (Lind 1967: 68). The employment opportunities thus created quickly drew workers off the plantations and into the urban areas, principally Honolulu. In just a decade, the plantation labor force was cut in half, from over 51,000 workers in 1932 to roughly 26,000 (Lind 1967: 71). A diversified economy providing jobs at better wages than those the plantations offered laid the foundation for a middle class in Hawaiian society. Of the immigrant groups, the Chinese, Portuguese and Japanese, in particular, moved steadily into skilled, clerical, and professional positions. This shift was paralleled in their language usage as well, with a greater proportion of speakers from these groups coming to represent the more decreolized segment of the community.

With World War II came an unprecedented expansion of US defense industries and, predictably, a concerted drive toward Americanization. The Japanese were especially vigorous, necessarily so, in demonstrating their American patriotism. Language schools, both Japanese and Chinese, were closed down throughout the war years, and other forms of cultural maintenance considerably curtailed. Generational conflicts between immigrant parents and local-born children worsened as a result of opposing national and, hence, linguistic loyalties. For the latter group, the adoption of English played a greater role than ever before in exemplifying affinity with the American way of life. Certainly, opportunities to use SE had dramatically increased with the arrival of a large group of military and civilian personnel from the mainland.

It was in this context that HCE was foregrounded as a marker of socioeconomic status in Hawaiian society. Being labelled a 'Pidgin' [i.e., HCE] speaker was considered by many a liability in the job market, associated as it was with the plantation and with the minimal intelligence assumed necessary for manual labor. It is important to note that the negative value was attached, not to being a HCE speaker, but to being *labelled* as such. Many individuals who thought of themselves as American or who simply aspired to the middle class made a conscious effort to suppress their HCE and their ancestral languages in favor of English.

Increased contact with English speakers, then, created both a convergence and a polarization in Hawaiian society. HCE's movement towards SE was reflected in the more frequent appearance of English features in the speech of locals, particularly those whose occupation and or social networks included mainland English speakers. At the same time, as the middle class's identity with SE developed, so the working class's alienation from it increased. More than ever before, HCE came to delineate class as well as ethnic differences among the people of Hawaii.

In 1959, American statehood was conferred upon the islands. The escalation of tourism and resort development followed, exacerbating existing resentment among many locals toward tourists, real estate speculators, and outside corporate investors. 'Tawking laik wan *haole*' associated one with the economic and political exploitation practiced by such outsiders and was therefore behavior to be avoided. Speaking HCE became a salient indicator of ethnic—i.e., 'local' as opposed to mainland *haole*—in-groupness that overlapped with its correlation with economic status as well. In Reinecke's (1969: 174) terms, HCE "emphasize[d] doubly the consciousness of kind".

Unfortunately, the rejection of SE that accompanied the affirmation of HCE often locked many HCE speakers into the vicious cycle of educational failure, socioeconomic stagnation, and political powerlessness. The alternative—switching more or less permanently to SE—effectively removed people from their primary social networks and often created tension within these networks. This, then, has been the dilemma confronting HCE speakers for the past three generations.

The assimilationist pressures intensified by the wartime experience have remained a factor in the language socialization of island children. As in many colonial situations where the less prestigious code in the community is explicitly devalued (see Sankoff 1980), many HCE speakers have come to perceive their home language as a way of speaking to be corrected and eventually overcome, like a bad habit. While HCE-speaking children display positive attitudes toward their home language upon entering school, recent research by Day (1980) has shown a switch taking place, to more positive attitudes toward SE, after only two years of schooling. In other words, it is in the educational context that these children are being made aware of community and/or institutional stereotypes of both HCE and SE. The question arises, then, of how Hawaii's schools have dealt with the language development of HCE-speaking children.

Recall that, over the years, HCE has been treated as a foreign language, forbidden in the classroom, declared *not* a language, branded un-American, and so on. Pedagogical practice seems to have shifted from proscription to prescription until, in the last decade or so, HCE has been officially recognized as a legitimate mother tongue. This recognition of HCE, however, has not led to its active maintenance in the educational context. To the contrary, curriculum development projects in the 1960s (e.g., those described in Nunes 1967; and Peterson 1967) clearly had as a goal transition from HCE to SE. HCE was seen as a starting point for instruction in SE, but its extension to the classroom was never given serious consideration.

Currently, the stance on HCE taken by the state Department of Education (DOE) is a contradictory one, as evidenced by its statements concerning HCE speaker's ineligibility for bilingual education programs. It seems, in essence, that the lack of resources, both human and financial, has forced the DOE to avoid confronting the 'Pidgin problem', primarily by denying that such a problem exists. This has involved a relabelling of HCE as a 'dialect' rather than a 'language', the implication being that differences between HCE and SE are so minimal as to obviate special programs, curricula, and/or materials. It remains to be seen how successful a devaluation of HCE's autonomy as a means of communication can be reconciled with the DOE's (Hawaii State DOA 1980: 4) explicit acknowledgement that HCE "is the first language for many children". At the very least, there has been a misunderstanding of the terms 'dialect' and 'language'; however, there may also have been a tendency to understate the linguistic uniqueness of HCE for the sake of administrative or pedagogical expediency. This interpretation of the situation is based in particular on the DOE's actions on two recent occasions where the issue of the educational needs of HCE speakers has been raised.

On the first of these occasions, HCE was explicitly judged a language that one could not be bilingual in. In order to determine the number and size of different first language groups among Hawaii's public school population, the DOE conducted a survey in 1977. The language categories in which students could be classified included Ilokano, Korean, and so forth. HCE speakers were not put into a separate category but classified as English speakers (Tyler 1978: 3). As a result, HCE speakers were denied consideration in the bilingual/bicultural program. While there are good arguments against the inclusion of HCE speakers in such programs, one argument cannot be that all HCE speakers are SE speakers anyway. To put it another way, the exclusion of HCE speakers from a bilingual education program does not justify totally ignoring this population of speakers, many of whom do have "sufficient difficulty speaking, reading, writing, or understanding the English language to deny them the opportunity to learn successfully in classrooms in which the language of instruction is English" (Hawaii State DOE 1980: 2).

In April, 1979, the problem was addressed in the legislative arena when the Hawaii House of Representatives (1979: 2) adopted a resolution requesting the DOE to "review its basis for the definition of the target group in Hawaii's bilingual education program and to reassess the needs of the Creole-speaking students with limited English-speaking ability and their eligibility for inclusion in the program".[10] The resolution also called for a report including the following data, none of which are yet available from any published research projects:

1. the number of students who learned first to speak Creole and have limited English-speaking ability, including the criteria for this assessment;
2. comparison and interpretation of standardized and other test scores of Creole-speaking students with LESA [Limited English Speaking Ability] and English-speaking students, including patterns of test results in reading comprehension, vocabulary, math computation, and word-problem solving;
3. comparison of the proportion of Creole-speaking students with LESA in the total student population who are in remedial reading classes, special education classes, and alternative programs, and those who have dropped out of school;
4. the extent to which positive or negative attitudes toward Creole and toward the Creole-speaking students are reflected by the school in rules, policies, and practices that encourage, allow, or discourage the use of Creole in class and on the playground;
5. the extent to which students are helped to make the transition from Creole to standard English through providing more extensive reading readiness activities for such students, by allowing the use of Creole in class discussions, storytelling, and creative writing, developing and adapting reading materials for the Creole-speaking students, and by providing more extensive instruction in vocabulary development; and
6. the number of Creole-speaking students with LESA who are using the Keaukaha Project and the Hawaii English Program (HEP) materials and an evaluation of their effectiveness . . . [11]

The point being made here is not that all of these data need to be gathered from massive research programs but that presently, virtually *none* of these questions about HCE-speaking children can be answered with respect to changes that might be made in the educational context.

In the DOE's (1980: 3) response to the resolution, it was claimed that HCE speakers could not be "classified as students of limited English proficiency" and, moreover, that the DOE's "curricula effectively treat the issue of the place of Pidgin English [i.e., HCE] in instruction and learning."

The lack of empirical evidence in support of this claim makes it difficult to ascertain the extent to which the needs of HCE speakers are actually being met.

Another shortcoming in the report is the claim (Hawaii State DOE, 1980: 2) that research by Day has shown "that the majority of Hawaii's children possess a great deal of fluency in both Pidgin [i.e., HCE] and English." In his extensive work on HCE, Day has not made such a generalization. Rather, he has made some specific observations, primarily of children at a laboratory school. In a paper reviewing the research of which Day's was a part, Gallimore and Tharp (1976) report the finding in question: that those children who performed well on a SE repetition test also tended to do well on a HCE repetition test. Hence, the inference that skill in SE is paralleled by skill in HCE. However, we cannot make the further inference that such parallel fluency is found in the 'majority' of Hawaii's children. At best, we might hypothesize that, if both repetition tests were administered to many HCE-speaking children, there would be some who would do well on both, some who would do poorly on both, and others who would do better on one test than the other.

It was, unfortunately, this kind of misinterpreted research finding that justified—from the DOE's point of view—the refusal to comply with the legislative resolution. Given the relative scarcity of research on language development in island children, the evidence that is available merits careful as well as critical scrutiny by those in a position to control the education of these children. Some of this evidence comes, for example, from studies of adult HPE and HCE conducted over the last decade (e.g., Bickerton 1977; Day 1972; Odo 1975; Peet 1978; Perlman 1973; Sato 1978). Were the DOE to examine this body of work it would have to acknowledge HCE's divergence from SE and, perhaps, reconsider its monolithic labelling of HCE as a 'dialect' of English.

Issues of labelling aside, island educators might find interesting recent work by Au (1980) and her colleagues at the Kamehameha Early Education Program (KEEP), where a major research effort has been directed at accommodating the needs of HCE-speaking children learning to read. Au (1980) reports on the success of a reading program incorporating culturally appropriate participation structures. Studies such as this one highlight the extension of HCE-SE differences into areas such as discourse style, e.g., question-answer patterns, joint performance of narratives, and other aspects of turntaking in group discussions. All of these features are potential difficulties for HCE-speaking children being instructed in a SE context and should at least be reviewed by the appropriate personnel in the DOE. The danger at this juncture is that island educators who have accepted the characterization of HCE as a minimally differing dialect of English will simply ignore relevant research of this type.

In the long run, what will need constant monitoring may not be the studies of HCE structure, i.e., syntax, morphology, and phonology, as much as the transmission and maintenance of *attitudes* toward HCE and SE in the educational context. The linguistic research has shown for HCE as well as other minority languages that 'there is nothing in such speech codes as linguistic systems that makes them any more or less desirable than SE" (Day 1980: 15). Rather, it seems to be the negative treatment of such varieties of speech and their speakers that fosters linguistic insecurity and academic failure.

To its credit, the DOE (1980: 3,4) his acknowledged the importance of a positive attitude toward HCE on the part of teachers in their 'handling' of HCE-speaking students. The responsibility for the cultivation and maintenance of positive attitudes in both teachers and students, however, rests largely in the hands of educational administrators, many of whom have chosen to avoid the HCE 'problem' altogether. It is not enough to endorse the rhetoric of educational equality by recognizing the legitimacy of a minority language. There must also be serious attempts to empirically describe the minority language and its relationship to the larger sociolinguistic context, the practical goal being the implementation of culturally appropriate pedagogy.

Conclusion

Over the last century, the locus of language contact and change in Hawaii has moved from the plantation to the schoolyard. In the process, Hawaii Pidgin English and Hawaii Creole English were created, the former facilitating interaction among immigrants and the latter serving as the first language of their children. In this paper, we have described the roles of HPE and HCE in the interplay of economic exploitation, ethnic identity, and language choice in Hawaii. We have focused on the institutionalization of linguistic discrimination against HCE and its speakers in the hope of revealing widely-held misconceptions and stimulating further consideration of HCE-speakers' needs in the formulation of educational policy.

Notes

* I am indebted to the late John Reinecke for providing historical perspective as well as encouragement and to Michael Long for helpful comments.
1. For the most comprehensive sociolinguistic history of Hawaii to date, see Reinecke (1969).
2. The term *haole*, Hawaiian for 'foreigner', has come to refer to Caucasians.

3. See Day (this volume) for an account of the decline of the Hawaiian language.
4. Hawaiian, meaning 'welcome' or 'enter'.
5. The literacy training made possible by the missionaries' orthography ultimately played a crucial role in the survival of the Hawaiian language. See Day (this volume).
6. MF64M is a *male*, *Filipino*, *64*-year-old from *Maui*. This example comes from the Nonstandard Hawaiian English Project corpus. (See Bickerton and Odo 1976: 173.)
7. MJ66H is a *male*, *Japanese*, *66*-year-old from *Hawaii*. The example is taken from the Nonstandard Hawaiian English Project corpus. (See Bickerton and Odo 1976: 274.)
8. The term 'dual-lingualism' is taken from Lincoln (1975).
9. MF45K is a *male*, *Filipino*, *45*-year-old from *Kauai*. The example is from the Nonstandard Hawaiian English Project corpus. (See Bickerton, 1977: 340.)
10. This action constitutes the first time that a legislative body has ever taken a stand in support of HCE speakers.
11. The Keaukaha Project and the Hawaii English Project are described in Peterson (1967) and Nunes (1967), respectively.

References

Adams, Romanzo. 1933. *The Peoples of Hawaii.* Honolulu: American Council, Institute of Pacific Relations.

Au, Kathryn H. P. 1980. Participation structures in a reading lesson with Hawaiian children: Analysis of a culturally appropriate instructional event. *Anthropology and Education Quarterly* XI, 2, 91-116.

Beechert, Edward. 1977. Labor relations in the Hawaiian sugar industry: 1850-1937. MS, University of Hawaii.

Bickerton, Derek. 1977. Change and variation in Hawaiian Pidgin and Creole English, II: Creole syntax. (Final Report on NSF Project No. GS-39748).

– 1981 *The Roots of Language.* Ann Arbor, Michigan: Karoma.

– and Talmy Givón. 1976. Pidginization and syntactic change: From SXV and VSX to SVX. Papers from the Parasession on Diachronic Syntax. Chicago: Chicago Linguistic Society.

– and Carol Odo. 1976. Change and variation in Hawaiian English, I: General phonology and Pidgin syntax. (Final Report on NSF Project No. GS-39748).

Day, Richard. 1972. Patterns of variation in copula one tense in the Hawaiian post-Creole continuum. Unpublished Ph. D. dissertation, University of Hawaii.

– 1980. The development of linguistic attitudes and preferences. *TESOL Quarterly* 14, 1, 27-37.

DeCamp, David. 1971. The study of pidgin and creole languages. In D. Hymes (ed.), *Pidginization and Creolization of Languages.* London: Cambridge University Press.

Fuchs, Lawrence. 1961. *Hawaii Pono: A Social History.* New York: Harcourt, Brace, and World.

Gallimore, Ronald and Roland Tharp. 1976. Studies of Standard English and Hawaiian Islands Creole English: KEEP linguistic research, 1971-1976. (Technical Report No. 59) Honolulu: Kamehameha Early Education Program.

Hawaii State Department of Education. 1980. Legislative Report relating to the needs of students with limited English speaking ability in the public schools of Hawaii. Honolulu: Hawaii State Department of Education.

Hawaii State Legislature House of Representatives. 1979. House Resolution No. 727 relating to the needs of students with limited English speaking ability in the public schools of Hawaii. Honolulu: Hawaii State Legislature House of Representatives.

Lincoln, Peter. 1975. Acknowledging dual-lingualism. *University of Hawaii Working Papers in Linguistics* 7, 4, 39-46.

Lind, Andrew, 1967. *Hawaii's People*. Honolulu: University Press of Hawaii.
Nordyke, Eleanor C. 1977. *The Peopling of Hawaii*. Honolulu: University Press of Hawaii.
Nunes, Shiho. 1967. The Hawaii English Program: Brave new venture. *Hawaii Schools* 4, 3, 14-17.
Odo, Carol. 1975. Phonological processes in the English dialects of Hawaii. Unpublished Ph.D. dissertation, University of Hawaii.
Peet, William. 1978. Relativization in a creole continuum. Unpublished Ph. D. dissertation, University of Hawaii.
Perlman, Alan. 1973. Grammatical structure and style shift in Hawaiian Pidgin and Creole. Unpublished Ph.D. dissertation, University of Chicago.
Peterson, Robert. 1967. The Hilo Language Development Project. *Elementary English*, XLIV, 7, 753-755, 774.
Reinecke, John. 1969. *Language and Dialect in Hawaii*. Honolulu: University Press of Hawaii.
Sankoff, Gillian. 1980. Political power and linguistic inequality in Papua New Guinea. In G. Sankoff, *The Social Life of Language*. Philadelphia: University of Pennsylvania Press.
Sato, Charlene. 1978. Variation in Hawaiian Pidgin and Creole English: *Go*+Verb constructions. Unpublished M.A. thesis, University of Hawaii.
Stueber, Ralph. 1965. Hawaii: A case study in development education, 1778-1960. Preliminary draft for the 'Cultural Factors in Educational Change' International Development Seminar, the East-West Center, Honolulu, Hawaii, August 16-September 3, 1965.
Tyler, Lois. 1978. The needs of the Pidgin English speaking students in the public schools of Hawaii who have limited proficiency in Standard English. MS, University of Hawaii.
Whinnom, Keith. 1971. Linguistic hybridization and the 'special' case of pidgins and creoles. In D. Hymes (ed.), *Pidginization and Creolization of Languages*. London: Cambridge University Press.

Dennis R. Craig

The Sociology of Language Learning
and Teaching in a Creole Situation*

1. Relevant characteristics of creole speech communities

A creole language is one that has come into existence, no matter by which of
several possible processes, as a result of the contact of speakers of different
languages. In defining a creole language in this way, however, we need to
exclude from consideration such languages as some of the standard European
languages, which started off in the same way as creole languages but which,
through centuries of national development, have achieved the status of
standard national languages. Creole languages, therefore, recognized in this
way, tend to be relatively new languages, spoken habitually mainly by
persons who happen to be natives of newly-developing socio-economic
communities; and in such communities there is usually some older, socio-
politically dominant and more prestigious language that has originally been,
or has become, the official language of the territorial area. A creole language
therefore tends to be of low social prestige, or to have a recently past history
of being so, with persons who possess it as their only language being
correspondingly low in the social hierarchy.

Based on the relationship between a creole language and the more-
extensively-accepted standard language that exists in the same territorial area,
two types of creole language situations may be distinguished. In the first type,
the creole language is lexically, and perhaps grammatically as well, related to
the more-extensively-accepted standard language. In the second type of
situation there is no lexical or grammatical relationship, except perhaps for
sporadic borrowings, between the creole and the relevant standard language.

Some countries that provide examples of the first type of situation are
Haiti and the French West Indies, where the official language is French and
the creole is French-based; Sierra Leone, New Guinea and the former British
West Indies where the official language has been English and the creoles have
English as one of their bases. Some examples of the second type of situation
are Surinam (Dutch Guiana) where the official language is Dutch and creoles
such as Saramaccan and Sraanan are English/African-based; St. Lucia (West
Indies) and the Seychelles, where the official language is English and the

Creoles are French-based. The vast majority of creole-language areas (cf. Hancock 1971) seem to be of the first type (Craig 1977).

2. Creole-standard bilingualism

From what has so far been outlined it is clear that creole speech communities will tend towards being bilingual communities. In such communities, whether a speaker naturally acquires the creole language alone, or the more-extensively-accepted standard language alone, or both of the latter forms of language, will depend on the pattern of social stratification in the community and the position of the particular speaker within that pattern. The situation may be roughly described as diagrammed in Figure 1 below.

Figure 1. Social class and language in a creole language community

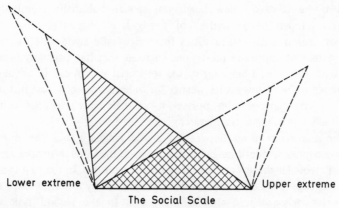

Lower extreme   Upper extreme
The Social Scale

Lower social class. Creole monolingualism

Lower and Upper social class. Creole – standard bilingualism

Upper social class. Standard monolingualism

— — — — Form of possible adjustments in the model, to accommodate different proportional relationships between upper and lower-social-class populations and creole-standard bilingualism and monolingualism.

As a general rule, the lower the socioeconomic status of the individual, the more likely he or she is to be a monolingual creole speaker; conversely, the higher the socioeconomic status, the more likely is it that the individual will acquire the more-extensively-accepted standard. Within this general rule, whether there will be individuals who naturally acquire both the creole and the more-extensively-accepted standard will depend on factors such as the nature and extent of the interaction between social classes, and the motivations that are generated within the community to use each form of language in different functional roles.

In general, the more-extensively-accepted standard language will tend to function as the medium of the official and formal business of the community, the indicator of social distance, education, high status and importance; the creole language, on the other hand, will tend to be the language of informality and intimacy, and of identification with the uniquely indigenous cultural tradition.

The development of creole-standard bilingual proficiency is, however, not likely to be equally distributed between social-class extremes. Most often, it seems to be the creole language that is more widely diffused across the community, while the more-extensively-accepted standard tends to remain the preserve of the upper social class and those who attain such status through education. This happens because of the numerical superiority of the lower social classes, and the fact that the dominant direction of social mobility is from lower to upper with the result that lower-social-class individuals moving to a higher status, with or without achieving a command of standard language, take their creole language with them; in addition to this, the proportion of the upper-social, standard-speaking class which tends to achieve a proficiency in creole through childhood contact with creole-speaking children and providers of services and by other means will be larger than the comparable proportion of lower-social, creole speakers who achieve standard language proficiency. These proportional relationships can be adequately represented in a model of the kind constructed at Figure 1.

The generalizations so far suggested in discussion and in the model seem valid for creole-standard speech communities as far removed and different as those of Jamaica (cf LePage and DeCamp 1960; Cassidy 1961; Bailey 1966), Haiti (cf. Valdman 1969), urban Nigeria (cf. Adekunle 1972; Vincent 1972) and Papua New Guinea (cf. Sankoff and Laberge 1974; Wurm 1977), to mention just a few.

The tendencies of creole-standard bilingualism outlined above account, by implication, for what can be expected to happen when a creole language becomes accepted in its territory as the standard language or a standard language, as has happened contemporaneously in Papua New Guinea, for example. The creole takes on additional functions as a medium of the official and formal business of the community; this occurrence, however, is likely to be accompanied by significant attitudinal changes and conflicts in the language community as a whole. Some proficient users of the standard will see the new status of creole as representing a decline in the cultural values that are associated with education and refined literacy; others will see it as signifying the emergence of a more egalitarian type of society and the end of the socioeconomic and political discrimination which has language as one of its bases. No matter how it is viewed, however, the achieving of standard-language status by a creole will be accompanied, if not preceded, by a strengthening of its role as a preserver of the indigenous culture, including the folk tradition in song, narrative and humour; and there will tend to be an increase in its use for communicating these aspects of culture in advertising and other uses of the popular media.

It may be noted however, that even in some places where, unlike Papua New Guinea, the creole has been accorded no official status, as in the West Indies, the achieving of political independence by indigenous communities has often led to a similar intensification of the indigenous culture-preserving and culture-communicating role of the creole.

Whether or not a creole language is accorded an offical status in its territory, however, it seems unlikely that a creole-speaking community will ever be able to move, under present-day conditions, to a position of completely abandoning the older and more-extensively-accepted standard language that originally served as the official language. The reason for this is the advantage to the community of possessing a national language which is at the same time international in its acceptability.

3. Social awareness, creole and standard language

From what has already been said, it is not surprising to find speakers in creole-standard speech communities, if they achieve a bilingual competence, tend to switch from one language to the other, often in the process of a single discourse, according to the varied social factors and personal interrelationships that impinge upon the discourse. Thus, a conversation between friends that began spontaneously in creole might change, equally spontaneously, to standard language because a stranger of some importance has joined the group; or an indigenous speaker to a largely indigenous group on a public occasion might begin in standard language and either switch occasionally into creole, deliberately in order to gain desired effects, or might lapse into creole without being aware of it if he or she gets carried away by the heat of the discourse. Occurrences of the latter types have long been reported for

Caribbean and some other creoles (Craig 1966; Bickerton 1971, 1973; Valdman 1969).

Much of the code-switching and 'diglossia' (Ferguson 1959) that has been reported in creole-standard situations, however, involves, not a clear movement from one type of language to the other, but a complex blending or mixing of the two forms of language. In some creole-speech situations, like that of Haiti (cf. Valdman 1969), this blending of creole and standard, if it occurs at all, seems to be purely idiosyncratic and is not known to result in a discretely describable form of language that can be said to have a population of speakers. In some other creole-speech situations, however, notably in the English-speaking Caribbean, apart from the mixing of creole and standard items that occurs in code-switching and diglossia, there is a fossilized blend of creole and standard features that constitutes the sole language of some speakers and that has become known as the 'mesolect' (cf. Bickerton 1973; Rickford 1974; Craig 1978a).

The phenomenon of mesolectal language is quite complex. Undoubtedly it represents the fossilization of an interlanguage, to use the terms of Selinker 1972 which are now well known. But why a mesolect should develop between creole (basilect) and standard (acrolect) (cf. Stewart 1962) in the territories of the English-based Caribbean creoles, but not similarly develop, as has been reported, in the territories of the French-based creoles has not yet been clearly accounted for. If the reports are correct, then the explanation probably rests in the differences between patterns of social mobility in the former British territories and those in the French territories. It would appear that, in the British territories, the motivation of the lower social classes towards upward social mobility was strong enough and elementary educational opportunities sufficiently available for there to be a constant striving towards the acquisition of Standard English, since the latter was the most immediately apparent passport to higher social status (cf. Bailey 1964) relevant to Jamaica; the result of such striving was, in many cases, an interlanguage between creole and standard. The persistence of this interlanguage, with all the attendant implications that are now understood relevant to interlanguages (cf. Selinker 1972; Richards 1972; Schumann 1974; Craig 1978a) is responsible for the range of language variation, that is known as the Caribbean creole-language continuum (cf. DeCamp 1971; Bickerton 1973).

In summary, it may be said that the awareness of social stratification, of its implications, and of its correlation with the possession of creole or standard language provides, in creole-language communities, a constantly strong motivation, not always successfully realized, towards the acquisition of a bilingual proficiency. Most often, the striving towards bilingualism is by creole speakers aspiring to possess the standard; but if the community develops recognizable function roles for a creole language, like, for example:

its use by Ghanaian youths as an in-group language (cf. Ansre 1978), its use in Haiti as the language of adult literacy (cf. Pompilus 1973), and so on, then the striving towards bilingualism might also proceed from standard-language speakers wishing to be proficient in Creole.

4. Language learning and teaching

The natural acquisition and informal learning of language in creole situations is determined by the factors which have just been outlined in the preceding sections of this paper: the correlation between social class and type of language, the effects of social awareness and of possibilities of social mobility, the allocation by the community of different functional roles to different types of language, and the language attitudes that provide a basis for that allocation. Any formal attempt to teach language in such situations must therefore take cognizance of the latter factors and of the ways in which they can affect (a) the choice of language-education alternatives for the community as a whole, and (b) the educational strategies and materials that should be used in implementing any chosen alternative.

Decisions in relation to (a) and (b) preceding will involve language planning and will determine the conditions to be observed in the use of language in education at all levels. However, for most creole situations, the most crucial level for the implementation of such decisions is that of primary education, since whatever is decided upon at this level, in terms of planning for the community as a whole, will become the basis of continuing strategies for other levels. The issues that are relevant to language learning and teaching in primary education in creole situations have been discussed at some length in Craig 1977 and can be no more than merely referred to here.

First of all, the conditions that govern creole-standard bilingualism and that have been discussed in Section Two of this paper necessitate that, for any creole speech community, alternatives in bilingual education such as those discussed, for example, in Fishman and Lovas 1970 be considered relative to creole and standard language. The decisions involved concern the following:

2(i) whether the creole will be used in early education to the extent necessary to allow children to adjust to formal schooling and to learn sufficient of the community's standard language for it to become the medium of instruction (Transitional Bilingualism), (ii) whether both creole and standard are to be developed in school for aural-oral skills, but with literacy being aimed at only in the standard language (Monoliterate Bilingualism), (iii) whether aural-oral fluency and literacy are to be developed in the creole for certain types of subject-matter and in the standard language for certain other types of subject-matter (Partial Bilingualism), and (iv) whether all skills are to be developed in both creole and standard in all domains (Full Bilingualism). There are two other alternatives that are also possible in creole situations; these are:

3(v) whether the creole is to be ignored completely, as has traditionally been the case in many parts of the world, and education be attempted solely in the standard language, and (vi) whether education is to be attempted in the creole language solely, even if at the primary level only.

Which of these alternatives a creole-speaking community will choose will be determined by the ways in which attitudes and motivations have been influenced by the background of factors such as have been outlined in the previous sections of the paper. It has been shown, however, in Craig 1977 for example, that no matter how communities make their choices, certain generalizations seem applicable to all creole language situations. These generalizations are as follows: (a) in all situations, even where the professed educational policy is monolingualism in the standard language, there will be varying degrees of oral usage of creole by indigenous children and teachers in schools; (b) there will be literacy in creole at the primary level only in cases where there is a clear educational policy of full or partial bilingualism and such case are rare, and (c) there will be an attempt at oral fluency and literacy in the more-extensively-acceptable standard language, at least at an upper primary level, in most cases.

What seems most significant in the generalizations is the fact of the pervasiveness and persistence of oral fluency in creole on the one hand, and an equally pervasive and persistent striving after literacy in the standard language on the other. The implication of this is that, so far as language teaching is concerned, the most common problem in all creole situations is that of teaching a standard language (other than the creole itself, if it has achieved such status) to creole speakers.

The problem differs according to the two types of creole situation discussed in Section One. If the creole bears no significant lexical and grammatical relationship to the standard language, then the problem of teaching the standard is essentially that of teaching a foreign language and, as Stewart 1962 pointed out, the attitudes of the community towards creole in such situations are generally more favourable than they would otherwise be. In such situations therefore, school programmes tend to be more realistic and more rationally designed to achieve results in terms of conferring proficiency in the standard; this happens because the child tends to be fully recognized as a foreign learner of the standard and therefore needing to be schooled within the context of one of the first four alternatives, which are clear bilingual alternatives, outlined in illustration (2) above. In this situation, the problems to be faced do not derive from the factors discussed in the sections preceding this, but are more socio-economic having to do with the underdevelopment of creole-language communities and the poor provision of basic communal necessities, including education.

If, however, the creole situation is of the other type, where there is significant lexical or grammatical relationship between the creole and the standard, then the educational problem tends to assume different proportions. The status of the child as a foreign learner of the standard language is not likely to be clearly recognized, even though the linguistic differences between creole and standard will be obvious, but the traditional attitude of regarding creole as a debased form of the standard is likely to hinder the design and implementation of adequate educational policies; in a majority of actual cases what happens is that alternative five (see 3v., above), viz. to ignore the creole completely in education, tends to be accepted.

However, in the latter type of situation, even if the obvious differences between the creole and the standard language suggest a foreign-language approach to the teaching of the standard, and therefore a bilingual type of educational programme generally, there are still likely to be special problems of the kind discussed in Craig 1976.

Firstly, apart from the attitudinal problem already referred to in respect of the relationship between the creole and the standard, there will tend to be a problem of low motivation in creole-speaking children attempting to learn the standard. Part of this problem will derive from the child's perception of a relationship between the creole language and the one the child is supposed to be learning in school; this perception has been shown (Craig 1976) to create in the child the illusion that the standard language is already known, and the result is that the child fails to obtain the equivalent of the satisfaction and learning reinforcement of the foreign learner who knows that something new has been learned and is available for use.

Another part of the motivational problem has to do with the fact that, although the age of social awareness referred to in Labov 1964 probably occurs earlier for some creole-speaking children, judging from the early development of code-switching (Craig 1976), creole-speaking children in the type of situation under discussion, like most non-standard-speaking children attempting to learn a standard, fail to see the relevance of the standard language to them, and fail to find any compelling reason for formally learning it. A similar phenomenon has been reported in relation to non-standard-speaking children learning English in the U.S.A. (e.g. Kochman 1969).

Still another part of the motivational problem, however, has to do with learners, in the type of situation being considered, not merely failing to see the relevance of learning the standard language, but actually having a negative attitude to the standard language itself, regarding it as the language of an oppressive elite, for example, or (among boys) regarding it as a language for 'sissies'. Phenomena of the latter kind have been referred to in Craig 1976 and it is clear that similar attitudes sometimes inhere in advocates of improved status for creoles in places like Haiti, Jamaica and New Guinea.

Secondly, there are problems that are largely methodological and that derive from the fact that speakers of a creole which bears a significant lexical or grammatical relationship to the standard are in the position of attempting to learn neither a native language nor a foreign language, but something half-way between the two when they approach the standard. This factor has important implications for teaching methodology, and these implications have been discussed elsewhere (Craig 1976, 1977, 1978a). One particular aspect of these implications, however, is relevant here, and this is the sociological one that learners of the standard, in the type of situation being discussed, need more than other learners to be put through processes that would sensitize them to the standard-language requirements of different social-class roles, and condition them to standard forms of communication when they are performing those roles. Teaching methods based on role-playing, with all their sociological and psychological implications, therefore assume particular importance in this type of situation.

Finally, in this type of situation, there are language-learning and teaching problems which have to do with the fact that the relevant learners, like some other types of non-standard speakers, are accustomed to a different format of communication from the one that is dominant in standard language. In the early work of Bernstein (e.g. 1961a, 1961b, 1961c), the kind of communication format that has since been referred to as characteristic of creole speakers was regarded as being characteristically low-social-class and termed a restricted code, to indicate its assumed limitations as a mode of communication. Since then, in Labov 1969, Craig 1971 and elsewhere, the latter position has been disputed and even the more recent work of Bernstein (e.g. 1972) seems to take a different stand from that originally taken. What now seems apparent is that the communication format of the lower social class, including creole speakers, employs strategies that are different from the preferred ones in standard languages which have been influenced by a long tradition of written style; but the strategies of the lower-social communication format can achieve the same cognitive results as the strategies that are characteristic of standard language (Craig, in press).

The differences in communication formats that have been referred to seem to achieve added importance in the more advanced stages of language learning and language use when they can constitute significant barriers to the efficient reception and processing of information. However, they also seem to be related to wider issues that have to do with the universal conceptual structures that underlie creole and probably all languages recently discussed in work such as Kay and Sankoff 1974; Bickerton 1977; Craig 1975, 1978b. The significance of these wider issues for the sociology of language learning and teaching is that they suggest on the one hand the universal commonalities underlying the structure and the functioning of the human being, but suggest at the same time the selective procedures that are put into effect by social groupings even in relation to factors as subtle, intangible and little understood as linguistic structure.

Notes

* State-of-the-art paper presented in the session 'The Sociology of Language Learning and Teaching' of the Ninth World Congress of Sociology, Uppsala Sweden, 14-19 August, 1978. First published in *Caribbean Journal of Education*, vol. 5, no. 3.

References

Aarons, B. and Stewart, W.A. (eds.), 1969. Linguistic-cultural differences and American education. *The Florida FL Reporter*, Anthology issue.
Adekunle, M.A. 1972. Sociolinguistic problems in English language instruction in Nigeria. In Smith and Shuy (eds.).
Ansre, G. 1978. Campus pidginization and accommodation in Ghana. Paper presented at the Conference on English in Non-Native Contexts, LSA Linguistic Institute, University of Illinois, July 1978.
Bailey, B.L. 1964. Social problems in the language teaching situation in Jamaica. In *Social Dialects and Language Learning*, ed. Roger W. Shuy, Champaign, Illinois, National Council of Teachers of English.
— 1966. *Jamaica Creole Syntax: A Transformational Approach*. Cambridge: Cambridge University Press.
Bernstein, B. 1961a. Social structure, language and learning. *Educational Research*. 3.
— 1961b. Social class and linguistic development: a theory of social learning. In *Economy, Education and Society*, ed. A.H. Halsey, J. Floud, and A. Anderson, New York: Free Press.
— 1961c. Aspects of language and learning in the genesis of the social process. *Journal of Child Psychology and Psychiatry*, 1, 313. Reprinted pp. 251-63 in *Language, in Culture and Society*, ed. D. Hymes, New York: Harper and Row 1964.
— 1972. A critique of the concept of compensatory education. In Cazden, John and Hymes (eds.).
Bickerton, D. 1971. Guyanes Speech. Manuscript, University of Guyana.
— 1973. On the nature of a creole continuum. *Language* 49(3).
— 1977. Pidginization and creolization: Language acquisition and language universals. In Valdman (ed.).
Cassidy, F. 1961. *Jamaica Talk: 300 Years of English Language in Jamaica*. London: Macmillan.
Cazden, C.B., John, V.P. and Hymes, D. (eds.). 1972. *Functions of Language in the Classroom*. New York: Columbia University, Teachers College Press.
Craig, D. 1966. Teaching English to Jamaican creole speakers: A model of multi-dialect situation. *Language Learning*, 16 (1-2).

- 1971. Education and creole English in the West Indies: some socio-linguistic factors. In Hymes (ed.).
- 1974. Developmental and social class differences in language. *Caribbean Journal of Education,* 1:2, University of the West Indies, Jamaica.
- 1975. A Creole English continuum and the theory of grammar. Paper presented at the International Conference on Pidgins and Creoles, University of Hawaii. To appear, Hawaii University Press.
- 1976. Bidialectal education: Creole and standard in the West Indies. *International Journal of the Sociology of Language,* 8, The Hague: Mouton.
- 1977. Creole languages and primary education. In Valdman, (ed.).
- 1978a. Creole and standard: partial learning, base grammar; and the mesolect. Paper presented at the Annual Roundtable Meeting, Georgetown University, Georgetown University Press. (Forthcoming).
- 1978b. Language Education in a post-creole society. In Spolsky and Cooper (eds.).
- In press. *The Language Jamaican Children speak: A study in social class distinctions.* Rowley, Massachusetts: Newbury House.
DeCamp, D. 1971. Towards a generative analysis of a post-creole speech continuum. In Hymes (ed.).
- and Hancock, I. (eds.). 1974. *Pidgins and Creoles: Current Trends and Prospects.* Washington D.C.: Georgetown University Press.
Ferguson, C. 1959. Diglossia. *Word,* 15: 2, 325-40.
Fishman, J.A. and Lovas, J. 1970. Bilingual Education in Sociolinguistic Perspective. *TESOL Quarterly,* 4, 215-22.
Hancock, I.F. 1971. A survey of the pidgins and creoles of the world. In Hymes (ed.).
Hymes, D., (ed.). 1971. *Pidginization and creolization of languages,* London: Cambridge University Press.
Kay, P. and Sankoff, G. 1974. A language-universals approach to pidgins and creoles. In DeCamp and Hancock (eds.).
Kochman. 1969. Social factors in the consideration of teaching standard English. In Aarons and Stewart (eds.).
Labov, W. 1964. Stages in the acquisition of standard English. In Shuy (ed.).
- 1969. The logic of Non-standard English. Twentieth Annual Roundtable Meeting. No. 22, ed. J.E. Alatis, Georgetown University, School of Languages and Linguistics.
Lepage, R. and DeCamp, David. 1960. *Jamaican creole: An historical Introduction.* London: Macmillan.
Pompilus, P. 1973. Contribution à l'étude comparée du créole et du francais à partir du créole haitein. *Editions Caraïbes,* Port-au-Prince, Haiti.
Rice, F.A. (ed.). 1962. *Study of the role of second languages in Asia, Africa and Latin America,* Center for Applied Linguistics, Washington D.C.
Richards, J.C. 1972. Social factors, interlanguage and language learning. *Language Learning,* 22:2.
Rickford, J. 1974. The insights of the mesolect. In DeCamp and Hancock (eds.).
Selinker, L. 1972. Interlanguage. *IRAL,* 10:3.
Sankoff, G. and Laberge, S. 1974. On the acquisition of native speakers by a language. In DeCamp and Hancock (eds.).
Schaedel, R. (ed.) 1969. *Research and Resources of Haiti.* New York: Research Institute for the Study of Man.
Schumann, J.H. 1974. The implications of inter-language, pidginization and creolization for the study of adult second language acquisition. *TESOL Quarterly,* 8:2.
Shuy, R.W. (ed.) 1964. *Social dialects and language learning.* Champaign, Illinois: NCTE.
Smith, D.M. and Shuy, R.W. 1972. *Sociolinguistics in Cross-cultural Analysis.* Washington D.C.: Georgetown University Press.
Spolsky, B. and Cooper, R.L. 1978. *Case studies in bilingual education,* Rowley, Massachusetts: Newbury House.

Stewart, W.A. 1962. Creole languages in the Caribbean. In Rice (ed.).
Valdman, A. 1969. The Language situation in Haiti. In Schaedel, R. (ed.).
— (ed.). 1977. *Pidgin and creole linguistics.* Bloomington and London: Indiana University Press.
Vincent, T. 1972. Pidgin in Nigerian literature. Paper presented at the Conference on Creole languages and Educational Development, University of the West Indies. ALSED Programme of UNESCO, Paris.
Wurm, S.A. 1977. Pidgins, Creoles, Lingue Frenche, and National Development. In Valdman (ed.).

Ayorinde Dada

The New Language Policy in Nigeria:
Its Problems and Its Chances of·Success*

Introduction

The colonial administrators in pre-independence Nigeria failed in many
respects when their policies are examined from the point of view of the
governed. Like many other countries of the defunct British empire, Nigeria
never "escaped the imposition of artificial colonial boundaries whereby
diverse cultures, languages, religions and social forms were lumped together
under colonially convenient administrators" (Das Gupta 1968: 17). In fact,
the only unifying factor in Nigeria was the British colonial might.

Of course the problem of communication was a capital one for the
colonial government's success and a certain number of choices were open to
this government. They could undertake to literally impose the metropolitan
tongue by teaching it in schools and making it the *lingua franca* among the
various 'nationalities' of the country as the French did through the policy of
assimilation in their overseas territories.[1] On the other hand, they could
develop orthography and pedagogical materials for the teaching of a few
languages particularly the now famous three major languages of Nigeria—
Hausa, Igbo and Yoruba—which would then be imposed on the other ethnic
groups for purposes of wider communication. They could even decide to let
spread only one indigenous language—probably the one spoken by the largest
single ethnic group.

But their language policy, if what existed could be so described, was at
best nebulous and at worst chaotic. The enthusiasm shown by many colonial
administrators (Omolewa 1978: 87) to spread the English language was
dampened "by strong apprehensions about the political consequences of the
propagation of the language" (Ubahakwe 1973). Such consequences included
the negative effects of the 'civilizing mission' which could precipitate agitation
for decolonization by a large section of the population whose common
instrument of attack would now be the English language. Thus, the majority
of school products only had enough of a smattering of the English language
to fit them into their assigned roles of clerical officers, waiters, interpreters,
etc.

As for the imposition of a single national indigenous language, this was out of the question because such an imposition would most likely generate protests from scores of other linguistic groups, the magnitude of which might be too much for the British government which was anxious to maintain peace in the colonial territories. Moreover, such a common language would not augur well for the British policy of 'divide and rule'.

Encouraging the use of regional languages in the form of the three major languages was a compromise. But even here, there were only sporadic attempts at producing regional bilinguals because the different Christian missions that were mainly in charge of education did not pursue a consistent language education programme. In some schools it was 'straight for English' while in others it was 'vernacular' for the first three years as they were anxious that 'natives' should learn to read the Bible in their own languages.

The British language education practice can then be summed up as follows:

1. An educated elite who were expected to assist the British administration were taught good English in a few 'model institutions' like King's College, Lagos. There were British examinations and certificates to crown the efforts of hardworking candidates.
2. The English language was made a requirement for entry into certain cadres of the civil and public service.
3. English was the language of instruction in addition to being taught as a subject at the secondary school level.
4. Mother tongue education was encouraged in many primary schools alongside the learning of English. It was the practice in many schools to teach in the mother tongue in the first three years while teaching it as a subject subsequently. It should be noted that the number of such mother tongues was limited to only a handful (out of the 400-odd languages) in which the writing system was developed.
5. In some other primary schools, especially private schools in urban centres, it was a 'straight for English' practice.

Language in Society in Colonial Nigeria

The language practice in society was a reflection of the language education practice. There was a cream of the elite who worked hand in hand with the British administration and who later formed the corps of politicians and administrators that took over from the British government at independence. These spoke good English and used it mainly as instrument of communication in their official capacities, English being the official language of the country. At a lower level were the lesser officers who were able to manage a form of communication in English while speaking mostly the mother tongue in less official contexts.

Communication from the government to the local level of administration and back was through interpreters while communication at the local level was carried on in the local languages. Horizontal communication was not smooth between one ethnic group and the other especially at the local level. The few educated members of the community were able to communicate in one form of English or the other (Banjo 1971) including the pidgin English in urban centres. But the majority of the people being monolingual and illiterate had difficulty in communicating with those illiterate monolinguals from other parts of the country. In areas of language contact there were bilinguals in indigenous languages while there were a few English/mother tongue/other tongue bilinguals (trilinguals).

Of the over 400 languages in the country (census figures 1963) three languages were officially recognized as the major Nigerian languages: *Hausa* (over 20 million speakers), *Igbo* (about 10 million/speakers) and *Yoruba* (about 10 million speakers). News was translated and broadcast in these languages. At independence, the major languages recognized increased to nine.

There was thus no single national language spoken by the whole population. English which had the official stamp was a minority tongue spoken by less than 10 percent of the population. The three major languages were regional tongues spoken by different nationalities although a few others spoke each as a second language while alongside these three were hundreds of languages spoken by minority groups some of them as large as over one million and others much smaller.

The New National Policy on Language Education

An educational language policy has been defined as one which "concerns what languages will be used as media of instruction and as subjects of study at the various levels of public and private education" (Karam 1974). Statements on the educational language policy in Nigeria can be found in the *Nigerian National Policy on Education* (1977), not as a separate policy statement but running through the document.

The main points of the language policy are as follows:

(a) ... the (Federal) Government considers it to be in the interest of national unity that each child should be encouraged to learn one of the three major languages other than his own mother tongue (the major languages in Nigeria being identified as Hausa, Igbo and Yoruba).

(b) Medium of instruction at the pre-primary level will be principally the mother tongue or the language of the immediate community. This would oblige the government to (i) develop the orthography of many Nigerian languages, (ii) produce textbooks and other materials in Nigerian languages.

(c) The government will see to it that the medium of instruction in the primary school is initially the mother tongue or the language of the immediate community and, at a later stage, English.

(d) A promise by the government to supply specialist teachers via the Teacher Training Colleges.

(e) At the Secondary level, English fully becomes the language of instruction while Nigerian languages are taught as subjects.

(f) Foreign languages like French may be taught later at the secondary level.

This document can be regarded as the first of its kind, spelling out as it does, a language policy for the whole country. However, a few comments are pertinent here concerning the likely problems to be encountered in its implementation and its chances of success.

Clause (a) implies that each child will eventually become a bilingual in two Nigerian languages i.e., mother tongue/major language or (where the mother tongue is a major language) in two major languages. If successfully carried out, this means that about two-thirds of the school leavers would be able to communicate with one another in one Nigerian language or the other. With the learning of English later, the product of the educational system becomes trilingual.

Certain problems arise from this clause however. (1) First, there is the problem of which language to teach to which group. Ideally, a child should be free to learn any of the major languages of his choice in each school. But it is unlikely that any single school will be blessed with specialists in the three major languages at the same time. Thus all children in each school may have to be forced to learn one and the same second Nigerian language. This may not yield the desired result. (2) Second, many pupils from minority areas may find themselves learning more than two Nigerian languages before going on to learn English. This represents a heavy language load for each of such learners. This heavy language load is also likely to affect adversely other subjects on the curriculum or perhaps only a few periods per week will be devoted to the learning of other Nigerian languages. The result of all these problems might be a low level of achievement in the languages learnt at school. If one realises that success in language learning depends on certain factors: aptitude, attitude, motivation, copious practice and opportunity to use the language in its sociocultural context, one would appreciate the difficulty of achieving any considerable measure of success in any of the languages.

The second clause is built on a very sound pedagogical principle. At the pre-primary level, pupils should learn in their mother tongues. In doing so, they are likely to be able to form and understand concepts much faster than when they use any kind of second language. In addition, the break between the home and school caused by a sudden change to a second language and leading to undesirable inhibitions is not likely to occur at this level.

However, the pre-primary school is at present a luxury which can be afforded by only a few parents in Nigeria and in fact it is only in this document that the government has acknowledged the existence of such schools. In this light, the present provision can be regarded as only a project for the rather distant future.

The third clause appears to be the most problematic one. At the primary level, pupils are expected to learn initially in their mother tongues or the language of their immediate community. First, there are about four hundred languages in Nigeria and learning in all these languages would be like re-creating the tower of Babel in the country. But there is the other alternative which is using the language of the immediate community. This definitely means using the second language for many pupils. For these pupils this might mean learning the language and learning in the language at the same time.

Then there is to be a switch over to English as medium of instruction later. How late? This is not specified but the custom of changing over after three years is well known in many parts of the country. The Ife project[2] is however experimenting on the use of mother tongue for instruction throughout the primary level while English is taught as a subject. The problem of language load is also important at this stage. Given the other additional Nigerian languages to be learnt and the involvement of the language learner in the attendant process of acculturation, the magnitude of children's difficulty becomes obvious.

Above all, the promise of a supply of specialist teachers via the Teacher Training Colleges is easier made than executed. At present in Nigeria, speaking generally, there is no specialist teacher for any subject at the primary school level. A teacher is trained to teach all subjects. A switch over to the system of specialist teachers even for one subject is bound to take some years to realise bearing in mind how difficult it is to recruit and keep teachers at this level.

At the secondary level English fully takes over as language of instruction with all the other languages being taught as subjects including foreign languages which might be taught at the latter part of the school course. At this level, language study becomes more academic and learners hardly practice speaking outside the classroom especially when there is no social need to do so.

It will thus be seen that the language policy in Nigeria as it exists at present has little to offer in terms of nation-building:

1. The use of a single language as a national language through which the people's identity can be adequately expressed is difficult to achieve. English apparently has the potential of fulfilling this role: its propagation might probably cost less than that of any other language in Nigeria. It would be widely used across peoples and cultures. It is a language of international communication. It is also a means through which the Nigerian culture can be collectively expressed. But it fails very much to satisfy the Nigerian's quest for the African identity. Besides, it will still remain for long a minority language given the new focus on indigenous languages and the fact that for many school pupils, the primary level is terminal and the knowledge of English at this level is minimal. This leaves only the elite to communicate effectively in English. No single Nigerian language is likely to emerge as Nigeria's *lingua franca* given the number of choices open to each learner.

2. The posibility of developing regional bilingualism seems more realistic in the situation. Such bilingualism is likely to include the following language combinations: English/major language, major language/other major language, mother tongue/major language, English/mother tongue, etc. The problem with this kind of bilingualism concerns the level of speaker's competence in what to him constitutes the second language and the language skills involved in such competence.

3. The new focus on mother tongue education is likely to intensify both linguistic and cultural awareness of hundreds of minority groups and correspondingly decrease their motivation for the learning of 'dominant' Nigerian languages. This then, in spite of the pedagogical advantage, seems to be a divisive element that can delay the nation-building process.

4. In terms of costs, it would perhaps be much cheaper to implement a policy that encourages much fewer languages than to embark on such a centrifugal and 'permissive' policy. Production of materials, development of the writing systems, provision of specialist teachers and the standardization and coordination of various dialects for such a large quantity of languages could constitute a major setback in the implementation of the programme.

The main advantage, of the policy lies in its attempt to systematize what had been hitherto a sporadic and chaotic language education venture. Second, as a written document, it has greater chances of being scrutinized, criticized and ameliorated, yielding a more progressive instrument of nation-building and national integration. Finally an attempt to implement it will definitely reveal all its weaknesses and strengths—an essential feedback for its originators.

Need for Opinion Poll

A significant oversight of the policy makers was their failure to sample the opinions of those for whom the policy was being formulated. Reactions to certain propositions could have probably led to the formulation of a more unifying language policy. But this opinion poll can always be done at any stage of the implementation process leading to a review of the policy and a reorientation in its implementation. This kind of opinion poll was undertaken by the present writer on a rather small scale and within a restricted area. A sample of 245 Yoruba-speaking subjects was randomly selected in Ibadan town (population over a million). Question touching on the national language issue were presented and the following results were obtained:

1. For easy communication in Nigeria, it is important
   (a) to have a single national language—126 subjects i.e. 51.4 percent
   (b) to use the three major languages—40 subjects i.e. 16.3 percent
   (c) to use 9 languages of the FRCN[3] —1 subject i.e. 2.83 percent
   (d) to use all the various languages—65 subjects i.e. 26.5 percent
2. The adoption of English as a national language is:
   desirable and possible—171 i.e. 69.6 percent
   desirable but impossible—35 i.e. 14.2 percent
   undesirable but possible—24 i.e. 9.79 percent
   undesirable and impossible—8 i.e. 3.26 percent
3. Popularity index of Nigerian languages recommended as national language:
   Yoruba—3.09
   Hausa—2.51
   Igbo—1.70
   Others—0.33
4. Which Nigerian languages would like to learn? (Given to a group of Yoruba speakers).
   Hausa—164 .e. 66.9 percent
   Igbo—25 i.e. 10.63 percent
   Others—4 i.e. 1.6 percent

From the above result, it can be seen that the idea of having a single national language in Nigeria is quite a popular one as indicated in the first item although some people would either wish that the so called three major languages be used or prefer that each group uses its own language.

There seems also to be a popular desire that English should continue to be used as a national language judging from item two. A total of 206 think it is a desirable thing, while a total of 195 think it is possible to achieve this. On the other hand, if a single Nigerian language should become the national language, the order of preference is indicated in item three. Yoruba tops the list because subjects are Yoruba-speaking. This trend is likely to persist if other language groups were interviewed. Hausa is ranked quite highly. Looking at item 4, it would appear that the Hausa language would be popular as a national language. This is not to say however that it would be accepted unquestioningly at a nationwide level.

A pointer to the fact that a single Nigerian language is unlikely to be acceptable as a national language is the fact that the greatest number of the Yoruba subjects interviewed here would want Yoruba to be adopted as the national language. From here one could see that other ethnic groups too would prefer their own language even if these are minority groups.

Recent events in the National Assembly are indicative of the complex nature of the language problem in Nigeria. The Nigerian Constitution stipulates that:

> The business of the National Assembly shall be conducted in English, and in Hausa, Igo and Yoruba when adequate arrangements have been made therefore . . .
>
> (Part IB, Section 5).

An attempt to give expression to this clause recently by discussing a bill that would expressly permit Assemblymen to use any of these three languages for the conduct of the business of the house generated such emotions from 'minority groups' that it was immediately withdrawn.

One cannot exclude this kind of reaction from minority groups at the implementation stage of the language in education policy when school pupils would be required to learn at least one other major language apart from one's mother tongue or the language of the immediate community. People are likely to read a kind of linguistic imperialism into this action.

The English language, which has been highly favoured in this study, although not so favoured by many of the educated Nigerians who are behind a lot of cultural and linguistic revival, may eventually remain with us for a longer time than we envisage—not because it might gain more admirers but because it is probably the least of all practicable linguistic evils.

Conclusion

This paper examined the new language in education policy as contained in the new National Policy in Education in Nigeria. In the light of the sociolinguistic situation in the country and the language problems of the school pupils, it was found that the relevant clauses of the policy would be difficult to implement.

A more practicable language policy should be based on general consultation with the people and a large measure of acceptance by them. The results of an example of such a consultation as reported here, while far from being sufficient to warrant any valid judgement, clearly underscores the necessity to undertake such an opinion poll at regular intervals, in order to direct the course of the evolution of (a) national language(s). Meanwhile, the easiest path to tread would be to continue with the use of English in all situations that bring together various ethnic groups at the national level.

Notes

* Paper read at the AILA World Conference 1981, University of Lund, Sweden.
1. 'Nationality' here is taken in the sense offered by Fishman (1968) as a socio-cultural entity that may have no politico-geographic realization but marked by authenticity and solidarity of group behaviour and group values.
2. For a full report see Afolayan (1976).
3. FRCN = Federal Radio Corporation of Nigeria.

References

Afolayan, A. 1976. The six-year *Primary Project* in Nigeria. In Bamgbose (ed.) *Mother Tongue Education: The West African Experience.* UNESCO 111-134.
Bamgbose, A. 1971. The English language in Nigeria. In Spencer (ed.) *The English Language in West Africa.* London: Longman. 35-48.
Banjo, A. 1971. Standards of correctness in Nigerian English. In *West African Journal of Education* June 1971. 123-127.
Das Gupta, J. 1968. Language Diversity and national development. In Fishman (ed.) *Language Problems of Developing Nations.* New York: Willey, 17-26.
Karam, F.X. 1974. Towards a definition of language planning. In Fishman (ed.) *Advances in Languages Planning.* The Hague: Mouton.
Nigeria: 1977. *National Policy on Education.*
Omolewa, M.A. 1978. The ascendancy of English in Nigerian schools 1882-1960. *West African Journal of Modern Languages,* 3, 86-97.
Ubahakwe, E. 1973. Towards a national policy in Nigerian education. *Ikenga:* A Journal of African Studies. II, 1: 79-91.

CLASSROOM INTERACTION AND EDUCATIONAL POLICY

Lucy T. Briggs

Bilingual Education in Peru and Bolivia*

Introduction

This chapter surveys the situation in bilingual education in two neighboring
Andean countries, Peru and Bolivia, focusing on recent efforts and projects of
which the author has personal knowledge.

Peru and Bolivia are multilingual, multicultural countries. More than a
third of the population of Peru, and more than two-thirds of the population
of Bolivia, speak an indigenous, vernacular language as their mother tongue.
Since the Spanish conquest in the sixteenth century, Spanish has been the
official language in both countries, and their traditional educational systems
make no provision for teaching children in vernacular languages. Although in
1972 Peru embarked upon a national educational reform that provided for
bilingual education, it has not yet been widely implemented. In both
countries, literacy is usually thought to be synonymous with Spanish literacy,
but there is no provision for teaching children whose native language is not
Spanish to speak and understand it before teaching them to read and write
it; as a result illiteracy is widespread. Teachers who speak the native language
of the child will sometimes use it in the first two or three grades, but they
tend to view it as at best a one-way bridge to Spanish and at worst a barrier to
learning that should be eliminated. The mixed use of the stigmatized native
language and Spanish in the classroom (especially when the teacher's Spanish
is imperfect, as it often is) leads to a weak bilingualism that fades once the
student leaves the school and returns to a monolingual community. Drop-out
rates are high, and the disparity between educational levels in urban
(Spanish-speaking) and rural (non-Spanish-speaking) areas continues to grow.

In order to understand the need for bilingual education in the two
countries, it will be helpful to look at some statistics, even though those
available may not be entirely reliable. The Peruvian census of 1972 indicates
that of a total population of 11,337,194 aged five years and older, 3.5
million, or approximately a third of the population, gave an indigenous
language as their mother tongue. Of these, 3,015,210 gave Quechua, 332,595
gave Aymara, and 119,337 gave other vernacular languages. Spanish was
claimed as mother tongue by 7,740,945 (República del Perú 1974: Vol. 2,

Cuadro 2). According to the census 11 percent of the total population in 1972 were monolingual Quechua speakers, 1.2 percent were monolingual Aymara speakers, 14.5 percent were bilingual in Quechua and Spanish, and 1.5 percent were bilingual in Aymara and Spanish (República del Perú 1974: Cuadro 8, as reported in Escobar, Matos Mar, and Alberti 1975: 100–101). No breakdowns on monolingualism and bilingualism were given for the other indigenous languages spoken in Peru, of which there are approximately 24, according to Larson and Davis (1981). It must also be kept in mind that in Peru Quechua is not just one language, but rather a family of related but not all mutually intelligible languages.

A detailed description of the sociolinguistic situation in Bolivia is found in *Lengua y sociedad en Bolivia 1976*, an analysis of the Bolivian census of 1976 as it pertains to language and society (Albó 1980). In that census, the following language-related questions were asked:

1. What Bolivian languages do you know how to speak? (asked of all respondents), and
2. What is the language spoken most frequently in your family? (asked of heads of families only).

The results were as follows. Of the total Bolivian population of 4,613,000, 1,753,000 (38 percent) reported they spoke Quechua, and 1,186,000 said it was the language of the family; 1,156,000 (28 percent) indicated they spoke Aymara, though only 892,000 gave it as the language of the family; 3,209,000 (69 percent) claimed to speak Spanish, 2,494,000 (54 percent) saying it was the language of the family; and 57,000 said they spoke other indigenous languages, 41,700 claiming one of them as the language of the family.

Albó cautions that the census figures for Quechua, Aymara, and the other indigenous languages must be taken as *minimums*, and the figures for Spanish as *maximums*, due to the fact that Spanish is the prestige language vis-à-vis the others, the language that all wish to speak or to be thought to speak, while the vernacular languages are correspondingly stigmatized, so that people may deny they speak them. It is also necessary to bear in mind that Quechua is generally of higher prestige than Aymara and the other vernacular languages (in Peru, the Cuzco variety of Quechua has more prestige than other varieties), leading to less underestimation of the number of speakers of Quechua than of the other indigenous languages.

Still, Albó points out that comparisons with earlier census data for both Peru and Bolivia do show that knowledge of Spanish is increasing, although perhaps not quite so fast as people would like to believe. And although the trend may eventually lead to loss of the vernacular languages and to general monolingualism in Spanish, this is not imminent, due to natural population growth. That is, while the percentage of monolingual speakers of vernacular languages may be falling as more of them become bilingual in Spanish, the absolute numbers of persons who speak the vernaculars is rising. Also, the bilingualism being attained is in many cases only rudimentary or incipient (Diebold 1961), and is not accompanied by literacy in either the native language or Spanish.

Bilingual education projects have been designed under government and other auspices to address these problems, but they have had little impact so far and their future is uncertain. They may be divided into projects for small language groups in lowland areas, and projects for larger groups of Quechua and Aymara speakers in the highlands. They are all transitional in orientation, designed to prepare children to transfer into all-Spanish classrooms after three or four years. While the primary goal of most projects is assimilation into the dominant Hispanic society, some of them recognize (at least in principle) a parallel need to preserve cultural and linguistic pluralism as a valuable national heritage.

Lowland jungle areas

Bilingual education projects for small language groups in eastern lowland areas of Bolivia and Peru have been conducted for some 30 years under the joint auspices of the Summer Institute of Linguistics (SIL, known in Spanish as the Instituto Lingüístico de Verano) and the government of each country. A detailed report of the SIL's projects in Peru, with examples of methods and materials, is given in Larson and Davis (1981). The SIL is a US-based organization that (despite its name, which implies that it operates only in summer) sends linguistic missionaries to spend years in remote places, analyzing, describing, and developing alphabets for hitherto unwritten languages with the aim of translating the Bible into them and thereby coverting their speakers to Christianity. As a corollary of missionary activities, the SIL develops literacy materials and trains native speakers to use them in schools established and run with the approval of the government.

Based to a large extent on the SIL's experience in Amazonian Peru, a national bilingual education policy was adopted by the Peruvian government in 1972 as part of the educational reform of that year. Eventually, the decentralization of education that resulted from the reform led to fragmentation among 34 educational districts of the SIL's bilingual education program in Amazonian Peru, with negative results for the program, according to Larson and Davis, who hold that bilingual education should have been exempted from decentralization.

As primarily a missionary institution, the SIL has come in for attacks that range from criticism of failure to train native speakers of vernacular languages in linguistics, thereby not preparing them to conduct their own continuing and independent research, to more politically-motivated accusations of a variety of misdeeds aimed at the expulsion of SIL from Peru and other countries where it works. According to SIL's defenders, the response of many language groups has been favorable, the Aguaruna being a frequently-given example in Peru. In any case, the SIL is now beginning to phase out of lowland Peru, having completed grammars, literacy materials, and Bible translations.

Meanwhile, SIL linguists in lowland Bolivia have been working on 16 minority languages of the 26 that have been identified (Instituto Lingüístico de Verano 1980). At my request, the SIL arranged for me to visit two of their schools in Bolivia, one for speakers of Ese Ejja in Portachuelo Alto, a very small community in northern Beni department, and the other for speakers of Cavineña in the even smaller and more inaccessible settlement of Las Mercedes, further south in the Beni. To reach both, I traveled on small planes flown by SIL pilots, paying my own fare. The schools in each place were small thatched-roof buildings with dirt floors and sides of woven straw and bamboo, clean, airy, and appropriate to the tropical climate. Each school was multigrade, with 12 to 15 students in three grades all under one teacher. The Ese Ejja school had been rebuilt by the children's fathers for my visit (erroneously billed as that of a World Bank official; I was, in fact, working as an adviser to a Bolivian government project funded by a World Bank loan, in the highlands). At Las Mercedes, a teacher from another school four and a half miles away brought her students on foot so that they might also demonstrate their knowledge to the visitor.

At both schools the children sang songs in their own language and Spanish, read from books in both languages, took dictation and did arithmetic problems at the blackboard, and eagerly showed their skills. Their number work was accurate, and their oral reading far superior to that which I had heard in traditional rural schools in other parts of Bolivia, where children learn to read haltingly, if at all, after years of frustrating effort. The three teachers (two men and a woman) had received training at the SIL headquarters at Tumi Chucua, near the northern Beni city of Riberalta, and they were obviously in control of the material and of their students.

The SIL linguists are now phasing out of lowland Bolivia, having completed most of their work there. As in Peru, the future of the SIL schools is now in doubt. Unfortunately, SIL-trained teachers lack the normal school degrees that would assure them of career status comparable to that of graduates of Bolivian normal schools, although the latter do not have the SIL teachers' special linguistic and cultural skills. Once the SIL presence is gone, it is likely that the schools will be reintegrated into the national systems and receive teachers from other parts of the country who have no knowledge of the local languages and cultures, as occurs in non-SIL schools in the area.[1] I was told that such teachers are often poorly motivated and frequently leave before finishing the school year. Rapid teacher turnover is also common in rural schools in highland areas of Bolivia and Peru.

Highland areas

The high valleys and arid, windswept altiplano of Bolivia and Peru, at altitudes of up to 14,000 feet above sea level, are home to the majority of the indigenous peoples of both countries today. The highlanders are a hardy race of farmers, miners, and herders, accustomed to trading and owning land over a wide area at different ecological levels. Their ancestors created the buildings and monuments of Tiahuanaco, a center yet to be fully understood by scholars; developed the cultivation by elaborate terracing and irrigation, and preservation by freeze-drying, of the potato, a staple unknown in Europe before the Spanish conquest; wove exquisitely fine tapestry and crafted beautiful objects in gold and silver; and were accomplished musicians and dancers, as their descendants still are. But these accomplishments are often forgotten today, or alluded to only in the promotional literature of tourism.

In the highland Peruvian department of Ayacucho, bilingual education projects in Quechua and Spanish were conducted under the auspices of SIL in 1965–70 (Burns 1971) and of the Universidad Nacional de San Marcos of Lima, Cornell University, and the Ford Foundation in 1965–68 (Escobar, Matos Mar, and Alberti 1975). As an outgrowth of the educational reform of 1972, in 1975 Quechua was declared an official language of Peru on a par with Spanish. In 1975–78 another Quechua/Spanish project was mounted in Cuzco under the auspices of the Peruvian government, the US Agency for International Development (USAID), and Cornell University (Weber and Solá 1980). These projects used different methods, but were all short-lived.

As of 1977, a program in Aymara, Quechua, and Spanish was underway in the department of Puno on Lake Titicaca, under the sponsorship of the government of Peru and of the Federal Republic of Germany. This is the Proyecto Experimental de Educación Bilingüe en la Región de Educación ORDEPUNO, which I will refer to here as the Puno project. For a full description of it see Sánchez Garrafa and Riedmiller (1980).

The Puno project is the largest bilingual education effort so far undertaken in the altiplano area. Although I was unable to visit any of the schools where it is in effect, I visited its headquarters in Puno twice, and in Lima once, during 1980, and in 1981 heard a report updating it (Komarek and López 1981). Beginning in 1977 with detailed sociolinguistic surveys of Aymara- and Quechua-speaking areas of Puno department, the project is designed to continue until 1984, and thus is the most extensive in time for the area. According to the 1977 surveys, the department of Puno then had a population of 800,000 of whom 40 percent were dominant in Aymara and 50 percent in Quechua, thus constituting together 90 percent of the population; 70 percent to 80 percent of children entering school were monolingual in Quechua or Aymara, and 50 percent of teachers in the area were native speakers of Quechua or Aymara while 30 percent more spoke one or both of them as a second language.

According to Komarek and López (1981) the project's objective is not assimilation, but integration with maintenance of cultural pluralism. In line with this objective, although the project originally planned to transfer students to all-Spanish programs by fifth grade, as of 1981 it was decided to continue the use of the mother tongue for a longer period of time (López, personal communication). This is in line with the recommendations of such bilingual education researchers as Skutnabb-Kangas (1979) and Cummins (1979), who stress the effectiveness, for children who speak a low-prestige language as their native tongue, of elementary education in that language with instruction in the prestige language as a subject (i.e., taught as a second language).

As of 1980, the Puno project had completed sociolinguistic surveys, attitudinal surveys of teachers and parents, collections of children's vocabularies in Quechua and Aymara, selection of 60 schools in Quechua-speaking areas and 40 schools in Aymara-speaking areas to participate in the project, several training courses for teachers in the program, and basic reading tests and second grade texts in both languages. A teachers' guide for Spanish as a second language was also completed, and materials for teaching Spanish were being developed so that it could be taught "gradually and systematically" (Komarek and López 1981). A series of radio soap operas was created and newsletters were published in Spanish/Quechua and Spanish/Aymara to disseminate information about bilingual education to teachers and parents. By the end of 1984 the program is expected to involve grades one through four in 83 schools with 332 teachers and 1,000 students (Komarek, personal communication, May 1982).

This project is clearly the most detailed and elaborately planned of the projects discussed in this article, but like others, it faces problems. Constant transfers of teachers undermine continuity and necessitate training new ones. Government policy has shifted since the program started. Quechua lost its official status in 1980, and in that year Peru underwent a period of deemphasis of education in general and bilingual education in particular, according to a former member of the Puno project staff (Riedmiller, personal communication). The question arises with this project as with the others: What will happen when the foreigners leave? One difference is that a number of Peruvians, some with advanced degrees, have served on the project staff and may be expected to provide expertise after the non-Peruvian technicians have departed.

In Bolivia, a project similar in method and model to the Puno project, though of shorter duration and smaller scope, was the bilingual education component of Rural Education Project I, a project funded by USAID and administered under the auspices of the Bolivian Ministry of Education and the University of New Mexico, in 22 school districts in Cochabamba, Bolivia, each serving small communities (2,000 or less) of Quechua speakers. Begun in 1978, the project used materials and methods adapted from those developed by former SIL linguists in Ayacucho, Peru and was designed to accomplish the transition to all-Spanish classes by fourth grade. Further information about this project may be found in Solá and Weber (1978), Development Associates (1979), and Briggs (1983).

After the *coup d'etat* of July 1980, new Bolivian authorities, not understanding bilingual education and opposed to it, instigated many teacher transfers and thus weakened the program. However, the project was able to continue bilingual education in six school districts. In late 1981, the Ministry of Education passed a Ministerial Resolution continuing project efforts, including bilingual education, for two more years. In early 1982, the former chief of the bilingual component was named District Director for Rural Education in Cochabamba, and continued to promote bilingual education from that position. Nevertheless, the future for this bilingual education program remains in doubt, because, first, nearly all educational authorities do not understand and consequently oppose, bilingual education, and second, neither the Ministry of Education nor any other organization has continued to publish the bilingual education materials produced under the program.[2] This is unfortunate, as video tape recordings of several classrooms using the method show children reading and writing fluently in both languages.

The Aymara/Spanish bilingual education experiment of the Proyecto Educativo Integrado del Altiplano (PEIA) a joint project of the World Bank and the Bolivian Ministry of Education, was intended to be the counterpart of Rural Education Project I. This experiment, which lasted for less than a full year in 1979 and was applied in only 15 schools, is described elsewhere (Briggs 1981a and 1983). It suffered from lack of coordination with its counterpart in Cochabamba (which had expertise lacking to the PEIA), lack of planning, lack of trained personnel, and lack of support on the part of project administrators—all factors related to the unstable Bolivian political situation. The project did serve to bring concepts of bilingual education to the awareness of some rural teachers and parents. An evaluation written a few months after the project's demise (Mamani et al. 1980, in which I participated) concluded that the program had some positive aspects and should be tried again, with improved planning and methods. The basic problem with the method was that children were taught to read a mixture of Aymara and Spanish, the idea being to replace the written Aymara with Spanish during the first year of instruction, and the materials failed to take into account important linguistic and cultural factors, using some words and expressions that could be offensive to rural Aymara speakers.

A project that did take linguistic and cultural factors into account, although not calling itself bilingual education, was a small-scale effort undertaken by a teacher in a rural school in Cochabamba for children who spoke a dialect of Spanish with a heavy admixture of Quechua. I have analyzed this project elsewhere on the basis of a description by its creator (Briggs 1981b). It received support from the Centro Pedagógico y Cultural de Portales, a prestigious educational institution in Cochabamba that is funded by the Patiño Foundation, and continued for two or three years. I do not know what its present status may be.

Another case of individual effort over a longer period is the work of an Aymara-speaking rural teacher, Pedro Copana, who at one time was associated with the Aymara Language Materials Project at the University at Florida (and was one of my Aymara instructors). After returning to Bolivia, Copana developed a method of teaching reading using short dialogues in Aymara and Spanish which he introduced in the primary and secondary schools in Compi, a community on the shores of Lake Titicaca, in the mid-1970s. It proved successful for both young children and teenagers (Copana 1981a). In 1980, Copana was transferred to an elementary school in Coaquipa, a town virtually monolingual in Aymara, where from March to June 1980 he again undertook to apply his method. The following is taken from an unpublished report he prepared on the experience in late 1981 (Copana 1981b).

First, he held a meeting with parents during which he discussed why their children were failing to learn to read or to speak Spanish by traditional methods. He told them about the experiences of other countries in using the children's native language in school, and proposed to teach the Coaquipa children in Aymara, while also teaching them Spanish. Then, with the parents' full consent, Copana taught the children the three Aymara vowel letters a, i, and u, and then the consonants, using words the children themselves suggested, for family members, farm animals and activities, and things in and around the home. With these and appropriate verbs the children could soon write and read short sentences reflecting real-life situations, such as:

Utax janq'uwa.	'The house is white.'
Tatax yap luri.	'The father prepared the field for planting.'
Mamax away sawu.	'The mother wove a shawl.'
Wawax jachiwa.	'The baby cried.'
Yuqallax qut sari.	'The boy went to the lake.'
Imillax nin p''ayi.	'The girl cooked on the fire.'

He also taught them the equivalents of the sentences in Spanish. The children soon learned to write some words in Spanish also, and their parents were pleased with their progress.

After the *coup d'etat* of July 1980, however, the newly-appointed officials of the school district prohibited any further teaching in Aymara, indicating that insistence on doing so would be taken as evidence of leftist sympathies, and as a result Copana stopped the experiment. (Ironically, in Bolivia the use of Aymara in the classroom has also been attacked by the political left, as allegedly preventing children from learning Spanish). Copana remains convinced of the value of using. Aymara in the classroom. He paints a bleak picture of what happens to children under the present system (here translated from the Spanish original):

Problems of an Aymara Child in School

1. When they first enter school, Aymara children cannot easily distinguish [Spanish] letters. They have great difficulty with the pronunciation of Spanish vowels. For them e and i, o and u are the same; they are unable to differentiate them easily.[3] In order to learn them, they must repeat the sounds over and over, and even then they do not grasp the pronunciation and quickly forget it. I have had the opportunity of teaching in Aymara. Children can then learn without any difficulty, and without problems in speaking. It has been my experience that children are [then] able to distinguish vowels both in Aymara and Spanish.
2. Aymara-speaking children are cheerful when they enter the classroom for the first time. When the teacher begins to speak in Spanish, they immediately become demoralized and stop paying attention. They start acting up and fighting among themselves because they do not understand what is being said to them. At times the teacher will have to explain in Aymara if the children are to understand the lessons.
3. Spanish-speaking teachers who do not know Aymara suffer in trying to explain the lessons to the students. I do not know how they accomplish this. They would have to use many teaching aids and materials and mimicry to make the children understand even part of the lessons.

[Translator's note: Such aids are usually completely lacking in rural schools.]

4. Teachers who speak Aymara and Spanish teach reading in Spanish, without understanding the linguistic aspects. They try to 'Hispanicize' the children by force, having them repeat letters and words until they learn to pronounce them. Many times the majority of students forget; only one or two remember the letters and words. Seeing the consequences, some teachers give explanations in both Aymara and Spanish so that the children will better understand the lessons.

5. After six years in the school system, Aymara children cannot speak Spanish as well as city children. They have great difficulty with pronunciation. It is not their language. In most cases, they speak Aymara at home. When they do speak Spanish they are criticized for not pronouncing it correctly, and they become even more frightened of speaking. [End of Copana report]

Criteria for Evaluation of Bilingual Education in Bolivia and Peru

Had the efforts of Copana received official tolerance, might they have continued to have positive results? In the absence of continuity, evaluation becomes very difficult, but not impossible, if projects are compared to the experiences of bilingual education in other parts of the world. In the first place, the involvement of parents and community leaders seems to be crucial. No matter how carefully and systematically planned a bilingual education project may be, it will fail without the informed consent of the children's parents. Copana thus receives high marks for parental involvement. Secondly Copana understands the differences between the sound patterns of Aymara and Spanish and their implications for reading and writing. He uses an alphabet for Aymara that accurately reflects its sound system, instead of trying to write the language as if it were Spanish.[4] Third, Copana understands that children learn to read faster when given meaningful materials that interest them. The words they learn to read should be words they understand and use in normal speech, in familiar and culturally appropriate contexts. The fourth principle that Copana understands is that children who have pride in their native language and culture and learn to read and write in their native tongue will be able to transfer their literacy skills to a second language that is being learned orally.

This is not to imply that all elements of Copana's method were ideal or that they could not be improved, as for example in techniques of teaching Spanish as a second language. But in their basic essentials, they had the stamp of success. Copana is convinced of the correctness of his position on the basis of his own personal experience, which in turn is grounded upon his understanding of linguistic principles, in particular as they relate to the linguistic structures of Aymara and Spanish. He knows that Aymara, as a language, is an intricate system of rules, grammatical and stylistic, in no way inferior to Spanish. He knows why monolingual Aymara speakers have difficulty pronouncing the five Spanish vowels: Aymara has only three, two of which overlap the areas of four in Spanish.[5] There is thus a scientific explanation for the Aymara speakers' difficulty, and it is not due to their stupidity as has been alleged for centuries by the Spanish-speaking elite. The teacher's conviction of the underlying equality of high prestige and stigmatized languages, regardless of the social status history may have conferred on them, leads to a sense of dignity and worth that is essential, I believe, for successful teaching of those who have borne the burden of the stigma. It is precisely this sense of dignity and worth that is often lacking in teachers who are asked to use bilingual education materials. The ambivalence of such teachers toward the vernacular language (even or perhaps especially if it is their native language) can only be dissipated by access to basic linguistic facts. In this context, knowledge of linguistics is a necessary prerequisite to a teacher's, and therefore, to students', success.

The four principles or criteria for successful bilingual education projects in circumstances like those pertaining in Bolivia and Peru may be restated briefly as follows.

1. Include parents in planning, explain new methods to them, obtain their support.
2. Inform teachers on the differences between the structures of the native language and the second language, in the context of basic linguistics.
3. Begin reading instruction in the native language with materials that are linguistically and culturally appropriate, so that children and parents understand what they are about.
4. Be aware that cognitive and affective achievement in the native language is a prerequisite for effective learning of a second language and for transfer of literacy skills to that language.

Of the large-scale efforts, the Puno project appears to score highest on these criteria. However, an analysis of the Aymara materials produced by the project shows weaknesses in principles 2 and 3. Although the books are brightly colored and appealing, reflecting scenes of rural Aymara life, the pictures of Aymara people are cartoonlike, and there have been objections to some pictures on cultural grounds (for example, a scene showing a dog inside a house and a donkey looking through a school window).[6] Moreover, the linguistic and cultural content of the texts leaves something to be desired, perhaps due to insufficient participation in the elaboration of the materials of persons knowledgeable in Aymara linguistic and cultural norms. It is to be hoped that these weaknesses will be remedied in later editions of the materials. A more detailed discussion of the Aymara materials of the Puno project and others may be found in Briggs (1981a).

Conclusion

The present situation in bilingual education in Bolivia and Peru is characterized by uncertainty. Projects that have been suspended are unlikely to resume soon, and new projects may be impossible for some time to come. Projects administered by foreign technicians do not often survive their departure. In such a climate, efforts should focus on dissemination of information to teachers, parents, and administrators on the aims and benefits of bilingual education and on the linguistic and cultural structures of the languages concerned. The highest priority should be given to the dissemination of materials in Spanish and the vernacular languages that can be useful to teachers, both native speakers of vernacular languages and non-speakers, whether or not they are using the languages in the classroom. (See, for example, Boynton 1980).

If teachers were receiving the necessary background in basic linguistics, and in the linguistics of Spanish and the language of their students; if they were helped to understand that learning to read and learning a second language are separate skills requiring different methods; in short, if they were better prepared, they could develop their own materials and methods to deal with the varied situations they face. No one method or model can fit all schools or situations. Moreover, whenever there is a change of government or a new method bursts upon the scene, previously mass-produced texts are relegated to warehouses, if not the dustbin. This can be avoided by focusing on the teacher instead of the production of materials that too often are wasted. Teachers also need to be prepared to explain the purposes and benefits of bilingual education not only to parents, but to other teachers and administrators, so that within the limits of each situation, vernacular languages are used to the extent practicable, the falsity of the assumption that they are inferior is demonstrated, and the speakers of stigmatized languages develop skills in both their native language and the national language, Spanish.

Notes

*   An earlier version of this article was read at the 79th Annual Meeting of the American Anthropological Association in Washington D.C. on December 6, 1980.

1.   In an effort to prevent this from happening, in 1981 SIL and the US Agency for International Development (USAID) office in Bolivia (see the section on highland projects) obtained a Supreme Resolution from the Bolivian government that guaranteed the jobs of indigenous teachers (it included all their names) and provided for them to receive teaching certificates based on their training and experience in bilingual schools. The law also required them to file certificates of exemption from military service due to geographical isolation. According to Dr. Jean Meadowcroft of USAID, who provided this information in early 1982, it was doubtful that this measure would save all the teachers' jobs, but it was hoped that it would help many of them. In my view, however, experience suggests that the law may be more honored in the breach than in the observance.

3.   The information to this point in this paragraph, like that in Note 1, was provided by Dr. Jean Meadowcroft of USAID, La Paz, Bolivia, for whose help I wish to express my appreciation.

3.   What Copana means is that to an Aymara speaker, Spanish e and i sound alike, and Spanish o and u sound alike. See Notes 4 and 5, below.

4.   There is at present no one standard alphabet for either Quechua or Aymara. The Aymara alphabet Copana uses was developed by an Aymara linguist, Juan de Dios Yapita, and is now used in universities as well as by increasing numbers of Aymara speakers. It is the only Aymara alphabet that has only one letter for each distinctive sound of the language. For example, it has only three vowels (a, i, u) while the other alphabets use the five Spanish vowels (a, e, i, o, u) to write the three Aymara sounds, creating spelling difficulties.

5.   This difficulty parallels the difficulty a Spanish speaker has in hearing the difference or producing the difference between the initial sounds of *doze* and *those* in English. In Spanish, the beginning sounds of the two words are variants of one sound written *d*, not two distinct sounds. That is, *doze* and *those* sound the same to Spanish speakers learning English; they cannot hear any difference. Both English and Spanish speakers, on the other hand, have trouble distinguishing certain Aymara consonants, such as the *t* sounds that occur in the following: tanta 'bushy tail', t"ant"a 'old rags', and t'ant'a 'bread'. The first has a plain t, the second t is aspirated (with a puff of air), and the third is glottalized (accompanied by closure of the vocal cords). A native speaker of Aymara distinguishes them easily and cannot believe that to us they 'sound alike'. This is not to say that one cannot learn to pronounce and distinguish the sounds of a foreign language, but it is not automatic, even for children, and may be very difficult when the sociocultural circumstances place the learner in a position of inferiority with respect to the language and culture being learned.

6.   The Aymara language sharply distinguishes the human category from the non-human. For example, there are separate human and non-human pronouns. Human pronouns may be used for anthropomorphized (humanized) animals in stories, but use of the non-human pronouns to refer to people is insulting. Similarly, in Aymara culture domestic animals and humans do not share indoor living space. Exceptions may be made in the case of individual baby animals (such as a lamb or a calf) which may be kept inside at night during cold weather, but adult dogs are *not* allowed in kitchens or bedrooms. Indeed, the dog is considered the antithesis of human being, and an angry retort is "Treat me like a person, not like a dog!" (This is not to imply that the Aymara mistreat their dogs; rather, they treat them and other domestic animals humanely, as a rule.) Thus, the presence of a dog inside a house and of a donkey at school (the latter with its added European connotation of stupidity) are culturally aberrant to the Aymara.

References

Albó, Javier. 1980. *Lengua y sociedad en Bolivia 1976.* La Paz: Instituto Nacional de Estadística.

Boynton, Sylvia. 1980. *Análisis contrastivo de la fonología del aymara y del castellano.* (Translated by Pedro Plaza Martínez from *A contrastive analysis of Spanish and Aymara phonology: Spanish as a goal language.*) La Paz: Instituto Nacional de Estudios Lingüísticos.

Briggs, Lucy T. 1981a. ¿Somos ratones o gente? (Are we mice or people?)–A comparison of introductory reading texts in bilingual education programs for Aymara speakers in Bolivia and Peru. Paper read at the Fifth International Workshop on Andean Linguistics, Cornell University, Ithaca, New York, July 30, 1981.

– 1981b. Progressive language differentiation in bilingual education: Two case studies. Proceedings of the Tenth PILEI Symposium, Cornell University, Ithaca, New York.

– 1983. Bilingual education in Bolivia. In *Bilingualism: Social issues and policy implications*, ed. Andrew Miracle, Jr. Southern Anthropology Society Proceedings, No. 16., Robert Blakely, Series ed., Athens, Georgia: University of Georgia Press.

Burns, Donald. 1971. *Cinco años de educación bilingüe en los Andes del Perú, 1965-70.* Lima: Instituto Lingüístico de Verano.

Copana, Pedro. 1981a. Linguistics and education in rural schools among the Aymara. In *the Aymara language in its social and cultural context*, ed. M.J. Hardman. Gainesville, Fl.: University Presses of Florida (Social Sciences Monograph No. 67).

– 1981b. Report, dated September 25, 1981. (Unpublished typed manuscript).

Cummins, James. 1979. Linguistic interdependence and the educational development of bilingual children. Review of Educational Research 492, 222-251.

Development Associates, Inc. 1979. A final report: Bilingual education grant project paper development AID/SOD/PDC-C-0193, Bolivia. Arlington, Va.: Development Associates, Inc.

Diebold, A. Richard, Jr. 1961. Incipient bilingualism. *Language* 37: 77-112. Also in *Language in culture and society*, ed. Dell Hymes, 1964. New York: Harper and Row.

Escobar, Alberto, José Matos Mar, and Giorgio Alberti. 1975. *Perú, ¿país bilingüe?* Lima: Instituto de Estudios Peruanos.

Instituto Lingüístico de Verano. 1980. *Veinticinco años de servicio al pueblo boliviano.* La Paz: Instituto Lingüístico de Verano.

Komarek, Kurt and Luis Enrique López. 1981. Sociolinguistic problems in the area of Puno and an attempt to change the existing situation. Paper read at Tenth PILEI Symposium, Cornell University, Ithaca, New York, July 31, 1981.

Larson, Mildred L. and Patricia Davis, eds. 1981. *Bilingual education: An experience in Peruvian Amazonia.* Dallas: Summer Institute of Linguistics.

Mamani, Andrés, et al. 1980. Informe de evaluación–Educación bilingüe. OF-PR-INF-75-80. La Paz: Ministerio de Educación y Cultura/Proyecto Educativo Integrado del Altiplano/Crédito 1404-80, MEC/BIRF.

República del Perú. 1974. Censos Nacionales VII de Población, II de Vivienda, 4 de junio de 1972. Lima: Oficina Nacional de Estadística y Censos.

Sánchez Garrafa, Rodolfo and Sybille Riedmiller. 1980. Bases y elementos de planificación del Proyecto Experimental de Educación Bilingüe Puno (Convenio PERU-R.F.A.). Lima: Ministerior de Educación, Instituto Nacional de Investigación y Desarrollo de la Educación (INIDE).

Skutnabb-Kangas, Tove. 1979. *Language in the process of cultural assimilation and structural incorporation of linguistic minorities.* Rosslyn, Va.: National Clearinghouse for Bilingual Education.

Solá, Donald F. and Rose-Marie Weber. 1978. Educational planning in multilingual countries: A report on a working conference. Ithaca, N.Y.: Cornell University Language Policy Research Program Report No. 2.

Weber, Rose-Marie and Donald F. Solá. 1980. Developing instructional materials for a bilingual education program in the Peruvian Andes. *The Reading Teacher* 34: 296-302, December 1980.

Susan U. Philips

Indian Children in Anglo Classrooms

The purpose of this paper is to describe some communicative processes in the American classroom that contribute to the continued lesser status of ethnic minority children when compared with Anglo children in that context. More concretely, I argue that Warm Springs Indian children's efforts to get the floor in the classroom are less often ratified, or incorporated by the teacher into the construction of the social reality generated through classroom talk, than is true of Anglo children's efforts to get the floor. Such differences in ratification and non-ratification are accomplished in a variety of ways, some of which are documented in this paper. This documentation is based on a comparison of Indian grade school classrooms on the Warm Springs Indian Reservation, in Central Oregon, with Anglo classrooms in a school just outside of that reservation.

The children of Warm Springs inherit a tradition of inequality or lack of equality with their non-Indian peers in the American classroom that goes back many generations. In discussing the position of Indians in American society, Vine Deloria compares them with Blacks in the following way:

> Both groups had been defined as animals with whom the white had to have some relation and around whom some attitude must be formed. Blacks were ex-draft animals . . . Indians were the ex-wild animals . . . . (Deloria, 1970: 171-172)

Deloria's point may be used here to focus attention on the following matters: (1) that non-Indians have always had and had to have some social definition of Indians that is linked to their way of behaving toward them; (2) that because of white men's control over Indians' lives, the white social definition of Indians has in most contexts prevailed over the Indians' social definition of themselves and of non-Indians in determining the nature and quality ot the relation between Indians and non-Indians; and (3) that because 'education' is a socializing process designed to transform creatures with one kind of social definition (i.e., normally 'children') into creatures with another kind of social definition (i.e., normally 'adults'), the nature of the social definitions assigned to Indians by whites has considerably influenced the educational ideology and attendant programs in Indian education.

Until the West was 'won', Indians were for the most part defined as *outside* of the American social context, and the framework within which they were perceived was, broadly speaking, that of the social evolutionists of the nineteenth century—i.e., Indians were savages, at a lower state of social development than the 'civilized' people who conquered them.

However, with the winning of the West, the remaining Indian groups were encompassed and surrounded by American society. With this development there arose the need to locate and define them socially as persons within as well as external to our societal structure.

The most crucial defining of Indians in relation to internal others was worked out in detail through the establishment of reservations. Indians were defined as 'wards' of the federal government, with the Bureau of Indian Affairs as the 'guardian'. Legally and socially the Bureau of Indian Affairs was thus in the position of "one who has, or is entitled to, the care and management of the person or property, or both, of another, as of a minor or person *incapable of managing his own affairs*" (Webster 1938: 442).

Indians were thus defined, as many other categories of persons have been, as defective and in this sense not fully human, and hence as not entitled to all of the legal and civil rights of those who are deemed fully human. Others who shared this status with them in different respects included (and still include) criminals, the insane, the mentally retarded, immigrants, Blacks, women, and children.

Those defined as defective or not fully human were differentiated according to: (1) the specific ways in which they were lacking; (2) variation in the rights of which they were deprived along lines felt to be in keeping with the specific ways in which they were lacking; (3) theories specifying the cause and possibility of cure for their deficiencies as persons; and (4) programs for what to do with them based on the foregoing.

What provided the distinguishing characteristics of the program for Indians derived from the stereotypes of social evolution and the categorization of Indians as savages within those stereotypes. Different lifestyles were assigned to different social evolutionary stages, but the societies at any given stage were not necessarily *permanently* stuck at any given stage. It was held possible for the Indians to rise to the white level of civilization. Indians, then, were not viewed as permanently disabled persons, as the mentally retarded and physically handicapped are, but as potentially educable, like children. Formal education was viewed as the process to bring them from savagery to civilization. And the education was to be tailored specifically to counteract those features of their lifestyle that most clearly distinguished them as savages: their geographical mobility and their hunting economy. Proposals for Indian education and the Bureau of Indian Affairs' land policies during the 1880s stressed the need to teach the Indians to live a *settled* life as *farmers* (settled farming being a diagnostic marker of civilization).

Although the causal framework used in accounting for the inadequacy of Indians as full-fledged human beings was distinctive, the approach adopted for transforming them was very much in keeping with that applied to the other categories of persons who likewise were defined as not fully human and hence wards of the state without full rights of citizenship.

Fey and McNickle have described the classic form of education that evolved during the 1800s under the auspices of the Bureau of Indian Affairs:

> The era of the large off-reservation boarding school started with the establishment of the United States Indian Training and Industrial School at Carlisle, Pennsylvania, in 1878. It was followed by schools at Chemawa, Oregon, in 1880; and Genoa, Nebraska; Lawrence, Kansas (Haskell Institute); and Chilocco, Indian Territory, all in 1884. These schools were modeled on the manual labor schools, providing part-time instruction and part-time maintenance labor.
>
> To this basic pattern were added military discipline and the complete regimentation of the child's waking hours. Moreover, the schools were dedicated to the ultimate eradication of all traits of Indian culture. The location of the schools at distances far removed from the reservations from which children were selected was deliberate policy. Children were often no more than five or six years old when they arrived at these schools. If the child could be taken young enough and moved far enough away from the influences of family and tribe, the odds against his ever again becoming a part of his environment were considered remote. (Fey and McNickle 1959: 129)

The boarding schools have been characterized as military in their organization, but it would be more appropriate to see them as sharing many of the features of prisons and insane asylums specifically, and of total institutions in general as these have been characterized by Erving Goffman (1961).

The institutionalization of Indian children in Bureau of Indian Affairs boarding schools was similar to that of criminals and the mentally ill in that the social behavior of persons in all three of these groups was defined as disruptive of normal social interaction. For all three groups the response to this disruption was to confine and isolate the people from what was defined as normal ongoing life. (In this respect, the reservation as a whole, not the school, may be viewed as similar to a prison).

But mere *isolation* of such persons was viewed as insufficient. There should be, in addition, a way of transforming them so that they would no longer be disruptive. The incarceration of abnormal persons' for this second purpose was thus viewed as serving two additional purposes: (1) the removal of such persons from the social environment that had made them abnormal, and (2) the transformation of such abnormal into normal persons through education or involvement in a normal social environment. It is important to point out that once these persons had been or were defined as not fully human, deprivation of rights accorded to people defined as fully human automatically took place. More concretely, the Indians (and prisoners and insane) had no choice in the matters of their being isolated, removed from their socializing environment, and resocialized to become different (normal) kinds of persons. They were forced to comply.

Bureau of Indian Affairs boarding schools were like the prisons and insane asylums (and other total institutions) of that period in organization in the following respects: (1) there were two significant categories of persons—those doing the socializing or educating and those being socialized; (2) the authority and control of the former over the latter was complete—there was no recourse to influences or sources of authority outside of the institution such as Indian family or community leaders; (3) the activities of every hour of every day were defined within the framework of the institution; (4) the institution was made as self-sustaining and self-sufficient as possible and its maintenance by the persons being socialized was justified as a part of their socialization. Thus, in boarding schools, the Indian children worked in the gardens, sewing rooms, hospital clinics and dairies half of each day, and this work was defined as occupational training.

One important part of the BIA educational policy of transformation of Indians was the replacement of Indian languages with English. Indian children were punished by school personnel if they were caught speaking their own Indian language in any setting of the BIA school. The policy of bringing together Indian children from diverse cultural backgrounds in itself led to the greater use of English between children who spoke different languages. But the blanket condemnation of *any* use of one's native language inhibited its use even between speakers of the same native language.

This classic form of total institutional 'rehabilitation' of Indians has been gradually disappearing in recent decades as the public school systems have increasingly assumed responsibility for educating Indian children. The admission of Indian children into the public school system may be interpreted as an indication of a change in the kind of social persons they are now defined as being. As a result of the total institutional habilitation of the entire Indian population, they are no longer deviant; no longer is there a need to separate them from 'normal' children.

It is the official and explicit policy of the public school systems to have a single framework for the definition of personhood. And this framework is applied to all children. Operationally, then, the public school system defines Indians as 'just like anybody else', and their behavior is interpreted within the framework of social expectations that holds for white children.

Where the federal government continues to have a direct involvement in Indian education, however, the Indian continues to be defined as deviant, but the interpretive framework through which he is defined as defiant has shifted from one which was special and uniquely applied to Indians (i.e., the social evolutionary perspective) to one which he shares with certain non-Indian groups. The Indian has now been assimilated to the poverty-minority category. The federal government's educational policy in relationship to poverty and minority groups is based on their definition as 'culturally deprived', or lacking normal socialization experiences in their pre-school years. In keeping with this definition the educational policy is, as it was in the heyday of boarding schools, to take them out of the abnormal environment and place them in one where the socializing influences are normal—i.e. in Head Start Programs and federally funded day care centers. The federal government's social definition of the Indian child as abnormal in relation to white children has not, then, changed. What has changed is the interpretive framework within which this definition is made (i.e., the Indian has been shifted from the social evolutionary framework to the minority-poverty framework).

We have then two conflicting contemporary social definitions of the Indian that are relevant in education: the definition of the public schools that he is a normal person 'just like us' and the definition of the federal government that he is an abnormal person when compared to 'us'.

But Indians define *themselves* neither as just like whites nor as abnormal persons deprived of culture. They continue to resist such definitions, and persist in seeing themselves as 'Indians'—which means they see themselves as a different kind of people separate and different from, but *equal to,* whites, and consequently worthy of the same human and civil rights. Their view of themselves has, however, had little effect on the kind of education their children receive, something which has been and continues to be largely outside their control.

Their Indian point of view *does* have a *small* voice in the academic literature on Indian education. One sometimes finds the position taken that in the public school classroom the Indian child experiences 'cultural conflict' (Berry 1968: 69—70). In his own Indian social environment he has been taught to do things one way; in the classroom he is expected to do things a different way—the white way. Here, then, is a situation in which two cultures are in conflict.

This cultural conflict perspective has had little influence in the real world of schools, in part because no one has pursued what practical implications it might have. As Berry points out:

> While no small amount of research has been done on the content of the Indian cultural heritage, and on the extent to which this has survived into the present, relatively little seems to have been done on the problem of how this impinges upon the school situation, and on the question of how the problems might be resolved. (Berry 1968: 77)

This failure in turn, is surely due in part to the fact that if were pursued, very expensive and far-reaching changes would be required in Indian education. While there is concern enough to mouth the point of view, there is not enough concern to back it financially.

But, in addition, the notion of cultural conflict is inadequate in its characterization of what the Indian child experiences. This view is egalitarian and relativistic in so far as it allows for there being more than one kind of person, and more than one way of doing things, and it does not make judgments that one way is more normal than or superior to the other. However, although this relativism seems laudable when compared to the demeaning-to-Indians idea of abnormality deriving from the cultural deprivation perspective, it obscures one very important aspect of what is going on in a classroom where the Indian child's culture is in conflict with that of the teacher—namely the extent to which *the teacher's interpretive framework is dominant in that context.* Teacher and student do not meet on an equal basis and work out between them what is meaningful, or what is right and wrong. It is the teacher who defines what is meaningful, what is appropriate, what is true and what is false. She does so within a framework of classroom procedure that derives from white middle-class culture, and she derives her authority to define what is real and meaningful from the power structure that sustains that culture. More specifically, her power is derived from the combined authority of her statuses of white person, adult, and teacher.

In considering her status as a white person, I refer back to the point made earlier that in the public school system there is room for only one cultural standard for social persons, and that is a white standard. The teacher as a representative of that standard is defined as a full or normal person.

In relation to the teacher as an adult, the children are not full persons, but rather on their way to becoming such. Adults usually define what is socially meaningful for children. It is basic to the socialization process that children learn to communicate in ways that are meaningful to adults—that they learn what *is* meaningful from adults. One might then want to say that while adults *always* have this authority in relationship to children, they are not always and continuously exercising it. There are, for example, times when children are on their own, playing and working together and mutually defining a system of communication.

The teacher-student relationship, however, is one in which regardless of ethnic and age differences the expectation holds that it will be the teacher who ultimately authorizes or determines what is right or wrong, meaningful or meaningless, true or false.

The teacher in our public schools, then, derives her authority to define what is meaningful from sources that are given considerable validation and support in our society. And because of the extent to which the teacher has the far greater power in determining the meaningful system of communication in the classroom, in the American public school system, Indian children who experience cultural conflict in the classroom also experience *effacement* of their culture in that context.

At the same time, it is important to note that cultural effacement does not often take the form of obvious rejection of Indian culture by the teacher. On the Warm Springs Reservation even examples of more subtle evidence of a teacher's relative ignorance of Indian culture are not common. But Warm Springs Indian students' behavior is more often defined as inappropriate by teachers than off-reservation Anglo students' behavior. More particularly, Indian children's contributions to classroom discussions are less often ratified.

In classroom interaction, the teacher's speech provides evidence of having heard the speech of *some* students, but not others. And in this way, some students' talk is ratified and incorporated in the sequence of discourse while other students' speech is not, Not all ratification or failure to ratify is intentional. In general, however, that which is ratified or responded to has been judged by the teacher to be acceptable and appropriate. And generally that which is *not* ratified or responded to has either not been heard or understood by the teacher or has been judged inappropriate by the teacher.

There are several very common ways in which teachers ratify students' utterances, and incorporate features of those utterances into their own utterances. First, and most obviously, there is very direct ratification of student utterances, which occurs quite often when students are responding to questions the teacher has asked.

(1) Teacher: They are :::. They're on what?
    Student: On wheels.
    Teacher: Right you are, Barbara. They're on wheels.
                    (#7 (2) – WS1 – 626)[1]

(2) Teacher: Alright, Larry? Why would you rather sleep in a camper than a tent?
    Student: Cause if you sleep in a tent all the animals can get in.
    Teacher: Alright, Shane?
                    (#7 (2) – WS1 – 626)

Second, teachers use the same linking devices that pervade the use of English in discourse and give evidence that the speaker has heard what the last speaker said. They substitute pronouns for units of speech that appear in the student's utterances. For example, the teachers frequently use the demonstrative pronoun 'that' to refer back to what a student has said:

(3) Teacher: Mark started using his imagination and now he wants Daddy to use/Daddy's imagination/to tell some more/of the story/.
    Student: /On the moon?/ /On the moon?/
    Teacher: That's right. Daddy's gonna tell some more about Mark on the moon.
                    (6 (1) –WS1 – 900)

(4) Student: And then when she gets there, she's gonna stop it.
    Teacher: Yes. What does Dick think of that, Allen? Would you read what Dick said?

$$(9 (1) - M \ 1/2 - 828)$$

Teachers also commonly substitute pronouns for nouns in the student's speech.

(5) Student: We always sleep in a *camper* that has a white thing, cause it hases beds.
    Teacher: Do you sleep in *it* every night?

$$(7 (2) - WS1 - 602)$$

(6) Teacher: Who do you see in the picture, Danny?
    Student[1]: Dick
    Student[2]: Pete and Dick.
    Student[3]: Pete and Dick.
    Teacher: What do they have?

$$(9 (1) - M1 - 896)$$

Third, while ellipsis is common in the students' speech, when *they* are building on the teacher's speech, it is much less common in the teacher's speech, at least at the first grade level. However, teacher *expansion* of the child's often elliptical speech is a very common form of *ratification,* and it is a common device for incorporating the child's utterance into the teacher's utterance.

(7) Teacher: Remember—who's using his imagination now?
    Student: Daddy
    Teacher: Daddy's using his imagination and he's telling part of the same story that Mark is telling. . . .

$$(\#6 (1) - WS1 - 126)$$

A fourth way in which teachers ratify student speech is by simple repetition of part or all of the child's response.

(8) Teacher: It's something you do every year until you get as/big as you're going to get./
    Students: /Grow. Grow/Grow.
    Teacher: Grow. Right.

$$(\#7 (1) - WS1 - 38)$$

This characterization of ratification is not comprehensive. Rather, it identifies some of the most *common* ways in which teachers verbally acknowledge and incorporate student's utterances into their own.

Teachers also *fail to ratify* the utterances of students in several common ways, singly and in combination.

First, teachers sometimes directly reject the utterances of the children, particularly when questioning them to determine their grasp of curriculum materials:

(9) Teacher: Is that what he said to the someone? "I whizzed around and around?"

    Student: Yeh.

    Teacher: No, that isn't what he said to the someone. Find the words that tell what he said to the someone.

                  (#6 (1) WS1 – 997)

Sometimes the teachers indicate a lack of ratification by providing a correct response where the student has given no response or an unacceptable response. Such modification is sometimes similar to the expansion of acceptable responses discussed earlier, and both sorts of responses can accordingly be ambiguous in intent.

(10) Teacher: The lark what to the tree?

     Student: Song.

     Teacher: *Flew to the tree.* It's a bird. It flew to the tree.

                  (#6 (1) – WS1 – 55)

It is also common for teachers to indicate non-incorporation of students' utterances by repetition of their own previous utterance.

Repetition of one's own utterance, where there has been *no* response from the person addressed, is widespread in verbal interaction. We hear it in the classroom, from both teacher *and* student.

(11) Teacher: What would he say if he were surprised? ( )
What would the spacemen say if he were surprised to see Mark?

                  (#6 (1) – SE1 – 150)

(12) Teacher: Write your name, but don't make any other marks on this paper.

     Student: (Write) your last name? Miz Thomas, write our last name?

                  (#6 (2) – WS1 – 894)

The repetition here indicates that the repeater has not heard anything that can be interpreted as a response. But, there is also such repetition from the teacher when an utterance from a student *can* be heard and interpreted as an answer to the teacher. When this occurs, we must infer that the teacher has not heard what we have heard, or is rejecting the response as inappropriate:

(13) Teacher: The last one says the lark did what to the tree. The lark.
     Student: Ate.
     Teacher: The lark what to the tree?

               (#6 (1) – WS1 – 55)

(14) Teacher: Let's look now at number–eleven. Can you read that for us//uh, Les?
     Student[1]:   /Yes.?
     Teacher: Can you find the (letters) for us and read it?
     Student[2]:   Salmon–Salmon
     Student[3]:   I can read it.
     Student[2]:   Salmon eggs ( ).
     Teacher: I don't hear Les, Les count eleven. Look down at eleven. . . .

               (#8 (2) – M1 – 498)

The repetition has the effect of holding the interaction in place. The teacher will not move the action forward until its elements are properly constituted. This process essentially involves cycling back through a segment of interaction. Schegloff (1972) has identified such re-cycling as evidence that a conversation is being repaired.[2]

From this discussion, it should be evident that while the turn economies and the participant structures are designed to equalize students' access to the floor, the teacher's response patterns are not. Instead, the teacher's response patterns *selectively incorporate* student's utterances heard and judged to be appropriate or correct, and ignore incorrect and inappropriate student utterances. This, when we consider not just who spoke, but who was heard and *verbally* defined by the teacher as having contributed to the interaction, it is apparent that some children's speech may be ratified more often than others.

This basic ratification process is the heart of the children's learning experience. It is the teacher's primary means for letting the children know when they are responding as she thinks they should. At the same time, there can be many reasons for the absence of ratification, which the teacher does not always articulate. Thus, children must somehow be able to make inferences from the patterning to the teacher's ratification and non-ratification that will inform them as to what sorts of mistakes they are making.

For *Warm Springs Indian students, talk is less often ratified than it is for Anglo students* (Philips 1982). The teachers more often judge their talk to be inappropriate. It is in this sense that Indian children's contributions are judged lacking, and in this sense they are indirectly defined systematically as less than or not equal to their Anglo peers. And finally, it is through this process that the educational tradition of assignment of a negative identity of Indian children is perpetuated.

Some of the failure to ratify and incorporate Indian students' responses to teachers' questions is due to the fact that Indian students' notions of a culturally appropriate response are different, by virtue of their Indianness, from the teachers' notions of appropriateness. I will illustrate this claim with evidence from three different aspects of language use in response to questions. First, Warm Springs Indian children have a culturally distinctive approach to the *regulation of turns at talk*. One of the things teachers are teaching at the first grade level is how to take turns getting the floor, and children who talk out of turn are often not ratified, even if they give a 'correct' answer, as in example 14. Warm Springs children rarely called out answers when other children's names were called, but they did something else that was in violation of the system the teacher was enculcating: When Indian students were asked a question, they often did not respond within the time the teacher allotted before she repeated the question, changed its form, or went on to a new question, but often answered just as the teacher was repeating the question, so that the impression one gets is that of the teacher and the student speaking at the same time. The teacher rarely ratified such student responses. Evidence from both in and outside the classroom indicated that what was going on was simply a slight difference in the timing of responses, in which Indian children and adults allowed slightly more time to pass after a person stopped speaking, before they spoke themselves.

Second, Indian children had culturally different notions from the teacher of *when humorous uses of language were appropriate* in the classroom, as the following example illustrates:

Teacher:	What else smells good?
Student:	Me.
Student:	My nose
	(students laugh)
Teacher:	(Do) all flowers smell good?

(#7 (2) – WS1 – 11)

Note the teacher here completely ignores the clever pun of the sort that is so common in daily Warm Springs life. The Indian children more often attempted such humor than the Anglo children of comparative age in the off-reservation town of Madras. They were often also ignored or scolded by the teachers when they did so. The teachers seemed to see such behavior as evidence that the children were not taking the learning experience seriously. But punning is common in the Indian community (Philips 1980).

Third, the Indian children had *daily experiences and forms of common knowledge that were different from that of the teacher*, and her limited ability to assimilate, comprehend and respond appropriately to them in many instances seemed due to that difference. Thus when an Indian child shyly told her teacher that she had been 'joined' in the war dancing over the weekend, the teacher had nothing to say in return. She couldn't say, "Who joined you?" or, "What did they give away?" to develop the conversation, because she didn't know that children were joined *by* someone and she didn't know that this person gave away goods to those present at the dancing. She certainly couldn't comment on the event, because she wasn't there, although she could have been.

I do not want to convey the impression that such cultural differences are the only reason Indian children more often find their answers to teachers' questions rejected by the teacher. When the book says 'The lark flew to the tree', and the student says it says 'The lark ate the tree', the teacher *cannot* ratify such a statement without furthering the child's confusion regarding what is going on, and one cannot readily attribute the child's response to a cultural difference in background. Such responses were more common among Indian children in my study and I cannot as yet fully explain why. At the same time *some* of the teacher's non-ratification of Indian children's contribution *is* due to cultural differences in notions of socially appropriate speech, and this is something we *can* do something about, now, through the development of a multicultural model of child development and socialization.

Some of the Indian children's utterances are defined as inappropriate or as nonexistant because teachers in our schools are still being trained to have a monocultural view of children's development, and to respond to anything that doesn't fit into their single cultural framework as if it didn't exist, rather than to recognize and to build for themselves local multicultural models of child development. As a consequence of this continued failure on the part of our systems of higher education to train teachers in a multicultural model of learning, Indian children continue to be defined as socially inappropriate and hence as less than equal to their Anglo peers just as they have since the beginning of an American tradition of Indian education.

Notes

1. WS1 means Warm Springs first grade. M1 means Madras first grade. The other numbers refer to locations on tape transcripts. Empty parentheses ( ) mean speech couldn't be transcribed. Full parentheses (Do) means transcriber *thinks* that was what was said.
2. The teacher's use of repair techniques to instruct the children makes it clear that although it is her own utterance that is being repeated, the teacher can rarely be said to be engaged in self-correction.

References

Berry, B. 1968. *The Education of American Indians.* Washington, D.C.: Office of Education, Bureau of Research.

Deloria, V. 1970. *We Talk, You Listen.* New York: Delta Publishing.

Fey, H. E., and D. McNickle. 1959. *Indians and Other Americans.* New York: Harper and Row.

Goffman, E. 1961. *Encounters.* New York: Bobbs Merrill.

Philips, S. 1980. Teasing, punning, and putting people on. In R. Bauman (ed.), *Language and Speech in American Society.* Austin: Southwest Educational Development Laboratory.

— 1982. *The Invisible Culture: Communication in Classroom and Community in the Warm Springs Indian Reservation.* New York: Longman.

Schegloff, E. 1972. Sequencing in Conversational Openings. In J. Gumperz and D. Hymes (eds.), *Directions in Sociolinguistics.* New York: Holt, Rinehart and Winston, 346-380.

— *Webster's Collegiate Dictionary.* 1938. Springfield, Mass.: G. and C. Merrian Co.

Viv Edwards

Expressing Alienation: Creole in the Classroom

The arrival of large numbers of West Indian migrants in Britain during the nineteen fifties and sixties created an interesting sociolinguistic situation. Their orientation towards British society was very positive. Although they tended towards fundamentalist worship, retained many distinctively Caribbean traits and spoke a very different variety of English, they were nonetheless Christian and the product of institutions and an education system modelled on the British system. They felt as if they were returning to the mother country. Many of the ingredients for social and linguistic assimilation were thus present, and if the host population had proved as welcoming as West Indian migrants anticipated this would no doubt have been the most likely course. The events of the last twenty-five years, however, have made assimilation a totally unacceptable course for most sections of the Black British community.

Workers from the Caribbean arrived at first to fill a vacuum created in the work force by post-war expansion. The net effect was an upward mobility for indigenous British workers and a serious shortage of manpower for low paid jobs with anti-social hours. Caribbean workers often accepted jobs of a lower status than those they had held, or been qualified to hold, in the West Indies (Peach 1968), but were generally confident that their ambitions would be realised by their children as they made their way through the education system. As we drift into the third decade since West Indian migration began, it is becoming increasingly clear that their hopes, by and large, have been frustrated. West Indians still tend to hold low status positions; their average weekly earnings are substantially below those of other groups of workers; they are under-represented among professional and white collar workers and over-represented among unskilled and semi-skilled workers (Smith 1977). A disproportionate number of West Indian families live in crowded, unmodernised conditions (CRE 1977).

Equally worrying, West Indian children as a group are seriously underperforming in British schools. By the early seventies a hierarchical situation had emerged in which non-immigrants were doing better than immigrants and all immigrants were doing better than West Indians (Townsend 1971). Even when ethnic minority children had received all their education in Britain, their performance was below that of the indigenous population. The figures which produced the greatest protest, however, were those which revealed the over-representation of West Indian children in schools for the educational subnormal (Coard 1971). On a national level there were four times as many West Indian children in ESN schools as indigenous children, and in Greater London these figures were higher still. The collection of educational statistics upon which these findings were based ceased in 1973 but indications are that underperformance among West Indian children is still widespread (Edwards 1979).

Attitudes towards West Indian speech

One of the most obvious early difficulties which faced West Indian migrants and the British host community alike was that, despite their colonial history, West Indians spoke a variety of English very different from any indigenous dialect. The precise form of this variety varies from island to island, but there is nonetheless a core of features common to all or most of the English-based Creole speaking territories which makes it realistic to talk in terms of 'West Indian Creole'.

Actual conversational data contain a mixture of standard English and Creole forms, the relative proportions affected by complex considerations of formality. Many writers (e.g., Le Page 1960; Edwards 1979) have therefore chosen to describe the situation in terms of a continuum between Broad Creole and English. The complexity of West Indian language, however, in no way detracts from its rule-governed nature, or the range of communicative possibilities it fulfills. West Indians have become very lively in recent years, poets like Bennett and Johnson, and novelists like Selvon have produced a good deal of Creole literature.

Attitudes towards West Indian Creole, however, do not always reflect linguistic objectivity. Like many other non-standard dialects, Creole is often felt to be lazy, sub-standard and inferior. One teacher's report on West Indian pupils (ATEPO 1970) described their language as 'babyish', 'careless and slovenly', 'lacking proper grammar' and even 'very relaxed like the way they walk'. There is a 'glut of speech' but a 'poverty of correct expression'. Children are even reputed to communicate by sign language. Fagan (1967) talks in terms of West Indian Creole being 'merely broken English' while Mordecai (1966) attributes the 'very simple language patterns' of West Indian children to their 'lack of interplay of language'. Situational restraints on children's language are sometimes overlooked altogether. Pollak (1972), for instance, remarks on the astonishingly small number of three-year-old

West Indians who could provide their own names and sex in developmental screening tests, but does not discuss the inhibiting effect which the formal test situation may have had on her young subjects or the fact that they may simply have been puzzled at being asked such obvious questions. She also demonstrates an ignorance of West Indian oral literature when she concludes that, because of their lack of response to her giving the first line of nursery rhymes, West Indian children have no tradition of children's rhymes.

Edwards (1978) offers the only empirical analysis to date of this area and confirms the negative attitudes generally held towards Creole. She also points to the role which these attitudes may be playing in educational underperformance. In experiments with student teachers and middle and working class English secondary school children, a hierarchy of preferences emerged. When played recordings of five children (a middle class boy, two working class children and two West Indian children) all talking fluently for a period of thirty seconds on the subject of a visit to the dentist, the middle class boy was considered to be the most intelligent, most interesting, best behaved and friendliest of the speakers. Listeners failed to distinguish between the working class children, whom they viewed less favourably than the middle class boy but nonetheless more favourably than the West Indian children. It was not revealed to the listeners, however, that one of the children, a West Indian girl, spoke twcie—once in the Barbadian accent which she used at home and with friends, and once in the working class English accent which she used at school. Significantly, she was viewed far more favourably when she spoke with an English accent than when she used a West Indian accent. There can be little doubt, therefore, that the low status of West Indians in society is faithfully reflected in the low status of their speech. And, although it is impossible to predict how teachers will behave towards West Indian children in the classroom, we cannot overlook the possibility that they will convey their negative feelings to the children.

But how do West Indians view their own speech? The views of West Indian adolescents who also took part in the testing above largely coincided with those of the English subjects. The low status of West Indian speech is no secret and it is not surprising that West Indians should be acutely aware of the situation. Moreover, there is a long history of cultural indoctrination which lends support to notions of the inferiority of Creole (Le Page 1968; DeCamp 1971). Negative attitudes towards vernacular speech are also a recurrent feature of West Indian literature. Sealey, for instance, in 'The Professor', describes a girl who admires her boyfriend because he could "talk English so good that when he finish you ain't understand a word he said". Amongst the most severe critics of West Indian speech are thus West Indians, and particularly educated West Indians. As Hymes (1971) shrewdly remarks, "Not the least of the crimes of colonization has been to persuade the colonized that they are in some way inferior, to convince the stigmatized that the stigma is deserved."

There is, however, an interesting ambivalence in West Indian attitudes towards their speech. On the one hand, Creole is felt to be 'bad talk' fit only for peasants, but it does have the sanction of being "intrinsically felt to be the code of the genuine, it symbolizes what is natural and deeply felt" (Reisman 1970). It is also something very personal and private and can be used most effectively for excluding outsiders. This last feeling was expressed very clearly by a West Indian girl who, when asked for the meaning of some remark she had made in Creole, waited for the teacher to leave the room before writing on the blackboard: "Sir is nosey about black people's language" (Jeffcoate 1979).

This linguistic ambivalence can usefully be discussed in the wider context of the remodelling activities of Afro-American and Afro-Caribbean communities which have been widely commented upon (Reisman 1970; Levine 1977). One of the responses to a life of oppression has been to remodel or transform words or symbols from one social order into something quite different. In this way both expressions and actions can refer simultaneously to a completely separate set of alternately held values. Reisman (1970) cites two examples of this kind of behaviour, 'break' and 'make noise'. Creole is often called 'broken' or 'broke up' language and yet when people 'break away' into Creole this is felt to symbolize deep and sincere feeling. Similarly, speaking Creole is sometimes called 'making noise', but in various contexts it can be seen to mean quite simply 'to express oneself'.

Adaptation to life in Britain

Although there is evidence of a great degree of adaptation to British speech norms, it would seem that many children have retained remarkably tenacious West Indian speech patterns. Creole features have been shown to persist in the speech, writing and oral reading of West Indian children who have been born in Britain (see Edwards 1980, for a review of the literature in this area). A survey of the writing of West Indian children between the ages of 6 and 14 contained the following:

Unmarked plural: My mum and his mum are the best of *friend*–Roslyn, 10
Unmarked possessive: He never took one of the *man sheep*–Michael, 10
Unmarked past tense: Nosy old Hilda *knok* on our back door–Jennifer, 14
Unmarked 3rd pers.sg.present: It *smell* very nice–Arlene, 13
Unmarked passive: Some had to have their picker *take*–Donna, 10
Unmarked copula: *It frightening* and *scarey*–Paul, 6
Creole plural marker: *The people them* was their–Donovan, 10

There were also examples of hypercorrection, in which children had obviously identified areas where their dialect deviated from the standard, but overgeneralized the relevant standard rule and applied it in inappropriate situations.

Then he *meated* a crocodile–Julian, 8
One day there was a *elephants*–Karen, 8
The slides *makes* the sugar *canes turns* into the box–Paul, 6
Jane's *dad's* was a detective–Peter, 9
It is *sticked* with its sticky legs–Alison, 9
He got out the tools from the *booth* of the car–Erma, 14

This kind of hypercorrection points to a considerable degree of confusion and insecurity. It seems highly likely that inconsistency and a failure to systematically explain differences between Creole and British English on the part of the teacher may have played a large role in producing this state. The teacher cannot possibly 'correct' everything and so tends to mark selectively. This approach, however, can hardly be expected to convey to a child that 's' is added to *all* third person singular present tense verbs, or that plural nouns are marked with an 's' in all but a very small number of cases in standard English.

The insistence of British schools on standard English has done nothing to help the West Indian child. In addition to the linguistic insecurity and confusion to which it has sometimes given rise, it has conveyed very clearly the message that his own language, which, after all, is the most valuable resource which he brings to school, is inacceptable.

Richmond (1979) has made an interesting contribution to this debate. He offes a very interesting analysis of the writing of Pat, a 14-year-old second generation Jamaican girl. Adopting a simple system of indicating errors, miscues or confusions (EMCs) in grammaticality, meaning, punctuation and spelling with numbers, and non-standard features with letters, he shows that EMCs occur four times as frequently as non-standard features in examples of Pat's work. Underlining the links between language and identity he suggests that teachers should concentrate on ways of improving writing which are unrelated to dialect. If dialect features are still to be found in the work of older pupils it should be possible to point out at this later stage those features and their standard English equivalents and to provide information about the existence of many dialects within a language if this has not been done already.

Youth culture orientation and language

There appears to be some confusion about the extent to which West Indian children in Britain can and do use Creole. Rosen and Burgess (1980) in a survey of eleven and twelve year old pupils in London schools suggest that as few as 20 percent of Jamaican (and 10 percent of children from Eastern Caribbean territories) have Jamaican (or other Caribbean Creoles) as their dominant speech or use it regularly in certain contexts, while 80 percent of Jamaican (and 90 percent of children from other Caribbean Creoles) are basically London or standard speakers who occasionally 'deepen' the dialect features. Both Sutcliffe (1977, 1983) and Hadi (1976), however, found that over 70 percent of the children in their samples admitted speaking Creole of a broadness equivalent to: 'mi aks di man fi put mi money eena im pockit'. The most probable explanation for this discrepancy lies in methodology. The Rosen and Burgess assessments rely on discussions between teachers and children which, given the low status and ambivalent attitudes towards Creole discussed above, may conceivably have resulted in under-reporting. The introduction of an actual Creole sentence in the Hadi and Sutcliffe surveys, in contrast, may well have established the researcher's positive orientation towards Creole and made it easier for children to admit that they use it in certain situations. It would also have served as an objective point of comparison for their own language use.

More interestingly for present purposes, however, than the extent to which West Indian children use Creole is the increasing number of reports from teachers that the speech of many Black children becomes more noticeably West Indian at adolescence. Such reports are, as yet, anecdotal but come from such a wide range of sources that there can be little doubt of their authenticity. In any community adolescence is a time of inter-generational conflict, but the problems which currently exist within the Black British community are particularly acute. Black parents have tended to be extremely accommodating to British society, often accepting jobs below their qualifications in the hope that their English educated children would do better. Many Black youths, on the other hand, are angry and frustrated that they are expected to occupy the same low status positions in society as their parents.

The move from Church to Rastafarianism has proved the source of considerable tension in some families (Louden 1977). The Rastafarian movement has its roots in Jamaica but has become widely known in Britain through the lyrics of reggae music. In a Jamaican context the themes of reggae are the everyday experience of a large section of the population—poverty, unemployment, crime and rebellion. In recent years, however, reggae has begun to deal with the situation of young Blacks in

Britain. Troyna (1977) has shown how it is possible to trace the deterioration of relations between Black youths and the police by studying reggae records. "Streets of Ladbroke Grove", "Fight to the End". "Police and Youth in the Grove" and many other titles and lyrics reflect a growing political awareness of the situation of Blacks in Britain. Reggae has also done a great deal to popularize Rastafarianism (Troyna 1978). A basic tenet of the faith is that Black people's destiny lies in Africa and Black people living outside the continent are in exile. Very important, Rastafarians see the necessity for Blacks to shape their future free from European influence. It promotes as something positive the very Blackness which British society as a whole rejects and it is easy to undeistand its appeal to young Blacks trying to establish an alternative cultural identity.

The linguistic implications of this development are far-reaching and Crump's (1979) study of the language of Black adolescents in a London school is particularly illuminating inasmuch as it relates language use to involvement in youth culture. Children's comments together with observations of the classroom and the playground suggest that it is only when pupils develop an orientation towards one or another of the major youth cultural groupings that differences in language use become apparent. Those who by the age of fourteen or fifteen take pride in 'talking Black' are those who turn to the all Black world of reggae and 'sound systems' or mobile discotheques. A likely explanation is that children, consciously or unconsciously, are martialling this Creole speech as a defense mechanism, a symbol of defiance of and alienation from mainstream society. As Hebdige (1976) remarks:

> As a living index of the extent of the Black's alienation from the cultural norms and goals of those who occupy higher positions in the social structure, the Creole language is unique.

The level of children's consciousness of their linguistic behaviour varies a great deal, but there is universal agreement that Creole is a means of defining one's own group and excluding others. Children questioned about their use of Creole reply, for instance, that they use it 'when I don't want people to understand' and 'when I don't want a white person to understand what I'm saying'. That West Indian children should feel a need to develop or maintain a separate identity poses very serious questions both for British schools and society at large.

The British schools' response

There has been a long history in British schools of ignorance and indifference to the linguistic and cultural needs of West Indian and other ethnic minority children. Official recognition of these needs came with the publication of the Department of Education and Science *Statistics of Education* for 1970 which revealed widespread underperformance among non-indigenous pupils, yet Black children had been present in British schools for over ten years by this time. Developments in the curriculum which reflect the changed composition of the classroom have been even slower. The publication of *Multiracial Education: Curriculum and Context 5–13* (jointly sponsored by the Schools Council and the National Foundation for Educational Research and the first large scale research programme of its kind) has been blocked since 1977 by representatives of the National Union of Teachers who felt parts of the report were unduly critical of teachers and politically biased. Individual researchers have resorted to publishing parts of their work independently (Worrall 1978; Jeffcoate 1979).

This is not to suggest, however, that all educators are insensitive to the situation of West Indian children, nor that they lack imagination in responding to their needs. The Inner London Education Authority, in a radical reappraisal of its policies for multicultural education, have been attempting since 1978 to develop a greater understanding of West Indian language on the part of teachers and encouraging the use of Creole in poetry and drama. Many individual teachers, too, have been discovering that Creole (and other non-standard speech) can be used to great effect in the classroom (see, for instance, Richmond 1978; Rosen 1978; Edwards 1979).

Those who have introduced West Indian language and culture into the curriculum argue that a recognition of the child's background is likely to have a favourable effect on his attitudes to school and his progress in learning. Their ideas, however, have sometimes been seriously misunderstood and misrepresented. The headmaster of one London comprehensive school with a large proportion of West Indian pupils is quoted in the *Sunday Times* of October 16th, 1977 as saying:

> Should I create a Black curriculum? Should I put Creole on the timetable? Over my dead body and the majority of my parents would cheer me to the skies. They want their children to get jobs. I will not even allow patois plays in the school. It must not be elevated to linguistic status at the expense of English.

This headteacher, like many other educationalists, has chosen to polarize the main issue in terms of either Creole or standard English. He had failed to recognize that acceptance of a child's language and background is likely to make him feel less threatened and therefore more motivated to learn and use standard English as well as the language he brings to the classroom.

Criticism of another person's speech seems to give a veneer of respectability to deeply seated negative feelings about the person himself. Those who cannot accept the speech of another group of people need to be quite clear that this is tantamount to rejection of that group and all it stands for; and this is certainly the way in which criticism is likely to be perceived by those at whom it is aimed. The retention of West Indian speech patterns and the development by some children of a distinctly Black British speech style in adolescence points strongly to the failure of the education system, and society as a whole, to meet the legitimate needs of West Indians. We must take heed of the warning signs and act positively. Complacency or resistance to any change in our present attitudes is potentially disastrous.

References

Abrahams, R. D. 1970. Patterns of performance in the British West Indies. In *Afro-American Anthropology*, ed. N. Whitten and J. Szwed. New York: Free Press.
– 1972. The training of the man of words in talking sweet. *Language in Society*, 1 (1): 15-30.
Association of Teachers of English to Pupils from Overseas (Birmingham Branch). 1970. *Work Group on West Indian Pupils Report.*
Bailey, B. L. 1966. *A Transformational Grammar of Jamaican Creole.* Cambridge: Cambridge University Press.
– 1971. Can dialect boundaries be defined? In *Pidgmization and Creolization* ed. D. Hymes. Cambridge: Cambridge University Press.
Cassidy, F. G. 1970. Teaching Standard English to speakers of Creole in Jamaica, West Indies. In *20th Annual Round Table Meeting on Linguistics.*
Coard, B. 1971. *How the West Indian Child is Made Educationally Sub-Normal in the British School System.* London: New Beacon Books.
Commission for Racial Equality. 1977. *Urban Deprivation, Racial Inequality and Social Policy: A Report.* London: HMSO.
Crump, S. 1979. The Language of West Indian Children and its Relevance for Schools. Unpublished M.Ed. dissertation, University of London, Institute of Education.
De Camp, D. 1971. The Study of Pidgin and Creole Languages. In Hymes (ed.), 13-39.
Edwards, V.K. 1978. Language attitudes and underperformance in West Indian children. *Educational Review*, 30 (1): 51-58.
– 1979. *The West Indian Language Issue in British Schools.* London: Routledge and Kegan Paul.
– 1980. Black British English: A bibliographical essay on the language of children of West Indian origin. *Sage Race Relations Abstracts*, 5 (3/4): 1-25.
Fagan, S. F. W. 1967. Analysis of the Written English of some Jamaican City Children. Unpublished M.A. thesis, University of London.
Hadi, S. 1976. Some Language Issues. Unpublished paper based on a survey undertaken as part of the Schools Council/NFER Education for a Multiracial Society project.
Hebdige, D. 1976. Reggae, Rastas and Rudies. In *Youth Sub-Cultures in Post-war Britain*, ed. S. Hall and T. Jefferson. London: Hutchinson, 135-54.
Hymes, D. (ed.) 1971. *Pidginization and Creolization.* Cambridge: Cambridge University Press.
Jeffcoate, R. 1979. *Positive Image: Towards a Multicultural Curriculum.* Writers and Readers Publishing Cooperative in association with Chameleon.

Le Page, R. B. (ed.) 1960. *Jamaican Creole.* Creole Language Studies, 1. London: Macmillan.

1968. 'Problems to be faced in the use of English as a medium education in four West Indian Territories. In *Language Problems of Developing Nations,* ed. J. A. Fishman, New York: Wiley.

Levine, L. W. 1977. *Black Culture and Black Consciousness.* New York: Oxford University Press.

Louden, D. 1977. Conflict and change among West Indian parents in Britain. *Educational Research,* 20 (1): 44-53.

Mordecai, J. 1966. West Indian Children's Language Study. Dissertation, School of Education, University of Birmingham.

Peach, C. 1968. *West Indian Migration to Britain: a Social Geography.* Oxford: Oxford University Press.

Pollak, M. 1972. *Today's Three-Year-Olds in London.* London: Heinemann.

Reisman, K. 1970. Cultural and linguistic ambiguity in a West Indian village. In *Afro-American Anthropology,* ed. N. Whitten and J. Szwed. New York: Free Press, 129-221.

Richmond, J. 1978. Jennifer and Brixton Blues. *New Approaches to Multiracial Education,* 6 (3): 10-15.

– 1979. Dialect Features in Mainstream School Writing. *New Approaches to Multiracial Education,* 8 (1): 9-15.

Rosen, H. and Burgess, T. 1980. *Languages and Dialects of London School Children.* London: Ward Lock.

Rosen, M. 1978. In their own voice. *Issues in Race and Education,* 16.

Smith, D. 1977. *Racial Disadvantage in Britain.* Harmondsworth: Penguin.

Sutcliffe, D. 1977. The Language of First and Second Generation West Indian Children in Bedfordshire. Unpublished M.Ed. thesis, University of Leicester.

– 1983. *British Black English.* Oxford: Basil Blackwell.

Townsend, H. E. R. 1971. *Immigrant Pupils in England: the L.E.A. Response.* Windsor: National Foundation for Educational Research.

Troyna, B. 1977. The Reggae War. *New Society* 39: 490-1.

– 1978. Race and Streaming: a case study. *Educational Review,* 30 (1).

Worrall, M. 1978. Race and teachers: the Schools Council study. *New Society,* 16 February 366-8.

LANGUAGE DEVELOPMENT AND THE FUNCTIONS OF MULTILINGUALISM

Eddie C. Y. Kuo

Language and Social Mobility in Singapore*

Introduction: The Singapore Society

The Republic of Singapore is small in size and short in history, yet
heterogeneous in ethnic and linguistic composition. Since its modern
inception in the early nineteenth century, Singapore has grown from a small
village of a few hundred inhabitants to a modern city of over 2.4 million
population. Each influx of immigrants in the past 160 years has added to the
ethnic and linguistic complexity of the island. Presently, the population of
Singapore is composed of about 77 percent Chinese, 15 percent Malays, 6
percent Indians[1] and 2 percent from other ethnic origins. Such ethnic
heterogeneity is paralleled by a still more diversified language structure since
each of the three major ethnic groups also retains a variety of dialects of
linguistic variants. For instance, most of the Chinese speak one of the southern Chinese dialects, including Hokkien, Teochew, Cantonese, Hainanese
and Hakka, at home. Similarly, Indians in Singapore can be divided into
Tamil, Malayali, and Punjabi language groups. It should be noted that there
does not exist in Singapore a strong indigenous host culture and ethnic group,
and each of the three major ethnic communities is characterized by its
distinctive cultural and literary tradition. It would seem that any rapid
assimilation, culturally or linguistically, among the heterogeneous population
with the Singaporte society as a 'melting pot' is unlikely.

Geographically, Singapore is a small island (588 square kilometres) located
at the center of an international crossroads in Southeast Asia. The compact
size of the Republic means that the population can easily be reached, either
through mass media or personal contact, unlike other Southeast Asian
countries with their vastly scattered lands and islands. This eases the problem
of communication and partly explains the efficiency of policy
implementation in Singapore. On the other hand, Singapore's geographical
location and its consequent emphasis on international trade and tourism
make Singapore an international city and encourage the use and status of
English.

Economically, Singapore is the most developed in Southeast Asia. Its
economy depends heavily on international trade, foreign investment and

careful planning. While dependence on international trade and foreign investment favours the use of English as a dominant language, the success in economic planning has resulted into what can be termed a 'planning mentality'. Politically, Singapore has been under a strong, stable and efficient government for more than fifteen years. There is strong confidence among the leaders that planning plays an important role and the government can achieve what it plans to achieve. This is reflected not only in economic planning but also in various aspects of social planning such as family planning, urban planning, educational planning, and manpower planning. All of the above directly or indirectly have some bearing upon language planning and the sociolinguistic situation in Singapore.

Singapore is a highly urbanized society, well-known for its efficient urban renewal scheme implemented by the Housing and Development Board over the years. Presently, over 70 percent of the population in Singapore live in ethnically integrated public housing estates. With the removal of slums and kampongs through urban renewal, there remain few isolated ethnic 'colonies' in Singapore today. People of different ethnic background now live in integrated public housing estates with frequent daily contact with one another. There is apparently a growing need for effective means of interethnic communication.

Sociolinguistic Background

Linguistically, the Singapore society represents a prototype of what Rustow (1968: 102) describes as a language pattern involving "a variety of unrelated languages each with its own literary tradition", and what Fishman (1972) designates as a 'multimodal nation'. An earlier study by Kuo (1976) identifies five major languages, using Ferguson's definitions (1971), and three minor languages in Singapore. The former are Malay, Mandarin, Tamil, English and Hokkien; the latter, Teochew, Cantonese and Hainanese.

As a compromise among the three major ethnic groups, the government of Singapore decided at the time of independence in 1965 that there would be four official languages in the new Republic[2]—Malay, Chinese (Mandarin) and Tamil to represent the three 'great traditions' in Singapore, and English because of its colonial background and the international status of the language. Such is thus the basis of the policy of multilingualism.

Of the four official languages, Malay is designated the national language. The decision reflects the political history and geographical location of the island-state, as Singapore was once a part of the Federation of Malaysia in 1963—65 and is surrounded by the Malay-speaking population of Malaysia and Indonesia. While the official role of Malay is almost purely ceremonial,[3] a pidginised form of Malay, 'Bazaar Malay', has long been used as a *lingua franca* among people from different ethnic backgrounds in the market place and other more traditional domains.

Mandarin Chinese which is the national language of China, is not a mother tongue for the great majority of Chinese in Singapore, but was chosen and accepted for historical and political reasons, to represent the largest ethnic community. Since the late 1970s, the government has launched a long-term campaign to promote the use of Mandarin (instead of Chinese dialects) as the common language among the Chinese. The campaign has boosted Mandarin as a 'high language' in the Chinese community. Simply because of the dominant size of the Chinese population in Singapore, if nothing else, Mandarin securely ranks second after English as a dominant language in Singapore.

As a contrast, Tamil as the ethnic language to represent the Indian community is rather weak due to the small size of the Indian community which in itself is diversified linguistically and culturally. The Tamil language does not seem to be receiving sufficient support from the Indian community not only because it is not the mother tongue for a large portion of the Indians, but also because it has never achieved a status symbolic of Indian identity either in South Asia or in Singapore. There is generally little sentimental attachment associated with Tamil among Indians in Singapore.

English, in contrast to the other three official languages, is associated with the colonial history and not connected with any of the Asian cultures. It is the only official language which is not an 'ethnic mother tongue'.[4] It is not associated with any of the three major ethnic groups in terms of ethnic-linguistic identity. Consequently, the language has many non-native speakers (more than half of the population) but only a small number of native speakers (probably not more than 5 percent). Despite, or perhaps because of, such unique characteristics, for all practical purposes English has become the *de facto* dominant working language. Administratively, it is the language of government bureaucracy. Legally, it is the language for 'the authoritative texts of all legislation and the judgement of courts of record' (Hickling 1975: 137). Commercially, English is the language of international trade and socially its use carries the most prestige.

The language policy of Singapore may be seen as a response to the competing multiplicity of cultural and linguistic traditions. The situation fits strikingly well with what Fishman (1972: 204) describes as decisions typical in a multimodal nation, whereby,

> In order to avoid giving any party an advantage – and in order to avoid constant rivalry for greater national prominence among the various contenders – a foreign Language of Wider Communication is frequently selected *de jure* or utilized *de facto* as (co)official or as working language (W) at the national level (sometimes in conjunction with an indigenous national language which may actually be little employed by those who are ostensibly its guardians).

English as a Dominant Working Language

As the dominant working language in Singapore, English has been gaining status and ground in the past few decades in terms of the number of speakers and literates.[5] The 1957 population census shows that 22.2 percent of Singapore population aged 15 and over claimed they could speak English (Table 1). A 1972 ECAFE national survey (Chen 1973) of 2,500 married persons reveals that 26.3 percent of the respondents reported that they could speak English 'fairly well', presumably a higher standard than that used in the 1957 census.[6] Furthermore, a 1978 national sample survey (Survey Research Singapore 1978)[7] shows that 61.7 percent of the adult population claimed that they could understand English. From Table 1, it is apparent that, among the five major languages in Singapore, English and Mandarin are the only two that are definitely gaining strength, with Mandarin gaining at an even faster rate than English.

Table 1: Percentage of population competent in various major languages, Singapore.

	English	Malay	Mandarin	Tamil	Hokkien
Percentage who can speak, 1957[a]	22.2	48.0	19.9	8.2	*
Percentage who can speak fairly well, 1972[b]	26.0	47.2	35.4	6.2	*
Percentage who can understand, 1978[c]	61.7	67.3	63.9	6.0	77.9

* Data not available.
Sources: a. Computed from Chua (1964), Tables 44-47, pp. 162-165, referring to population aged 15 and over.
b. Based on Chen (1973), Table 4.7, p. 41, referring to married population.
c. Computed from Survey Research Singapore. (1978), Vol. 1 and 2, Table 6A, referring to population aged 15 and over.

The increasing status of English is more clearly shown from the growth of the English literacy rate between 1957 and 1980. Statistics from the last three censuses (Table 2) show that English made the greatest gain among the four official languages during the past decades. Significantly, this is true not only for the total population, but also for each of the three major ethnic communities. In fact, from 1957 to 1980, Malays, Chinese and Indians in Singapore made more literacy progress in English than in their respective ethnic languages. In view of the present educational and occupational structure of Singapore, the trend of growing English literacy seems certain to continue. Indians as a group were by 1970 already more literate in English than in Tamil. Should the present trend continue as expected, it is likely that both Chinese and Malay populations will eventually become at least equally literate in English and in their respective ethnic languages.

Table 2:   Literacy rate (percent) in various official languages in Singapore by ethnicity, 1957, 1970 and 1980.

Population aged 10 and over who were	1957	1970	1980*
Literate in Malay			
Malays	59.7	70.2	82.7
Chinese	0.8	1.0	1.1
Indians	4.5	10.1	15.9
Others	13.6	16.9	15.1
All	9.1	11.4	14.1
Literate in English			
Malays	20.3	33.0	54.4
Chinese	17.6	31.2	42.4
Indians	30.8	48.0	60.1
Others	87.3	89.4	82.6
All	21.0	33.7	46.2
Literate in Chinese			
Malays	b	a	0.3
Chinese	35.6	46.0	63.8
Indians	b	0.1	0.4
Others	b	1.3	2.3
All	26.7	35.6	49.2
Literate in Tamil			
Malays	b	a	0.1
Chinese	b	a	a
Indians	48.6	38.8	42.5
Others	b	0.2	0.2
All	4.8	2.8	2.8

*   Data in Khoo (1981) do not provide precise figures for calculation of literacy rate in respective official languages. The rates given are estimates only. The error margins are believed to be less than 1 percent except in the case of Indians which may have a wider margin of underestimation.
a   Less than 0.1 percent
b   Data not available
Source: Computed from Arumainathan (1973), Table 6,8, p. 52, and Table 9.4, p. 103, and Khoo (1981), Table 24, p. 36.

The above observation is supported by the statistics of biliteracy (officially reported as 'bilingualism' in the census) in 1970 and 1980. Statistics reveal that, of the population aged 10 and over, 13.8 percent in 1970 and 31.5 percent in 1980 were biliterate in at least two official languages. Among them, almost all were biliterate in English and one of the other three official languages. This reflects the success of the bilingual education program and the crucial function of cross-ethnic communication played by the English language in Singapore (cf. Kuo 1976, 1979).

While we have shown that more of the population in Singapore is gaining competence in English—and that the language is more frequently used and more functional in many domains—we also find that competence in English is associated with social mobility and socioeconomic status. English, as the language of administration and trade in Singapore, is without doubt a prestigious language. Competence in English has become an important requirement for career advancement and occupational mobility.

The most direct and relevant set of data for placing the status of English into the perspective of social stratification comes from a 1975 national survey. The relation between language competence and household income is presented in Table 3. The most significant finding noted from Table 3 is that consistently more of the higher income population was competent in each of the major languages except Tamil than those from the lower income group. Competence in major languages is clearly associated with economic status. Moreover, it is also apparent that a large proportion of the population could understand at least two or three major languages, the higher income group being the more bilingual.

A closer look at Table 3 reveals that, while people from the more wealthy families were more likely to be competent in a given language (except Tamil) than those from the poorer families, the case of the English language shows the sharpest contrast. We find more than three-quarters of those with over S$ 1,000 monthly household incomes could understand English, contrasting with less than two-fifths among those with household incomes of less than S$ 300. To a lesser degree, this is also true with Mandarin (66.5 percent and 43.7 percent). Both English and Mandarin, then, are discriminative of social-economic status, though the former is the more so. It should be noted that while the association between household income and competence in a given language may have been confounded with the factor of ethnicity (further analysis is not possible for want of relevant data), the contrast in the case of English is too strong to be challenged.

The occupational structure in Singapore generally favours the English-educated, i.e., those who have gone through schools using English as the major language of instruction. They enjoy better job opportunity, and they are also more likely to receive higher pay. Table 4 shows that in 1978,

Table 3: Percentage of population aged 15 and over who can understand various major languages by monthly household income, Singapore, 1975*.

Monthly Household Income	Percentage who can understand major languages				
	English	Malay	Mandarin	Tamil	Hokkien
Over S$1,000	77.5	68.4	66.5	4.1	77.5
S$501 – 1,000	60.0	60.3	63.5	6.8	77.2
S$301 – 500	43.3	56.8	54.6	6.0	71.3
S$1 – 300	35.3	62.1	43.7	12.1	60.0
Total	56.6	61.3	59.4	6.7	73.7

* Excluding 'income unknown' and 'no income' cases.
Source: Survey Research Singapore (1975), Vols. 1 and 2, Tables 6B.

except among those with the lowest level of education, the English-educated consistently earned a higher monthly income than the Chinese-educated of the same level of education. The difference was greater among the better educated. It is evident that the occupational structure under rapid industrialization attributes much weight to competence in English as a criterion of recruitment and reward.

Table 4: Median monthly income of men by stream of education and educational level, 1978.

unit = Singapore $

Level of Education	Stream of Education	
	Chinese	English
No schooling/ some primary	251	251
Completed primary/ some secondary	275	299
Completed secondary	325	386
Tertiary	1,004	1,388

Source: Pang 1980: 171.

Language, Education and Social Mobility

In order to have a fuller understanding of the connection between language and social mobility, it is imperative to look at the language in the educational context in Singapore. Two phenomena are especially relevant: first, the formulation and implementation of the bilingual program in the educational system, and second, the shift in student enrolment from ethnic schools to English-medium schools.

Before independence in 1965, four more or less independent school systems had evolved in Singapore, each with a different language as the major medium of instruction. At the time of independence, the government adopted a policy of parity of treatment for the four official language streams in its educational structure. One major achievement of the Ministry of Education, however, is the consolidation of the schools of different language streams into a national educational system. At present, while the four language streams still exist in name, all schools follow somewhat standardized curricula. Textbooks are now locally produced, and most teachers are locally trained.

Under the policy of bilingual education, all students in Singapore are required to take lessons in English and one of the ethnic languages. The two languages are used not only in language courses, but also as languages of instruction for specific subjects. The bilingual curriculum begins from Primary One (or even pre-primary classes in some selected schools). Following the 'personality principle' (McRae 1975), the parent chooses the ethnic language for his child to study in addition to English, which is required for all. In actual practice, the Chinese are expected to choose Chinese, the Malays are to choose Malay, and the Indians, Tamil, although there are also cases of Malay and Indian students taking Chinese as the second school language.

The ratio of instruction time for the two languages ranges from 50:50 to 70:30. Many Chinese-medium schools and almost all of the Malay- and Tamil-medium schools allocate more than half of the instruction hours for subjects using English as the medium of instruction. The label of 'Chinese-medium' or 'Malay-medium' therefore indicates only the history and tradition of a school, and not necessarily the dominant language used in instruction.

In the system of bilingual education in Singapore, English and the ethnic language are taught for different subjects and functions. As a general principle English is used in mathematics, science and other technology-related subjects, while the ethnic language is used in civics (or moral education) and humanity-related subjects. The practice fits into what Mackey (1972: 160) classifies as the Dual-Medium Differential Maintenance Type, a relatively rare pattern of bilingual education. The rationale behind it.

which is also the *raison d'être* of the policy of bilingualism in Singapore, is to utilize English as an instrument for Western science and technology and to learn the ethnic language for the retention of the traditional culture and values.

The language element has long been a major component in the educational policy and its implementation in Singapore. As an extension of such concern, language instruction (and learning) has also become the primary objective of the system, and language achievement the major criterion of student performance.

In the present educational system, pupils are assessed and streamed at the end of their Primary Three (aged 9–10) year into 'normal bilingual course', 'extended bilingual course' or 'monolingual course'. It is significant to note that Chinese pupils in the 'monolingual course' have Chinese (Mandarin) as the medium of instruction, while pupils of other ethnic background use English as the teaching language.

Moreover, minimum language ability requirements for English and the ethnic language are also imposed at different levels of standard examinations as a basis for admission to secondary schools, pre-university classes, and the university. While this practice ensures that a minimum level of language capability is maintained at each level of education, it is also obvious that language capability (and to some extent, language aptitude) has become an important element in social mobility.

Since it is mostly up to the parents to choose the language stream for their children, at least at the primary level, student enrolment in the various language-medium schools to a great extent reflects the view of their parents on the relative importance of various languages. The parents' consideration and decision will therefore considerably affect the future status of the official languages in Singapore. Table 5 summarises the statistics of Primary One student enrolment in the four language streams from 1960 to 1976. The data clearly show that there has been an enormous change in the relative intake of pupils over the years. Consistent with the observation previously made, the English stream has been gaining ground over the years, with 86 percent of Primary One pupils enrolled in English-medium schools by 1976. The English schools are attended by students from all three major ethnic communities, while the other language-medium schools are attended mostly, if not exclusively, by students from corresponding ethnic-language groups. The statistics thus clearly indicate that there have been more and more parents from all three major ethnic communities sending their children to English schools. The present trend, coupled with the tendency for the English-educated to be less ethnocentric, presents an optimistic picture of the emergence of a supra-ethnic, integrative identity in Singapore.

Table 5:   Percentage of primary one registration by language stream, 1960-1976.

Year of Registration	Language Streams				Total	
	English	Chinese	Malay	Tamil	%	N
1960	51.81	39.32	8.64	0.23	100	52,560
1961	55.37	36.45	7.89	0.29	100	55,234
1962	60.27	31.01	8.43	0.29	100	57,878
1963	62.07	29.30	8.41	0.22	100	59,084
1964	63.05	27.90	8.84	0.21	100	61,015
1965	62.28	28.59	8.94	0.19	100	61,931
1966	60.24	32.80	6.76	0.20	100	59,128
1967	61.28	33.19	5.36	0.17	100	56,736
1968	63.09	33.06	3.66	0.19	100	55,526
1969	66.42	30.92	2.51	0.15	100	56,152
1970	69.30	28.98	1.60	0.12	100	54,730
1971	71.42	27.44	1.06	0.08	100	52,284
1972	74.89	24.26	0.79	0.06	100	51,747
1973	77.88	21.46	0.61	0.05	100	47,599
1974	78.51	21.03	0.43	0.03	100	44,918
1975	82.52	17.16	0.32	–	100	42,409
1976	86.06	13.75	0.19	–	100	43,730

Source: Prime Minister's speech to Parliament, 23 February 1977; reported in *Straits Times,* 26 February 1977.

The current trend toward increasing enrolment in the English schools seems irreversible unless there is a dramatic change of educational policy in Singapore. It is doubtful that the Malay- and Tamil-medium schools can survive under such pressure.

The trend is consistent with the series of changes that occurred to the traditionally Chinese-medium Nanyang University. The first sign of change appeared in 1975 when the major medium of instruction of Nanyang University was switched from Mandarin to English. Then in 1980, it was announced that Nanyang University was to merge with the University of Singapore (which has always used English for instruction) to become part of the new National University of Singapore. Now that the only university in the Republic uses English as the medium of instruction, and since university education is a valued goal aspired to by most mobility-conscious parents, the parents are further motivated to send their children to English-medium primary and secondary schools to better prepare them for university education. Moreover, since university graduates are likely to be among the leaders of society in the future, the present educational system is likely to perpetuate the dominant position of English.

The Language Paradox

English is a Western language. As such it is associated with Western culture and Western values, and thus is perceived to be the language of modernity, progress, technology and economic development. At the same time, a prevalent view in Singapore sees that English is related to the decadent 'Western' values of materialism, 'hippy-ism', sex, drugs and violence. This ambivalent attitude is consistently displayed in the speeches of political and intellectual leaders of Singapore and its existence is confirmed by the observations of social scientists.

The status and function of English in Singapore are most clearly delineated in relation to economic development and modernization. It is often pointed out that Singapore lives by trade and that the language of that trade is English. The use of English in Singapore thus greatly aids the attraction of overseas capital, trade and industrial investment. As a dominant international language, English is also believed to provide access to the vast range of technical and organizational knowledge of the West. In Singapore's bilingual programme, as we have noted, in both English and non-English schools, English is used as the medium of instruction in mathematics, science and technology. The purpose is clearly to prepare the younger generation for further economic and technological development.

That the use of English is functional to economic progress is not only part of the official thinking of the governing elite, but also the motivation behind parents' choice of language medium for their children. Parents choose English schools mainly because they reckon that an English education will provide their children with better opportunities in career advancement and social mobility. By comparison, those who send their children to Chinese schools do so for moral training and character building. According to Murray (1971: 156–7), the competition between 'economics' and (ethnic) 'identity' provides a general conceptual model that appears to explain most of the pattern of choice of language medium by Chinese parents. The pattern is clearly one of English for economic reasons and ethnic language for identity reasons.

In Singapore today, competence in English is such an important qualification for career achievement and social mobility that those lacking that ability are typically pessimistic in their outlook towards their future. This is supported both by a 1969 survey of Nanyang University students (Lind: 1974) and a comparative study of two small groups of Nanyang and Singapore University students in 1974 (Cheng and Lim 1975). In the 1969 study, Lind (1974: 169) points out that one major set of factors of pessimism among Nanyang University students centred around the language issue and the way this has been defined by the government. The impression appears widespread that Nanyang graduates are invariably rated inferior to the graduates from Singapore University in the competition for jobs with both the government and many business firms, and that this discrimination is chiefly a consequence of a deficient command of the English language and of the associated but questionable notion that the qualification in other respects must likewise be inferior.

The utilitarian value of English is well recognised by policy-makers, parents and students. In his study of Chinese students, Murray (1971: 750) found that 10.3 percent of his pre-university sample from Chinese schools indicated they were 'sorry' they had attended secondary schools in Chinese, while only 1.6 percent of the English-educated took this view of their education in the English language. Murray found that this tendency appeared to rise with age and/or education level: over 18 percent of all first-year students in Nanyang University regretted their Chinese secondary education, compared with just over 2 percent at the University of Singapore who regretted their English schooling.

English, which is not an ethnic mother tongue, is promoted in Singapore as the *lingua franca* of interethnic communication. In fact, many researchers have found that the learning of English is associated with a loyalty to Singapore that can facilitate the emergence of a 'Singapore identity'. This view clearly existed during colonial times. Commenting on the colonial government's policy toward language education, Gopinathan (1974: 8) points out:

> English-medium education and the learning of English are treated as being synonymous with loyalty to Singapore, largely because the British saw that their interest would be best served by an English-educated elite and also because of the politicization of vernacular, especially Chinese, schools.[8]

While there is no empirical evidence to determine whether this kind of thinking still remains among the political elite in the new Republic, a national survey on 'Singapore National Identity' revealed that the English-educated actually showed a higher level of national identity than the 'vernacular educated' (see Chiew 1972).[9] In another study (Tan and Chew 1970), the English-educated in integrated schools were found to be less 'ethnocentric' and more 'tolerant' than students from the Chinese stream. According to Gopinathan (1974: 64):

> It has been demonstrated consistently that the English stream has the highest ratings for cultural and linguistic tolerance and the Chinese stream the least. . . . The racially integrated English stream, deculturalized as it may be, seems, perhaps by the very fact of deculturalization, to have made the greatest inroads into breaking down cultural intolerance.

This stronger feeling of Singapore identity and the lower level of ethnocentrism are achieved at the cost of a more superficial association with the ethnic culture. It seems that only when one is free from sentimental attachments to one's own ethnic tradition can one progressively look forward and develop a new identity at the supra-ethnic level. The dilemma is that, while it is desirable to maintain certain sentimental attachments to ethnic-cultural tradition, this may hinder the development of a new identity, which can best be built initially only on an instrumental basis.[10] It is therefore not surprising that there is a stereotype in Singapore of the English-educated which characterizes them as more Anglicised, as weak in their sentimental attachments to their ethnic traditions but strong in their instrumental attachments to the new nation-state. The danger is, as the Prime Minister Mr. Lee Kuan Yew pointed out several years ago, that too much emphasis on English may lead to the "detrimental effects of deculturalization", of producing "anaemic, uprooted floating citizens without the social cohesiveness and the cultural impetus that give the people the drive and the will to succeed as a group" (quoted in Josey 1971 : 346).

An obvious way of dealing with this problem is bilingual education—the learning of English and one of the ethnic mother tongues. While bilingual education has been forcefully implemented in Singapore since the early 1970s, the underlying dilemma still remains.

English as a medium of communication opens the door to modern technology and skills. At the same time, it makes available to its speakers the mass culture of the West, which often conflicts with traditional cultural values. English language and English education therefore are taken to be associated with modern values and the modern style of life, while the ethnic language and education represent tradition. The contrast exists in the family, the school, the mass media, and other social situations. The difference is so great that the English-educated are believed to possess different personality characteristics from the non-English educated. With the English language playing a dominant role in Singapore, it is a common concern among parents with Chinese educational background that the younger generation are being assimilated or even 'corrupted'. Typical comments from them—which may or may not be valid—regarding the English-educated are that they are naive, proud, selfish, immature, and unstable, with no respect for parents and elders (see Lee 1967).

The stereotype in fact is so well accepted by the Chinese-educated community that being English-educated has come to mean being outgoing, carefree, fun-seeking, irresponsible and even hedonistic. In contrast, being Chinese-educated implies a shy, introvert, withdrawn, but diligent, hardworking, and mature personality. In her study of factory workers in Singapore, Heyzer (1974) found that factory girls are often labelled English-educated or Chinese-educated, not according to their actual educational background, but according to their style of life and value-orientation. An English-educated girl in this context may have little formal education and speak little English. Yet she is referred to as English-educated by her colleagues because of certain behaviour and attitude characteristics. In this connection, it is relevant that Heyzer also points out that competence in English was one crucial factor relating to promotion and social mobility in the factory she studied. Those with poor English accepted their lot with a pessimistic outlook, saying they could not expect much because they did not speak English. The feeling is not too different from that reported by Lind (1974) among Nanyang University students.

Conclusion

From the above discussion, it is clear that English is at the same time both good and bad, loved and hated, in Singapore. This ambivalence exists as part of the collective thinking and ideology of the elite group and is possibly a potent force behind the government's policies on the language issue. At the same time, this love-hate complex also exists at the individual level and is closely associated with motivations and decisions regarding language learning. It is also an important element in the explanation of certain sociolinguistic patterns in Singapore. This is an area to be further explored by sociolinguists.

Parallel to this psychological dilemma is the social dilemma resulting from the seeming functional incompatibility between English and ethnic languages. While English is promoted for its utilitarian functions and for its role in the development of a supra-ethnic Singapore identity, the ethnic languages are encouraged for cultural foundation and for the retention of traditional values. Here we find a dilemma between modern progressiveness and traditional values, between supra-ethnic identity and ethnic-cultural rooting,[11] between instrumental association and sentimental commitment—all entangled with the language issue.

As a manifestations of this dilemma, several seemingly contradictory language policy decisions were observed in late 1970s and early 1980s. One was the merger of Nanyang University with the University of Singapore, making English the sole language used in tertiary education. At the same time, an all-out long-term mass campaign was launched to promote Mandarin as the common language in the Chinese community. Then at the primary education level, the less capable pupils are streamed at the end of Primary Three into the 'monolingual course', in which the Chinese school children are to revert to using Mandarin as the language medium, while all others are to take courses in English.

What is obvious of the present language policy is that English remains the language of social mobility and interethnic communication. Since the English language continues to be the major medium of instruction at the secondary and tertiary levels, the middle- and upper-class population in Singapore in the future would be mainly English-educated and (hopefully) bilingual. As a result, the upper stratum of the population would be ethnically heterogeneous but linguistically homogeneous, with English as the *lingua franca*. This however would not be true with the lower stratum since many of them would probably be from the monolingual Chinese stream and may have even reverted back to dialects as their daily languages. The language of interethnic communication for this category of population would probably remain as Bazaar Malay, Hokkien, or some form of basilect[12] variety of Singapore English.

This situation can be problematic if the lower-class population are ethnocentric and consider themselves deprived, with strong sentimental associations with their respective ethnic cultures. Under such circumstances the maintenance of communicative integration would depend much on the solution of the problems of vertical inter-class communication and of horizontal interethnic communication among the lower-class group. Because of the increasing numbers of English-educated citizens, their better chance of upward social mobility, and the increased usefulness of English, linguistic homogeneity would spread from the top level of society. This expansion of linguistic, and to some extent cultural, homogeneity would mean more political and social stability in Singapore so long as contact and mobility between this group and the lower stratum could be effectively maintained with the help of social brokers. The social broker role (Murray 1971) of the bilinguals becomes extremely important and will remain so for a long time to come.

Notes

* The author is thankful to Survey Research Singapore, Ltd. for permission to use some statistics from SRM Media Index.
1. The 'official' ethnic category of 'Indians' includes people of Pakistan, Bangladesh and Sri Lanka origin.
2. The Republic of Singapore Independence Act of 1965 includes the following section laying out the language policy of the new Republic:
    7. (1)   Malay, Mandarin, Tamil and English shall be the four official languages in Singapore.
    (2)   The national language shall be the Malay language and shall be in the Roman script: provided that—
    (a)   no person shall be prohibited or prevented from using or from teaching or learning any other language; and,

(b)   nothing in this section shall prejudice the right of the Government to preserve and sustain the use and study of the language of any other community in Singapore. (*Government Gazette Acts Supplement,* no. 2, 1965, pp. 99-100).

3. In Singapore, the national anthem is sung, and military commands are given, in the Malay language. Until early 1981, a person applying for citizenship was required to pass a simple oral Malay language test. The requirement was modified and a person can now take an oral test in any of the four official languages.

4. We use the term 'ethnic mother tongue', or 'ethnic mother language', to refer to the major languages associated each with a specific major ethnic community in Singapore. The ethnic mother tongue of the Chinese is Mandarin Chinese, that of the Malay community is Malay, and that of the Indian community is Tamil. The ethnic mother tongue in this sense does not necessarily mean the first language learnt, in fact it may never be learnt. Most Chinese in Singapore speak one of the southern Chinese dialects as a mother tongue. And perhaps up to half of the Indians are not Tamil speakers. Nevertheless, an ethnic mother tongue is socially accepted as the language to represent the respective ethnic identity. In Singapore, these three languages are officially referred to as 'mother tongues', which is a misnomer.

5. The gain however is not exclusive to English: it is also true of Mandarin Chinese. See Table 1.

6. The 1972 ECAFE study applies a non-proportionate stratified sampling scheme. As a result, the sample included 71.6 percent Chinese, 19.9 percent Malays, and 7.0 percent Indians. The relevant percentages in Table 1 are based on the unadjusted original sample.

7. Survey Research Singapore is a private market-research group. The 1978 survey was carried out among a representative cross-sectional sample of the adult population aged 15 and over in Singapore, using the multi-stage random sampling procedure. A total of 4,617 persons were interviewed between July 1977 and June 1978.

8. Commenting on the tendency toward political radicalisation among the Chinese-educated in 1965, Franke (1965: 186) perceptively points out that it was a disadvantage in occupational opportunity that led to political frustration: it is actually not Chinese education as such, but resentment and frustration that are leading people towards radical political doctrines.

9. In a study of 3,316 secondary students in Singapore in 1969-70, Busch (1974) found that the Chinese stream students were less loyal than those from the non-elite English schools but more loyal than students from the selected elite English schools. This indicates that the category of 'English-educated' is perhaps too general and simplistic for many purposes. Busch's study also found that both 'ability in Mandarin' and 'ability in English', as perceived by the students, are positively related to national loyalty. It cannot be determined whether the association is confounded by socioeconomic status.

10. The concepts, 'sentimental attachment' and 'instrumental attachment', are used following Kelman (1971).

11. Commenting on a related issue, Benjamin (1976: 122) points out that Singapore's emphasis on multi-racialism brings about "a marked degree of cultural involution. . . in which each 'culture' turns in on itself in a cannibalistic manner, struggling to bring forth further manifestation of its distinctiveness." Similarly, Gopinathan (1974: 64) comments: "Pride in the achievements of several thousand years of one's own culture. . . need not necessarily lead to an appreciation of the value of other cultures."

12. Platt and Weber (1980: 271) define 'basilect' as the "lowest sub-variety of a speech continuum. . . spoken mainly by those of little or no formal education".

References

Arumainathan, P. 1973. *Report on the Census of Population, 1970 Singapore*, vol. 1, Singapore: Department of Statistics, Republic of Singapore.

Benjamin, G. 1976. The cultural logic of 'multiracialism'. In Riaz Hassan ed., *Singapore: A Society in Transition*. Kuala Lumpur: Oxford University Press, pp. 115-133.

Busch, Peter A. 1974. *Legitimacy and Ethnicity: A Case of Singapore.* Lexington, Mass: Lexington Books.

Chen, Peter S. J. 1973. National Reports on A Comparative Study of Husband-Wife Communication and Practice of Family-Planning (Report 1: Singapore). Bangkok: ECAFE, United Nations (mimeo.).

Cheng, Ai Teng and Lim Luan Keow 1975. University Students: Their Self-Images and Images of Society. Unpublished Academic Exercise, Department of Sociology, University of Singapore.

Chiew, Seen Kong 1972. Singapore National Identity. Unpublished M. Soc. Sci. Thesis, Department of Sociology, University of Singapore.

Chua, S.C. 1964. *State of Singapore: Report on the Census of Population, 1957.* Singapore: Government Printing Office.

Ferguson, Charles A. 1971. National sociolinguistic profile formulas. In C.A. Ferguson, *Language Structure and Language Use.* Stanford, California: Stanford University Press, pp. 157-170.

Fishman, Joshua A. 1972. National languages and languages of wider communication in the developing nations. In J.A. Fishman, *Language in Sociocultural Change,* Stanford, California: Stanford University Press, pp. 191-223.

Franke, Wolfgang. 1965. The problem of Chinese education in Singapore and Malaysia. *Malaysian Journal of Education,* 2: 182-191.

Gopinathan, Saravanan. 1974. *Towards a National System of Education in Singapore, 1945-1973.* Singapore: Oxford University Press.

Government Gazette Acts Supplement. Singapore.

Heyzer, Noreen. 1974. A Factory Situation in Singapore, seminar paper presented at the Department of Sociology, University of Singapore, 11 December.

Hickling, R.H. 1975. Language, law and Singapore. *Malayan Law Review,* 17: 136-148.

Josey, Alex. 1971. *Lee Kuan Yew,* rev. ed. Singapore: Asia Pacific Press.

Kelman, Herbert C. 1971. Language as an aid and barrier to involvement in the national system. In Joan Rubin and Bjorn H. Jernudd, eds., *Can Language be Planned?* Honolulu: The University Press of Hawaii, pp. 21-51.

Khoo, Chian Kim. 1981. *Census of Population 1980 Singapore,* Release no. 3, Department of Statistics, Singapore.

Kuo, Eddie C.Y. 1976. A sociolinguistic profile. In Riaz Hassan, ed., *Singapore: A Society in Transition,* Kuala Lumpur; Oxford University Press, pp. 134-148.

– 1979 Measuring communicativity in multilingual societies: The cases of Singapore and West Malaysia. *Anthropological Linguistics,* 21: 327-40.

Lee Chong Kau. 1967. Choice of Education among the Singapore Chinese. Unpublished Academic Exercise, Department of Social Work, University of Singapore.

Lind, Andrew W. 1974. *Nanyang Perspective: Chinese Students in Multiracial Singapore.* Honolulu: The University Press of Hawaii.

Mackey, William F. 1972. A Typology of Bilingual Education. In W.F. Mackey, *Bilingual Education in a Bilingual School.* Rowley, Mass.: Newbury House, pp. 149-21.

McRae, Kenneth D. 1975. The principle of territoriality and the principle of personality in multilingual states. *International Journal of the Sociology of Language,* no. 4: 33-54.

Murray, Douglas. 1971. Multilanguage Education and Bilingualism: The Formation of Social Brokers in Singapore. Unpublished Ph.D. Dissertation, Stanford University.

Pang, Eng Fong. 1980. Returns to schooling and training in Singapore: Postscript. In E. Afendras and E. Kuo (eds.) *Language and Society in Singapore.* Singapore: Singapore University Press, pp. 168-72.

Rustow, Dankwart A. 1968. Language, modernization and nationhood–An attempt at typology. In J.A. Fishman, C.A. Ferguson and J. Das Gupta, eds., *Language Problems of Developing Nations*. New York: Wiley, pp. 87-106.

Platt, John, and Weber, Heide. 1980. *English in Singapore and Malaysia*. Kuala Lumpur: Oxford University Press.

Straits Times, Singapore.

Sunday Times, Singapore.

Survey Research Singapore. 1975. *SRM Media Index*, 1975, *General Report for Singapore*, Vol. 1 and 2, Singapore.

— 1978. *SRM Media Index*, 1978, *General Report for Singapore*, Vol. 1 and 2, Singapore.

Tan, Renee and Chew, Sock Foon. 1970. An Analysis of the Attitudes of Pupils in Chinese Medium, English Medium and Integrated Schools on Selected Variables. Unpublished Academic Exercise, Department of Sociology, University of Singapore.

Hans R. Dua

Sociolinguistic Inequality and Language Problems of Linguistic
Minorities in India

Introduction

Though the languages of minority groups may be accorded constitutional
recognition, protection and equal status for use in administration and
education, the implementation of policy regarding their use and development
raises several complex problems. In this paper we have considered a wide
range of problems faced by linguistic minorities in terms of sociolinguistic
inequality. We have characterized the notion of sociolinguistic inequality in
terms of nature and degree of variation in the comparative status of language
development and use, demographic distribution, sociocultural history and
mobilization and intergroup attitudes and relationships. The factors that
contribute to sociolinguistic inequality of minority languages in different
settings further constrain their effective use under the forces of change that
operate in both the minority and majority communities, but affect the
minority communities more deeply than the majoriy since the former face
both internal pressures from within their community and external pressures
in the society as a whole. It is argued that the variation in sociolinguistic
situation and the forces of change may require not only the involvement and
participation on the part of minorities and sincere efforts by the majority
but also a differential treatment in the solution of language problems of the
minorities. The issues raised in the present paper are discussed with special
reference to the multilingual situation in India.

Demographic Distribution

The numerical strength of minority language speakers varies from 3.98
percent of the total state population in Kerala to 85.74 percent in Nagaland
according to Census 1971. In order to understand the implications of
variation in the numerical strength it would be useful to distinguish between
two types of linguistic minorities. First, there are language groups in minority

in all states and union territories whose language is included in schedule VIII.[1] For instance, in Assam, Karnataka, Maharashtra, Punjab, Chandigarh, Delhi and Goa, Daman and Diu the speakers of the scheduled languages are in minority ranging from 20 percent to 43.53 percent of the total population of the state or union territory. Among the minority speakers of scheduled languages Sindhi and Urdu speakers demand special attention and will be discussed at length. However, the focus of the paper is on the problems of the other type of linguistic minorities.

The second type of linguistic minorities are the speakers of tribal, or non-tribal and non-schedule languages. The concentration of such minorities is found in Manipur, Meghalaya, Nagaland, Tripura, Andaman and Micobar islands and Arunachal Pradesh. It is interesting to note that though tribal language speakers are in majority on the whole, the extent of ethnic and linguistic diversity renders various groups into minority status in comparison to others. For instance, in Nagaland 72.11 percent of the population speak 14 major languages, the largest group being Ao speakers with 14.26 percent of total population. Similarly, in Arunachal Pradesh there are 82 ethnic groups speaking their own dialects out of which about 20 groups are quite large. The Adi speakers constitute the largest group with 21.06 percent of the total population. Though Nagaland and Arunachal Pradesh are similar as far as ethnic and linguistic diversity is concerned, they show a contrasting situation regarding the use and development of tribal languages which brings out the relevance of sociocultural and historical factors that define sociolinguistic inequality. Besides discussing this situation in detail below, we will focus on the language problems of the minority speakers of other tribal languages also.

The demographic variation in the strength and distribution of minority speakers of different tribal and scheduled languages raises three important issues regarding their use and development for educational and administrative purposes.

First, it has been suggested that the mother tongue of the tribal communities having one *lakh* (one hundred thousand) or more population in any state should be recognized as the medium of instruction in the primary stage and that of the communities having 2000 or more population should be recognized as bridge languages during the first two years of the primary stage to be ultimatedly switched over to the regional languages concerned (NCERT 1967). This suggestion may be considered as unrealistic from the point of view of the number of languages that might have to be used and developed. It may also be rejected on the ground that merely numerical strength of the minority group would not seem to be an adequate reason for the use of its language without considering its sociolinguistic context and its relationship with the majority community. For instance, Gonds constitute 46.3 percent of the total tribal population in India, but as explained below, Gondi is not used as a medium of instruction. As opposed to this, Chakhasang speakers in Nagaland are only nine thousand but their language is used as medium of instruction up to standard IV.

Second, the presence of different types of ethnic and linguistic minority groups in a region creates a unique configuration. Without understanding the sociocultural and linguistic contact factors in a particular setting any policy regarding the development and use of minority language will not have the desired effects. For instance, Tulu and Kodagu speakers have accepted Kannada as a culture language and have not found it necessary to have instruction through their mother tongue, though there have been some attempts due to political and social pressures to recognize their languages as markers of separate identity and language.

Finally, from the point of view of geographical concentration, the language minorities may be characterized as block minorities, diffused minorities or border minorities. The implications of this will become clear below. Here it needs to be pointed out that the tribal minorities which speak languages different from the regional language of the state and are split in more than one state face more complex problems of language use, and social and ethnic identity, than those which are found in a single state, though they speak a different language from the regional. In this respect the Santhali and Gondi speakers, spread over different states, present ian interesting study in the processes of social mobilization, identity formation and language policy.

Sociolinguistic Context of Linguistic Minorities

The sociolinguistic contexts of linguistic minorities show variation not only in terms of demographic and geographical distribution, about which some issues were raised above, but also in terms of sociocultural, historical and political factors. This will be discussed with reference to both scheduled and tribal language minorities in different settings.

Among the scheduled languages Urdu and Sindhi speakers in minority in states show a contrasting situation. The Urdu speakers constitute 5.22 percent of total population of India according to Census 1971. The majority of them are found in Andhra Pradesh, Karnataka, Maharashtra, Bihar and Uttar Pradesh which account for 83.41 percent of total Urdu speakers. The language problems of Urdu speakers in Uttar Pradesh and Bihar would seem to be different from those in the other states for various reasons. First, in Karnataka and Andhra Pradesh the Urdu speakers come in contact with the majority speakers of Kannada and Telugu respectively which are non-cognates to Urdu. They not only speak the majority languages for intergroup communication, but also a variety of Urdu known as Dakkhini Urdu which differs from the standard Urdu at both the phonological and grammatical levels. They accept standard Urdu as a super-posed variety for national identity, show a varying degree of competence in it as well as interference of Dakkhini Urdu, and want to retain Dakkhini Urdu for local identity, though under the increasing use of standard Urdu and highly favourable attitudes towards it, it is not very unlikely that the Dakkhini Urdu may be lost in future (Dua 1980a). As opposed to this in Bihar and Uttar Pradesh, Urdu shows a cognate relationship with Hindi. Both Hindi and Urdu are mutually intelligible having the same grammatical structure. But both are written in different scripts and show an increasing tendency of divergence in the literary styles and processes of lexical elaboration and development of new forms of discourse.

Secondly, the issue of Urdu speaking minority has become complicated because of its symbolic significance for identity for Muslims. The total number of Muslims who report Urdu as their mother tongue according to Census 1971 is 46.57 percent at all-India level, and this percentage varies from state to state due to demographic and social reasons. Thus, while in West Bengal 10.48 percent of total Muslim population are Urdu speakers, the percentage is as high as 93.74 percent in Andhra Pradesh. The variation in the percentage of Muslims who claim Urdu as their mother tongue has implications for the mobilization of those Muslims who do not report Urdu as their mother tongue. This issue has been more prominent in Uttar Pradesh and Bihar because of historical and political reasons than in Karnataka and Andhra Pradesh (Brass 1975).

Finally, in Jammu and Kashmir Urdu has been declared as the official language of the state, though the majority of Muslims speaks Kashmiri as their mother tongue, and non-Muslim population other languages. This has serious consequences for the use and development of Kashmiri as well as other minority languages. Thus, the Urdu speaking minorities spread all over India face different kinds of problems due to differences in the nature of language contact, sociopolitical and religious mobilization, demographic distribution and historical background.

The Sindhi speaking minority, like Urdu speakers, is spread all over India, though mainly concentrated in Maharashtra, Gujarat, Rajasthan and Delhi. However, unlike Urdu speakers, the Sindhi speakers show a greater tendency for assimilation. First, the link between language and religion is missing in the case of Sindhi speakers and, as Brass (1975) has observed, language without reinforcement by religion is not a sufficient criterion for separate community. Second, a majority of Sindhi community seems to have readily accepted the regional language of the state for economic reasons. It was after twenty years of partition of India that Sindhi was recognized as one of the languages of schedule VIII. Though this imparted "a sense of a constitutional culture identity", it is felt it may not have achieved much (Daswani 1979). It is found that the third generation Indian Sindhis consider Sindhi to have low value for instrumental function and a limited role for intra-group communication (Daswani and Parchani 1978). Finally, the Sindhi community is divided over the issue of script; one group favors the adoption of Devanagari,[2] and the other wants to retain Perso-Arabic script in which Sindhi was written before partition of India in 1947. Thus the Sindhi speaking minority shows less unity and a greater degree of assimilation than the Urdu speaking minority.

The variability in the factors that create sociolinguistic inequality in the use and development of minority languages not only is more obvious but also has serious consequences in the case of tribal or non-scheduled, non-tribal languages than the languages of schedule VIII in minority status in different settings. The case of the languages of Nagaland, Arúnachal Pradesh and other languages such as Gondi, Santhali will substantiate this point. In Nagaland 14 Naga languages are used as media of instruction ranging from two to eleven years depending upon the strength of the ethnic group and language development. Historically though different Naga groups had relations of hostility and friendship among them, they showed a sense of identity and solidarity in their continuous conflict with the British. They also came under the influence of Christianity. (NIC 1970: Sinha 1972). Thus they have had a deep awareness of their separate identity of language and culture and the significance of education through mother tongue.

Arunachal Pradesh on the other hand shows an opposite situation. For one thing the various ethnic groups there were untouched by the British administration leaving their traditional culture and political organization undisturbed. Second, they "remained in a state of perpetual flux in their internal relationship and were not integrated into a single polity" (Roy Burman 1973). Finally, Arunachal Pradesh has passed through a vacilating policy of language use in education. Until 1965 Assamese was the medium of instruction up to the primary stage, and Hindi was introduced after that. In some schools Hindi was the medium from primary stage. A large number of textbooks in tribal languages for the primary schools were also prepared and printed in Devanagari script. But in 1965 teaching of tribal books was discontinued, and English was introduced at the earliest stage along with Hindi, as there was opposition of Assamese medium of instruction (Roy Burman 1972). In 1971 English was made the medium of instruction from the primary stage. Thus the use and development of tribal languages in education in Arunachal Pradesh was very much restricted, though recently some attempts are being made for the development and use of the major tribal languages like Adi, Nocte, Apatani, Nishi, etc.

The case of Gondi seems to be similar to the tribal languages of Arunachal Pradesh in some respects. Though Gondi speakers constitute 46.3 percent of the total tribal population in India as mentioned above, Gondi is not used as medium of instruction for various reasons. First, Gondi speakers are spread mainly in Madhya Pradesh, Maharashtra and Andhra Pradesh. They frequently live interspersed with general population and economically depend on it. Second, Gond is a generic term used for such tribes as Raj Gond, Abujh-Maria, Bishon-horn, Meria, Maria, Konds, etc. in different states, which show different degrees of assimilation. For instance the Gonds in the eastern part of Madhya Pradesh speak Chattisgarhi, a dialect of Hindi, and Koya according to Grigson (1947) are a Teluguised tribe of Gond or of Maria Gond and speak fundamentally a Gondi dialect strongly influenced in inflexion and vocabulary by Telugu. Third, Gondi is not only influenced by different regional languages, it shows a great deal of regional and ethnic variation. In a study conducted by the Central Institute of Indian Languages five regional varieties were recognized in terms of distinct phonological, grammatical and lexical features on the basis of data collected from seventeen points in Madhya Pradesh. Finally while no concerted efforts seem to have been made in Madhya Pradesh as compared to the Gond education scheme started by Haimendorf in 1944, the scheme in Andhra Pradesh was dropped before it could make any impact. Gondi was used as a medium of instruction under this scheme and textbooks were prepared in simplified Devanagari script. Though Gondi is a Dravidian language and could be written in Telugu script, Haimendorf made a choice for Devanagari partly because he found Telugu script as "one of the most complicated of Indian scripts" and partly because Gonds outside would not have been able to use Gondi books in Telugu script. However, a few years after the formation of Andhra Pradesh in 1956, instruction through Gondi medium was dropped and Telugu medium was introduced. The Gondi speakers seem to have welcomed this change as they considered the knowledge of the regional language more useful for economic reasons. They seem more inclined to adopt the official language as Haimendorf had also noted that Gonds clamoured for instruction in Urdu for practical reasons when it was the official language of Hyderabad State (1944: 100). Thus, demographic, geographic, ethnic and linguistic diversity among Gondi speaking population, lack of sociopolitical mobilization and greater propensity for assimilation have all contributed to almost total neglect and apathy in the development and use of one of the minority languages with a large population.

The policy of the state government may also put constraints on the use of minority languages. For instance, Assam government maintained until 1975 that it was the right of the state government to recognize any language or dialect for the medium of instruction, even though there was constitutional provision for the use of minority languages. In Manipur only Manipuri is used as a medium of instruction up to standard VIII and other tribal languages such as Thado, Thangkhul are beginning to be used as media. It is interesting to note that while Hmar is not used as medium of instruction in Manipur, where its 22,800 speakers constitute 2.13 percent of the population, it is recognized in Assam, where it has only 15,000 speakers and constitutes a mere 0.10 percent of the population. Similarly, Garo is used as a medium of instruction in Assam, though it has less than 10,000, but not in Meghalaya where it is one of the major languages, its speakers making up a full 32.48 percent of the population. Thus, the differences in the policies followed by the state governments and in the mobilization of the same linguistic groups in different states contribute to inequality in the sociolinguistic situation of various minority languages. The case of Santhali discussed below presents an interesting study in this respect.

Problems of Language Development

The range and the complexity of problems in the development of minority languages would differ in relation to the degree of sociolinguistic inequality discussed above. In the case of scheduled languages in minority states in different states the major problems would be the provision of schools, teachers and textbooks at the demand of the minority community for which reports of the Commissioner of Linguistic Minorities provide a detailed description. In the case of tribal or non-tribal, non-scheduled minority languages, besides these problems, three specific issues need to be considered in some detail. The first major problem concerns the writing system as most of such minority languages do not have any tradition of writing. In this respect four alternative systems of writing have been considered in some detail. The first two choices relate to the selection of Devanagari or Roman script for the minority languages. The case for and against them has been argued in the broader context of adopting a single script for all major Indian languages as well as in the context of tribal, and non-scheduled non-tribal minority languages (Daswani 1975; Pattanayak 1979; Ray 1963). The third choice involves the adoption of any one of the script systems used for writing the regional languages. It has been argued that the adoption of the script of the dominant regional language of the state would be in the interest of minority language speakers in the particular state or region for socioeconomic and educational reasons. (NCERT 1967; CIIL 1971; De Silva 1975; Government of India 1966). Finally, an already existing indigenous script can be adopted for the minority language as such scripts are found to exist in the case of some languages. For instance, Khampti, one of the tribal languages in Arunachal Pradesh, is written in Tai script, and Santhali is written in Ol script.

Each choice involves some modification in the script system to make it suitable for the minority language in question, and each has its own advantages and disadvantages. The issue of selecting any particular script system for any minority group cannot be simply decided on the basis of technical, educational or economic reasons. Since script is considered as a symbol of separate identity and group distinctiveness, and since it has significance from the view point of religion, it can easily become an issue for political conflict and rivalry making any choice difficult on rational grounds. Two specific cases will illustrate the nature of complexity involved in the selection of script for minority language. In one case Assamese script was being used for minority language Bodo in Assam. However, the conflict between Bodo and Assamese speakers over the sharing of socioeconomic advantages in the process of economic development in the state became associated with the opposition of Assamese script by the Bodo speakers. The issue of script as a symbol for assertation of distinct identity assumed a central importance in the conflict leading to violence. Ultimately the prominent leaders of Bodo community were persuaded to accept the Devanagari script, though some still favor Roman script. The other case is related to the Santhali speakers and is more complex than that of Bodo speakers. The Santhali speakers are found in four states of Assam, Bihar, Orissa and West Bengal. If the principal of adopting the script of the dominant regional language for socioeconomic and educational reasons is accepted, four script systems will have to be adopted in different regions. There are some groups among the Santhali speakers who are in favour of adopting any one of the three revealed scripts of indigenous origin. Again in terms of social divisions and religious affiliations some Santhali speakers want to adopt Roman script and others Devanagari script. The choice of one script from amongst the revealed scripts, Devanagari or Roman would accelerate the process of social mobilization and group solidarity and promote the use and development of Santhali language. This alternative has been suggested by the Commissioner of Linguistic Minorities. However, the various State governments involved in this case have raised objections to this suggestion for administrative, socioeconomic and educational reasons. Thus the situation remains in flux as it was making concerted efforts extremely difficult in the use and development of Santhali language by the speakers spread in different regions.

The second problem concerns the choice of variety for the purpose of standardization. It has been pointed out above that Gondi shows dialect variation due to historical, geographical and cultural reasons. Similarly, in Arunachal Pradesh such ethnic groups as Minyong, Gallong, Padam, Bokar, etc., speak a variety of Adi, though descriptive account of variation between different varieties is not available. Such dialect variation is quite common in the case of many minority languages. In the case of dialect variation there seem to be three alternatives as far as the problem of standardization is concerned. We may select one variety as the base form for standardization. This may create competition and rivalry among different dialect or ethnic groups making choice difficult. As opposed to the unitary base variety we may accept all varieties for standardization to avoid conflict and rivalry. This will lead not only to the multiplicity of minority languages but also to the distribution of meagre resources in the development of several varieties with comparatively slow progress in standardization in each case. The third alternative would be to select and blend elements from different dialects. This would involve the creation of a variety which may not only be artificial but also unacceptable to various dialect groups of the community. In cases of ethnic and linguistic diversity of a minority language unless one group or variety emerges as dominant and central, and the other groups accept the particular variety as a norm, the process of standardization of the language in question would be slow, divided and protracted.

The third issue concerns vocabulary expansion and development of suitable forms of discourse which may show conflicting tendencies. In particular the different sources of vocabulary expansion have created conflicting currents of opinions not only in the case of fastly developing major Indian languages like Hindi, Urdu, Tamil etc. but also the minority languages. There is likely to be an influx of borrowings in the minority language from the regional languages or from Hindi and English. The case of Tripuri spoken in Tripura presents an interesting study in this respect. In a survey of active recall vocabulary among Tripuri speaking children was found that while 4+ age group children show almost no loan words from Bengali, the 8+ and 10+ age group children use not only a number of Bengali content words but also structural words for *who, which, until*, and numerals and colour terms. In preparing textbooks it would be useful to incorporate such loan words. But a caution is necessary here. If we heavily rely on borrowings in the expansion of the lexical stock of a minority language it may create a feeling of inferiority and inadequacy of the minority language among the speakers. This may also hasten the process of what is referred to as 'alloglotticisation' which involves influx of vocabulary from the dominant language. Price (1979: 34) has noted the specific examples of this process such as "anglicization in Wales, Ireland and Scotland, gallicization in Brittany and other French provinces and germanicization in the Romansh valleys". On the other hand, the minority language speakers may place too much emphasis on the native resources for lexical expansion, and thus widen the gap not only between the spoken and written forms of the language, but also between the minority language and the majority language. In the case of Tripuri while there is a movement for rejecting the Bengali script in which it is written, it is not clear how far there is emphasis on rejection of Bengali vocabulary.

Problems in the use of minority languages

While it would be useful to study how the problems in the use of minority languages in education, mass communication and administration relate to sociolinguistic inequality and comparative status of language development, it would be essential to consider several other issues relevant from the point of view of planning their use in various domains. Some of these issues pertain to the duration of their use, their function and position in the educational structure, the availability of trained teachers and textbooks, the content of the curriculum and intergroup attitudes towards education, the nature and extent of use in mass communication etc. As regards the duration of the use of minority languages, we find a great deal of diversity in various states and union territories (Chaturvedi and Mohale 1976; Dua 1980c). Most of the minority languages are used as media of instruction in the pre-primary, primary or middle stage of education. Only Ao, Angami, Lushai, Sadari, Santhali, Mathili and Manipuri are used as media of instruction for ten or eleven years. None of the minority languages is used as medium at the University level, though some of them are taught as subjects. It is essential to understand the reasons for variation in the number of years for which minority languages are used not only for language development and planning but also for social and psychological reasons. It is essential to find out the minimum time limit and the nature of use which would be required for concept formation and development of learning strategies to understand the utility of mother tongue medium for academic achievement. This needs to be related to the level of competence required in mother tongue and its function for group solidarity and language maintenance.

In the use of minority languages for restricted number of years as media of instruction, two other important issues have implications for educational methodology and policy. Since the minority children are required to switch from their mother tongue medium to another medium of instruction at the stage of secondary or higher education, it must be made sure that they are not put to disadvantage in this process. They must have adequate competence in the language which they adopt as second medium. This does not necessarily mean that the teaching of second language to be adopted as medium should be pushed in the early stages of education. Similarly the dropping of the mother tongue medium should neither be too soon nor too sudden. Thus the nature and degree of use of mother tongue medium, teaching of second language, modes of shifting from one medium to another, the problems of preparation of suitable learning materials and training of teachers, are the major methodological issues which have occupied the attention of scholars in the transfer model of bilingual education suggested for the linguistic minorities (Biligiri 1969; Annamalai 1973; Pattanayak 1977).

The issue regarding educational policy is related to the complex multilingual character of Indian situation which requires the study of English, Hindi and any one of the major languages of the state. This is one of the reasons that most of the minority languages used until the end of middle stage of education are not continued as subject afterwards. For instance, only Ho, Maithili, Mundari, Oraon and Santhali are taught as compulsory second languages and only Lushai, Sadari and Santhali as compulsory third languages. We must clearly understand the implication of continuation or discontinuation of the teaching of mother tongue after its use as medium in the earlier stages. The continuation beyond middle stages involves not only the burden of learning more languages by the minority children, but also a higher degree of language planning for minority languages. Their discontinuation may restrict their development as well as their function.

The production of pedagogically sound and well-designed textbooks and the range and quality of textbooks raise several issues related to the comparative status of development of minority languages, duration of their use in education and availability of both financial and personnel resources. It has been reported by Roy Burman (1968) that books are produced in sixty tribal languages which consist of mostly dictionaries, word books, textbooks and religious literature. However, books on creative literature and such subjects as philosophy, history and economics are being produced only in some tribal languages. Thus, we find works in drama, novels and other forms of literature in Khasi, Hmar, Paite, Thadau, Angami, Ao, Kabui, Oraon, Munda and Santhali. The books on philosophy, history, economics and other related subjects can be found in Garo, Kachari, Khasi, Paite, Thadau, Angami, Sema, and Tangkhul. An interesting phenomenon has been noted by Roy Burman (1974) regarding the attitudes of the tribals toward the production of books in tribal languages and their use in education. He observes that in Manipur while the tribal languages carry a vigorous stream of adult literature and journals, textbooks written in these languages by educated Christians are not used even in the missionary schools. Some sections of the educated tribals are reported to consider their language to be a medium of culture rather than of education. The implications of this orientation need to be examined in detail, according to Roy Burman. However, the production of creative literature and books on a wide range of topics provides a useful resource for textbooks, for extensive use of minority languages in education and for the expression and interpretation of ideas, values, and beliefs of both minority and majority cultures in the context of modern life and conditions.

As regards the problems related to financial and personnel resources, central and state governments and tribal departments subsidize the publication of textbooks in minority languages and provide facilities for the training of resource persons. The Central Institute of Indian languages has organised several workshops for the training of tribal graduates and preparation of primers and readers in several tribal languages for the purpose of adult literacy and primary education. It need not be pointed out that besides the active support and encouragement by the government, the willingness and commitment of the minority to devote time and efforts and the expertise and funding of the research institutes are essential components in the preparation and publication of textbooks in tribal minority languages.

The availability of trained teachers poses a great challenge for the effective implementation of the role of minority languages in education. For one thing, the rate of literacy among the tribal or non-tribal non scheduled minority languages is generally low and we do not find enough teachers to teach through the mother tongue medium. Second, even if enough educated speakers are available, they prefer jobs in other fields of life to the teaching profession. Whether the teachers speak the mother tongue of the minority children or not, they need to be trained not only for pedagogical purposes but also for sociolinguistic reasons. For it has been found that the attitudes of the teachers and the pupils toward the minority as well as majority languages and cultures have indirect implications for the minority children's proficiency in their mother tongues and bilingualism and for the maintenance of their language and culture (Dua 1979).

The intergroup attitudes towards the problems of using minority languages in education and other domains require a deep understanding of the subtle and complex issues involved and a balanced and integrated approach to resolve them. It needs to be ascertained whether the use of minority languages in education is encouraged simply as a symbol of minority status, recognition and identity or as an effective medium of education for the preservation and transmission of cultural heritage. In the latter case the minority community needs not only to lend its active support and involvement in the development of educational institutions, but also be clear as to what values of the community, and what elements of its history, way of life, religion and culture are to be transmitted through the use of language. This requires evaluation and interpretation of its own culture as well as the acceptance of majority culture and its values for the minority group. If the minority community lays too much emphasis on its own culture, it may not only isolate itself from the main stream of social life in the society, but also alienate its members who may see more advantages accruing to them from majority language and culture. On the other hand, if it puts too much emphasis on the values and norms of majority culture, it may hasten the process of assimilation and lose its distinctive character in course of time. It is therefore essential for the minority community to strike a subtle balance between the selection and transmission of the contents of the two cultures when conflicting demands are made on it.

The attitudes of the majority community towards minority language and culture are no less significant for the growth of a pluralistic society. The majority community may accept the right of the minority to education through its language at the primary stage or even at the secondary stage but follow a policy of cultural assimilation rather than integration without assimilation through the use of its language and other subject courses at the higher level of education. It may covertly denounce the values of minority culture and religion, and try to impose its own view of history, culture and life under the pretext of social development, modernization and national integration. It may perceive the provision of education through minority language as a waste of time and money or as a source of group solidarity leading to assertion of special rights and privileges and even separate statehood by the minority community. Thus it is clear that both the minority and majority communities may display a wide range of positive and negative attitudes towards each others' culture, language and institutions. The vitality and function of education through minority languages depends on the nature and understanding of mutual attitudes. Sutherland rightly remarks (1979: 48):

> Educational provision for minority groups therefore depends on a multitude of inter-related factors both of cultural values and of administrative and economic considerations. It is affected by the majority group's estimate of its own position and future as well as by the minority group's self-perception and wishes.

The use of minority languages in education is found to be incompatible with their use in mass communication and administration for political, economic, social and administrative reasons. For instance, though in Nagaland 14 languages are used as media of instruction at various levels, only English is recognized as the official language, and governments do not entertain application for official purposes in any of the Naga languages. The only minority language reported to be in use at the lower level of administration in relation to the population distribution is Khasi in Meghalaya. The use of minority languages in radio broadcasts is better, but shows another dimension of incompatibility in language use. For instance, in Arunachal Pradesh news and programs are broadcast in Tangsa, Nocte, Idu-Mishmi, Wanchoo, Nishi,

Adi Apatani and Monpa, but none of them is used in education at any level. The consequences of incompatibility in the use of minority languages in relation to different domains and for different purposes need to be understood for planning their use and development.

Apart from the question of compatibility of the use of minority languages in mass communication with their use in education, some serious constraints on their use in mass communication require careful attention and understanding. First the control and organization of the programmes and the key personnel in their production are more likely to be in the hands of members drawn from the majority community and this implies that majority attitudes and values are likely to get more prominence in comparison to minority interests (Husband 1977). Second, the news and programmes in minority languages are likely to be overshadowed by the quality and range of programmes broadcast in majority language leading to the marginal function of minority languages (Misra and Dua 1980; Dua 1980b). Third, the effective mass circulation of minority papers seems to be a rare phenomenon. For instance, among the newspapers printed in 42 languages other than the schedule VIII languages during 1976, the total circulation of dailies, weeklies, fortnightlies and monthlies does not exceed 3000 copies in each case except in the case of Manipuri, Khasi, Nepali, Konkani and Lushai. Finally, from the point of view of content the minority language journals and papers come under the pressure of majority language and culture in subtle forms. In terms of the categories for the classification of the contents of newspapers, the minority papers are mainly devoted to literary and cultural themes, religion and philosophy and news and current affairs. The educated minority speakers do not subscribe to the minority papers as their needs and interests are not catered for by the limited range fof topics covered by them. The minority papers cannot cater to the demands of the educated minority speakers partly because they cannot compete with the papers in majority language in terms of coverage of topics and circulation, partly because they cannot give more place to the themes of majority culture than those of their own culture and religion and partly because the minority speakers are more inclined to majority language papers, journals and books for educational, social and economic reasons. Under these subtle pressures and constraints the role of minority languages in mass communication seems to be either minimal or rendered ineffective in promoting their use and development, in transmitting the knowledge and values of the culture, in strengthening the cultural identity and literary creativeness and in developing political awareness and group solidarity.

In short, the survey of the problems involved in the use of minority languages in different domains brings out issues that have theoretical and practical aspects and that have political, social and cultural implications. They require balanced policy decisions regarding the function and position of minority languages and an understanding of intergroup attitudes, perceptions and aspirations.

Forces of Change

Apart from the subtle pressures on the minority language and culture as seen in the discussion of intergroup attitudes above, the minority community may be subjected to forces of change within their own community and in the society as a whole. The minority community may be assimilated by the majority language and culture for socioeconomic reasons depending upon mobility and rate of organization of different sections of the community. For instance, Brass (1975) finds that the educated elite among the Maithili speakers has been assimilated by Hindi or English speaking elite groups, and this process of assimilation has been further accelerated due to the rapid social mobilization of adjoining Magahi speaking districts where the use of Hindi is dominant. This has contributed to the failure of Maithili language movement among other reasons. Again, the minority community may be under constant pressures of immigration for seeking employment opportunities. Roy Burman (1969) reports that many Oraon speakers have moved to the tea plantation areas of North Bengaland and adopted *lingua franca* Sadari for speaking with their children. Thus he feels it necessary to make a distinction between ancestral language which the parents speak among themselves and the mother tongue which the children use with their parents and in other situations. This may lead ultimately to loss of the ancestral language. Finally, the minority community may be divided in their opinion regarding the economic, social, and educational advantages in the use of their languages. When the elite members of the community are divided among themselves due to their self-interest, they cannot provide leadership for social and political mobilization conducive to the development and use of their language. This can be seen not only in the case of minority languages vis-à-vis major Indian languages, but also major Indian languages vis-à-vis English which has constrained the extensive use of major Indian languages.

The external pressures in the society as a whole govern and regulate the forces of change within the minority community and may prove too strong to withstand. They are the product of the modern centralised and rapidly industrialising societies which favour the expansion of standardized national languages at the cost of minor languages. The multiplicity of languages, in particular the minor languages, is considered on obstacle to trade, mobility of labour and development of technology and business. The national networks of mass communication, education and administration encourage the use of national standardised languages to promote uniformity of ideology and culture and centralised planning for economic development and national modernization. They generate and support the processes of acculturation and assimilation which pose a great threat to the survival of minority languages and cultures. In a recent survey Dressler and Wodak-Leodolter (1977) have drawn attention to the detrimental effect of modern, centralised societies on the underpriveleged minority languages. They show how the function of the minority languages at first is reduced to religion and home and how the functional domains of majority languages are extended through mass media and education leading to its penetration in private domains and ultimately to the loss of minority language. The rapid loss of the minority languages of the immigrant and native populations in the United States under the pressure of Government policy and centralised modern society is too well known to be repeated here. What needs to be pointed out is that unless the minority and majority languages perform complementary roles in both private and public domains, the survival of minority languages will always be in danger under the forces of change generated by the use of national, standard language. The recent emphasis on bilingual education in the educational policy in various parts of the world including the United States seems to be based on the recognition of this fact.

In view of the forces of change within the minority community as well as the society as a whole, the legal and constitutional protection of minority languages may not be adequate for their development and use. Alcock (1970) draws attention to this issue when he remarks that there was no greater inequality than to treat equally unequal things. He goes on to say that if an effective socioeconomic equality between the minority and majority community is to be achieved "the minority should have the facility and possibility of satisfying its own interests and spiritual, cultural, economic administrative and political needs with means as effective as those by the majority." In order to achieve this goal a differential treatment of linguistic and ethnic minorities is considered essential for establishing an equilibrium of power and status between the majority and minority communities. The characterization of the nature of the differential treatment and development of mechanisms to ensure its effective implementation place an extra burden of responsibility, understanding and cooperation of the part of both minority and majority communities.

Conclusion

We have considered a wide range of complex problems of linguistic minorities with a special reference to the multilingual situation in India. We have discussed these problems in relation to the concept of sociolinguistic inequality characterised in terms of variation in the comparative status of development and use of minority languages, the demographic distribution, sociocultural history and mobilization of intergroup attitudes and relationships between the minority and majority communities. We have shown that the minority communities are subject to subtle pressure and forces of change generated by centralised industrialising societies. For a viable language policy for use and development of minority languages it is essential not only to develop the complementary roles of both minority and majority languages in various domains for use but also to evolve a measure of differential treatment for the effective use and development of minority languages.

Notes

1. The schedule VIII includes the following languages: Assamese, Bengali, Gujrati, Hindi, Kannada, Kashmiri, Malayalam, Marathi, Oriya, Punjabi, Sanskrit, Sindhi, Tamil, Telugu and Urdu.
2. Devangari is the name for the script system in which Hindi is written, just as the Roman alphabet is used for writing English or other languages.

References

Alcock, A.E. 1971. *The History of the South Tyrol Question.* London: Michael Joseph Ltd.
– and Brian K. Taylor and John M. Welton (eds.). 1979. *The Future of Cultural Minorities.* London: Macmillan.
Annamalai, E. 1973. A programme for bilingual education in India. In Kelkar, A.R. et al. (eds.), Proceedings of the Fourth All India Conference of Linguistics, Agra.
– 1979. On devising an alphabet for unwritten languages. In G. Sambasiva Rao (ed.), *Literacy Methodology.* Mysore: Central Institute of Indian Languages.
and Society in India. Simla: Indian Institute of Advanced Study.
Brass, Paul. 1975. *Language, Religion and Politics in India.* Delhi: Vikas.
Chaturvedi, M.G. and B.V. Mohale. 1976. *The Position of Languages in School Curriculum in India.* New Delhi: National Council of Educational Research and Training.
CIIL. 1971. Conference of Heads of Tribal Research Bureaus/Institutions. Mysore (Mimeo).
Daswani, C.J. 1975. The question of one script for Indian languages: Devanagari or Roman. *Indian Linguistics.* 36 (3): 182-185..
– 1979. Movement for the recognition of Sindhi and for the choice of a script for Sindhi. In Annamalai, E. (ed.), *Language Movements in India.* Mysore: Central Institute of Indian Languages.
– and S. Parchani. 1978. *A Sociolinguistic Survey of Indian Sindhi.* Mysore: Central Institute of Indian Languages.
De Silva, M.W.S. 1975. Language, Style and Literacy. Paper presented in the Orientation Workshop in Adult Literacy, Mysore. (Mimeo).
Dressler, W. and R. Wodak-Leodolter. 1977. Language death. *International Journal of Sociology of Language.* No. 12 pp. 5-11.
Dua, Hans R. 1979. The contribution of sociolinguistics to educational theory and practice. *Indian Journal of Linguistics* Vol. 6 pp. 18-41.
– 1980a Language identity, language functions and social status. *York Papers in Linguistics,* 9. pp. 87-97.
– 1980b Planning language use in radio broadcasts in a multilingual country. *Indian Linguistics.* 41 (1): 1-9.

- 1980c. Language Planning and Linguistic Minorities. Paper presented in the International Summer Institute in Language Planning. Mysore: Central Institute of Indian Languages.
Dube, S.C. (ed). *Tribal Heritage of India.* New Delhi: Vikas.
Fuerer-Haimevdorf, C. von. 1944. Aboriginal education in Hyderabad. *Indian Journal of Social Work*, 5 (2).
Grigson, W.V. 1947. The Challenge of Backwardness. Nydenabad: Government Press.
Husband, C. 1977. News media, language and race relations: A case study in identity maintenance. In Giles,. H (ed.), *Language, Ethnicity and Intergroup Relations.* London: Academic Press.
India, Government. 1966. Report of the Education Commission New Delhi: Ministry of Education.
India, Government 1975. The Sixteenth Report of the Commissioner of Linguistic Minorities. New Delhi: Ministry of Home Affairs.
Jeyapaul, V.Y. A report of the Survey of the Active Vocabulary and structures of Tripuri children. Mysore: Central Institute of Indian Languages (mimeo).
Jones, D. 1942. *The problem of a National script for India.* Hertford. England.
Khubchandani, L.M. 1978. Multilingual education India. In Bernard Spolsky and Robert L. Cooper (eds.), *Case Studies in Bilingual Education.* Rowley Massachusetts: Newbury House.
Mishra, B.G. and Hans Raj Dua. 1980. Language Use in Himachal Pradesh. Mysore: Central Institute of Indian Languages.
NCERT. 1967. Tribal Education in India. Report of the National seminar on Tribal Education in India.
Naga Institute of Culture. 1970. A Brief Historical Account of Nagaland.
Pattanayak, D.P. 1977. Minority mother-tongues: A plea for bilingual elementary education. In *Language Curriculum: An Approach to the Structure of Curriculum in India Languages.* (Revised edition.) Mysore: Central Institute of Indian Languages.
- 1979. The problem and planning of scripts. In G. Sambasiva Rao (ed.), *Literacy Methodology.* Mysore: Central Institute of Indian Languages.
Price, G. 1979. The present position and viability of minority languages. In Alcock, Taylor and Welton (eds.), *The Future of Cultural Minorities.*
Rathnaiah E.V. 1977. *Structural Constraints in Tribal Education: A Regional Study.* New Delhi: Sterling.
Ray, P.S. 1963. *Language Standardization.* The Hague: Mouton.
Roy Burman, B.K. 1968. *Bibliography of Publication in Tribal Languages.* New Delhi: The Registrar General of India.
- 1969. Languages of the tribal communities of India and their use in primary education. In Poddar, A. (ed.), *Language and Society in India.* Simla: Indian Institute of Advanced Study.
- 1972. Integrated area approach to the problems of hill tribes of north-eastern India. In Kumar Suresh Singh (ed.), *Tribal Situation in India.* Simla: Indian Institute of Advanced Study.
- 1973. Rupa: A Sherdukpen village in Arunachal Pradesh. Census of India village Monograph series New Delhi: Office of the Registrar General of India (unpublished).
- 1974. Cultural policy and tribal population. In Saberwal, Satish (ed.), *Towards a cultural Policy.* Delhi: Vikas.
Sinha, A.P. 1972. Politics of economic development in the hill districts of Assam. In K. Suresh Singh (ed.), *Tribal Situation in India.* Simla: Indian Institute of Advanced Study.
Sutherland, Margaret B. 1979. Comparative perspectives on the education of cultural minorities. In Alcock, Taylor and Welton (eds.), *The Future of Cultural Minorities.*
UNESCO. 1947. Document E/CN 4152 Section V.
Verdoodt, Albert. 1975. Ethnic minority and United Nations. In Mackey W.F. and Verdoodt (eds.), *The Multinational Society.* Rowley, Massachusetts: Newbury House.

Stephen A. Wurm

The Status of New Guinea Pidgin
(Neo-Melanesian) and Attitudes Towards It

Introductory Remarks

New Guinea Pidgin, commonly known as Tok Pisin and, years ago, also as Neo-Melanesian (though this term remained confined to linguistic literature and never really gained any currency in New Guinea itself) is the major *lingua franca* of Papua New Guinea. It has well over 1,500,000 speakers which is over half the population of the country—with this number increasing rapidly. It has the official status of one of the three major languages of Papua New Guinea—the other two being Hiri Motu (or Police Motu) with about 200,000 speakers and English which has approximately the same number of speakers. The language is, in its vocabulary, predominantly English-based, with about 15 percent of its vocabulary derived from the Austronesian (Melanesian) Tolai language of New Britain, and 5 percent from German and a few other sources such as Malay and Portuguese. In its structure, it is quite unlike English, and much more like an Austronesian language. Its grammar is quite complex, and it is certainly not just a simplified and jargonised form of English as used to be popularly believed by many in the past. The language is quite highly developed today and adequate for the expression of a range of sophisticated thoughts, and often used by Papua New-Guineans in preference to their own language, even if they share a common tongue. In spite of this, only a small fraction (perhaps 30,000 or so) of its large number of speakers speak New Guinea Pidgin as their first language—in other words, the language has been creolized only to a very minor extent. At the same time, a great proportion of its speakers have a first-language mastery of it and speak it with greater proficiency than any other language they know, including their mother-tongues. This is understandable in a country with about 760 distinct local languages (Wurm 1977c) in which New Guinea Pidgin is the major means of intercommunication between speakers of different languages, and is used by a large proportion of the population more often than any other language.

New Guinea Pidgin has, in recent years, undergone a considerable reorientation of its status and functional role. This is in line with developments in other parts of the world in which pidgins and creoles are spoken and in which there have been fundamental political and social changes in recent years. The social positions of the speakers of such pidgins and creoles have, in such areas, undergone radical changes, and this has had far-reaching effects upon the standing, functions, and use of these languages. In particular, some langages that until recently carried the stigma of low-caste language—and continue to do so in the eyes of some members of the new social setups—have suddenly been elevated to much higher social and functional levels than has hitherto been the case. (Wurm 1977a). In this, it has to be kept in mind that pidgin and creole languages traditionally occupy clearly definable positions in the linguistic hierarchy of a society that is strongly stratified linguistically and socially, and their functions and role are determined by the class standing of their speakers and the social situations in which they are used within and across class boundaries.

History of the Development of New Guinea Pidgin

For the understanding of the specific situation concerning New Guinea Pidgin, a brief discussion of its origin and development to the present day may be of value (Mühlhäusler forthcoming).

As early as the 1880s, New Guinea Pidgin had become stabilized in a form from which present-day New Guinea Pidgin is directly derived, and in contrast to many other pidgin languages in other parts of the world, became nativized almost from the beginning, i.e. had become a language used primarily for communication between members of the indigenous population rather than one used for intercommunication between whites and indigenes. As a result of this, it quickly developed into a language with close to the same range of expression and social functions as an indigenous first language. It had been established by Mühlhäusler (1978) that the earliest form of a stable New Guinea Pidgin was spoken in the Duke of York Islands, to the north of New Britain, around 1882. Mühlhäusler suggests that this earliest form of New Guinea Pidgin owes its origin to the development of a stabilized plantation pidgin on Samoa. After 1879, labourers were recruited for the Samoa plantations from the Duke of York area, and the first labourers returned there from Samoa in 1882. In this year the first plantations were established in the Blanche Bay area of the Gazelle Peninsula of New Britain, with labourers from Bougainville and New Ireland, and it seems that experienced ex-Samoan labourers were employed as overseers on these new plantations. The vocabulary of the newly stabilized language seems to have subsequently been enriched with Tolai and German words in the administrative centre of

Rabaul on the Gazelle Peninsula. With the rapid spread of administrative control and the resulting inter-tribal pacification through much of what was then German New Guinea, intercommunication across tribal boundaries became important, and New Guinea Pidgin became nativized and firmly established in the area.

When German New Guinea was taken over by the British and Australian forces in 1914, New Guinea Pidgin continued to spread, and regional dialects and distinct social dialects began to develop. However, it remained strictly a low-caste language, and there was almost no social intimacy between indigenes and Europeans.

The Second World War fundamentally affected the social setup in Papua New Guinea and brought about new social patterns in which New Guinea Pidgin was to have new functions. Its importance was recognized by the Australian authorities, and the prewar social barriers between indigenes and Europeans broke down, especially with members of the armed forces. New Guinea Pidgin assumed the function of a means of expressing solidarity among all racial groups in Papua New Guinea. These events can be regarded as more or less deliberate acts of external language planning—but much more deliberate acts were performed in the extensive use of Pidgin in war propaganda, with a view to strong social control. Also, large-scale recruiting of indigenes from many, often remote, areas as carriers and labourers produced a sharp increase in the number of speakers of the language and led to its spread into new areas.

After the end of World War II, New Guinea Pidgin accelerated its spread through Papua New Guinea, a regional dialect became stabilized and nativized in the highlands, and the language started to make inroads into areas where Police Motu (now called Hiri Motu) functioned as a *lingua franca*—this development had already begun during the war years. The breakdown of social barriers between indigenes and Europeans continued and led to the gradual change of New Guinea Pidgin from a caste language to that of a language with new roles in the changed Papua New Guinea society.

In the early nineteen-fifties, English began to play a major role for the indigenous population as a result of primary schools switching to English as the main—and in the Government schools the sole—medium of instruction. At the same time, the United Nations Organization called upon Australia in 1953 (Hall 1955) to discontinue the use of New Guinea Pidgin in the then Trust Territory of New Guinea. This was an amazingly unrealistic and ill-informed pronouncement because the Australian administration was obviously in no position to control the use of a fully nativized *lingua franca* whose primary function was to serve as a means of intercommunication among the indigenous population. The pronouncement did have the effect of strengthening the pro-English language policies of the administration, but the spread of New

Guinea Pidgin continued at an ever-increasing rate, both geographically and with regard to its social functions. A new sociolect of New Guinea Pidgin, called Urban Pidgin, which already had had a limited existence, became well established and developed. New styles such as written style, radio announcing, etc. emerged in the language. Regional dialect development first reached a peak during the early nineteen sixties, especially in the highlands, but a gradual neutralization of regional variants began subsequently as a result of the increasing mobility of the population and the increasing impact of mass media. English influence on New Guinea Pidgin steadily increased, particularly in Urban Pidgin. The language began to become creolized in some areas. However, this had little influence upon the form of language for sociolinguistic reasons. To be understood, the children who were and are the speakers of creolized New Guinea Pidgin had to conform to the nativized forms of the language which were already in constant daily use in internative communication situations.

During the 1970s and the rapid political changes which took place in that decade in Papua New Guinea, two major developments occurred in the function and role of New Guinea Pidgin (called Pidgin from here on for the sake of brevity):

A new contact culture developed in Papua New Guinea which moved away from the traditional culture, though it incorporated elements from it and also adopted many elements from the Western culture. Nevertheless, it was basically quite distinct from both and typically modern Papua New Guinean. In its development, Pidgin became its intrinsic means of expression. The rapid spreading of this sub-culture in recent years, predominantly in urban environments, but also to some considerable extent in some rural areas, has resulted in a dramatic increase of the functional role and geographical importance of Pidgin which is now in a diglossic relationship with English in urban settings, i.e., the two languages exist side by side, with Pidgin and English fulfilling mutually exclusive, specific social roles and functions. In several areas, Pidgin is beginning to replace, or has already replaced, the local vernaculars on its way toward creolization (Mühlhäusler 1977).

Recent political developments on the Papua New Guinea scene during the rapid progress of the country toward its present independence have created a situation in which there has been a dramatic extension of the use and functions of Pidgin on what may be termed the public level: quite large groups in Papua New Guinea expected Pidgin to expand its role and functions into areas of expression and communication in which it had not been used previously. Such areas are, for instance, (a) its very predominant use as a debate language in the Papua New Guinea Parliament on issues that traditionally have been discussed in English; (b) its increasing use in broadcasting, where it is used to report on world news and for the discussion of political, economic, social, and other concerns that sometimes require quite high levels of complexity of expression; (c) its similar use in writing in the press; (d) its widening role in education.

Attitudes Towards New Guinea Pidgin

Against this history of the development of Pidgin and of its use and function, a discussion of earlier and present attitudes toward the language may be of interest.

Earlier Attitudes Towards New Guinea Pidgin

Earlier European attitudes towards Pidgin were mostly strongly negative and based largely on misinformation and language prejudice (Wurm 1969, 1973) and constitute an interesting illustration of European attitudes towards indigenous concerns in a colonial setting. There were essentially two main types of criticism of Pidgin on the part of Europeans (Wurm 1977b):

The essence of the first of these criticisms was that Pidgin constituted a corruption of English: Pidgin was described by critics as a disgusting, debased corruption of English, full of insulting words, and sounding quite ridiculous to listeners.

This criticism is based on erroneous premises. Pidgin is not English, just as English is not French though it contains an abundance of words of French origin. In its structure and basic principles, Pidgin is much more like an Austronesian language than English. As such it is quite different from English, just as English is structurally different from French. It is true that the percentage of the English-based lexicon of Pidgin is considerably greater than that of the French-based lexicon of English, but it is not greater than the Latin-based vocabulary of French and Italian. Nevertheless, present-day French or Italian are not regarded today as corruptions of Latin, though it may be argued that they owe their historical origin to exactly that, just as it may be argued that Pidgin owes its origin ultimately to a corruption of English even though the situation relating to Pidgin was in many respects quite different from that leading to the emergence of French or Italian. However, in its present-day form, Pidgin constitutes an established language when judged from the linguistic point of view.

To describe Pidgin as disgusting and debased, as being full of insulting words, and sounding ridiculous to listeners, is the result of looking at it from an outside point of view, i.e., one based on a different language, namely, English. In such a fashion, any language closely related to another in a portion of its vocabulary, or in both structure and vocabulary, could, when looked at from the point of view of this other language, be said to be debased, full of insulting words, and as sounding ridiculous to listeners—i.e., to listeners speaking this other language, and not the language in question itself. Speakers of Dutch and German, Spanish and Portuguese, the various Slavic languages and others could potentially find themselves in such situations quite frequently—quite a number of the words in such closely related languages are similar or near-identical in form and appear to be easily recognisable to speakers of one such language when uttered by speakers of the other language, but their meanings are often rather different, and a quite harmless word in one language can be a highly insulting one in the other, but, as has been pointed out, it may sound nearly the same. Educated members of two such speech communities who realise this problem do not usually have the habit of describing each other's languages as being full of insulting words. Why is it then that speakers of English described Pidgin as being full of insulting words, though if they had any knowledge of the language at all, they had to know that such words which were formally similar to insulting words in English, had harmless meanings in Pidgin? The traditional attitudes of the English-speaking whites towards the indigenes may well have had much to do with this, as well as the belief on the part of many of the former that Pidgin was a sort of 'baby-talk' fit to be used by and to the indigenes only, and not a real language. At the same time, it may also have to be taken into account that some English speakers were, because of their still lingering adherence to the Victorian heritage, perhaps more sensitive to and emotional about what they looked upon as insulting words, than speakers of most other languages. Also, English is not a member of a pair of very closely related major languages such as those referred to above. Because of this, most English speakers have not been exposed to a language which sounds much like theirs in many respects, though strangely, and sometimes embarrassingly, differing from it in many instances. (The only instances of such exposure are provided by the dialectal differences existing, for instance, between British and Australian English, or British and American English: these certainly provide a few examples similar to those referred to above.) If Pidgin is taken into account English can be looked upon as a member of just such a pair of languages that are closely related at least in one respect—i.e., in their lexicon. However, only a very small proportion of the speakers of English ever comes into contact or is familiar with the exact nature of Pidgin—this helps explain the over-reaction of many English-speakers on their first contact with this, to them, unfamiliar and strange sounding idiom. Characteristically, the most ardent, emotional, and articulate critics of Pidgin had been largely persons who knew very little about it, whereas quite a few of the European residents of Papua New Guinea who have a good knowledge of it regard it either impartially and dispassionately or may have a lot to say in its favour.

With regard to the argument that Pidgin sounds quite ridiculous to listeners, i.e., speakers of English unfamiliar or only a little familiar with it, it is interesting to note that a similar situation may well be said to exist between English and French if the numerous French loanwords in English and their diverse pronunciations and meanings in these two languages are taken into account. However, it is culturally and socially largely inappropriate for educated speakers of the two languages to regard the other language as ridiculous, whereas it was culturally and socially correct for speakers of English to regard Pidgin as a ridiculous language and at the same time as nothing more than a debased corruption of English.

Pidgin Regarded as Inadequate

The second argument against Pidgin is that it is an inadequate, restricted language unsuited for the expression of thoughts on anything but the most elementary level. In contrast to the arguments discussed above which are not often heard any more today, this argument is still frequently voiced. In this, it has to be pointed out that the question concerning the adequacy of a language is only meaningful if the culture is named for whose expression that language serves as a vehicle. Since every natural language constitutes a reference system for the culture within which it has developed, it follows that every language is basically adequate for the expression of and reference to the cultural concepts constituting the culture to which it belongs, and undergoes changes along with changes of this culture. It also follows that a language is inadequate for the expression of a culture to which it does not belong, and that this inadequacy increases in direct proportion with the degree of difference between the culture to which the language belongs, and the one which critics pointing to its alleged inadequacy expect it to express.

Examining Pidgin in this connection, the first question to be asked is whether Pidgin is a fully adequate medium for the expression of the cultural concepts of the people of Papua New Guinea who have been using it as their *lingua franca*. Pidgin is the major *lingua franca* employed by indigenes in multilanguage situations as the means of intercommunication in all situations concerning multilanguage groups as a whole or at least a multilanguage section of it. However, there are cultural and social situations involving members of a single homogeneous speech community only in which the language of intercommunication is not Pidgin, and for which Pidgin is inadequate—understandably so, because it has no connection with that specific part of the indigenous culture which may often be ritual in nature. At the same time, a language other than Pidgin would also be inadequate, English probably more so than Pidgin, because of the greater alienness of the culture to which English belongs, to the cultures of the indigenous population of Papua New Guinea, than is the case with Pidgin.

The cultures of the indigenous population of Papua New Guinea are rapidly changing, much of them getting lost and being replaced by something new that is approaching uniformity and is neither traditional nor European (see above). The language serving as a reference system for this new growing element in the cultures of the population is Pidgin, and being the means of expression of this new set of cultural concepts, it is intrinsically adequate for this task.

It is quite correct to say that Pidgin, in its present form, is not adequate for the expression of the range of concepts constituting a sophisticated Western culture such as the British-Australian toward an approximation of which the Papua New Guinea culture was thought to be heading. However, it seems quite unlikely now that the basic culture of the new Papua New Guinean nation will ever become a copy of the British-Australian model—it will certainly become something with a character entirely its own, and what will have been absorbed into it from the British-Australian culture will only be a component element that will have undergone drastic changes and adaptations. With the development of this basic culture, the language serving it as a means of expression may well be expected to have the inherent ability to develop with it and to become richer and more complex, in step with the culture to which it belongs. The exceedingly rapid development of this culture does, however, pose a problem for the language serving and maintaining it: for it to remain in step with the changes and advancement of the culture, numerous new terms have to become part of it at an accelerating rate. At present, most such new terms are loanwords from English—this constitutes the line of least resistance, with a language with a vast reservoir of terms readily available to be drawn upon. There is some justification for such a procedure provided the adoption of English loans does not exceed an unavoidable minimum. However, this is unfortunately not the case with Pidgin at present, though it does contain the necessary linguistic mechanisms for the creation of such needed additional terms, in conformity with the nature of the language itself, to ensure its adequacy (Mühlhäusler 1979).

A third criticism was often levelled against Pidgin in the not-too-distant and recent past, and sometimes even today: it has been said to constitute a bad heritage from the days of colonialism, and that it has been used for the purpose of accentuating, emphasising and perpetuating social and racial distinctions, i.e., it has been used by the European masters in speaking to members of the indigenous population to keep them in their place.

A part of this argument is certainly true for the past, though it has to be remembered that most of the use of Pidgin as a means of intercommunication was between indigenes and not between Europeans and indigenes. This criticism has been made by some European and quite a few non-European members of the United Nations Organisation, and has also been put forward by a few Europeans, as well as by some indigenous leaders, in Papua New Guinea itself. However, it seems unrealistic to hold this view in this form for the present or the future: several languages which in the past used to be stigmatised by the type of social features ascribed to Pidgin in this criticism have become the national languages of nations. Indonesian is a good example: until the middle of the last century, the local population in the then Dutch East Indies was forbidden by law even to learn Dutch, so that it could be kept linguistically and, in consequence, socially, clearly separated from the European rulers. Nevertheless, the linguistic tool used for this separation has now become the national language of the Indonesian nation.

By contrast to European attitudes, earlier indigenous attitudes towards Pidgin were predominantly favourable—except perhaps in areas in which Pidgin was encroaching upon the regions in which traditionally the other major *lingua franca* of Papua New Guinea, i.e., Hiri Motu (then called Police Motu) was holding sway—and they centred on the one hand around the important communicative role of Pidgin which made it possible for indigenes from different linguistic and cultural backgrounds to freely intercommunicate and act together. This gave them a feeling of unity and solidarity and made them look upon Pidgin as 'their' language giving them a level of identity which eventually laid the foundations for the new Papua New Guinean subculture mentioned above. On the other hand, the favourable attitude of indigenes towards Pidgin resulted from the advantage which it gave them in communicating with Europeans and the authorities, and in obtaining economically lucrative employment (Wurm 1977c).

Present-Day Attitudes Towards New Guinea Pidgin

Present-day attitudes towards Pidgin in Papua New Guinea are quite varied. Some of them reflect the views and vested interests of certain groups (Wurm 1977c).

Attitudes displayed by Europeans at present living in Papua New Guinea no longer have great relevance in contrast to European views in earlier days. It is of interest, however, to note that most of the Europeans in Papua New Guinea today take a stand toward Pidgin which is quite different from the traditional European view of earlier days: they regard Pidgin as a language in its own right without emotional bias and make serious efforts to learn it properly. This, in turn, strengthens positive attitudes of indigenes towards Pidgin and reinforces their growing expectation that Europeans resident Papua New Guinea have a good command of the language—which is by no means an easy task.

Unfavourable Attitudes Towards New Guinea Pidgin

At the same time, earlier negative European attitudes have become perpetuated among many educated Papua New Guineans who have gone through the indoctrination of an English-based education. They adopted the prejudices of earlier administrators and of their teachers, and they show a tendency to over-estimate the importance and potential of English for Papua New Guinea.

While these attitudes of the English-speaking elite are at least in part emotionally based, a large number of less educated Papua New Guineans frown upon the use of Pidgin, at least in the educational system, for what in their view are pragmatic reasons, and would not like to see the use of English cut down in favour of Pidgin in schools. This attitude stems from the great importance attached to English and education in English by the administration of Papua New Guinea during the last two decades of Australian rule which induced many Papua New Guinean parents to regard English as the sole key to wealth and economic progress. However, this view is gradually losing ground today as a result of the fact that such parents are often disappointed in their hopes. In present-day Papua New Guinea, knowledge of English is almost totally irrelevant for many school leavers. However, it is true that the exclusive use of Pidgin in elementary education would, in the present situation surrounding education in Papua New Guinea, produce serious problems for children wishing to proceed to higher education which is in English. However, the educational system is changing, and this unsatisfactory situation is likely to change too in the forseeable future as a result of suitable language policies.

Other Papua New Guineans with a vested interest who look upon Pidgin with disfavour are the supporters of regional nationalism and separatism in Papua who look upon Hiri Motu as their symbol of national and group identity. The existence of this group and their political movement which is now losing strength appears to have constituted one of the main reasons for the Papua New Guinea Government's disinclination and inability to give its full support to Pidgin as the main language of the country.

Favourable Attitudes Towards New Guinea Pidgin

The abovementioned instances of general or selective unfavourable attitudes towards Pidgin are far outweighed by a generally favourable attitude towards it on the part of a large part of the population, and of the majority of the political leaders. official support of Pidgin is very cautious, but unofficial support is much more powerful.

Favourable Attitudes Towards New Guinea
Pidgin Based On Pragmatic Reasons

For a very large proportion of the population and also for much of the administration, especially on the lower levels, but also among higher officials, the reasons for the positive attitude towards Pidgin and its support are essentially pragmatic (Mühlhäusler 1977). For the majority of the rural population, Pidgin is the only link which they have with the outside world and the only avenue which gives them access to new ideas. It is the linguistic tool which makes it possible for them to cooperate and function as higher units through the local government councils across language barriers. The records of the meetings of these councils are always kept in a *lingua franca*, very predominantly Pidgin, even if some of the council debates themselves may be held in local languages. For lower administration officials, Pidgin constitutes a totally indispensable tool for their work, and the rural population looks upon Pidgin as their only effective means of access to the Administration. Missions also see Pidgin in such a pragmatic light.

Higher government officials and political leaders recognize and use Pidgin as a linguistic tool of major communicative importance: of all the languages in Papua New Guinea, it can reach the highest percentage of the population, both on the oral and written levels. Mühlhäusler (1977) points out that statistical analyses have shown that on both these levels, Pidgin can reach over three times more people in Papua New Guinea than functional English and Hiri Motu put together.

The importance attached to Pidgin by the majority of the political leaders of the country is also reflected by the very predominant use of Pidgin as a debate language in the Papua New Guinea Parliament. However, the reasons underlying this use may also be emotional, in addition to being pragmatically based.

Members of the Pidgin-speaking population of Papua New Guinea who lack a knowledge of English often voice their apprehension that they would be left behind should English take over. One reaction to this is the insistence of many parents that their children should be educated in English, as has been

pointed out above. However, this feeling of apprehension also tends to reinforce the pro-Pidgin feelings and attitudes of many Papua New Guineans on
the emotional level.

Favourable Attitudes Towards New
Guinea Pidgin Based on Emotional Reasons

It has already been mentioned above that large portions of the rural
population of Papua New Guinea regard Pidgin as a unifying link which gives
them a feeling of solidarity, with this feeling reinforced by the feelings of
apprehension concerning English. From this it is only a short step to the
frequently observed attitudes of many Papua New Guineans who look upon
Pidgin as a means for their self-identification, as a language which is their own
and a distinguishing feature of all that is Papua New Guinean, and as
something of which they are justly proud. This attitude manifests itself in
many interrelated ways: Papua New Guineans expect Europeans who reside
in their country to know Pidgin well (its mastery, or that of Hiri Motu, is one
of the requirements of Papua New Guinea citizenship). They resent being
addressed by Europeans in bad Pidgin and they tend to speak Pidgin to each
other whenever possible, especially in situations in which the speaking of
Pidgin used to be frowned upon or banned until recently (such as High
Schools and the University of Papua New Guinea), and they look upon Pidgin
as the means for expressing their deepest feelings and as the vehicle of
national self-expression. These attitudes have produced the feeling in many
Papua New Guineans that Pidgin should be the national language of Papua
New Guinea and this has resulted in its very prevalent use in the parliament as
the language of debate (Hull 1968) (though pragmatic considerations also
seem to have played a part in this as has been said above), in the re-intro-
duction of Pidgin as a language of instruction in vocational training, in
the renewed general admissibility of Pidgin in elementary and adult education
(Wurm 1977b), and the emergence of indigenous Pidgin creative writing
(Laycock 1977).

Recent Developments and Future Outlooks

With its elevation to high social functions, the establishment of the subculture
mentioned before, and the need for, especially lexical, expansion of Pidgin to
meet the requirements of its new function, Pidgin has recently entered a new
phase of development. The main sociolects, Urban Pidgin and Rural Pidgin,
became clearly established, and are diverging rapidly. At the same time, the

stabilization of Pidgin and its regional and sociolectal uniformity in given areas and sociolects have begun to disappear, with fluidity and variability appearing at an increasing rate. This developing is largely attributable to the powerful influence of English, and to the fact that because of the lack of insight into the nature of Pidgin and insufficient coordination of language planning, the necessary linguistic elaboration accompanying the functional extensions of Pidgin have taken place in a haphazard way (Mühlhäusler 1979). These factors are disrupting the basic underlying rules of Pidgin and are beginning to threaten its existence as a separate language.

There seems to be little doubt that Pidgin is to remain the majority language of Papua New Guinea and that its geographical area and functional ranges will increase. The creolization of Pidgin has begun and can be expected to gain considerable momentum. Under these circumstances, and taking into account what has been said above about the recent developments of Pidgin and the destructive influence of English upon it, it seems clear that there is an urgent need of language planning actions. In the present writer's view (Wurm 1977d), Pidgin will be unable to fulfill satisfactorily its envisaged tasks in education and in being used for wider national purposes without its enrichment and standardization through internal language planning actions.

References

Hall, R.A. 1955. *Hands off Pidgin English!* Sydney: Pacific Publications.
Hull, B. 1968. The use of Pidgin in the House of Assembly. *Journal of the Papua New Guinea Society* 2 (1): 22-25.
Laycock, D.C. 1977. Creative Writing in New Guinea Pidgin. In Wurm, (ed.), 1977: 609-638.
Mühlhäusler, P. 1977. The social role of Pidgin in Papua New Guinea today. In Wurm, (ed.), 1977: 549-557.
– 1978. Samoan Plantation Pidgin English and the origin of New Guinea Pidgin. *Pacific Linguistics*, Series A. No. 54: 67-119.
– 1979. *Growth and structure of the lexicon of New Guinea Pidgin. Pacific Linguistics*, Series C, No. 52.
– Forthcoming. History of New Guinea Pidgin, I: the external history. In Wurm et al. (eds.).
Sibayan, B.P. and A.B. Gonzale, (eds.). 1977. *Language planning and the building of a national language: essays in honor of Santiago A. Fonacier on his ninety-second birthday*. Manila: Linguistic Society of the Philippines and Language Study Center, Philippine Normal College.
Valdman, A., (ed.). 1977. *Pidgin and creole linguistics*. Bloomington, Indiana: Indiana University Press.
Wurm, S.A. 1969. English, Pidgin and what else? *New Guinea Quarterly* 4 (2): 30-42.
– 1973. The problem of a national language in Papua New Guinea. *Linguistic Communications* 10: 117-146.
– 1977a. Pidgins, creoles, lingue franche, and national development. In Valdman, (ed.), 1977: 333-357.

- 1977b. Criticisms and attitudes towards Pidgin. In Wurm, (ed.), 1977: 539-548.
- 1977c. New Guinea Pidgin–today and tomorrow. In Sibayan and Gonzale, (eds.), 1977: 218-237.
- 1977d. Future outlooks and standardization of Pidgin. In Wurm, (ed.), 1977: 583-594.
- (ed.). 1977. *New Guinea area languages and language study*, vol. 3: *Language, culture, society, and the modern world. Pacific Linguistics*, Series C, No. 40 (two fascicles).
- Forthcoming. ed. with P. Mühlhäusler, D.C. Laycock and T.E. Dutton. *Handbook of New Guinea Pidgin. Pacific Linguistics*, Series C.

John Spencer

Language and Development in Africa:
The Unequal Equation

Africa is a vast continent and its languages many and various. Development
can mean a number of different things, and is certainly a complex process
however one looks at it. Inevitably therefore I shall be dealing in generalities.
I shall not attempt to present a particular case study, but rather some
perspectives; other contributions will consider more specific aspects of an
overall picture. By means of these perspectives it is possible we may be able
to perceive, a little more clearly, some of the relationships between language
use and the developmental process, and problems, in many of the new
African nations. Each national language situation is of course unique, but I
hope to extract some of their common characteristics.

The developmental process, however we define it, involves the penetration
of traditional life and institutions by modernising forces and influences. This
process has aspects which are political, economic, social and cultural; and the
changes which the societies undergo as a result relate crucially to questions of
group identity and national identity, questions of planning choice, questions
of intergovernmental relationships and cooperation, questions of education,
questions of vertical and horizontal mobility. I believe there is a relationship
between language use and all these aspects of development and change —
sometimes centrally, sometimes peripherally.

Africa, particularly sub-Saharan Africa, is probably the most linguistically
complex area of the world, if population is measured against languages. It is
possible that Africa contains well over a thousand languages. They cannot yet
be counted with any certainty or precision, for about many of them too little
is known. Language names alone are no guide: the seventh volume the *Current
Trends in Linguistics, Linguistics in Sub-Saharan Africa* (1971) contains a
checklist of over 5,000 language names from sub-Saharan Africa. No suggestion is made that all these names refer to separate languages—some are dialect
names, some toponyms, some synonyms, some tribal and ethnic names.
However, it sufficiently indicates the complexity and heterogeneity of
Africa's linguistic composition viewed demographically. The paucity of
knowledge about many of Africa's languages may be illustrated by quoting
from what was until quite recently, and certainly when I first began work in

the field, the most up-to-date compilation of information on the West African area: *The Handbook of African Languages*, Part II, *Languages of West Africa*, by Westermann and Bryan, published for the International African Institute by Oxford University Press in 1952. Here is one entry, admittedly a relatively obscure one, but not untypical of the state of knowledge two decades ago about the linguistic situation in some of the less frequented parts of Africa: in Section VII, collating information about 'Isolated Language Groups or Units (Non-class Languages) of Nigeria and the Cameroons', we find the following:

Isolated Unit? MBEMBE

MBEMBE (IZARE, NSARE) own name ǹcàlé, Dialect Cluster? *Note*: The name AKONTO has also been applied to this language.

Spoken by: *MBEMBE* (a collective name for several tribes or sections, also known as *TIGONG*).

Where spoken: British Cameroons, Bamenda Province, Mbembe District; also in Wukari Divison, Benue Province.

Number of speakers: 2,893 (tax payers).

According to E. Meyer there is considerable difference between the dialects (or languages) spoken by the Mbembe; Richardson, however, reports that the language is stated to be uniform.

Footnote to MBEMBE: Not to be confused with the *Mbembe* of Ogoja province (see p. 116), nor with the *Mbem* of Bamenda Province. The latter are said to speak a language related to that of the *Nfumte* (*Nfumte*), but nothing further is known of their speech. Both *Mbem* and *Nfumte*, together with the *Mbaw* (*Mbo*), were formerly known as *Kaka* or *Kakantem*.

Incidentally, Mbembe has now been investigated, and a successful doctoral thesis on it completed some years ago.

However, to view African linguistic complexity in terms of a two-dimensional map is to simplify. For its multilingualism is also layered, and we should need a stratigraphical map to see the situation more clearly. We may illustrate this by reference to a small language community, the Angass people, among whom I once did some fieldwork, and who live on the eastern escarpment of the Jos Plateau in Nigeria. One of the several dialects of Angass seemed to have a higher prestige than the others, and appeared to be used as a local *lingua franca*. However, outside the quite restricted Angass-speaking area some vehicular form of Hausa would be needed, in order to communicate with non-Angass speaking peoples on the Plateau and elsewhere in the North. In southern Nigeria an Angass traveller would have found a knowledge of Nigerian Pidgin useful; and education would have introduced him to standard written English, if he had been to school. This linguistic layering seems in the main the result of various languages having historically become *lingue franche*, vehicular languages, used beyond their home base; and of others becoming, perhaps, at some stage, pidginised and then possibly creolised, as they have extended themselves through contact with adjacent languages or through settlement and the continuous movement and mixture of peoples. Indeed, Africa's linguistic condition is a monument to innumerable conquests, incursions, peaceful interaction, hegemonies, vassaldoms, cultural or religious movements, migrations, from time immemorial. And European colonial rule in Africa, much of it during only a century or so—or less in certain areas—planted a bold and arbitrary superstructure of European languages, as well as arbitrary political boundaries, on top of an already stratified or layered multilingualism; and in some areas, where settlement of Europeans and other non-Africans was encouraged, also planting powerful minorities speaking non-African languages as mother tongues.

This complex multilingualism is sometimes obscured by the fallacious use of the French loan-words *anglophone* and *francophone*. English and French have of course not *replaced* African languages—nor have Portuguese or Spanish. They have been *superposed* (as second languages) upon the existing vernacular language mosaic. Nor will they replace the vernaculars for the foreseeable future. It will be necessary a little later to look at the nature and effects of this superposition.

We are aware, from our knowledge of other parts of the world, including Europe, that a plurality of languages within a nation state does not normally conduce to the peaceful and harmonious progress of its peoples. There are the inevitable battles for linguistic parity, or dominance, in national institutions, in law, in administration, in education; and cultural and ethnic divisions, often intensified by religious distinctions, focusing around language and linguistic loyalty, can seriously hamper or sometimes destroy the development of the larger national unity. Even more important, perhaps, is the practical question of social communication, as societies change and become more complex. In his study of the seventeenth century, the historian G.N. Clark write: "When a country was governed by a limited ruling class, it did not matter what language the masses spoke, as long as they kept their place". Today, in most parts of the world, the masses are not of course content to keep their place, and the ruling class is not usually limited (except in a sense which G.N. Clark did not mean!). And we might formulate an axiom: the more complex and interactive a socioeconomic organism becomes, the greater the handicap of linguistic complexity. Or put another way, as Fishman has it more succinctly, linguistic homogeneity has greater competitive efficiency.

It may be significant, I think, that high or medium per capita gross national product tends to correlate with linguistic homogeneity, viewed nationally. In other words, what the economists call 'developed' or 'intermediate' status in the rank order of development is normally to be found in linguistically homogeneous polities—to use a rather excruciating phrase. On the other hand, the correlation with linguistically heterogeneous polities tends the other way; multilingual states are characterised typically by low or very low per capita gross national product, and are consequently far down on the developmental rank scale. In particular, no developed or affluent nations, though many of these have minority languages, utilise a language for education and other national purposes which is of external origin and the mother tongue of none, or at most few, of its people. It may be that the characteristics shared by almost all affluent societies, as we know them today—large interactive urban populations, large-scale industrial and economic organisations, intricately articulated national institutions, high literacy rates, and administrative penetration and centralisation—can only be achieved if there has, historically, been some prior resolution of linguistic complexity.

How then can we best focus upon such problems in African societies undergoing rapid change? First, we can distinguish between what it has been found convenient to call the *structural,* the *functional* and the *symbolic* attributes of languages. The linguistic scholar has traditionally examined the structural attributes of languages: the phonology, the grammar, the lexicon. All the evidence we have from the structural descriptions of languages, in Africa and elsewhere, suggests that nowhere in the world are there any primitive languages in existence: no languages, that is, which provide any indication of what the prototypic language or languages of early *homo loquens* were like. All natural languages are fully formed, highly delicate in their grammatical and semantic systems, and capable, given the opportunity, of handling every aspect of the experience and thought and culture of the community to which they belong. It seems as if they all have, intrinsically, an equal capacity to expand their resources in order to accommodate to the developing communicative needs of their community. In this sense, then, from a structural point of view, all languages are equal; equal, that is, intrinsically. The extrinsic factors are, however, by no means equal.

We must thus make a distinction between language viewed as a structural system and language viewed as a communicative instrument. For not all languages have been, or are, given an equal opportunity to extend their resources in response to expanding communicative needs. And from a *functional* point of view, which accounts for our second range of attributes, the languages of the world are very unequal indeed. Here we need to pause for a moment, for the functional viewpoint is of relevance to our central question. It may be helpful to look at the basic stages of functional development, in relationship to a simple hypothetical model of a language community undergoing change. In the history of the functional development of languages there seem to be three important steps:

1. *Graphisation*—the development of a writing system.
2. *Standardisation*—the emergence of a supradialectal norm, superposed upon dialect variants, commonly a step or stage closely associated with graphisation.
3. *Elaboration*—the process whereby the lexical resources are expanded to cope with the needs of increasingly complex social, economic, cultural and technological domains, and the specialisation of styles and registers for various fields of activity.

Clearly, extensive communication networks, centralised government, mass education and technological development demand these steps, and are indeed the forces which induce functional elaboration in a language.

But we have said that this is a simple hypothetical model of the basic stages of functional development: simple in the sense that it presupposes a steady cumulative process, whereby a people's language accommodates itself to their changing needs, as their society and its communicative networks become more complex and demanding, without functional competition from other languages. Real linguistic history is rarely so neat, however. For one of the characteristics of a society in which there is more than one language, is the existence of competition between language communities for the functional development of their language, usually at the expense of others.

If we turn to Africa, we can see that by no means all of its languages have yet even been graphised. Some languages on the other hand have been provided with several competing orthographic systems: by German Lutherans, French Catholics and American Baptists, in one instance I can think of. Supradialectal norms — standard forms of languages for wider communication between dialectal groups — have not, in most cases, yet satisfactorily emerged. In some cases there are competing standards. And the process we have called elaboration, linguistic enrichment for specialised modern purposes and technical use, for Western-type law, for example, or technology, and all the modern as opposed to the traditional domains of life, has hardly begun to happen except in a few cases. And this functional restriction, the crippled state of functional development, which we see in relation to Africa's languages, is partly the result of unequal competition between them and the European languages introduced by the colonial powers, as well as the linguistic fragmentation which could not in any case permit all languages to proceed at an equal pace. These European languages were already written, standardised and technically elaborated. The process of social and economic modernisation, from a communication point of view, was largely preempted by the European language.

It is of course necessary to add that the continued dominance of English and French in the independent inheritor states of Africa, as far as certain communicative functions are concerned, is partly because they now are languages of worldwide currency. If much of Africa had been ruled by the Dutch and the Danes, instead of the British and the French, there might have been less reluctance after independence to find means to replace the colonial language. If Indonesia had been a British or French colony instead of part of the Dutch empire, the replacement of the colonial language by *bahasa Indonesia* might not have proceeded as rapidly or as successfully. To adapt a cliche, God today, more than ever before, appears to be on the side of the big linguistic battalions.

Thirdly, we need to recognise that languages have a symbolic value, both for their speakers and for those who come into contact with them. It is true to say generally that a community's sense of integrity and identity is bound up with its language, the primary vehicle for its culture. The strength of allegiance to its language — the degree to which group solidarity is focused upon language rather than other cultural attributes — will in part be determined by whatever threats there may be to the community's culture or way of life; but also by the language's functional value relative to that of other languages in the contact situation. In other words, prestige, in terms of language, often derives from a language's real or apparent functional power.

It is important to recall that in most parts of the world languages are in competition for functional roles. In modernising societies, not all languages can be permitted to play all the communicative roles availabe. Some languages will inevitably expand their functional capacity, while others will remain restricted to certain domains: the domestic, the local, the traditional, the interpersonal at the familiar level. Full linguistic self-determination for every language community is, in the modern world, not only not possible but also, in many cases, undesirable. For a minority language community to aim at making its people linguistically self-sufficient through the sole use of their mother tongue, is to impel themselves towards a linguistic and cultural ghetto, with all the economic and political disadvantage that this entails. And for a national government to encourage, or force, minority language communities too far in this direction is of course discriminatory; as is clearly the covert aim of South Africa's *Bantu Education Act*. This Act of the 1950s, which remains part of the apparatus of political *apartheid*, increased the use of African vernacular languages in African education, thus reducing in effect the African child's access to the two national languages: English and Afrikaans. It is also part of the strategy for segregating different African language communities from one another by intensifying linguistic and ethnic divisions among the African population of

South Africa, and preparing the way for the spurious 'independent ethnic homelands', such as Bophutatswana or Transkei, into which different groups are now being divided politically. In multilingual societies, what most minority speech communities will try to settle for is something rather different from total linguistic self-determination; a compromise between the ghetto and total linguistic relegation, as it were. They will normally expect some official recognition of their language, and some satisfactory functional roles for it: combined with adequate access through education to languages with wider, national roles. This therefore means bilingualism, functionally adjusted; satisfying the legitimate pride in the mother tongue, while supplying the linguistic means, through a second or third language, for playing a full and undisadvantaged part in the life of a wider community. But to achieve this kind of communicative equilibrium is never easy, and always expensive.

Bilingualism now appears to be a necessity for more and more people in Africa, as indeed elsewhere. For, as the socially mobilised sector of the population increases—as more and more people begin to be caught up in the modernising process through urbanisation, improved communications, large-scale institutions and educational expansion—the number of bilinguals increases. What is the typical nature of this bilingualism? Experience of bilingualism in Europe or the United States is very misleading in this context, if our mother tongue happens to be one of the major languages. For such, our own language gives access to, allows us to play roles in, any domain of life and activity, from the familiar and the domestic to the most technical and specialised. Competence in another language simply permits us to function in some of these domains; or if we are truly ambilingual, with virtually equivalent competence in mother tongue and another language, to function in either language in all domains. But in African societies, the required bilingualism is almost always that which we define as *diglossia*: the complementary distribution of functions between languages. This means that the linguistic or communicative life of bilinguals in African societies, at least those caught up in the modernised sector, is split between two or more languages. In some domains of life one language, say the mother tongue, is appropriate: in other domains, particularly those involving western-type activities and institutions, only the second language will serve. This is the reflex at the individual level of the communal effect of differential functional distribution as between languages—in particular between the European second languages and the mother tongues, the African languages.

This may be illustrated by a rough, schematic diagram, in which 'European-type' bilingualism, complete ambilingualism and diglossic bilingualism are compared in terms of the typical coverage of domains of the two languages, designated L^1 (first language) and L^2 (second language); and we may imagine that the vertical axis of domains runs from the familial, intragroup, and traditional areas of life at the top, dominated as they tend to be by oral communication, into the more specialised, technical and inter-group areas, what we have called the 'modern' domains, towards the bottom, the latter being closely associated with literacy. (See Figure 1.)

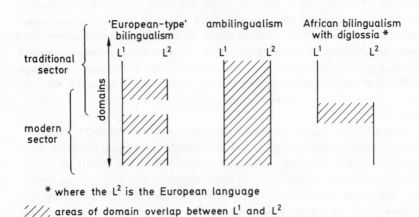

* where the L^2 is the European language

/// areas of domain overlap between L^1 and L^2

In diglossic bilingualism, the two language codes are in complementary distribution relative to the total range of domains. This is also accompanied, normally, by a difference of prestige between the languages, and often by literacy in only the second language. The language inherited from the colonial power not only has the prestige derived from a literate culture of long standing, but offers access to technology, to large communities of native speakers elsewhere, and so on. And the domains with which it is associated in national life are such as to give it an added prestige—because of its apparent power—far above that possessed by the mother tongue. Education through the European language entrenches this diglossia.

We can now begin to see some of the effects of colonialism upon the language situations of Africa. Not all these effects were disadvantageous, for, after all, two of the languages introduced into Africa by the colonial powers have turned out to be two of the most widely current and useful in the modern world. But that having been said, what were the effects? First, the introduction of the colonial languages into African societies, and their use as media of education and as communicative instruments for the modernising process, froze the opportunities for functional development of almost all the African languages. It also froze linguistic competition between languages for access to new domains, and to some extent the European language retarded the extension of existing African vehicular languages. Secondly, these European languages tended to be highly prized by the small élites which colonialism produced and to whom power passed. Only where a potential competitor remained--as with Swahili in Tanzania and Kenya, Arabic in the Sudan or Somali in Somalia--did it seem possible after independence to plan for an alternative. The majority of African languages thus remained boxed in, functionally restricted, with the cost of expanding their functions growing every day more expensive.

What now happens or is likely to happen? Much will depend on the speed of changes. Social and economic mobilisation was relatively slow under colonial rule. Educational opportunity was extremely limited. Up to independence, therefore, the viability for communicative purposes of what I have called, following Fishman, diglossic bilingualism was not by any means tested. But the small élites of the colonial period are now being rapidly expanded. If mobilisation accelerates, and more and more of the population becomes caught up in the modernising process, will the vernacular languages be forced to extend their functions so as to increase the overlap with the European languages? In so doing how will they extend their resources, through their continued contact, in the lives of more and people, with these European languages? It appears that in many cases this functional extension is already beginning to happen. Rapid social and economic change in multilingual societies, in all the instances so far examined by scholars, seems to *force* a reallocation of language functions. But this raises questions about codification, standardisation and literacy in the vernacular languages. This suggests that linguistic interventionism by governments is required. And politically this can be a very divisive and sensitive issue, of course, unless there is a general consensus about the languages selected, which is rarely the case.

Where we hear of a fall in the efficiency of European language use in African societies, what this really means is that mobilisation into the 'modernising sectors' is proceeding faster than the extension of competent bilingualism. Is there a breaking point, where efficiency in communication falls, in certain crucial domains, to an extent which impairs the viability of administration, organisation and institutional systems? Of course, in such situations, linguistic communication does not actually break down altogether. But there may be political, social and economic side-effects. If vernacular languages are forced to play wider roles, the *major* African languages may begin to appear a greater threat to *minor* language groups than European languages ever have. Educational pressures for a wider role to be given to major vernaculars may make themselves felt. And this means administrative decisions with very significant political consequences.

Extending the roles—and thus fostering and developing the resources—of some of the major African languages in any society, is I suspect inevitable, and is already beginning: indeed it was begun in some cases, not always successfully, during the colonial period by the British, though not by the French. Interventionism here, 'linguistic engineering' as some have called it, requires delicate handling and is expensive. Ultimately it means orthographic normalisation (cf. Igbo, whose orthography was only agreed after independence), development through agreement of a standard supradialectal norm; a translation programme, which itself requires the training of competent translators; a literacy programme; subsidised publishing; encouragement of creative writing, and so on. And yet, if encouragement of this kind succeeds in giving enhanced status and extended functions to certain languages, it could lock a language community into itself, and increasingly inhibit its members from playing a wider role in nationally integrative processes, unless the European language continues to be taught more efficiently and extensively as before.

As the lives of people change, as the traditional world is increasingly penetrated by the modern, the external, they find it necessary to talk of new things. Their language becomes accordingly modified, unless for everyone there is an alternative language to which they have access, which can serve for such new purposes. The diglossic separation of functions between vernacular and European language is bound to begin to blur. What we need to explore more fully, in particular case studies, is the interplay of forces which act upon language use, and upon attitudes towards languages, in various parts of Africa. Such studies must, I think, primarily be undertaken by African scholars themselves.

Parallels with Europe are, I know, dangerous and usually misleading. I only offer one for reflection. Since the end of the eighteenth century, the number of languages in Europe which have achieved the status of official recognition, which have had their use in education, law, and government legitimised, and in which in consequence there are now extensive literatures and textual material available, has increased very considerably; although of course some languages still struggle for this status today. This remains true even if we exclude languages in European Soviet Russia, where the number of languages officially recognised and sponsored has of course risen startlingly, as a result of a centrally directed policy since the Revolution. Whether such a development can be conjectured for many of the African languages, it would be unwise to say—and none of us will be here to make a count in a century's time!

But already the signs are that Hausa, Wolof and Akan, in West Africa, for example, Swahili in East Africa of course, and Amharic in Ethiopia, and some of the major Bantu languages, are beginning to tread this road. North and east of the Sahara Arabic is inevitably encroaching on the functions preempted a century or so ago by French in the Maghreb, and English in the Sudan. Somali is already established as the national language of Somalia, a rare and fortunate case of national unilingualism, In most cases I have mentioned, one does not think in terms of total replacement; but rather what I have called functional encroachment on the domains traditionally restricted to the colonially inherited language or languages of European origin. It is not an either/or equation, but a more/less equation. And the equation will take decades for solution. Much will depend on how social, economic and political change provokes—naturally or artificially—a reallocation of functions, a readjustment of roles, among the languages now in use in various parts of Africa. Only such reallocation can stimulate the development and elaboration of vernacular languages. And this in its turn will contribute to their relative symbolic status, their prestige, and the allegiance felt for them by their users. Only then, some generations in the future, will Africa's complex and unequal linguistic equation be on the way to resolution.

Bibliographic note

I am indebted to so much material, read since I first became involved with the problems of language in Africa almost twenty-five years ago, that I cannot provide a true bibliography to this sketchy and synoptic essay. Some indications may be had of possible further reading on the colonial language issue from the bibliography appended to my 'Colonial Language Policies and their Legacies' in Berry and Greenberg (eds.) below. I have also found helpful over the years many contributions in the following short list though I should also add that I am most indebted to my colleagues, friends and graduate students from Africa, if there is anything of value or perception in my essay, for their courteous and illuminating explanations, discussions and arguments over many years in many places.

References

J. Berry and J.H. Greenberg, (eds.), 1971. *Linguistics in Sub-Saharan Africa.* Current Trends in Linguistics VII. The Hague: Mouton.

J. Fishman (ed.) 1968. *Readings in the Sociology of Language.* Mouton.

— , C. Ferguson and J. Das Gupta (eds.). 1968. *Language Problems of Developing Nations.* Wiley.

— 1974. *Advances in Language Planning.* Mouton.

E. Haugen, 1972. *The Ecology of Language.* Stanford University Press.

Dell Hymes (ed.). 1964. *Language in Culture and Society.* Harper and Row.

— 1971. *Pidginization and Creolization of Languages.* Cambridge University Press.

W.H. Whitely (ed.). 1971. *Language Use and Social Change.* Oxford University Press.

D. P. Pattanayak

Diversity in Communication and Languages;
Predicament of a Multilingual Nation State:
India, A Case Study

Introduction

Like air and water, language is indispensable for human societies. When natural water is so parcelled out that a section of the people is deprived of even drinking water, or natural air is so polluted by a few so that the large majority of people cannot live in health and happiness, then this is the sign of an unequal society. Similarly when a society is denied full expression through the language which it uses naturally and its needs are instead sought to be met through a regulated or imposed language, then inequity sets in. In dominant monolingual countries the minorities are pressurized to melt their identities and join the main stream through the dominant tongue. In multilingual countries where many languages complement each other in different functions in defined domains, registers, and styles, when one language is sought to be imposed, it leads to obvious inequality. Asia, Africa and Latin America, which are multilingual, multicultural and multiethnic are under pressure to apply monomodels, which are sources of tension and inequity. It is in this context that a close scrutiny of problems of multilingual communication in the world has become imperative, not only to understand the ethos of multilingualism, but the nature and extent of inequality resulting from ignorant and intentional language use, misuse and disuse.

Today the multilingual multiethnic and multicultural world stands at the crossroads. It is unfortunately the developing world which has 75 percent of the world's population but 14 percent of the world's income. Population in these countries are in search of a good life, a life comparable with the West, but lack the resources to achieve it. The pattern of development over the past 25 years shows a tremendous income gap not only between developed and developing countries, but also within the developing countries themselves. The upper 20 percent received 55 percent of the benefit from the rise in national incomes in developing countries while the lowest 20 percent received only 5 percent of the benefit. These upper percentile are the highly schooled, oriented to the good life of the West and schooled in a language which creates a breach between their avowed feeling to the rest of their own population vis-à-vis their self interest and their actual feelings towards them. They speak of high technology rather than of appropriate technology, of transnational languages rather than of national and indigenous languages and they speak of translations and transplants rather than of original creations and innovations. They forget that development is the property and produce of the social system. With Trilling, one can say that in the present moment in these people "it is possible to observe the moral life in process of revising itself". This process can best be observed in India, a true representative of the multilingual pluricultural world.

Linguistic Colonialism and the Use of Transnational Languages

Doh Joon-Chien gives a lucid description of the process of intellectual colonization of the East and the role of the language of the erstwhile colonial masters in this process.[2] Use of language can become a major factor in creating unequal societies in the multilingual context. Differential and controlled language use in education, in administration, and in mass communication regulates access to rank, status and wealth in society and aids elite formation. Such elitism develops its own vested interest. The elite in India today is, by and large, an English speaking elite. A rural elite naturally wants to share power and privilege with the urban English-speaking elite and consequently makes compromises with them. Therefore, they are in favour of the English press, the large circulations of journals and newspapers, colour television and controlled reading. While languages like English in India, which are prized colonial heritages, do capture the interest, they do not capture the idiom of many in the respective countries. Therefore they often address an assumed audience. The regional and local languages, by virtue of being direct, intimate, warm and picturesque, cater to the real and immediate presence of the audience. English loses some of these qualities as often it is seen to be in competition with and therefore having an interest adverse to that of the many. English language in India has fostered western orientation and reduced the self-confidence of its users. Its dominant use in education has created a system which has bypassed the majority; in administration it has denied the majority participation in the socioeconomic reconstruction of the country and has made justice unjusticiable. Its use in the mass media threatens to homogenise cultures, obliterate languages and reduce people into a mass. Lack of definition of its role and domain vis-à-vis the local languages of communication seeks to replace the role relations of interdependence to one of dominance and subordination.

After relegating most languages as indigenous languages, after branding many local literate languages as minority languages, efforts are being made to focus attention on a national language in most multilingual countries. If this one language could be a transnational language identified with the developed countries, it is argued, it could save the bother of building *de novo*. We could then transplant not only the already-developed vocabulary, syntax and the rich scientific literature, but the economic development that goes with it. It is forgotten that a language develops as a result of the interaction of the individual with the society and of the society with the environment.

In the modern world, elitist communication, which is minority communication, receives maximum attention as mass communication. There is a gross under-access to media in the present-day world. For example, 90 percent of the radio frequencies of the world are used by 10 percent of the population and 90 percent of the population use 10 percent of the frequency. For another example, there are almost 800 million illiterates in the world. India, which has 50 percent of the world illiterates, has 30 percent literacy. The other 50 percent, constituting 400 million, are concentrated mostly in the multilingual, multiethnic developing Third World. In India out of 30 percent literates, only 2 percent have anything to do with the printed word. This shows the under-access of the print media. For a third example, there is a serious imbalance in the international news flow. Almost 80 percent of the total news flow emanates from West-based major transnational agencies. One-fifth of the total of the foreign correspondents of the western agencies are based in the developing nations where four-fifths of the world's population lives. No wonder that the western agencies devote only 20 to 30 percent of news coverage to developing countries. What is true of the international scene is true of national scenes in many countries of the East where minority elites socialised in the western molds of thinking are at the helm of affairs. For example, in India, as Madan Gopal says, "Taking all the modern media of communication into account, it can safely be stated that their reach is not more than 20 percent of the population."[1] In most such countries there is more discussion on coverage than on access, more discussion of the rights of the sender and ownership of channels than of the audience and the reactions of people and institutions to different signals or ideas. Even the McBride Commission[1] shows more concern for the conventional institutionalised forms of communication—radio, press, television and communication satellites—forgetting that communication is a social process.

Multilingualism vs. Monomodels

The Indian predicament is symptomatic of the predicament of the multi-lingual, multicultural and multiethnic developing world. The ethos of multi-lingualism is diametrically opposite to that of dominant monolingualism. For the latter, many languages are an absurdity whereas for the former they are a necessary condition of existence. There is an interesting parallel between agriculture and language. As Erik Eckholm says, "the more genetically homogeneous the fields, the higher their vulnerability to large-scale losses caused by pests, diseases and weather abnormalities". The dangers of uniformation through monocropping and through monoculture are of serious proportions. In the name of modernity genetic variability is being destroyed. By the same token, in the name of standardization and mass media, the cultural variability is being threatened. Both of these put serious constraints on economic planning and create cataclysmic spasms in the present world as well as threaten its future.

The ethos of predominantly monolingual and predominantly multilingual countries is qualitatively different. Therefore, the dynamics as well as economics of planning must be viewed differently in the two situations. From a predominantly monolingual point of view many languages are a nuisance as their acquisition is considered a load; they are uneconomical and politically untenable. Even translation services are computed to be more economical than use of an additional language. In the case of multilingual countries, the reverse is the case. For them, restrictions in the choice of languages they use is a nuisance, and one language is not only uneconomical, but it is politically untenable and socially absurd. The enormity of resources spent to produce the 4 percent of English-knowing persons in India over the past 200 years would prove the absurdity of the efforts to replace many languages by one under democratic planning. The cultural deprivation and sociopolitical inequality introduced by the approach of monolingual control of a multi-lingual polity makes nonsense of any talk of such economic benefit.

Linguistic or cultural homogeneity of even one group is in a sense a fiction. Both culture and language are hierarchical notions embodying in them elements which could be called sub-cultures or dialects, which viewed from another angle are cultures and languages. In countries with linguistic and cultural diversity, the situation is more complex. In such countries, indepen-dent languages sometimes belonging to more than one language family, create a complex web of relationships. Here, maintenance of identity of small groups and their integration with a larger national image constantly come into conflict. Any effort at standardisation or cultural universalism through reduction of multiplicity could give the impression of imposition of limita-tions on the cultural alternatives available to the community. As technological innovations may accord superiority to a group of people in the society by altering group relations, changes in the communicational network also could give advantage to a social group, who in turn appropriate to themselves benefits of technological innovations. These groups enter into dominant minority relationship with others in the society. The dominant group then starts taking decisions without any reference to the interests of the minority communities and thus the political cycle begins.

The fifteen dominant languages listed in schedule VIII of the Indian Constitution,[2] for example, enjoy certain privileges by virtue of their dominance which are often denied to the minority languages. They are recognised media for education and administration in states, where several hundred minority languages clamour for recognition. Whenever minority languages have been recognised as associated administrative languages in the states or even as media of primary education, they have been so recognised only after such groups generated sufficient pressure, and not as a result of policy planning.

Language politics is intimately connected with economics and resource planning. Unless resources are so developed that sub-groups within a region or culture or groups within a culturally diverse nation get equal opportunity for their creative fulfilment, language is bound to be used for divisive purposes. Bangladesh provides an excellent example of a country where resources planning resulting in unequal development of regions gave expression to its bitter frustration through the language movement. The resentment against regional imbalance found a rallying point around the language issue and ultimately resulted in the creation of a new nation.

In countries with diverse ethnic groups reinforcement of ethnic differences by parallel language differences may pose major problems. In developing countries, where scarce resources leave even the dominant group disadvantaged in its own region, it naturally becomes reluctant to share political and economic power with the minority groups. The minority politicians find a powerful weapon in the language to attack the adversary. Thus, Urdu in India identified with the Muslims, although it is the mother tongue of less than fifty percent of the Muslims, has often been used as a tool of communal disharmony. The communal riots in post-independent Malaya between the Malays on the one hand and the Chinese community on the other were triggered mainly by the issue of the use of language in education.

A very interesting development in such confrontations is the counter-reaction of the dominant group to the demands of the minority, whether it is the demand for the recognition of *Kuo yu* (Chinese) by the Malayan Chinese Association, the recognition of Tamil by the Sri Lanka Tamils, or Urdu by Muslims in some Indian states. The majority group, which consider their language as an essential marker not only of their group identity, but also of the national identity, expects the minority to prove their nationalism by accepting the language of the majority as the medium of education and administration. This in turn exacerbates relations and politics of confrontation continues. No planning, whether it is for a region or for a nation, can succeed unless a will to live together is generated among the people. A negative purpose such as fighting a common enemy can weld people together until the purpose is served, but without a conscious unity and will to live it is futile to talk of a planned society.

Position of Hindi

The American Constitution neither declares English as the one official language nor does it declare one official religion. The Indian Constitution writers in their wisdom decided that Hindi was to be the official language of the country. They also made English the associate official language for a limited number of years which is being extended with no end in sight. The history of India probably would have been different if it had been made clear that there was no harm in using different languages as long as people knew Hindi.

The love-hate relation existing between the dominant and minority languages on the one hand, and the standard and the non-standards on the other, are best exemplified by Hindi in India. The status of Hindi as a language has been questioned by scholars, it has been the cause of intense political action and because of its amorphous nature both scholars and politicians have been hard put to delimit the Hindi region.

The place of Hindi in the multilingual set-up has never been clearly spelled out. While the extreme enthusiasts consider Hindi as a replacement for all the other Indian languages, the detractors would not even accept Hindi as a link language in the scheme of national bilingualism. The Hindi question cannot be decided on the basis of majority. Only catholicity in dealing with its own dialects and varieties and alliance with the other Indian languages can meet the challenges of receding nationalism and maintain the multilingual and multicultural polity in India.

Although Hindi has been a subject of political debate both at the national and state levels in North India, one thing strikes a student of the Hindi movement. Hindi has made some progress whenever it is a movement from within and a movement through voluntary efforts. There seems to have been retrogression when it is conceived as a movement from the top and propped up by government effort. The government effort at the expense of non-governmental initiative smacks of imposition and consequently it becomes a handy tool for political movements.

Even when Hindi assumed dominance through official patronage, it did not carry any guarantee that conforming to Hindi and shedding the alien language would bring material prosperity. On the contrary, it was interpreted as a threat to social and economic position of small groups. A belief slowly gained ground that national unity is a convenient excuse for actions motivated by more selfish motives.

Hindi did not become an effective instrument of daily life in the Hindi zone itself. While Maithili, Bhojpuri, Magahi, Awadhi and Braj dialects of Hindi, continued to be powerful group symbols and used as media of vigorous literatures, the Hindi pandits and leaders complacently took things for granted.

Hindi did not become an emotional symbol for people of different cultural ancestries. In the realm of religion, Hinduism did provide such a pervasive emotional symbol. Even though Hinduism provided a cover for 12 philosophies, 6 believing in the existence of God and 6 not believing in the existence of God, to co-exist so as to encompass monism, dualism, triadism, animism, animatism and all kinds of worship including ancestor worship, Hindi failed to become such a common symbol. On the contrary, spread of Hindi was interpreted as Hinduisation rather than Indianisation. This left the large majority of the people on the fringe of Hindu society and those outside the Hindu society, almost out. This lack of identification of Hindi with Indianisation provided a convenient handle to politicians who wanted to create cleavages such as Hindi versus Urdu, Hindi versus English and Hindi versus other Indian languages.

In a country with multiple ethnic groups speaking languages belonging to four or five different language families, Hindi should have become an emotional refuge for the minorities. Hinduisation, on the contrary, is identified with rigid conservatism rather than with flexible pluralism.

While recognising competing factions in the delimitations of linguistic states, the permanent and aggregate interests of the Indian community were not sought to be linked with Hindi. As a result, in spite of massive input, no non-Hindi group as a whole has taken up the cause of Hindi. As a result, Hindi has remained as a symbol of North Indian identity rather than growing up as an Indian identity, unlike English in America which became a powerful symbol of American rather than Anglo-Saxon identity.

Hindi never attained the vitality which a language earns by being used in organised society. The pan-Indian Hindi sought to be created was so removed from the grassroots that it failed to draw sustenance from the various spoken languages as envisaged in Article 351 of the Constitution. Hindi, a latecomer as medium of education, administration and mass communication, at best remained a competitor to other Indian languages rather than providing useful insight and experience for extension of the use of other regional languages into newer domains.

From the common man's point of view, Hindi is neither the language of authority nor of convenience. Because of lack of planned action, Hindi has neither been a cohesive link to weld the country into a single cultural region, nor has it become a necessary concomitant of the national political personality of the country.

With six states and one union territory using some variety of Hindi, the Hindi speaking region provides a much larger ground for competition than any other single language area. The national second choice for any Indian language speaker therefore is bound to be Hindi provided channels of fair competition are kept open. English will remain as an ancillary language operating in irreplaceable defined domains irrespective of the Constitutional provision, not only because it provides a cultural link with the outside world, but also because it has become part of the Indian heritage. Restriction is as bad, if not worse, as imposition. The states as well as the centre will therefore do well to provide more opportunities to the younger generation to learn many languages rather than restricting them to language(s) of their choice. Only a multilingual approach to language planning can provide the answer to intrastate, interstate and centre-state problems in this regard.

Conclusion

Monolingual orientation in education not only forces the speakers of minority languages to seek identification with the mainstream through the dominant language, it makes them unequal to the task of searching for knowledge and opportunities. The identity crisis and poor self-image resulting in drop-out, stagnation and wastage raise important questions which need to be answered by educationists.

Should education pursue a policy insisting on a single loyalty, teaching a single language, attacking dual and multiple identities, thus trying to create a single language common culture? Do the people have to speak English, Spanish or a single national language to enjoy their constitutional rights? Is it correct to discriminate in education and employment because of language?

The world has pursued paths of suppression, imposition and discrimination in spite of preaching lofty ideals of creating a new man and culture. The question is can education guarantee the creation of new societies while being fair to the many ethnic, cultural and linguistic groups? A good deal depends on how these questions are answered.

References

1. Madan Gopal, 'Reaching Rural India'. In Mass Media in India 1979-80, Publications Division, Ministry of Information and Broadcasting, Government of India, 1980, p. 87.
2. Doh Joon-Chien, 'Eastern Intellectuals and Western Solutions', Vikas Publishing House Pvt. Ltd., Delhi, 1980.

Notes

1. The International Commission for the Study of Communication Problems had as its Chairman, Mr. Sean Macbride (Ireland), barrister and politician. The commission is named after him. There are 16 members from different countries in the Commission. The first session of the Commission was held in Paris on December 14, 1977 under the auspices of UNESCO. The terms of reference of the Commission, were as follows:
   (a) to study the current situation in the field of communication and information and identify problems which call for new action at the international level, taking into account the diversity of socioeconomic conditions and levels and types of development;
   (b) to pay particular attention, within the framework of this study, to problems relating to the free and balanced flow of information in the world, as well as the specific needs of developing countries;
   (c) to analyse communication problems in all their different aspects, within the perspective of the establishment of a new international economic order and the initiative to be undertaken to favour the installation of a 'a new world information order';
   (d) to define the role which communication might play in sensitising public opinion to the major problems confronting the world and in helping towards their progressive solution through concerted national and international action;
   (e) to define the new role which communication media of every kind could play in furthering the progress of education, science and culture, taking account of the diversity of situations in the world.
2. The languages listed under Schedule VIII of the Constitution of India are:
   1. Assamese, 2. Bengali, 3. Gujarati, 4. Hindi, 5. Kannada, 6. Kashmiri, 7. Malayalam, 8. Marathi, 9. Oriya, 10. Punjabi, 11. Sanskrit, 12. Sindhi, 13. Tamil, 14. Telugu, 15. Urdu.

List of Contributors

Dell H. Hymes
Dean, Graduate School of Education
University of Pennsylvania

Einar Haugen
Department of Germanic Languages and Literatures
Harvard University

John Fought
Department of Linguistics
University of Pennsylvania

Ana Celia Zentella
Head, Black and Puerto Rican Studies
Hunter College

Regna Darnell
Department of Anthropology
University of Alberta

Monica Heller
Department of Linguistics
University of California at Berkeley

Kathryn A. Woolard
Graduate School of Education
University of Pennsylvania

Joan Rubin
National Center for Bilingual Research
Los Alamitos, CA

Benji Wald
National Center for Bilingual Research
Los Alamitos, CA

John R. Rickford
Department of Linguistics
Stanford University

Richard R. Day
Chair, Department of English as a Second Language
University of Hawaii at Manoa

Martha Hardman de Bautista
Director, Aymara Language Materials Project
Center for Latin American Studies
University of Florida, Gainesville

Michael Clyne
Department of German
Monash University
Clayton, Victoria
Australia

Joshua A. Fishman
Distinguished University Research Professor
Social Sciences
Ferkauf Graduate School
Yeshiva University, New York

Franklin C. Southworth
Department of South Asian Studies
University of Pennsylvania

Jane Zuengler
Teachers College
Columbia University

Charlene J. Sato
Department of English as a Second Language
University of Hawaii at Manoa

Dennis R. Craig
School of Education
University of the West Indies
Jamaica

Ayorinde Dada
Department of Teacher Education
University of Ibadan
Nigeria

Lucy T. Briggs
Department of Spanish and Portuguese
Dartmouth College

Susan U. Philips
Department of Anthropology
University of Arizona

Viv Edwards
Faculty of Arts and Social Studies
University of Reading
U.K.

Eddie C.Y. Kuo
Head, Department of Sociology
National University of Singapore

H.R. Dua
Central Institute of Indian Language
Mysore, India

Stephen A. Wurm
Department of Linguistics
Research School of Pacific Studies
Australian National University
Canberra